SEVENTH EDITION

Stage Management

LAWRENCE STERN

ALLYN AND BACON
Boston   London   Toronto   Sydney   Tokyo   Singapore

In memory of Xenia Chekhov

Senior Editor: Molly Taylor
Editor in Chief, Social Sciences: Karen Hanson
Editorial Assistant: Sarah McGaughey
Marketing Manager: Jacqueline Aaron
Editorial-Production Administrator: Annette Joseph
Editorial-Production Coordinator: Holly Crawford
Editorial-Production Service: Lynda Griffiths, TKM Productions
Artist: Corinne Ovadia, Asterisk Inc.
Composition Buyer: Linda Cox
Electronic Composition: TKM Productions
Manufacturing Buyer: Julie McNeill
Cover Designer: Kristina Mose-Libon

Library of Congress Cataloging-in-Publication Data

Stern, Lawrence
    Stage management / Lawrence Stern.--7th ed.
      p. cm.
    Includes index.
    ISBN 0-205-33531-4
      1. Stage management.   I. Title

  PN2085 .S77 2001
  792'.023--dc21   2001016118

Printed in the United States of America

10   9   8   7   6   5   4   3   2   06   05   04   03   02   01

Contents

Foreword

The best way to introduce this book is to speak well and perfectly about the author. For you can't expect a stage manager like Lawrence Stern to stand up front and blow his own horn. Someone who knows him must do it for him, and I gladly assume the task.

Now there are all sorts of virtues a stage manager must have. You will find them listed and profusely described in the pages of this book. But the supreme virtue among many is: The stage manager must arrive before everyone and leave long after everyone else is gone.

Of course that is the essence of creativity in any field you may want to mention. Those who love writing stay up until dawn to finish a story. Those who love painting work around the clock until they drop dead in their tracks. Stage managers . . . ?

Lawrence Stern is one of those superb men who quietly go about their business, keep charts, arrive two hours early and, long after the play has closed or collapsed, or both, can be found carrying out the trash, cleaning up the lobby, filling in the final forms, or holding the flashlight while the author of the play crawls around on the floor of the ladies' room helping some poor blind thing find her lost contact lens.

All this Lawrence Stern has done, and more. His passions may be quiet, but they are there. Instead of your usual slob, found all too frequently in our unhappy society these days, Lawrence Stern is one of those who gives you 150 percent of himself. I know that sounds impossible, but I have seen him do it. And this book, with its incredible amount of detail and huge compilation of firsthand knowledge, is proof of all that I say.

Frankly, I don't know how your average stage manager ever got along without this book, just as my own Pandemonium Theatre Company was never the same once Lawrence Stern moved on to other fields.

There you have it—some sort of idea of the man who wrote this book. But you needn't take my word for it. Just leaf through the book swiftly, checking chapters, pages, paragraphs. You'll soon find that a subtitle of the book could well be More than You Ever Wanted to Know about Stage Managing. Except of course, that would be foolish: you can never know enough.

Let Lawrence Stern be the best teacher you ever had. He's here. *Listen* to him!

Ray Bradbury
Los Angeles

Preface to the Seventh Edition

Dear Readers:

During my first directing assignments, I found that those assigned to assist me did not know how to analyze a script, call sound cues, or spike set pieces. During rehearsals, a director wants to give his or her full attention to the cast—there's no time to instruct stage managers. Soon, I began gathering some of my past stage management forms and writing notes on procedures. I hoped that I would be able to say to my novice assistants, "Look over page 103, so that tomorrow you will know how to take blocking notation." That was the beginning.

Flash forward: computers and the Internet. I regard this seventh edition of *Stage Management* as the dot.com edition—with websites and e-mail addresses in every chapter—an updated resource for today's plugged-in generation.

My thanks to stage managers Bob Bones, Jane Bulnes-Fowles, Jill Gold, David Grindle, Johan Henckens, James T. McDermott, Cari Norton, Big J Peterson, Bradley Spinelli, and Chad Zadrow for sharing their expertise; to contributors from theaters and support industries—Richard Bergstresser and Garth Hemphill (ACT-SF), Steve Edmonds (Mountain Community Theater), Michael Ferguson (Theatre Projects Consultants), Jody Hanson and Scott A. Hochhalter (Electronic Theatre Controls), John Holly (Equity), Robert Jensen (Fullerton College), Ben Kato (Jeffrey Finn Productions), David Lindberg (Musson Theatrical), Mark E. Nelson (Ohlone College), Gary Parks (Clear-Com), Ivan Schwartz (Mackie Designs), and Steven Louis Shelley (Field Template); to Anya Finke and Sean McCullough (Cabrillo College) and David Sword (Santa Clara University); to Professor Elbin Cleveland of the University of South Carolina for a very useful critique of the sixth edition; to Molly Taylor and Karon Bowers, my editors at Allyn and Bacon, and to their assistant, Rebecca Sullivan; to Lynda Griffiths of TKM Productions; and to Ray Bradbury, THANK YOU!—your initial support and encouragement are not forgotten. I also thank the following reviewers of this seventh edition: William J. Byrnes, Florida State University; Elbin Cleveland, University of South Carolina; and Janet Rose, University of Oregon.

One of my greatest rewards has been feedback from readers. It's your continuing demand that makes possible this seventh-edition opportunity to make "the backstage bible" even more useful and practical. If you would like to contribute to future editions, your comments are always welcome. If you work in ballet, a theme park, dinner theater, ice shows, lounge acts, festivals, or any other theatrical environment, I hope you'll share the things you've learned along the way. On page 383 you'll find a Reader's Comments Form with my address. Thanks in advance for your help.

L. S.

Preface to the First Edition

In the many levels of live theater—educational, children's, community, showcase, and professional—there are few provisions for training in stage management. It is often assumed that anyone can do the job reasonably well who has a mind to, without previous training or experience, and the result of this is a great deal of trial and an enormous amount of error. A new stage manager typically makes his or her own kind of improvised performance, trying to carry out the functions of stage management without ever being able to find out for sure what those functions are, except by trial and error. Unfortunately, there are few places where anyone can find any written summary of useful principles or primary needs of stage management, and what they do find by gleaning from texts on directing, stagecraft, or the like is not usually appropriate to any one person's theater situation, much less to a reliable or professional standard for this kind of work. Most managers solve their problems with whatever organizational skill and inventiveness they possess—but at an unwarranted cost in time, effort, and uncertainty.

At the amateur levels of live theater, particularly in educational and community theater, the problems resulting from such a lack of guidelines for stage management are compounded by the fact that often the duties of the producer, director, stage manager, and even business manager are assumed by one person. This individual is frequently a faculty member or volunteer who has had little or no experience in stage management. It is this person who stands to profit most from this book. However, this guide is written in the hope that it will prove to be a valuable tool for all producers, directors, stage managers, and supervisors of theatrical programs, regardless of theater level or staging environment.

L. S.

1

Making Things Run Smoothly

Stage managing is like riding a bicycle. If you don't keep moving, you fall down.

—Elbin Cleveland

A Point of Departure

The cast, staff, and crew of a live theater work together toward a common goal: a good performance. Thus, theater is necessarily a group effort in professional, amateur, or educational theater. However, it is *never* a group effort of vague fellow committee members, but of associated autocrats—a playwright, a producer, a director, a stage manager, designers, and, above all, actors. Each accommodates the others, and may overlap others in function when necessary, considering the wide variety of differing conditions for each show and every kind and level of theater. But each autocrat assumes distinct responsibilities and accepts them completely: The *producer* is the general manager who has responsibility for obtaining the personnel and resources to make theater happen. The *actors* must serve as the most essential dramatic medium, without whom no theatrical ideas or emotions can be communicated to an audience. The *director* must interpret the playwright's script through the media of actors and designers. The person who has responsibility for making the entire production run smoothly, on stage and backstage, in prerehearsal, rehearsal, performance, and postperformance phases, is the *stage manager*.

Stage management, in general, involves more responsibilities and resources than any one manager ever needs to apply to any single production. So in this book, I will describe and give examples of many more methods for stage management than should be applied to any one production, and you will need to use your judgment to determine which will be most effective for you. However, at this point, you might also benefit from some overview of these functions to show how the responsibilities of stage management are needed and applied. I can provide this best through a personal anecdote about a situation in which I did not even act as stage manager.

The Care and Feeding of the Amateur Stage Manager: A True Tale of the Theater

The North Covina Theater Guild was about to present *Take Me Along*, and I had been asked to direct. Their producer, a homemaker, was Mrs. Betty Spelvin (all names changed to protect the very innocent). She had been with the group since its inception; to put it another way, she *was* the inception. She had statuettes on her desk from the Adult Drama Festival and on her bookcase a gavel that proclaimed her "Best Producer."

My first encounter with my producer concerned the absence of the stage manager. At the production conference prior to rehearsals, I asked where he was. When she told me he could not be there for the meeting, I shrugged and assumed that he would appear for the following nights' meetings, since his name appeared on the staff list.

At the first reading, I again asked for the stage manager. "Oh," said Betty, "he doesn't come in until production week." Production week was her term for the week of strenuous rehearsals prior to opening night.

"When he does come in, what does he do?"

"Why, he gives the actors their calls and pulls the curtain," said Betty.

From my five years as an Equity stage manager, I knew there was more to it than giving calls and pulling the curtain. I also knew that I could not function as stage manager if I waited until the week of technical and dress rehearsals to join the company. "Who gives the light and sound cues?" I asked.

"The light and sound men take their own cues. They can see from the booth in back. They're junior high school kids, but very dependable."

"Well, who is supposed to assist me during auditions?"

"You're doing just fine. You're really organized. If you need any help, just yell." And she dashed off before I could.

After the readings, I cornered her in the box office to ask who would be taking blocking notation during rehearsals. "The director always does that," she answered.

"Who calls the cues, warns the actors, and sets the furniture and props during rehearsals?"

"We all pitch in," smiled Betty reassuringly, "and it all gets done, so don't you worry."

"Who mimeographs and distributes the rehearsal schedule?"

"The girl in the box office. She's very good. She'll join us in two weeks. Listen, I know this isn't the way you're used to doing things in Hollywood, but believe me, it all comes together like magic on the night."

(When I was 6 years old, my 7-year-old neighbor attempted to saw a lady in half using a rusty saw and me as the lady. I don't believe in magic!)

"I must have a stage manager to assist me starting tomorrow night," I said.

"Impossible," she replied. "We just haven't been able to find reliable people to work as stage manager. We have no budget for them. It's always worked out that the director is better off doing it himself."

"Let me put it this way, Betty. Find me a stage manager or find yourself a new director."

Betty Spelvin, I found out later, had been running little theater groups in Little Rock, Arkansas; Omaha, Nebraska; Boulder, Colorado; Manila, the Philippines; and a few other places where her husband was stationed. She had been known to sew entire wardrobes overnight; paint complete sets after dress rehearsals; get up on lines in an afternoon to stand in for an ailing actress; and fire, replace, or take over for directors on the spot.

There must have been a short supply of directors in North Covina that week. Also, Betty was moving to a new home and her daughter was about to be married. And Betty was expedient. So the next night, I had a stage manager.

Paul Crowell was young and inexperienced but alert, intelligent, and personable. He was anxious to learn and caught on quickly. I gathered examples of work I'd done as a professional stage manager—schedules, promptbook, sign-in sheets, cast lists, scene-shift diagrams, and so on—and turned them over to him. I explained to him the only thing I thought essential.

"As stage manager, you will have total responsibility for making things run smoothly. As producer, Betty's function is to obtain the personnel and materials to make our production happen. As director, my function is to interpret the script. Both Betty and I are concerned that things run smoothly, but you are the only one on the staff who is totally in charge of smooth running. If there's a minute delay in rehearsal or production, it's your fault, and for every second within the schedule that you can deliver productive rehearsal time, you, personally, will be improving the quality of the group's performances."

Paul had been a class officer in high school. He'd lettered in baseball and football. He was efficient and had a way of getting people to move with him.

The North Covina Theater Guild was immediately responsive to what they assumed were innovations in making theater. The cast and staff had never had complete schedules and cast lists so early. Cast members were surprised when labeled prop boxes and backstage mapped prop tables appeared before they had even set aside their scripts. Most of all, they were shocked when they found rehearsals beginning at the moment called and ending at the time specified. At rehearsals, all the light and sound cues were called by the stage manager. Sound effects were used at rehearsals a week prior to the technical (tech) rehearsal. Costumes were paraded well before dress rehearsals. There were no last-minute rushes. There were no late rehearsals. The tech rehearsals ended at 11 P.M. And was I amused when I overheard cast members talking about "the new method from Hollywood."

A few years have passed since Paul stage-managed his first show in North Covina. While in the military, Paul wrote, "Tanks are less temperamental than actresses and easier to stage-manage." He is now a lawyer.

And Betty Spelvin, bless her heart, is still running the North Covina Theater Guild. With her husband retired from the military, she is probably dug in to stay—producing, directing, stage-managing, serving coffee in the lobby at intermission, and selling theater parties.

I know I've mellowed. I certainly realize that stage management is not understood at many amateur theaters. But I still think it's desirable. So for all the Betty Spelvins of the world, here are five suggestions for the care and feeding of the amateur stage manager.

Get a Firm Understanding of the Function of the Stage Manager

There is no definitive list of the duties of a stage manager that can apply to all theaters and staging environments. A stage manager for a comedy performed in a theater in the round might carry out specific duties that are totally different from those of a stage manager for a traveling pantomime troupe. But the function is the same. Regardless of specific duties, the stage manager is the individual who accepts responsibility for the smooth running of rehearsals and performances, on stage and backstage. If you understand this function, you can decide on the specific duties for your theater. (This book is intended to help you do this.)

Give your stage manager her or his rightful function and the responsibility to carry out that function—not just a list of duties.

In Betty's case, understanding the function of the stage manager might mean sharing some of her responsibility with him or her—not a bad idea. Betty felt that she had to do everything herself if she wanted it done right. As a result, she did everything. If she could get over her I-am-the-savior-of-the-theater complex, perhaps she could devote more of her creative energy to the producer's function of obtaining personnel and materials. Obtaining a capable stage manager would have saved Betty and her directors a lot of work.

Get Firmly into Your Mind the Qualities That Make a Good Stage Manager, and Don't Settle for Anything Less

Organizational ability is one of the primary qualities of a good stage manager. Leadership ability is another. The stage manager must be able to influence the staff, cast, and crew. He or she must be a take-charge type and a self-starter and must be the kind of person who has the capacity to accept responsibility. (This book describes and applies most of these qualities in detail.)

As a producer, you are expected to control quality in selecting your staff. You should select the stage manager with the same care that you use to select your director, scene designer, and costumer.

Motivate Your Stage Manager

If your stage manager is new to the work, you must make her or him see that everything she or he does contributes to the improvement of the production. It is not enough for the stage manager to understand his or her function and specific duties. Point out, for example, that in setting rehearsal furniture 15 minutes prior to rehearsal, three hours of cast time may be saved—time that can be devoted to rehearsing that will result in a more polished performance.

In short, make sure that your stage manager knows that every bit of work he or she does is desirable, necessary, and appreciated.

Collect the Work of Past Stage Managers as a Reference

It is much simpler to set up a rehearsal schedule if you have a well-ordered one in your hand. Likewise, it is easier to improve a rotating duty roster if you have a past example to imitate. It would save a new stage manager considerable time and energy in making a shift plot chart if she or he had an old form from which to work.

Collect such materials in a loose-leaf notebook arranged in the general order of their use: prerehearsal materials, rehearsal materials, production materials, and postproduction materials. (The material in this book provides a start in this direction.)

Reward Your Stage Manager

Cast members are generally rewarded by the response and applause of the audience. Directors clip their reviews. Producers count the money at the box office. But in most amateur theaters, the stage manager is forgotten.

Kind words and letters of praise would be a good start. But why not let your stage manager in on the rewards available to other cast and staff members? Give her or his name prominence in the program. Publish her or his biographical sketch along with those of the cast. At the annual banquet when your theater group gives out its awards for best actress, best director, and so forth, why not select a best stage manager, too? Could you place in the lobby a plaque that records the name of the outstanding stage manager of each year? Find other ways to honor your stage manager—and he or she might come back for another production.

Why are there awards for virtually every aspect of a theatrical endeavour *except* stage managing, when a stage management staff can literally make or break a production? We bear the responsibility of executing a lighting design with our cueing, an intricate scene design relies on an intelligent deck ASM, and a whole production relies on a PSM with the caring and experience to view the show with a directorial eye and to constantly work on the upkeep of the production. Is this recognized by anyone but other stage managers? Have you ever tried to explain what you do to anyone who hasn't done it themselves? And is it worth the stress and angst for what little recognition we get?

Personally, I firmly believe that it is, but I despair at the lack of basic understanding of the job that is all too common even within our own theater community. I love what I do. The rewards, I find, are usually well worth the struggles, and the thrill of each new production gives me the lift I need to do my best. But I tend to be overly Pollyanna-ish and wonder how other stage managers feel.

Jill Johnson
Production Stage Manager
Long Beach Civic Light Opera
Long Beach, CA

A new director, who finds on hand a stage manager who has been through several productions with a group, inherits an experience level that can get him or her off to a flying start.

Well, Betty, that's the way it should be. But if, as in so many amateur theater groups, you want to continue to distribute the stage manager's duties while holding on to the function—if you want to continue to bring in people at the last minute to pull the curtain and give the actors their calls, and call them stage managers—if you want to continue to paint scenery and sew costumes at the last minute because you haven't done your work of obtaining a professional stage manager who could schedule work calls—if you want to continue to make amateur theater amateurish—then that's your problem.

Suggested Classroom Exercise

Discuss with students the function of the stage manager. Try to express results of the discussion as a brief statement, beginning with an infinitive phrase. My statement is: "To make things run smoothly on stage and backstage before rehearsals begin, during rehearsals, during production, and after the production closes."

2

Characteristics of a Good Stage Manager

The ability to speak several languages is an asset, but the ability to keep your mouth shut in one is truly impressive.

—Anonymous

I have since learned what a stage manager does. Everything. In production he is master of all details, liaison with Actors' Equity and the hairdresser, maker of appointments and planner of time for the cast, assistant to the director, rehearser of understudies and replacements, supervisor of all moves in and out of theaters, confidant and hand holder of cast, director, and author. Once the play opens he's the man who runs the show, attends every performance and is responsible for the condition and upkeep of the set and costumes, the temperature of the theatre, as well as the cast, and is responsible for the level of performances. He's Big Daddy. And Porter (stage manager for *Any Wednesday*), unobtrusively but meticulously organized, highly efficient, funny, warm, and caring, was perfect casting.*

In this quotation, playwright Muriel Resnik praises her stage manager as "unobtrusively but meticulously organized, highly efficient, funny, warm, and caring." Are these the highest attributes? Let's examine eight qualities of a good stage manager. These tenets involve a professional attitude and certain personal traits.

Professional Attitude

1. Good stage managers assume responsibility.

Effective stage managers say to themselves, "I am the one who must make things run smoothly on stage and backstage. Beyond me the buck does not

---

*From the book by Muriel Resnik, *The Son of Any Wednesday*. Reprinted by permission of Muriel Resnik. Copyright © 1965 by Muriel Resnik.

pass." This is an active role, not passive. It is not merely coordination. It is not merely doing what one is told. It is not merely the sum total of the myriad little duties. It is taking charge. It is accepting responsibility.

The significant difference between professional and nonprofessional stage managers is not whether they are paid or are members of a union. The significant difference is whether they are willing and able to accept responsibility for making the production run smoothly on stage and backstage in prerehearsal, rehearsal, performance, and postperformance phases. Your professionalism will make a significant difference in your relationship to the theater staff. The producer, director, technical director, and other staff members are also concerned that things run smoothly. But they have higher-priority responsibilities. You are the only one on the staff for whom this is the primary responsibility. If you can and will accept this responsibility, you are an equal of the producer and director on the team that makes theater. If you do not accept this responsibility and simply carry out a number of assigned tasks (pulling the curtain, giving the actors their calls, etc.), then you are a subordinate of the producer and director. Which are you?

2. *Good stage managers keep their cool.*

Can you exercise emotional self-control during all phases of production?

You will be working with excitable, conceited, self-centered, temperamental, volatile, sensitive, nervous, explosive people. But you will serve them best by not becoming emotionally involved in their arguments, controversies, or displays of temper.

If the leading lady stalks out screaming and crying, hand her a tissue to show her you care, but don't tell her or the director who was right or wrong in their dispute. It's none of your business. They will resolve their problems without your help.

If the producer asks for the cooperation of the cast in nonacting chores (cleaning the dressing rooms, selling tickets, publicity, etc.), don't give a noncooperative cast member a five-minute harangue or diatribe on his or her responsibilities. It is your job to ensure that cast members know what the director and producer expect of them—the time, the place. You may post a duty roster. You may hand out written memos. You may phone them to remind them. You may explain. But you may not lose your temper with a cast member for any reason at all.

If a cast member is late for half-hour call, even habitually late, and fails to call the theater, you may remind, you may explain, you may plead, you may cajole, but thou shalt not lose thy cool.

In general, don't raise your voice to cast members. Reply to raised voices in calm, steady, controlled tones.

If a director or producer should reprimand you, privately or before the company, for your prompting technique (as an example) or anything else, don't sulk. Get on with the job the way she or he wants it done.

If you blow a cue, don't get upset. Concentrate on getting the next one right.

Know your own panic response. Then control it. You have reacted to crises in the past. You know you can survive the next one. In time of panic, there must be only one question in your mind: Is there any action I can take to alleviate this situation? If so, do it. If not, keep your cool. Don't get swept up in the panic. Errors tend to compound.

Example

During a performance, a telephone bell failed to sound. The actors started to ad-lib, thinking that the cue was simply late. The stage manager in the booth realized that it was not late, but a mechanical failure. There was absolutely no way for the stage manager to get the bell to ring. There was no way to inform the cast on stage that the bell was not about to ring. The cast continued to ad-lib until one actor picked up the phone saying, "Thought I heard it ring."

What should the stage manager have done?

Answer: nothing.

The stage manager in this case panicked, left the control booth, and ran backstage to repair the bell—even though it was not to be used again during the performance. As a result, the next two sound cues were omitted. The error was compounded.

It is terribly uncomfortable to watch a cast ad-lib around a mechanical failure. But that's the price of insufficient preparation.

1. Did the stage manager test the bell during the precurtain routine?
2. Did the stage manager make sure that the bell wire was out from under the feet of backstage actors and crew?
3. Did the stage manager check to see that all connections were soldered?
4. Did the stage manager have a separate emergency bell wired in? (Do you think this is going too far?)

A week later, during a performance of the same play, the bell failed again. It was unquestionable negligence on the part of the stage manager. But a bell was heard. A cast member had brought an emergency bell to ring offstage because she didn't want a repeat of that incident. (Apparently the cast member didn't think an emergency bell was going too far!)

Stage manager, if a cast member has to ring your bell for you, it's time to hang up your clipboard.

Keeping one's cool means never appearing harassed, belligerent, insecure, apologetic, or imposed upon. It's not enough to be doing your job well. You've got to let the cast know by your deportment and the relaxed smile on your face that everything is under control. This gives the cast confidence. In this way, your cool may often be a positive contributing factor to the overall quality of the production.

3. Good stage managers keep their mouths shut and their eyes and ears open.

Do you tend to be quiet and observant? If what you say always has to do with the immediate improvement of the rehearsal or production, the cast members, crew, and staff will listen to you. If you run off at the mouth endlessly, you will have to struggle to gain attention when you have something significant to contribute. Where between these two extremes are you?

If you have a choice between shouting across the stage to a subordinate to change some gel frames and crossing the stage yourself to deliver quiet instructions, choose the latter. The cast, staff, and crew will come to appreciate the fact you are the great mover without the vocal display.

Don't waste your own time promoting yourself. Efficient work is hard to hide, so you need not explain how efficient you are to staff members.

Be alert to what is going on around you. During breaks, stick with the director. In casual conversation with actors and staff, she or he will agree to changes in lines, props, cues, or design. You should make these changes, or cause them to be made, without further instruction.

Example

During a break, an actor approaches the director and asks if he may omit a line that's been troubling him. She agrees to the omission. You were getting a cup of coffee instead of staying at the director's side. At the next rehearsal of the scene, the actor omits the line. You prompt. The actor breaks character to advise you that the line was cut. You turn to the director for confirmation. The director doesn't remember since it has been three days since this scene was last run. The actor and director discuss it. They agree to omit the line, or the director decides at this time she wants the line delivered. The rehearsal resumes. But there has been a delay that you might have avoided if you had stuck with the director and kept your ears open.

There are no breaks for stage managers. If you must have refreshments, bring a thermos and pack a sandwich or snack in your kit.

Don't gossip with the cast. You will often be privileged to know things that are going on at the administrative level, or between the producer and the director, or between the conductor and the harp player, or about closing date, casting history, salaries, and much more. Keep it to yourself.

If a cast member should ask you what you think of the director, staff, crew, or another cast member, try the following, delivered by rote in a loud if not sincere voice: "X is the best director (producer, scene designer, publicist, actor, actress, etc.) I've ever had the pleasure of working with." When you are no longer associated with that production, you can say what you really think, but until then, a complete, beguiling display of "I-know-how-to-play-this-game" is the most effective response.

Don't align yourself with any clique of actors within a cast. The stage manager is a friend to the whole cast. If you choose to go out after the show with one group habitually, make it clear to the others in the cast that you would also like to be with them. Invite them to come along sometime.

4. *Good stage managers think ahead.*

Don't just sit there, anticipate!

What is the company going to be doing later today? Tomorrow? Next week? Does everyone know about it? Is everything ready? You have made a master calendar, schedules, do-lists, duty rosters, a prompt script, and checklists. All of these are instruments to help you think ahead. But there is no substitute for constant vigilance.

If something is changed suddenly, what future effects will the change have? What other changes must be made as a result of that change? Who must be notified?

One of your greatest contributions to the performance quality is making the most of every minute between first reading and final curtain. If there is any delay in rehearsal or production, it's your fault.

Stage-managing can be compared to flying a high-performance aircraft. Once you're in the air, you can't make repairs. Once the curtain goes up, you can't stop the performance to make changes in the location of set pieces and discovered props. So pilots and stage managers both must have extensive preflight checklists.

To land a high-performance aircraft, you must take several steps prior to entering the landing pattern, because the aircraft moves so fast there is no time to accomplish everything once into the pattern. To carry out a tight sequence of light changes and sound effects, the stage manager must also take several steps in advance, like ensuring that tapes are cued, that dimmer board presets are cranked in and patches made, and that all hands are rehearsed in the execution of that sequence and understand their cues. Once the sequence starts, there is no time to do all of the things that must be done in advance if the sequence is to be brought off successfully.

Although the comparison might be extended, the point is clear: Pilots and stage managers must have the same think-ahead discipline to function properly.

Serious emergencies call for both keeping cool and thinking ahead. A fire should be expected momentarily. Do you have a fire extinguisher in the control booth? Do you have another one backstage? Do you have a phone in the booth? If it's a pay phone, do you have emergency coins taped nearby? Do you know the number to call? Is there a clear unblocked space for you to get out from behind your equipment? Can you give calm instructions to your audience in a tone of voice that will convince them to leave the theater in an orderly fashion? In a huge theater, do you have a working microphone in the booth that will allow you to reach the entire audience via the public address system? Do you know evacuation procedures? Are all the exit aisles, doors, and alleys unblocked? Will the emergency exits open? Is your scenery flameproofed in accordance with city ordinances? Is all electrical equipment wired safely?

If the answer to any of these questions is no, the stage manager and the producer are derelict in their responsibility for the safety of the audience and the cast. They have not anticipated problems.

Stage managers must force themselves out of the rut of thinking that it can't happen here. It *can* happen here, and everyone in your theater will be safer if you will just assume that it *is* going to happen here within the next 30 seconds.

Plan ahead for the worst possible type of medical emergency. Assume that a member of the cast or crew will suffer a severe injury or heart attack in the course of mounting, rehearsing, or presenting.

Do you have a company doctor? Is her or his office or home near the theater? Do you know the location of an all-night clinic? Have you driven there on a test run from the theater? (It is maddening to find that the clinic entrance is located on a one-way street and you will have to drive three extra blocks because you didn't make the right approach—while your passenger is losing blood!)

What's your earthquake plan?

During such emergencies, keeping your cool and thinking ahead become traits of paramount importance.

Personal Traits

5. *Good stage managers are considerate.*

Do you have that quality of selfless caring that prompts you to give a friend your jacket when you know you'll be cold? Can you put the comfort of every cast member before your own comfort?

Is the theater warm enough? Is it possible to arrive there a little earlier to turn on the heat so that cast members don't walk into a cold theater? Can you turn on the lights so cast members won't have to enter dark dressing rooms?

Is the backstage area too drafty? Can you close some doors or make some baffles out of extra flats?

Do the actresses have to walk to their cars from the theater along a dimly lit street? Can you walk them to their cars or ask other cast members to do so? If it's raining, can you provide an umbrella?

Is there drinking water backstage and in the dressing rooms? Can you arrange for water service or provide pitchers and cups?

Have you dusted the rehearsal furniture before the cast sits down?

Do you really listen when cast members speak to you?

Can you offer your cast a natural affection?

Backstage in Hollywood theaters, I found the lavish affection and terms of endearment that pass between casual acquaintances to be quite surprising. It did not seem very natural to me. But insecurity seems to be a very common trait among theater people, and they find warmth and affection reassuring. This display of warmth does not come naturally to all people. It is certainly not recommended if it must be forced. But if you can display a natural affection for your cast, as if they were all dear old warm friends or members of your family, why not?

Are you considerate with respect to the creativity of others? Can you offer constructive criticism effectively without stamping out creative instinct? It's very difficult to do.

Many of the creative people—the scene designers, costume designers, choral directors, choreographers, and directors—carry their gifts wrapped preciously within thin skin. Yet, in the theater situation no creator can work alone. He or she must communicate with and gain the cooperation of all the others on the staff to see his or her creativity come to fruition. The stage manager, unfortunately, is frequently placed in the position of coordinating the creative efforts of the supersensitive. It requires much patience and tact.

Example

Set construction is running behind schedule. The technical director complains to you that the scene designer has no concept of economy in design, that he tries to present in total rather than suggesting. She complains that the designer is overburdening the shop with an unconscionable amount of work.

The scene designer complains to you that the technical director has ruined more scenery than a termite on a showboat, that inefficient methods are being used in the shop, and that for two nights running one of his ornamental set pieces has not been placed on stage because it is waiting to be repaired and that this ruins the entire aesthetic balance of the set.

Your chief concern as stage manager is to have the set for the next production ready for the take-in one night hence.

This is the type of situation that requires tactful soothing and massive doses of consideration. If you try to fix the blame at this point, you are likely to find your next production hung up. Cool off the technical director and the scene designer, separately. Commiserate with each, separately. Tell them what an incredibly good job they've been doing up to this point. Praise their strong points. Overlook their weaknesses. Sympathize with their problems. Pep them up and send them back to work. They'll get the scenery finished.

6. Good stage managers keep their sense of humor.

Making theater should be a happy experience for all concerned. Unfortunately, delays, deadlines, economic pressures, personality conflicts, and other factors sometimes make the process grim.

Don't contribute to the grimness. Leave your personal problems at home. Come to work with a resolve to stay happy.

"I find that most people are just as happy as they make up their minds to be," said Abraham Lincoln. Lincoln considered humor a "labor-saving device" and a "multiple-purpose tool."

"A sense of humor is part of the art of leadership, of getting along with people, of getting things done," said Dwight D. Eisenhower.

Try to keep a smile on your face, and have a good reason for its being there.

A cheerful stage manager can be a great asset to any theater group. Sometimes a cheerful word can get the whole company over a rough spot.

Knowing jokes is not a substitute for having a sense of humor. There are occasions, however, when a good theater story will put the company at ease. A successful director with whom I worked greeted each new cast with a story; it seemed to break the ice and to be very effective for him. Consult Appendix C for a few of my favorite stories.

A corollary of tenet 6 is that *good stage managers do not have personality conflicts with anyone.* Holding grudges or showing hostility toward any member of the company cannot be a part of your behavior. Go home and shred your philodendron, but don't let any member of the cast, staff, or crew feel that you dislike her or him. It simply does not expedite production.

7. *Good stage managers are organized and efficient.*

Throughout the chapters that follow, the emphasis will be on organization and efficiency, so no further comment should be needed here.

8. *Good stage managers are punctual and dependable.*

If you are not there on time or early, or cannot be depended on, you simply cannot be a stage manager.

In summary, good stage managers

Accept responsibility
Keep their cool
Keep their mouths shut, their eyes and ears open
Think ahead

In her mystery novel *The G-String Murders*, Gypsy Rose Lee writes, "As stage managers go, Sammy was about average, but that isn't saying much for him. I've worked for a lot of them and I haven't found one yet that didn't think he owned the theater and everybody in it."* What an unfortunate fictional portrait. I ask all of my student stage managers to read your book. I feel it encourages them to be efficient without being offensive or despotic.

> Billy C. Creamer
> Theater Director
> Rolling Hills High School
> Rolling Hills Estates, CA

*From Gypsy Rose Lee, *The G-String Murders* (New York: Penguin Books, 1984/ 1941).

Are considerate
Keep their sense of humor
Are organized and efficient
Are punctual and dependable

How do you compare?

Suggested Classroom Exercise

Ask students to pretend that each is a producer about to hire a stage manager. Tell them to write out three qualities that they would consider essential (e.g., organized, sense of humor, dependable) and rank order those three. Then combine the lists and discuss as a group which attributes of a stage manager are most important.

3

Getting the Play and Understanding It

Genius is one percent inspiration and ninety-nine percent perspiration.

—Thomas Alva Edison

During the readings, rehearsals, and production, you must have a copy of the script and a thorough understanding of it. In order to expedite readings and rehearsals, you should check to make sure that there are enough scripts on hand for actors and staff.

Usually, copies of the script are ordered when the rights of production are obtained from the play service (Samuel French, Tams-Witmark, etc.; see below). If, however, you are going into production with one copy of the script, or a vague memory of it, one of the first things you must do is make sure you have on hand an adequate number of scripts. This may possibly be limited to determining how many are necessary, or it may mean actually going to pick them up.

The following information will assist you in contacting major play publishing services in the United States. Some catalogs can be ordered via e-mail or the Internet.

Anchorage Press Plays
P.O. Box 2901
Louisville, KY 40201-2901
(502) 583-2288
fax: (502) 583-2281
e-mail: applays@bellsouth.net

Baker's Plays
P.O. Box 699222
Quincy, MA 02169-9222
(617) 745-0605
fax: (617) 745-9891
www.bakersplays.com

I. E. Clark Publications
P.O. Box 246
Schulenburg, TX 78956-0246
(979) 743-3232
fax: (979) 743-4765

Dramatic Publishing Co.
311 Washington Street, Box 129
Woodstock, IL 60098-3308
(815) 338-7170
fax: (815) 338-8981
e-mail:
    plays@dramaticpublishing.com
www.dramaticpublishing.com

Dramatists Play Service, Inc.
440 Park Avenue South
New York, NY 10016-8012
(212) 683-8960
fax: (212) 213-1539
e-mail:
    postmaster@dramatists.com
www.dramatists.com/dramatists

Eldridge Publishing Co.
P.O. Box 1595
Venice, FL 34284-1595
(800) HI STAGE
fax: (800) 453-5179
e-mail: info@histage.com
www.histage.com

Heuer Publishing Co.
P.O. Box 248
Cedar Rapids, IA 52406-0248
(319) 364-6311
fax: (319) 364-1771
e-mail: hitplays@netins.net
www.hitplays.com

Institute for Readers Theatre
P.O. Box 17193
San Diego, CA 92117-7193
(619) 276-1948
fax: (619) 576-7369
e-mail: info@readers-theatre.com
www.readers-theatre.com

Music Theatre International
421 West 54th Street
New York, NY 10019
(212) 541-4684
fax: (212) 397-4684
e-mail: Licensing@MTIShows.com
www.mtishows.com

Pioneer Drama Service
P.O. Box 4267
Englewood, CO 80155-4267
(303) 779-4035
fax: (800) 333-7262

The Rodgers & Hammerstein
    Theatre Library
1065 Avenue of the Americas, #2400
New York, NY 10018-2506
(212) 541-6600
fax: (212) 586-6155

Samuel French, Inc.
45 West 25th Street, Fl 2
New York, NY 10010-2003
(212) 206-8990
fax: (212) 206-1429

Tams-Witmark Music Library, Inc.
560 Lexington Avenue, Fl 12
New York, NY 10022-6828
(212) 688-2525
fax: (212) 688-3232

Check with your post office to determine the type of mail service that you must have to ensure that the scripts get to you on time. It is usually worth the cost of specifying overnight or second-day delivery, or at least first class, rather than the less expensive book rate, to make sure that your scripts won't be delayed in the mail. UPS is very reliable.

In determining the number of scripts you will need, consider:

1. Will all speaking parts need scripts? Check your visual display of characters on stage (discussed later in this chapter) to see whether a few pages of one script can be removed for one or two other speaking parts.
2. Will the costume designer, scene designer, property master, or any other staff member need a script? The publicity person can often make good use of a script.
3. Will a follow-spot operator or any other crew member need one?
4. Will understudies or replacements need them?
5. Can the budget allow for a few extra copies?
6. Do you have copying equipment, or easy access to it? Is it legal to photocopy? (See page 21.)

Sides, a part of a script giving only one character's lines, each preceded by the cue for the line, may be typed or hand-copied by apprentices or the actors, if necessary.

When script shipments arrive, immediately check the content against the invoice or manifest. Make sure you have what you need. If you wait until the first day of rehearsal, you have a potential disaster!

Lock up your scripts and let them out only on a sign-out basis. Otherwise, they will disappear. It's not usually criminal intent. It may be the chorus girl who wants to read for a principal part in next week's production who loses her script on a cast picnic. This does not mean to imply that she should not be permitted to see a script in advance of a reading, but she should have to sign it out.

All scripts and sides should be signed out when issued to cast members and staff. Lock up the sign-out sheet in the same cupboard as the scripts. Scripts, sides, and scores are usually due back from cast, staff, and musicians on the day preceding or coinciding with the close of the show. (This is payday in professional companies; the cost of lost materials can then be deducted on the spot.) Post a notice to this effect and a price list on the call board. Note your intent in the company rules.

Frequently, a cast member with just a few lines will elect to copy them rather than sign out a skimpy side, thus avoiding the possibility of losing it. You would be wise to encourage this.

Normally in musical stock and musical comedy, the scores, scripts, and sides are packaged and returned within a week after the close of the production in order to decrease rental costs. This task is usually assigned to an apprentice or the company "gopher" (a production assistant sent to "go fer" things). If a closing night review of the past year or season is to be presented, you may want to retain one score and one script from each of the shows.

On straight playbook shows, you may allow the actors to keep the scripts, or you may ask that they return or pay for them. Determine your policy and relay it to the cast.

All too frequently, you may be held responsible for missing scripts and asked to pay for them. It is a good idea, then, to mark each script with a number so that each can be accounted for.

Scripts sometimes get tied up for unusual reasons.

Example

In casting a big-name show, an actor might be sent a script even though there is no intent to cast that actor. You may even be called on to deliver the script to the actor's home. The script is never seen again until a few weeks after opening, when it comes back through the mail with a hard-to-read note, "Not my cup of tea," and the big-name actor's initials.

Agents for professional actors often beg directors or managers for scripts, and receive them, even though there is no intent to cast the agents' clients. The agents feel that showing the scripts to their clients is tangible proof that they are working and that their clients are being considered.

When a script is issued for any unusual reason, don't count on its being returned in time to meet your needs. It is best to replace that script immediately if you have on hand only the necessary minimum with which to begin rehearsals.

Although your responsibility for scripts may be very limited, you should know how to get, replace, reproduce, lock up, control, and retrieve scripts as part of your work in expediting auditions and rehearsals.

Of even greater concern is the processing of your own script—making it into a working tool.

The Prompt Script

Turning a script into a *prompt script* increases the size of the margins (see Figure 3.1). This allows you to make all of your cues and warns (warning alerts) large and clear, and it gives you adequate room to make clear blocking notations and diagrams. It also gives you sufficient room to make production notes.

Making a Promptbook

To make a promptbook, cut or "unbind" the pages of a script and mount each page on a standard size (8½"× 11") loose-leaf sheet (unruled) so that both sides of the script can be seen (see Figure 3.2).

If you are willing to use two printed scripts to produce one prompt script, this is by far the fastest method: You simply paste alternate printed pages to opposite sides of each loose-leaf 8½" × 11" page.

Whether your prompt script is made from two scripts or by the "economy" one-script method, you need to consider the best placement of loose-leaf page space around the printed script, and Figure 3.2 shows the alternatives. Note that for the one-script cutout method with a loose-leaf

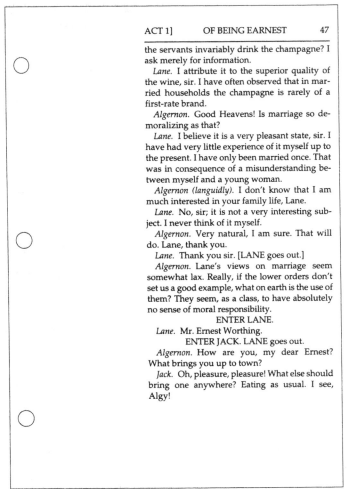

ACT 1]   OF BEING EARNEST   47

the servants invariably drink the champagne? I ask merely for information.

Lane. I attribute it to the superior quality of the wine, sir. I have often observed that in married households the champagne is rarely of a first-rate brand.

Algernon. Good Heavens! Is marriage so demoralizing as that?

Lane. I believe it is a very pleasant state, sir. I have had very little experience of it myself up to the present. I have only been married once. That was in consequence of a misunderstanding between myself and a young woman.

Algernon (languidly). I don't know that I am much interested in your family life, Lane.

Lane. No, sir; it is not a very interesting subject. I never think of it myself.

Algernon. Very natural, I am sure. That will do. Lane, thank you.

Lane. Thank you sir. [LANE goes out.]

Algernon. Lane's views on marriage seem somewhat lax. Really, if the lower orders don't set us a good example, what on earth is the use of them? They seem, as a class, to have absolutely no sense of moral responsibility.

ENTER LANE.

Lane. Mr. Ernest Worthing.

ENTER JACK. LANE goes out.

Algernon. How are you, my dear Ernest? What brings you up to town?

Jack. Oh, pleasure, pleasure! What else should bring one anywhere? Eating as usual. I see, Algy!

Figure 3.1   A Promptbook Page with Script Page Numbers Visible

page pasted around printed script edges, pattern 1 calls for rubber-cementing, taping, or gluing four sides of every page, whereas patterns 3 and 4 require that only two sides of each page be attached. I feel that pattern 2, which requires that three sides be attached, gives the most desirable distribution of additional space.

If you cannot spare an extra printed script and must paste loose-leaf paper around printed pages to show both sides of each printed sheet, then start by making a heavy cardboard template cut to show all the printed area of each script page (see Figure 3.2). With a single-edged or mounted razor, you can then cut about five loose-leaf sheets at a time to the correct size, making one loose-leaf cutout page for each two-sided leaf of printed script.

Use Scotch Magic Transparent Tape, a crayon-shaped glue stick, or rubber cement to attach script pages to the cutout loose-leaf sheets. Rubber

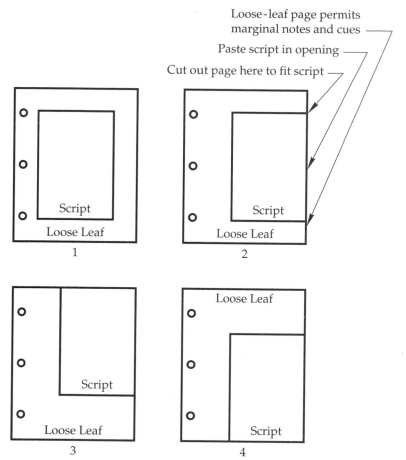

Figure 3.2 Four Patterns for Mounting Script Pages

cement is the most forgiving. Errors can be corrected without cutting, because rubber-cemented pages can be pulled apart and restuck without damage to the pages. Glue sticks are faster and more convenient. I have found the Avery Glue Stic to be excellent. Some liquid glue sticks wrinkle the paper when dry. It is best to experiment and find the right glue stick before pasting up your entire script.

With the help of a few apprentices, using assembly-line methods, you can assemble an "economy model" prompt script in less than one hour. Allow several hours if you are making your first script by yourself, and five hours if you have a hangover following a cast party.

To photocopy or not to photocopy, that is the question; and the question is asked here *only* with respect to the manufacture of the stage manager's prompt script.

Copyright law and the term *fair use,* are open to a wide range of legal interpretations. All of the publishers listed earlier in this chapter were asked for their policy with respect to making the stage manager's prompt script by photocopying. The replies ranged from "No photocopying" to "It's okay under fair use if a copy is purchased for the exclusive use of the stage manager."

With the intent of making each publisher's policy clear to stage managers who are considering photocopying rather than mounting pages on 8½" × 11" paper, here's what the publishers say:

Samuel French	"While our general policy is that we do not authorize the photocopying of our publications, there may well be circumstances that could alter that situation on individual bases."
Music Theatre International	"MTI does not permit or condone photocopying of scripts."
Tams-Witmark Music Library, Inc.	"Copyrighted works cannot be reproduced without the consent of the copyright proprietor. In any event, the scripts that we supply are already on 8½ × 11 paper, and, accordingly, no photocopying would be necessary."
The Rodgers & Hammerstein Theatre Library	"Photocopying a copyrighted work without the express prior consent of the copyright owners is not considered 'fair use' within the meaning of that term as defined by the United States Copyright Act. We are always happy to entertain requests to photocopy materials on a case-by-case basis. When a producing organization requests the right to photocopy a script for the purpose of creating a stage manager's prompt book, we are most often able to grant such permission. In such a case, we require that all photocopies be returned to us with the other materials when the production has closed."
Heuer Publishing Company	"Photocopying copyrighted scripts is illegal unless permission in writing is received from the publisher/agent. However, if a published script is purchased for the stage manager and the stage manager photocopies that script to enlarge the margins for his/her exclusive use and the photocopied script is destroyed after its use, we would consider this scenario 'fair use' and give the stage manager permission to photocopy the purchased script. You should always check with the publisher first and get permission in writing. Most requests are evaluated on a case-by-case basis."
Baker's Plays	"We ask that the stage manager write in advance asking permission. Most of the time we can allow, depending on the contract with the author."

Dramatists Play Service, Inc.	"Photocopying a work that is still protected under copyright laws and without the express permission of the authors or their representatives does not fall within the 'fair use' constraints of the United States Copyright Act. Dramatists Play Service, Inc., however, will consider requests for permission to photocopy a play script for the purpose of creating a stage manager's prompt script on a case by case basis."
Eldridge Publishing I. E. Clark Publications Institute for Readers Theatre Pioneer Drama Service	"If a script is purchased for exclusive use of the stage manager, and if the stage manager photocopies that script in order to enlarge the margins to make a prompt script for his/her exclusive use, then this falls under 'fair use' and is not a violation of copyright law."
Anchorage Press	"The necessity to have a prompt script that is adapted to the needs of the stage manager has made it common practice to copy and enlarge. It is important to have purchased a script for the exclusive use of the stage manager. We suggest that the script be archived with the prompt script following the production."

Make tabs for each scene so that you can quickly turn to any scene without thumbing through the script. You can purchase tabs at a stationery store or you can make your own, using tape. Each tab should be labeled (see Figure 3.3). Place the scene tabs on the last page of the previous scene, not the first or second page of the scene, so that the tab will open your script properly, with the desired scene immediately displayed.

Rehearsal schedule, pronunciation guide, plots, set sketches, and cast lists should also be tabbed so that you can turn immediately to whatever information you need during a rehearsal without wasting time by shuffling through a lot of paper.

A neat, well-made promptbook is an asset, but no critic will ever review your promptbook. Great paperwork does not necessarily make great theater. It might be possible for some people to keep all of their blocking notation in their heads and make sound-and-light cue notations in the margins of uncut scripts, but most managers could not work this way, and most wouldn't feel secure or comfortable. I advise you to do whatever works best for you, but I would suggest that super organization of your promptbook is a great system.

Keeping the Prompt Script in a Safe Place

Once a skilled stage manager has worked on a prompt script, it becomes a valuable tool and should therefore be safeguarded.

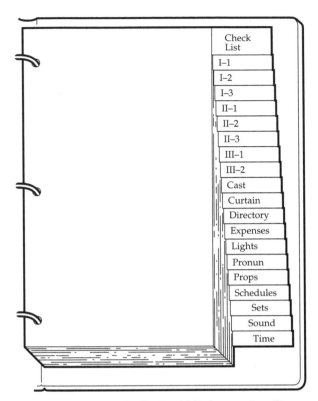

Figure 3.3   Page Tabs for Rapid Reference in a Prompt Script. Note that the tabs are in alphabetical order so that the stage manager has extremely easy access to any information that is needed during rehearsal or production.

There are two possible ways to do this. The first is that the prompt script is *always* with the stage manager; it even goes home with the stage manager. If anyone needs information from the prompt script in the middle of the night, he or she calls the stage manager. The stage manager is so prompt and so reliable that there is never any fear in anyone's mind that the prompt script might be missing when needed.

The other possibility is that the prompt script is kept in a secure place in the theater—locked up when the stage manager is not using it during rehearsals. The idea here is that if something should happen to the stage manager, someone else could pick up the prompt script and run the rehearsal or show.

You will have to decide which of these two possibilities is best for your theater.

Allowing Access to the Prompt Script

Anyone who needs information from the prompt script should ask the stage manager for that information. The prompt script is the stage manager's tool, and as a courtesy to the stage manager, no one should go into the prompt script without his or her permission.

Keying or Coding the Prompt Script

In educational theater, the stage manager is often advised to set up the prompt script so that anyone can read and understand all the cues and notes, as well as the blocking notation. The stage manager should be instructed to make a key for abbreviations and symbols on the front page of the prompt script.

Understanding the Script

You must understand the script, and you must understand it well before casting and before rehearsals begin if you are to be effective. To understand it, you must analyze it and identify its problems. The word *problem* is used to mean anything that must be done to run the show.

Try to allow a quiet time of intense concentration for your first reading. It can pay off in the accomplishment of a lot of work. All of this prerehearsal work can pay great dividends in time saved during rehearsals.

As you read, use light pencil in the margins of your script to identify all possible light cues, sound cues, special effects, costume changes, or peculiarities, properties, entrances, exits, and pronunciation questions. You might want to use the following code:

L—Light cue
S—Sound cue
Ef—Special effect
P—Property
E—Entrance or exit
?—Pronunciation question

Of course, any code that works for you is fine.

For every light, sound, and special effect, using a ruler and working in light pencil, you should draw a horizontal line closest to the line of dialogue preceding an oral cue, or under the description of a visual cue. This line should cross the entire promptbook page so that you can see it quite easily during rehearsals.

About a half page preceding the line, draw another horizontal line marked "warn lights" or "warn sound." In the case of two light cues and a sound cue in a tight sequence, you need put in only one warn line before the sequence, but it should be marked "warn light/sound series" (see Figure 3.4).

It is too early to number these cues or to write them in ink, since there may well be changes during rehearsals. You will use the penciled lines to call the light and sound cues during rehearsals.

accepts me. I am going to kill my brother, indeed I think I'll kill him in any case. Cecily is a little too much interested in him. It is rather a bore. So I am going to get rid of Ernest. And I strongly advise you to do the same with Mr. . . . with your invalid friend who has the absurd name.

Warn

Bell

Algernon. Nothing will induce me to part with Bunbury, and if you ever get married, which seems to me extremely problematic, you will be very glad to know Bunbury. A man who marries without knowing Bunbury has a very tedious time of it.

Jack. That is nonsense. If I marry a charming girl like Gwendolen, and she is the only girl I ever saw in my life that I would marry, I certainly won't want to know Bunbury.

Algernon. Then your wife will. You don't seem to realize, that in married life three is company and two is none.

Jack (sententiously). That, my dear young friend, is the theory that the corrupt French Drama has been propounding for the last fifty years.

Algernon. Yes; and that the happy English home has proved in half the time.

Jack. For heaven's sake, don't try to be cynical. It's perfectly easy to be cynical.

Algernon. My dear fellow, it isn't easy to be anything now-a-days. There's such a lot of

Bell

beastly‸competition about. *(The sound of an electric bell is heard.)* Ah! that must be Aunt Augusta. Only relatives, or creditors, ever ring in that Wagnerian manner. Now, if I get her out of the way for ten minutes, so that you can have

Figure 3.4 Lightly Penciled Cues and Warns for Use during Rehearsals

Plots

As you identify the problems and put in your light pencil lines, you might also wish to list the problems. A list of problems is a *plot*. A functional plot is one that allows your associates to obtain a complete grasp of the problems in their areas without having to refer to the script. In other words, *plots allow you to digest the script for others.*

In deciding whether making plots will be of practical value, ask yourself this question: If I were the sound technician on this production, would it help if I were handed a sound plot? In productions where the technical people come in just a few days before opening, having plots ready is particularly valuable.

Copies of your plots should be given to all staff members concerned. Your copy should be kept in your promptbook, properly tabbed, to be changed in rehearsals as necessary.

If, as you read, you list problems on separate sheets of paper headed "Light plot," "Sound plot," "Special effects," "Properties," and "Pronunciation," then you will now have rough plots ready.

Some acting editions of plays contain costume and property plots. They do not always contain all the information you will need, but you will be able to modify them easily (see Figure 3.5).

In general, you will want to cite on each plot for each entry the following: the page, the act and scene, and a full description of what happens.

COSTUME PLOT	Actor Provides	Borrow	Rent	Purchase	Responsible & Date
MRS. JONES:					
Green and white silk polka dot dress					
White shoes					
Long white gloves					
White bracelets and earrings					
Pink silk fringe dress and stole					
Pink shoes and white beaded evening bag					
FRED:					
Light blue shirt					
Grey flannel pants					
Dark red tie					
Black shoes					
Red wool school jacket (Monroe High School)					
FATHER:					
Pajamas, orange and white stripe cotton					
Black shoes					
Grey suit					
Print shirt					
White shirt					
Soft grey hat					
JANE:					
Green jumper and white blouse					
White low heel shoes					
White bag					
White dress					
Light blue suit					
White gloves					
White high heel shoes					
HENRY:					
Dark blue and white stripe shirt					
Print shirt					
White shirt					
Jeans					
Grey sneakers					
Grey socks					
Tan shoes					
Light brown double-breasted suit					
Blue apron					
JEEVES:					
Black double-breasted tuxedo					

Figure 3.5   Costume Plot as Modified from the Script

Light Plot

Leave plenty of room between entries on the light plot (see Figure 3.6). The director may add lighting effects not called for in the script and may add many dimmings and brightenings of areas during rehearsals.

Sound Plot

Frequently at sound recording sessions, the sound technician and staff members, each holding a copy of the sound plot (see Figure 3.7), select and

page	lt. effect	cue	cue #	inst dmmrs	int	timg
114/64	Shop up	after Foreman's entrance				
114/70	Shop out	David: "Whee" and Marvin's exit				
115/71	Dressing room in	following David's exit				
115/78	Dressing room out	David: "No, he's a hardware salesman!"				
116/78	Stage and Stage Manager's area (Now the foots!) (But no worklight!)	after entrance of cast				
116/82	Stage and Stage Manager's area out	David: "I am your older brother! By a former marriage!"				
117/82	Stage to general with worklight, no foots	when cast in place				
117/83	Stage down to effect of single worklight	Mother: "A very nice young man." & her exit				
117/84	Worklight out	David: "I trust I haven't kept you waiting too long."				
	Curtain calls lighting					
	Curtain lights out					
	House in					

Figure 3.6   Light Plot, Listing Cues. Note that cue numbers will not be established until the technical rehearsal. The columns left blank for "cue number," "instruments/dimmers," "intensity," and "timing" will normally be filled out by the light technician working with the stage manager. See Figure 11.1 for board operator's form.

	ACT SCENE PAGE	SOUND CUE SHEET	VOLUME	TONE	SPKR SLCTN	TIME	OTHER
1. Intro music		30 min prior to curtain in time	4	balance	1, 2, 3	30 min	fade out GENTLY
2. Fade out intro		to cue up 3rd cue (on "places")	—				
3. Roar of airplane	I-1	just prior to curtain	8		1	20 sec	
4. Thunder, lightning, heavy rain	I-1	"You won't be needing your raincoat."	7		2	90 sec	
5. Bells and light rain	I-2	"Hold on to my hand."	5	Treble	2	20 sec	
6. Car approach motor sick	I-6	"I don't hear anything."	6	balance	3	20 sec	
7. Motor strangles, car door slams	I-6	". . . His usual cheerful self."	8		2	10 sec	
8. Bicycles (like loud crickets)	I-10	"We'll meet you there." & ad libs (as they exit)	4-9 (fade up gently)		2	90 sec	

Figure 3.7   Sound Plot, Listing Cues. Space should be left between cues so that additional cues can be entered. The last five columns are set through coordination of director, stage manager, and sound technician during rehearsals.

rerecord, or create and record, sound effects. Ensure that all the needed sounds are recorded, in proper order and of appropriate length.

Costume Plot

Besides giving some indication of the clothes to be worn (see Figure 3.5), you should also identify quick changes that will require change booths in the wings or at the tops of aisles and/or a series of changes that will require that an actor be assisted (see Figure 3.8).

The costume plot published in the actor's edition of a contemporary noncostume play in which each cast member wears one costume throughout might require only the director's approval. But in a musical such as *Little Me*, in which the lead plays several roles and is forever making quick changes, you will need to write a meticulous plot with cues for costume assistants and presets for costumes.

Properties

Note whether the prop is discovered or carried on—if discovered, where, and if carried on, by whom (see Figure 3.9). During rehearsals, note whether the prop enters stage left or stage right, so that if there are two or more prop tables backstage, you will know where to preset that prop.

Property control is discussed at greater length in Chapter 10.

Atlanta Opera
COSI FAN TUTTE
Principal Costume Run - Last Changed on 5-28-00

Act, scene / est. time	I,1 — 35:00 - Dock & Café EN	(change)	XT	Shift CHANGE TIME/PLACE	I,2 — 67:00 - Drawing Room EN	(change)	XT	Shift CHANGE TIME/PLACE	I,3 — 85:30 - Garden EN	(change)	XT	INTERM 20:00 min CHANGE TIME/PLACE
FIORDILIGI (Harris)	12:30 / SL	Parasol, Locket	34:00 / SL	SL	35:30 / SL	Chg to underwear	43:30 / SL	SL or SR	67:00 / SR	Chg to Day Dress	85:30 / SR	
					47:30 / SL	add dr. gown, brush hair	60:00 / SL					
DESPINA (Reuter-Foss)					35:00 / SL	maid	43:30 / SR		67:00 / SR	maid	67:00 / SR	
					44:30 / SR		57:30 / SR		72:30 / SR	maid	73:30 / SL	
									76:00 / SL	Chg to Doctor	onstage	
DORABELLA (Ziegler)	12:30 / SL	Parasol, Locket	34:00 / SL	SL	35:30 / SL	Chg to underwear	43:30 / SL	SL	67:00 / SL	Chg to Day Dress	85:30 / SR	
					47:30 / SL	add dr. gown	60:00 / SL					
DON ALFONSO (Cokorinos)	onstage		15:30 / SL		43:30 / SR		61:30 / SR		68:30 / SL	no hat	onstage	
	17:30 / SL		35:00 / SR		66:00 / SL		67:00 / SL					
GUIGLIELMO (Barret)	onstage	casual look	15:30 / SL	Mo. Rm.	45:30 / SR	Albanian	65:30 / SR		70:00 / SL	Albanian	onstage	
	20:00 / SL	Chg SL to full dress uniform	29:30 / SR									
FERRANDO (Thomsen)	onstage	casual look	15:30 / SL	Mo. Rm.	45:30 / SR	Albanian	66:00 / SR		70:00 / SL	Albanian	onstage	
	20:00 / SL	Chg SL to full dress uniform	29:30 / SR									

Figure 3.8 Principal Costume Run Sheet, *Cosi Fan Tutti*. This form was generated using Microsoft Excel. The costume workers use stopwatches and the production stage manager gives 5-minute warnings: "Five-minute warning on Ms. Harris's quick change in the DL hallway." All warnings for costumes tell who, what, and where.

Courtesy Sean M. Griffin, ASM, The Atlanta Opera.

Entrances and Exits

Preparing for entrance warns

List each character, the scenes he or she is in, and the pages on which he or she enters and exits in the following way:

Irene:
I-1, 16–24; I-2, 26–30, 50–53;
II-1, 57–73, 78–83; II-2, 84–112

Constance:
II-1, 5–19; I-2, 26–45; etc.

PROP/SET PIECE	personal	preset	WHO/WHERE	work	SOURCE	final
coffee cup, white take-out	x		Quagmeyer	x		x
attache case	x		Hubris	x	Bill	x
script	x		Hubris/in attache	x	Lawrence	x
artist's smock	x		Hubris/in attache	x	Maria	
April Monkhood's picture	x		Hubris	x	Lawrence	x
phone, old beat up		x	on table	x		
radio, old beat up		x	on table	x		x
vase to hold brushes		x	on table	x		x
brushes		x	in vase	x	Dinah	x
small white paper bag		x	on table	x		x
push broom		x	behind easel	x		x
oil paintings		x	on chair	X		
abstract of woman		x	on easel			
bottle of whiskey in white bag	x		Quagmeyer	x		
easel, paint smeared						
table, beat up, paint smeared						
2 beat up, non matching chairs						

THE BEAUTY PART   Stage Right Prop Table

Act __I__ Scene __4__

Figure 3.9   Property Plot (May Double as Control Form)

(In Act I, Scene 1, Irene enters on page 16 and exits on page 24. In Scene 2 of Act I, she enters on page 26 and exits on page 30, then reenters on page 50 and exits again on page 53.)

You may wish to post your list of entrances and exits prior to a casting call so that actors may easily find lines to read for their parts.

You may also want to lightly pencil in warnings for entrances of actors, about a page preceding each entrance. It is not a stage manager's function to warn actors for their entrances during performance, but you will find that warning them during rehearsals is helpful. This aspect of rehearsal procedure is discussed in Chapter 8.

Long strips of paper rather than penciled lines may be used for entrance warns (see Figure 3.10). The marker warns are harder to miss than the light lines and can be completely removed from the prompt script prior to opening night. The marker can also be handed silently to an assistant to summon the actor.

From your notations of entrances and exits, you can now make up a visual display of characters on stage, a graph that shows at a glance which actors work together on what script pages (see Figure 3.11). This device

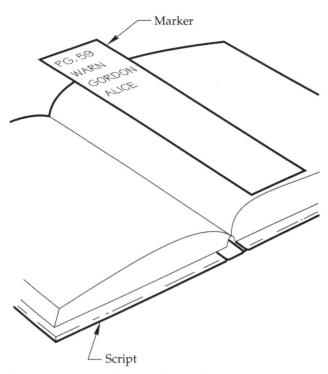

Marker

PG.59
WARN
GORDON
ALICE

Script

Figure 3.10   Actor Warn in Prompt Script for Quick Access during Rehearsal

will be invaluable to you in planning rehearsal schedules, finding appropriate pages for readings, double casting, and removing script pages to serve as sides for a minor role. The visual display should be placed in your prompt script as a reference tool.

Actors and their entrance cues

During performances, actors are responsible for making all their entrances on cue. They alone have this responsibility. This arises out of very understandable circumstances: During the performance, the stage manager can only be in one place—the work area—where she or he is busy following the book and cuing sound, lights, and curtain. Cues sometimes coincide with an actor's entrance (e.g., the doorbell rings prior to the entrance or the director calls for a subtle increase of light intensity on the door area as the actor enters). So the stage manager cannot be in two places at once, cueing and pushing the actor on stage. There might be several actors entering from more than one entrance. Therefore, out of very practical considerations, it is necessary that each actor be responsible for her or his own entrance. In professional theater, the union insists on this. In opera, however, cues for entrances and costume changes are given routinely (see Figure 3.8 and page 149 in Chapter 9).

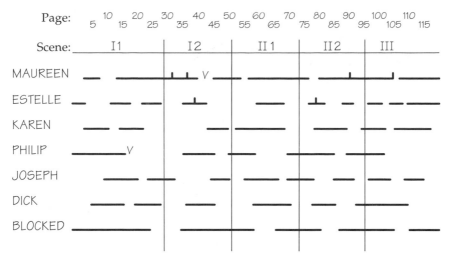

Figure 3.11   A Visual Display of Characters on Stage. Numbers denote script page numbers. Note that the "blocked" line allows you to see what scenes have yet to be blocked, and who's in them. The "v" denotes voice only.

As usual, there are some exceptions to this rule. The stage manager is responsible for actors being in place when they are discovered at the rise of the curtain and when they are offstage about to enter within the first few seconds after the curtain. After calling "Places, please," the stage manager checks that all discovered cast members are in their appropriate blocked positions. The procedure for checking this, in a theater-in-the-round example, is discussed in Chapter 12 under "Shift Inspection."

There are even some exceptional exceptions: Occasionally, a producer or director overrides normal procedure and asks that the stage manager "supervise" the entrances and exits of an actor who has particular difficulties. Such an exception is discussed as an example under "Calls" in Chapter 9.

During rehearsals, the situation is different. In the role of expeditor of rehearsals, the stage manager should closely supervise the entrances of cast members. In many theaters, there is no monitor system that broadcasts the rehearsals to offstage areas where the actors may wander off for fittings or to run lines. So the stage manager warns them of their entrances, following the procedures described under "Warning" in Chapter 8.

Pronunciation Questions

You may wish to make a list of all words in the script about which there is a question of pronunciation. Include the pronunciation of all proper names in the script that might be pronounced in more than one way.

Example

Middle of the Night by Paddy Chayefsky—"Mrs. Nieman." Obviously, all members of the cast should pronounce this name the same way. Should it be pronounced *Ne*-man or *Ni*-man?

List foreign words and phrases and give both the pronunciation and meaning.

Example

A Majority of One by Leonard Spigelgass—"mashugina"; *ma-shoog-i-na,* Yiddish meaning "crazy."

List unusual and uncommon words and give pronunciation and meaning.

Example

The Emperor by Hermann Gressieker—"trireme"; *tri-reem,* an ancient Roman galley with three banks of oars on each side.

Example

The Cherry Orchard by Anton Chekhov—"Epihodov"; *Ep-(i)-hoé-daff,* a clerk who proposes to Dunyasha.

This list may be posted as early as the readings for the benefit of those trying out for parts. But it is especially beneficial to you, since you must pronounce the words correctly while prompting. You should keep a copy in your prompt script. Also, cast members should be provided with pronunciations of characters' names.

Special Effects

If there is only one special effect in a play, there is obviously no need for writing a plot. But if you are doing a play that calls for many, you will want to list them for consideration by the scene designer and technical director. Such a list might include a heavy fog, walls shaking and dishes falling off shelves, a trapdoor disappearance accompanied by a flash of smoke, a sliding panel, firing of weapons, and so on. Use of fire or an open flame on stage requires a separate plot (see Figure 18.7).

Making plots and lists seems far removed from making theater happen. It is not recommended unless you can clearly see that it will expedite your production.

However, hard work in analyzing the script and identifying its problems before rehearsals begin pays off—your work becomes easier with every day that passes. Lack of preparation before rehearsals begin results in a terribly overworked and panicked feeling as opening night approaches—a feeling I've always preferred to avoid.

I feel that two or three weeks of work on material before rehearsals start is a must, depending on how fast you can type and organize.

Curtiss Marlowe
Stage Manager
Liberty Theatre
North Hollywood, CA

Suggested Classroom Exercise

Show the class a prompt script of a recent show. Discuss the pattern of mounting pages (Figure 3.2) that was used and explain why that pattern was selected.

4

Scheduling and Company Rules

If you're failing to plan, you're planning to fail.

—Anonymous

The Master Calendar

Time, management of time, and the coordination of the cast, crew, and staff are very important to every theater. In order to keep everyone on time and their efforts meshing smoothly, it is desirable to post a master calendar— and only one master calendar—in a convenient place so that it is available to everyone on the staff. The master calendar can be your most effective tool for coordinating the staff.

The master calendar (see Figure 4.1) should be large enough so that several lines can be written legibly in the space allotted for each day. It should, of course, be developed after consultation regarding the needs of the producer or management, the department heads in various phases of production, and, above all, the director, with whom you work in a direct supporting role. The calendar should list many of the following kinds of events, but not necessarily all of them, and not necessarily in the following order:

Deadline for set drawings/line drawings (Chapter 8)
Deadline for lighting plans (Chapter 11)
Deadline for cleaning/repairing lighting instruments (Chapter 11)
Deadline for obtaining sufficient copies of the script (Chapter 3)
Readings/auditions (Chapter 6)
Deadline for complete casting (Chapter 6)
Understudy casting (Chapters 6 and 16)
First rehearsal (Chapter 8)

SUN	MON	TUES	WED	THUR	FRI	SAT	NOTES
		1 10 STAFF CONF.	**2** 7:30 – Readings 9:30	**3** 2:00 – Readings 4:00 6:00 readings 7:30	**4** 2:00 – Readings – 5:30	**5** DEADLINE: SET DESIGN LINE DWGS.	Readings
6	**7** 1ST DAY THTR. AVAILABLE 10 AM 1ST Rehearsal (contracts) 2:00 Pub. Photos	**8** 10 AM Rehearsal 11:30 Staff conf.	**9** 10:00 Staff conf. 10:30 REHEARSAL	**10** 10 AM REHEARSAL 2:00 COSTUME FITTINGS	**11** 10:00 Rehearsal	**12** CAST DAY OFF 10:00 WORK CALL	
13 10:00 WORK CALL	**14** 10:00 rehearsal	**15** 10:00 Rehearsal	**16** 10:00 Staff conf. 10:30 REHEARSAL	**17** Deadline: Live sound effects obtained 10 AM Rehearsal	**18** DEADLINE ALL REHEARSAL PROPS 10:00 Rehearsal	**19** cast day off 10:00 WORK CALL	
20 10:00 WORK CALL	**21** CAST DAY OFF 8:00 TAPE ALL SOUND CUES MUSIC	**22** 10:00 AM Rehearsal 10:30 Staff Meet.	**23** REHRSL 10 AM Staff Conf. deadline: Research Opening night & invitations	**24** 11:30 Rehearsal DEADLINE ALL PROPS final	**25** DEADLINE: All lines memorized 10 Rehearsal Integrate Sound	**26** Take-in Day: 10 Work call 8:00 REHEARSAL RUN THROUGH	
27 9:00 Work Call SET COMPLETE 8:00 Rehearsal Run Through	**28** cast day off 10:00 Focus lights 2:00 Flame proof sets	**29** 10:00 STAFF Conf. 8:00 Tech Rehearsal	**30** DEADLINE: All costume complete 8:00 Tech Rehearsal				

Figure 4.1   A Master Calendar

All subsequent rehearsals (Chapter 8)
Work calls (Chapters 4 and 12)
Staff conferences (Chapters 4 and 8)
Deadline for memorization of lines (by act) (Chapter 8)
Deadline for obtaining all rehearsal props (Chapters 8 and 10)
Take-in day (Chapter 12)
Deadline for completion of sets (Chapter 13)
Deadline for completion of sound effects (Chapter 13)
Focus lights (Chapter 13)
Fittings of costumes (Chapters 8 and 13)
Publicity picture calls (Chapter 8)
Publicity interviews (Chapter 8)
Deadline for reservation of opening-night tickets
Deadline for obtaining all final props (Chapter 10)
Integration of sound effects into rehearsals (Chapter 13)
Integration of film effects into rehearsals (Chapter 13)
Costume parade (Chapters 8 and 13)
Special costume rehearsal
First rehearsal with musicians
No-actor tech/all set changes (Chapter 13)
First technical rehearsal (Chapter 13)
Second tech (Chapter 13)
First dress rehearsal (Chapter 8)
Second dress
Invitational dress/previews
Flameproofing of set (Chapters 8, 15, and 18)
Fire inspection (Chapter 18)
Opening night (Chapter 18)
All performances (Chapters 14 and 16)
Understudy rehearsals (Chapter 16)
Closing night (Chapter 17)
Strike (Chapter 17)
Take-out day/sets and props returned (Chapter 17)
All other use of the stage (Chapter 17)

If you plan to have every aspect of the production in its final shape all at the same time, you are likely to have problems. But by spacing deadlines for various aspects of the production, you may check on, and overcome, small crises rather than have to face (and optimally surmount) total panic.

Example

If you wait until the technical ("tech") rehearsal (Chapter 13) to check on the progress of your sound effects, you may find that the tape is not ready and the source records that the sound technician expected to tape at the last minute are missing. At the second tech, the sound technician finds that wires to a back-stage speaker are missing and there is no spare wire in the theater. So you may get your sound effects working by dress rehearsal, if then.

But if you put your sound tape completion deadline two days before your target date for sound integration at a rehearsal, and put the date of integration two days before your technical rehearsal is scheduled to run, you can afford to slip one day, even two or three, and still be ready for tech with all sound ready for plug-in. Similarly, you must try to plan checkpoints in other areas and get your coworkers to try to meet these checkpoints so that everything shapes up neatly for the first technical rehearsal.

Some deadline dates must naturally fall before others. "Take-in" day, for instance, must come before "focus lights" day, since focusing of instruments is dependent on placement and shape of set pieces. Rehearsal props deadline (Chapter 10) should precede line memorization deadline so that actors can pick up their props (or substitutes for them) as they set down their scripts.

If all staff members are required to post their requirements for use of stage and rehearsal space on the master calendar, conflicts will be avoided.

Example
The crew arrives for a work call and finds the cast on stage for an extra rehearsal. After it is determined whose needs are greater, cast or crew depart, losing time. If all of the stage requirements had been posted on the master calendar, this situation would have been avoided.

The master calendar should not be placed on the callboard or made available to the cast under normal circumstances. It is kept away from cast members so that actors do not become confused about their rehearsal schedule or concerned about technical deadlines. All information that cast members need from the master calendar should be made available to them by other means, particularly the rehearsal schedule (see upcoming section). WordPerfect, Print Master, and Calendar Creator are three of many computer programs that can help in the fast manufacture of calendars.

Staff Meetings

Some theaters have regularly scheduled staff conferences; most do not. If conferences have not been held in the past, you should initiate them. Having everyone on the staff sit down together at a designated time to discuss problems and progress can save a lot of time and grief.

At the preproduction or first staff meeting, get the director's concept expressed, honed, understood, and preferably summarized in writing.

During staff meetings, ask intelligent questions that will urge your coworkers to reveal specifics about what they are doing. "Everything is going just fine and on schedule" is not a satisfactory contribution to a staff meeting from any department head. It should be show-and-tell time, with every member showing diagrams and drawings and discussing the specifics.

Example

At dress rehearsal, it is found that the leading lady's costume blends perfectly into the set designer's flats to the point where all but her face and hands disappear when she stands against them. Her hoop skirt won't fit through any door on the set. Some things will have to be changed at the last minute. These problems would have been avoided if the set designer and costume designer had done "due diligence show-and-tell" at a staff meeting.

A full review of the master calendar is a good way to start the first staff meeting.

One main reason for having a production meeting with all designers, production manager, tech director and director, as well as the stage manager, is to make sure that the schedule is tailored to fit not only the tech side of things but also the cast and director's needs. Without a representative from the rehearsal point of view, many things can be overlooked, such as time built into a schedule for a spacing rehearsal on stage before tech, adding wardrobe pieces before dress rehearsal if they affect actor business, and special cue light and quick change booth needs backstage.

For a musical, especially in theatres that don't specialize in them, it's important to remind the tech crew of requirements for that type of show. Power requirements in the pit, front of house sound mixer location, pit setup and other "musical" specific details need to be discussed early on in the process and built into the schedule and budget.

Aside from the mundane business aspects of production meetings, it's a nice chance for the creative team and tech crew to get to meet each other and start to feel like they're working together toward a common goal. The relationships that come out of that meeting can help avoid problems that occur when all the designers have been working single-mindedly only to collide with each other at first tech. It makes a stage manager's life a lot easier too!

Jill Gold
PSM
Pasadena Playhouse

Rehearsal Schedules

Carefully oversee the preparation, posting, and distribution of the rehearsal schedule. If possible, the schedule should be posted at the very first reading and distributed before the first rehearsal.

This takes a lot of coordination with everyone in a supervisory position. If you are working with amateurs who are not expected to be at the total disposition of the rehearsal schedule, you will have to coordinate the schedule with the cast as well. If you are working with professionals who are at the total disposal of union restrictions, you will have to work into the schedule the exact union requirements, specifying days off as well as required coffee breaks on more complicated schedules.

Once content is determined, clarity should be your chief concern in writing the schedule (see Figure 4.2). Make sure that for each entry you give the time, date, place, and scenes to be rehearsed. It is not enough to identify the act (Roman numeral) and scene (Arabic numeral)—that is, II-1, III-2. You must list the names of the cast members involved. Do not assume that cast members will know which scenes they are in. Assume the worst— that cast members will find ways to misinterpret the schedule. Take the time to make reading and understanding the schedule easy for cast mem-

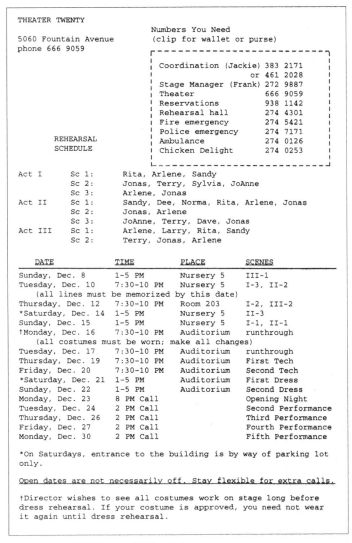

```
THEATER TWENTY
                         Numbers You Need
5060 Fountain Avenue     (clip for wallet or purse)
phone 666 9059         r----------------------------┐
                       |  Coordination (Jackie) 383 2171  |
                       |             or 461 2028  |
                       |  Stage Manager (Frank) 272 9887  |
                       |  Theater              666 9059  |
                       |  Reservations         938 1142  |
                       |  Rehearsal hall       274 4301  |
            REHEARSAL   |  Fire emergency       274 5421  |
            SCHEDULE    |  Police emergency     274 7171  |
                       |  Ambulance            274 0126  |
                       |  Chicken Delight      274 0253  |
                       L----------------------------┘

Act I      Sc 1:    Rita, Arlene, Sandy
           Sc 2:    Jonas, Terry, Sylvia, JoAnne
           Sc 3:    Arlene, Jonas
Act II     Sc 1:    Sandy, Dee, Norma, Rita, Arlene, Jonas
           Sc 2:    Jonas, Arlene
           Sc 3:    JoAnne, Terry, Dave, Jonas
Act III    Sc 1:    Arlene, Larry, Rita, Sandy
           Sc 2:    Terry, Jonas, Arlene
```

DATE	TIME	PLACE	SCENES
Sunday, Dec. 8	1-5 PM	Nursery 5	III-1
Tuesday, Dec. 10	7:30-10 PM	Nursery 5	I-3, II-2
(all lines must be memorized by this date)			
Thursday, Dec. 12	7:30-10 PM	Room 203	I-2, III-2
*Saturday, Dec. 14	1-5 PM	Nursery 5	II-3
Sunday, Dec. 15	1-5 PM	Nursery 5	I-1, II-1
†Monday, Dec. 16	7:30-10 PM	Auditorium	runthrough
(all costumes must be worn; make all changes)			
Tuesday, Dec. 17	7:30-10 PM	Auditorium	runthrough
Thursday, Dec. 19	7:30-10 PM	Auditorium	First Tech
Friday, Dec. 20	7:30-10 PM	Auditorium	Second Tech
*Saturday, Dec. 21	1-5 PM	Auditorium	First Dress
Sunday, Dec. 22	1-5 PM	Auditorium	Second Dress
Monday, Dec. 23	8 PM Call		Opening Night
Tuesday, Dec. 24	2 PM Call		Second Performance
Thursday, Dec. 26	2 PM Call		Third Performance
Friday, Dec. 27	2 PM Call		Fourth Performance
Monday, Dec. 30	2 PM Call		Fifth Performance

*On Saturdays, entrance to the building is by way of parking lot only.

<u>Open dates are not necessarily off. Stay flexible for extra calls.</u>

†Director wishes to see all costumes work on stage long before dress rehearsal. If your costume is approved, you need not wear it again until dress rehearsal.

Figure 4.2 A Rehearsal Schedule

bers. This is not done out of contempt for actors, but out of respect: If you can free them from the mechanics of production, you may allow them greater concentration on their primary function.

Your schedule might also include a wallet-sized area with important telephone numbers that can be clipped for the cast member's wallet or purse. Numbers to be listed are (1) a coordination number or numbers that cast members can call to leave messages when supervisory personnel cannot be reached directly, (2) your home phone number, (3) the home phone numbers of any other staff or supervisory personnel whose assistance may be required by members of the theater group, (4) the theater number, (5) rehearsal hall number (if different from theater number), (6) police emergency, (7) fire emergency, (8) ambulance emergency, (9) food service, (10) ticket reservations (if different from theater number), and (11) any other numbers that might be helpful as quick reference to the cast.

The rehearsal schedule need not (and probably should not) include any of the technical deadlines for staff members posted on the master calendar. This might be confusing to cast members. But line memorization deadlines should be included and dress rehearsals noted. Notes on parking, access to the theater and rehearsal areas, and other helpful information would also be appreciated by cast members.

If you are unable to fill the entire rehearsal schedule with specifics, it is best to post a tentative schedule, so labeled, with dates and blank spaces for the unknown variables, so that cast members can fill in the blanks (see Figure 4.3).

Sometimes it is effective to staple a second copy of the rehearsal schedule into each cast member's script on the premise that the script is less likely to be lost than a single sheet of paper.

It may be desirable for you to print the following lines at the bottom of your schedule: "Open dates are not off! They haven't been set yet. Please keep your personal schedule open for additional rehearsals as called." Keep in mind, when first making up the rehearsal schedule, that to include extra "safety" rehearsals initially and then cancel them when they are determined to be unnecessary is easier than to call extra, nonscheduled rehearsals as opening night looms closer.

In some amateur theaters, the cast may be told halfway into rehearsals that they will have to come to previously unscheduled work calls if they want to have scenery. This generally is met with much unhappiness. To avoid this, stage managers in amateur situations should plan work calls before rehearsals begin and put them on the schedule with a note that cast members will be expected to attend in work clothes.

When rehearsing a musical in one week, it becomes necessary to juggle principals, chorus, dancers, and extras between five or more different areas and still retain one's sanity. This calls for extremely careful planning of a more sophisticated schedule (see Figure 4.4) and the determination of all concerned to meet the schedule.

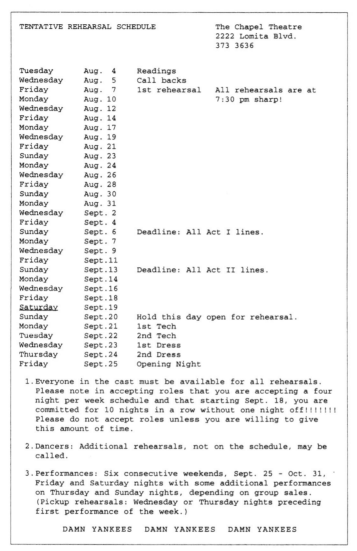

```
TENTATIVE REHEARSAL SCHEDULE              The Chapel Theatre
                                          2222 Lomita Blvd.
                                          373 3636


Tuesday       Aug.  4    Readings
Wednesday     Aug.  5    Call backs
Friday        Aug.  7    1st rehearsal    All rehearsals are at
Monday        Aug. 10                     7:30 pm sharp!
Wednesday     Aug. 12
Friday        Aug. 14
Monday        Aug. 17
Wednesday     Aug. 19
Friday        Aug. 21
Sunday        Aug. 23
Monday        Aug. 24
Wednesday     Aug. 26
Friday        Aug. 28
Sunday        Aug. 30
Monday        Aug. 31
Wednesday     Sept. 2
Friday        Sept. 4
Sunday        Sept. 6    Deadline: All Act I lines.
Monday        Sept. 7
Wednesday     Sept. 9
Friday        Sept.11
Sunday        Sept.13    Deadline: All Act II lines.
Monday        Sept.14
Wednesday     Sept.16
Friday        Sept.18
Saturday      Sept.19
Sunday        Sept.20    Hold this day open for rehearsal.
Monday        Sept.21    1st Tech
Tuesday       Sept.22    2nd Tech
Wednesday     Sept.23    1st Dress
Thursday      Sept.24    2nd Dress
Friday        Sept.25    Opening Night

  1.Everyone in the cast must be available for all rehearsals.
    Please note in accepting roles that you are accepting a four
    night per week schedule and that starting Sept. 18, you are
    committed for 10 nights in a row without one night off!!!!!!!
    Please do not accept roles unless you are willing to give
    this amount of time.

  2.Dancers: Additional rehearsals, not on the schedule, may be
    called.

  3.Performances: Six consecutive weekends, Sept. 25 - Oct. 31,
    Friday and Saturday nights with some additional performances
    on Thursday and Sunday nights, depending on group sales.
    (Pickup rehearsals: Wednesday or Thursday nights preceding
    first performance of the week.)

        DAMN YANKEES   DAMN YANKEES   DAMN YANKEES
```

Figure 4.3   A Tentative Rehearsal Schedule

The worst problem in keeping to such a complicated schedule, where work periods are broken down to the hour and even half hour, is that the staff members—musical director, chorus director, choreographer, and costume designer—are unwilling to release the cast members they are working with at the end of the specified time period. They are always in the middle of something very important and need five minutes more. It becomes difficult to cajole these creative people into keeping to the schedule.

REHEARSAL SCHEDULE

TUESDAY – JULY 14

TIME	AUDITORIUM	TENT	CHORUS ROOM	MUSIC ROOM	COSTUME SHOP
10:00		Frank			
10:30		II-5		Julie	Ravenal
11:00		II-5	Girl Sing. Dancers	Ravenal	Male Danc.
11:30	Frank, Karen	Ravenal Magnolia	Girl Sing. Dancers Male Danc.	Julie	Andy
12:00	I-1	(Lunch)	Girl Sing. (All Danc. to lunch)	(Lunch)	(Lunch)
12:30	I-2	(Lunch)	" "	(Lunch)	Parthy
1:00	(Lunch)	All Danc.	(Lunch)	Joe	Magnolia
1:30	(Lunch)	" "	(Lunch)	Andy, Parthy	Steve
2:00	I-3	" "	Girl Sing	Ravenal	Joe, Frank
2:30	I-3	Male Danc.	" "	Queenie	Girl Danc.
3:00	I-4	All Danc., Girl Sing.		Ellie, Frank	Julie
3:30	Andy	" "		Magnolia	Queenie, Ellie
4:00	Pict. Call				
4:30					
5:00		I-2			
5:30					Local Chorus
6:00	Joe, Queenie		Local Chorus		
6:30	Ellie, Frank		" "		

Notes: Today is day off for Male Singing Ensemble. Picture Call: 4 p.m. Aud. – Check sep. picture call sheet to see if you are needed. Report to costume shop, then aud.

Figure 4.4   A Single-Day Rehearsal Schedule

A second problem is that a lot of cast time is lost in shepherding members between rehearsal areas. With many work areas and short work periods, a certain amount of confusion and delay cannot be avoided, but clear and careful scheduling can help to minimize it.

Is it desirable to duplicate schedules? Yes, it is. It is one of the ways in which you can assist the cast beyond the minimum requirements of announcing the next call. It also saves cast members the trouble of individually copying the schedule.

Sometimes it is not enough to distribute the schedule, staple a duplicate in each script, post a copy on the callboard, and announce the next call at each rehearsal. You must "mother-hen" the schedule even beyond this. If a cast member is late, you must check to find out why, in the hope of eliminating future tardiness. If a cast member is absent, you must call to make sure that the actor knows the next call. If there is any change in the schedule, it is your responsibility to see that every person concerned is informed of the change.

Keep several extra copies of the rehearsal schedule in your prompt script, always ready to hand one to a cast member who has misplaced his or hers, one to the upholsterer who wants to know when the stage will be free so that she or he can recover the sofa, one to the lady who lives above the theater and wants to know when not to play her TV, and more to all others concerned, ad infinitum. Of course, every staff member should be on your initial distribution.

Company Rules

A handout of company rules is a helpful device to let cast, staff, and crew know what is expected of them (see Figure 4.5). Categories of rules that you will want to include are:

Backstage behavior, noise, and cleanliness
Tardiness
Guests backstage and complimentary tickets
Costume upkeep

When the rules are approved, distribute them to all concerned, preferably at the initial meeting of the company. Post a copy on the callboard.

Just as you want to know what is expected of you, actors want to know what is expected of them. Take time at the first company meeting to review the rules and explain the reasons for them.

Example

Tent theater rule: "Cast members must sit in the last two rows of the theater when not on stage during rehearsals." This brief rule alone seemed unjustifiable; after all, the empty seats in front were a much more convenient waiting place. The rule could have been explained in just a few lines: The asphalt surface of the center of the tent became so hot during rehearsal hours that the chair legs sank into and destroyed the surface. The back rows were not surfaced and were thus practically indestructible.

If there are good reasons for rules, try to make the reasons clear to cast members. This will result in greater cooperation on their part. Reasons for rules that seem obvious to you are not always so obvious to cast members—such as the fire hazard of smoking backstage. Be patient in explaining.

If there are not good reasons for rules, the rules are probably not necessary!

Player's Ring Gallery
8325 Santa Monica Blvd.
December 13

The Company of
ONE FLEW OVER THE CUCKOO'S NEST

1. You must sign in each night. Never sign in for another actor.
2. Please call 555-2424 if you expect to be late for half hour call.
3. Please use the stage door, not the front door.
4. Please open and close the stage door quietly.
5. Please stay backstage after 8 pm (7:30 pm Sat.).
6. Cast members are not allowed in the box office.
7. Extremely important and emergency messages can get to you by calling 650-6920 during performances, and only that number.
8. Please leave costume laundry with SM on Sunday night after performance. You must fill out laundry slip.
9. Please stay out of the light booth.
10. Please do not speak to SM during light cues, sound cues, and set changes.
11. All cast members must take curtain call in complete costume.
12. Please smoke behind theater & not in the backstage hallways.
13. No visitors are allowed in dressing rooms during perf.
14. Please be alert to the monitors for your cues. The SM is responsible for warns only before acts, not before individual cues once the act has begun. (See your Equity rules.)
15. Please do not talk during perf. while backstage. If you must communicate, please whisper. The wall between aud. and dressing room is not sound proof.
16. Keep theater doors closed because of air conditioning.
17. Please do not congregate with aud. during intermission.
18. Please wear appropriate clothing backstage.
19. Please do not use the pay phone during the performance (because of noise).
20. Please help in Saturday night buffet cleanup.
21. Please stay out of the entrance areas during entrances & exits of other actors & during crew shifts. You can be seen by the audience.
22. Please do not use the men's room during the performance. It is noisy and near an entrance. Both men and women may use the women's room during perf., but please wait until the water has stopped running before opening the door, and hold the door to prevent slamming.
23. Use good judgment about not using the water fountain during silent moments of performance.

THANK YOU IN ADVANCE FOR YOUR HELP AND COOPERATION!

Lawrence S.
stage manager

Figure 4.5   An Example of Company Rules

The following rules worked well during a L-O-N-G H-O-T summer in Georgia:

The fine system:
1. No bare feet at any time in the theatre offices, scene shop, set or dressing rooms. First offense: $5.00 fine; second offense, $10.00 fine; third offense, dismissal.
2. Showing up at rehearsal intoxicated: immediate and irrevocable dismissal.
3. Late for rehearsals. First offense: $5.00 fine (waived if SM called); second offense, $10.00 fine; third offense, dismissal.
4. Chewing gum or smoking in rehearsal hall during rehearsal: $15.00 fine, doubled at recurring offenses.
5. Summer clothing not deemed appropriate (too revealing) for rehearsal (no air conditioning in rehearsal space): $15.00 fine, doubled at each offense.

The SM did not collect a single dime between May 23 and August 13.

> Scott Ross, Stage Manager
> Gaye Markley, House Manager
> Georgia Shakespeare Festival, 1989
> Atlanta, GA

The Callboard

The callboard has already been mentioned as the place to post the rehearsal schedule and company rules. Let's take a closer look at it.

The callboard is a backstage bulletin board for cast, crew, and staff (see Figure 4.6). It is usually located near the stage door where cast members can't miss it when they arrive and depart.

The basic items that every member of the company must be able to find are:

Emergency phone numbers (Figure 4.7)
The next call (Chapter 8)
The rehearsal schedule (described earlier)
The sign-in sheet (Chapter 9)
Closing notice (Chapters 13 and 17)
Company rules (described earlier)
Names of company members qualified in CPR and first aid (Chapter 8)

Figure 4.6   A View of a Well-Organized Callboard. Jill Gold, Production Stage Manager, posts a notice on the callboard of the Pasadena Playhouse. Note that the callboard is spacious and well lit. It is divided into three areas: Equity, Messages, and Sign-In.

Courtesy Jill Gold, PSM, Pasadena Playhouse. Photo by Rato.

> First-aid information (Figure 4.8) and location of first-aid kit
> Blood-borne pathogens advisory and location of cleanup kit (Chapter 15)
> Location of fire extinguishers (Chapter 15)

Some other items that you might wish to post are:

> Helpful phone numbers (cab service, food service, and nearby restaurants and hotels if cast members are from out of town)
> Cast list (Chapter 6)
> Favorable reviews (if favorable to *all* cast members)
> Invitations to other theaters
> Advertisements of lessons and services of special interest to cast members
> Telegrams and letters to the cast
> Duty roster (Chapter 15)
> Curtain call order (Chapter 14)
> VIP list (Chapter 15)
> Firearms safety tips (Figure 10.5)

EMERGENCY

FIRE ## 555-2419

POLICE ## 555-4711

AMBULANCE ## 555-3210

ALL NIGHT CLINIC and how to get there 555 3699

White Memorial Medical Center
414 North Boyle
(West on Brooklyn past Soto to Boyle
turn left on Boyle)

DIAL-A-PRAYER for producer's use only 555 2783

courtesy Lawrence Stern, stage manager 555 3179

Figure 4.7   Emergency Phone Numbers for Callboard Display

When casting is complete, take down the notes regarding readings. Also, items on the callboard that are no longer timely should be removed.

Bring your organizational skill and artistic ability to the arrangement of items on the callboard so that cast members can find what they want quickly. It might be advisable to divide the callboard into three areas: permanent, temporary, and urgent.

The callboard should be large enough to accommodate all the bulletins that must be posted without having them overlap. Make sure that extra pins are available to put up additional material, and attach a pencil to your callboard so that cast members can initial bulletins and the sign-in sheet, as well as make notes for themselves, without having to search for a pencil.

With your master calendar discussed and posted, staff meetings arranged, rehearsal schedules coordinated and distributed, company rules determined and explained, and the callboard made orderly, you have made a good start at making things run smoothly.

Figure 4.8   Example of First-Aid Information Poster That Might Be Placed on a Callboard

Courtesy Zee Medical, Inc., Irvine, California. www.lifeessentialsbyzee.com.

Suggested Classroom Exercise

Have the class brainstorm all of the events that should be included in a master calendar. Write them on the board in chronological order. Compare the list to the one on page 36.

5

Getting Acquainted with Your Theater

A real handyman needs only three things: WD-40 to make things go, duct tape to make things stop, and a big hammer for those delicate adjustments.

—Anonymous

Who Does What?

The stage manager should know who reports to whom in *her* or *his* theater. Not only should the stage manager know to whom she or he is responsible, but also to whom everyone else on the staff is responsible. In the role of personnel coordinator, this information is important.

The easiest way to find this out is to talk to people on the staff. If you are still uncertain, bring up the question at the earliest staff meeting. Even in theaters in which the distribution of tasks has been codified over the years, time may be taken at the first production meeting of a season to review and adjust for current staffing, personal preferences and capabilities of staff, and staff members' available time.

Figure 5.1 shows an idealized organizational chart for a hypothetical theater. I can readily guess that it does not apply to your theater. There are so many variations in staff organization that it would be impossible to provide in this book charts for every theater. Several factors causing variation are discussed in this chapter.

Designing an organizational chart for your theater might be desirable if you have a high turnover in personnel and you need to brief incoming personnel quickly. The more your organizational chart differs from what might normally be expected, the more your theater needs an organizational chart.

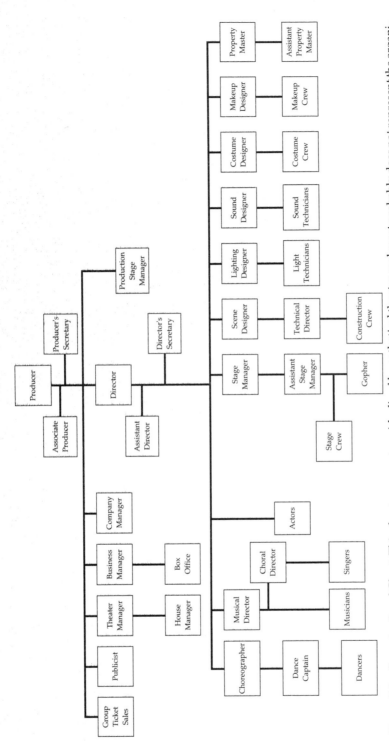

Figure 5.1 Organizational Chart. This chart represents an idealized hypothetical theater and most probably does not represent the organization at your theater. There are an infinite number of variations in the organization of a theater's staff. Some of the causes of variation are discussed in the text. This chart shows primary lines of responsibility only. The stage manager, for example, reports to the production stage manager and to the director. This chart shows primary lines of responsibility only. The stage manager, for example, reports to the production stage manager and to the director. This chart shows primary lines of responsibility only. Also, the organization shifts *when the curtain goes up*. Actors who reported to the director now report to the stage manager, and light and sound technicians who reported to designers now report to the stage manager.

The chart is not as important as is knowing who does what. Authority in the theater generally stems from function. The authority of the lighting designer over the lighting technician stems from their relative functions. The function of the lighting technician is to repair, gel, hang, wire, and focus lighting instruments. Obviously, the lighting technician takes orders from, and is responsible to, the lighting designer.

As succinctly as possible, here are the functions of the theater staff:

The *producer* is to obtain the personnel and materials to make theater.

The *director* is to interpret the script through the use of actors and designers.

The *stage manager* is to ensure that everything runs smoothly backstage and onstage.

The *actor* is to deliver the playwright's words, emotions, actions, and characterization, as interpreted by the director, to the audience.

The *technical director* is to execute scene designs and staging devices. (Confusion about the role of the technical director is discussed below. If you, as stage manager, have any doubts about your working relationship with the technical director, talk it out with him or her. If you're unable to resolve the conflict, talk with the producer.)

The *theater manager* is to ensure the safe, efficient, and clean operation of the theater. (This includes care of the physical plant, box-office operations, restrooms, garbage disposal, gas, electricity, water services, and compliance with city regulations concerning the health and safety of the audience. It may include parking lot operations.)

The *house manager* is to greet and to seat the audience and to attend to the audience's comfort.

The *designer* (costumes, lighting, scene, sound, or makeup) is to design plans, turning the director's and playwright's concepts into the realities that make stage illusion.

The *technicians* (master carpenter, master electrician, stagehand, etc.) are to turn designs into reality and to operate equipment before, during, and after performances.

The *company manager* is to supervise the transportation and housing of the company.

There may be several other titles, real or honorary, on your staff. If you are uncertain about what they do, ask them.

The title of *production stage manager* may take on different meanings. In some theaters, it is simply an honorary title for the stage manager. Sometimes this title is assigned only when there is more than one show being rehearsed and presented in the same theater or theater complex. In this case, the function of the production stage manager is to coordinate and supervise the use of the theater's facilities, crews, and subordinate stage managers.

I have a major disagreement with the manner in which the relationship between the director and the designers is portrayed. Currently, designers and directors collaborate in order to establish a point of view about a play (or dance or whatever). Working together we decide on what we believe the playwright is trying to communicate, and therefore how we want the audience to feel or what we hope they will understand or learn through our production. After the point of view is established, the designers strive to create the world of this particular production of the play. Ongoing communication with the director and other members of the design team is vital to the success of the production. Designers strive to get to the essence of a piece, and a tremendous amount of time, energy, research, imagination, and creativity is necessary. A designer may go through hundreds of doodles, sketches, and/or models before the final design is decided upon. The director is ultimately in charge, and has final say on all matters, but it is the designer who creates the design, and would implement any changes to the design before and during the run. It would be inappropriate for the stage manager to make changes to a design without the designer's consent, even if requested to do so by the director.

Lori Dawson
Lighting Designer
Stephens College, MO

[I applaud producers and directors who can draw out the best from their designers through collaborative process. All of my experience, however, was with "name above the title"-type directors who wanted it done their way and attempted to focus creative input of designers within the limited parameters that the director established. In the end, we all want the best production we can get, whether we arrive there via collaborative process or under the whip of a dictatorial director. The stage manager does not establish the relationships between producer/director and designers. I'm not sure that recognizing the distinction in process is necessary to the successful functioning of a stage manager. But it's certainly worth thinking about, especially if a stage manager has a choice in selecting the atmosphere in which he or she wants to work. For an excellent discussion of designer relationships in the creative process of making theater, see Chapter 2 of *The Lighting Art,* second edition, by Richard H. Palmer. Also see page 140.]

Sometimes the title of production stage manager is assigned to the producer's assistant. In this case, the production stage manager has no specific duties relevant to any one show but troubleshoots and supervises, reporting only to the producer.

Sometimes the production stage manager and stage manager divide duties. The stage manager works rehearsals and turns the prompt script over to the production stage manager at tech rehearsal. Then, the production stage manager calls the show while the stage manager runs the stage

I have stage-managed four more shows now. I finally know the first prereq-uisite for finding an assistant stage manager: confidence. You must be able to trust this person. When you can trust your ASM, a great weight is lifted from your shoulders. Then it seems logical as to what duties you can assign.

Violet E. Horvath
Stage Manager
Arrow Rock, MO

crew. In some theaters, the production stage manager runs rehearsals and then turns the prompt script over to the stage manager who runs the show; the assistant stage manager supervises the crew, and the production stage manager sits in the audience and gives notes to the cast after each perfor-mance. This sharing of duties is common in musical theater and opera.

There is no single correct distribution of duties between the production stage manager and the stage manager, or between the stage manager and the assistant stage manager.

Some of the factors that determine the distribution are the same factors that might influence the distribution of duties between the technical direc-tor and the stage manager:

1. Will of the producer or director
2. Tradition of the particular theater
3. Number of people available
4. Layout of the theater
5. Personality of individuals filling the slots

Again, the stage manager gains an understanding of who reports to whom by talking with coworkers. She or he tries to avoid problems by anticipating work that will have to be done and ensuring that everyone involved knows his or her specific duties in getting that work done.

Some general principles to keep in mind:

1. Treat everyone on the staff with respect for his or her function.
2. Many hands make light work.
3. If you have subordinates, one of your responsibilities is to ensure that they are not overworked. (Sometimes a stage manager feels that since she or he served as assistant stage manager and got the work done, she or he can now lean on the assistant stage manager. If you are the assistant stage manager, you have to appeal to the stage manager's ego. Explain that you are not the same terrific, out-standing, well-organized, industrious assistant stage manager that he or she was, and that you need help.)

Examples of Problems

1. The technical director (TD) tells you that he is in charge of the lighting designer, the sound designer, the shop foreman, the makeup crew, as well as the stage manager. He states that he runs the crew during performances and that you (SM) call the cues. He says that you will report to him for work in the shop on scenery construction prior to rehearsals.

   Could be. In some educational and community theaters, the TD has extensive responsibility. If you feel that a different system would improve the operation of your theater, speak to the producer. If you feel that you are being overworked and/or need help (an ASM or gopher), speak to the TD and/or the producer.

2. The production stage manager (PSM) tells you that your first duty as the new ASM is to help build a fence around the theater.

   Probably. Your duties are what the PSM says they are, even if those duties don't fit your mental picture of the job. If you are a member of a union, you might complain to your union rep. Will building the fence interfere with your other duties? If so, you need to make that clear to the PSM.

3. The director's secretary tells you, the new SM, "I will be holding book (prompting) during rehearsals and will also supervise understudy rehearsals."

   How do you feel about it? Do you feel that you have lost some of the authority that goes with your title, or do you welcome the help? Or do you have mixed feelings? Perhaps you welcome the help at rehearsals yet feel that the director's secretary is not as capable of supervising understudy rehearsals as you are. Perhaps you feel that you really need to hold book during rehearsals in order to prepare yourself for running the show successfully.

   This is a typical problem of the distribution of tasks among a theater's staff. The same type of problem might occur between the PSM and SM, or between the SM and ASM, or between the TD and SM. There is no correct answer for all theaters. What will work best for your theater?

   Talk to the director's secretary about your feelings and discuss what is best for getting the show on most efficiently. If you fail to resolve the conflict, speak to the director and/or producer, and then abide by their judgment.

In all these examples of problems, you will generally find that as the stage manager gains experience and reputation, more responsibility is given to him or her. As the stage manager moves on to other theaters, experience, reputation, and clout follow along, and the stage manager knows enough to stipulate in advance what specific duties he or she will not surrender to, or take from, others on the staff.

In Appendix A, you will find a production checklist from a stage manager's point of view. Please be cautioned before turning to this appendix that THE STAGE MANAGER NEED NOT DO EVERYTHING ON THIS LIST! At professional and educational levels of theater, there are many people on theater staffs to accept responsibility for doing most of the tasks on this list. Some productions, regardless of theater level, do not require that the task be done. As you review this list, check off the things that you know you personally need to do to get the show on the road. Use another symbol (?) to indicate those items you are not sure about. Then, talk to your producer and director to decide if the task needs to be done and who will do it.

Personal Equipment for Stage Managers

In addition to your prompt script, what else do you keep handy? Actually, there is no end of little things to keep on hand to keep the show going, and it is amazing to see how the absence of a small thing at the crucial time can create havoc. For instance, it hardly seems possible that responsible people would allow a shortage of pencils to delay a rehearsal. But it happens time and again in amateur as well as professional productions.

Consider Hildegard Knef's comments on the rehearsal of the 1954 Broadway musical *Silk Stockings:*

> Today was the first reading. The whole cast sat in half-circle on the stage with their manuscripts in their hands, a paper cup of coffee beside each chair.... Nobody had a pencil. Unbelievable that actors never have pencils at first readings. Henry, the stage manager, lent his and it went from hand to hand until finally Cy Feuer's temper snapped. "I'm well aware that you don't get paid till the opening but you could at least buy one little pencil.... We've wasted hours already."... I'd love to be able to invite a German student of Theatrical Science to attend rehearsals.*

Let's consider some items of personal equipment you are likely to need in running the rehearsal and the show.

Over a period of time, you will find that you may be able to use one or two items in the mounting of one play and one or two items in mounting another. It is not mandatory that you own or buy these items. It is simply handy to collect things.

As the items accumulate with each successive play, they'll overflow from your pockets and briefcase. You'll want a kit—a cardboard carton, tool box, or tackle box—to keep everything conveniently near you in the rehearsal area.

The items listed here are, for the most part, self-explanatory. Some of their uses have been mentioned already, and you are invited to imagine a likely use for the others:

> Paraffin (When a tooth filling is suddenly lost, a small piece of paraffin may allow an actor to complete a rehearsal.)
> Lighter flints and fluid

---

*From *The Gift Horse* by Hildegard Knef, translated by David Anthony Palastanga (New York: McGraw-Hill Book Company, 1971). English translation copyright © 1971 by Hildegard Knef.

Matches
Paper clips
Sewing needles
Thread, black and white
Razor blade, single-edge
Masking tape, two widths
Electric tape
Two-sided tape
Scotch mending tape
Safety pins
Straight pins
Hair pins
Carpet tacks
Tacks
One-inch brads
Chalk
Pencils, *many*, #2
Pencil sharpener
Large eraser, art gum
Flashlight
Candle
Black ballpoint pen
Marking pens
Luminous paint and brush
Luminous paint solvent
Tape label maker
Graphite lock lubricant
Electric extension cord
Stopwatch
Sixty-minute timer
Ruler, 12"
Measuring tape, 50'
Architect's ruler, ½" = 1' scale
Tailor's measuring tape
Note cards, 3" × 5"
Oil, small can
Working bell and buzzer
Whistle
First-aid kit
Change, $5 in nickels, dimes, and quarters
Duplicate keys to everything
Rubber cement
Plastic cement
Plasti-tak (a putty-like adhesive)
Rubber bands

Good stage managers are equipped to handle anything. I suggest that you add an adjustable wrench, a collection of miscellaneous hardware (screws, nails, bolts, etc.), Post-It note pad, glo-tape, a 3-plug tap, string, soap, and garbage bags.

> Neill McKay
> Stage Manager
> Tom Morrison Theatre
>   and Memorial Hall
> Fredrickton, N.B., Canada

I would add saline solution to the list of what a SM should have and what should be in a first-aid box; lost contacts can delay rehearsals and stop shows.

> Jane Bulnes-Fowles
> Stage Manager
> Reed College
> Portland, OR

Nail polish remover—either normal or acetone-free. It's a great solvent. I've removed magic marker graffiti, paint from my shoes, and accumulated dirt from the bottom of my makeup case.

> Big J Peterson
> Actor/Tech
> Georgia Renaissance Festival/
> Six Flags over Georgia
> Lilburn, GA

In my brief theatre experience I have been asked for ponytail holders, barrettes, clips, or something to hold hair in place and out of the way. I do not go to rehearsals without them.

> Chad Zodrow
> Stage Manager
> Northwestern University
> Evanston, IL

Magnifying glass
AC-DC current tester
Welding gloves (great for handling hot instruments)
Gel books
Cough drops
Throat lozenges and troches
Aspirin
Aspergum
Can opener

Salt, sugar, tea, coffee, powdered cream, bouillon, packaged soup, honey, hot chocolate
Wash'n Dri Towelettes
Paper towels
Paper cups
Nail file
Kleenex
Toothbrush and paste
Toothpicks
Dental floss
Comb
Mouthwash
Water heating element
Gummed reinforcements
Telephone extension
Dust cloth
Tweezers

You will enjoy those moments when you can dip into your kit and save someone, particularly yourself, a long walk.

Stage Diagrams

If you are starting to work in a new theater, you will want to check out the plant, record the information, be able to analyze and apply this to your production needs, and pass on that information in a convenient, usable form. The easiest way to do this is by making a series of diagrams. Of course, if you've already done a show in this house, you should have all the information where it can be referred to quickly.

How big is your stage? Where are the sight lines? How high is the proscenium? Is there fly space and flying equipment? These are but a few of the questions that your *stage diagram* should answer.

Usually the stage wings and significant surrounding space—apron, stairs leading to the stage, backstage area, and so forth—are drawn to scale. The scale of ½" = 1' is recommended, but any scale that is serviceable will do (see Figure 5.2).

When you have finished your drawing, list at the bottom the significant dimensions:

1. What is the width of the stage?
2. What is the depth (curtain line to back wall)?
3. What is the height of the proscenium arch?
4. What are the height, width, and diagonal measurements of the largest door through which scenery may pass to get from an outside street onto the stage, or in from the scene shop to the stage?

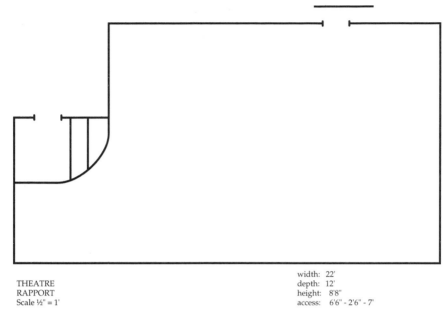

THEATRE
RAPPORT
Scale ½" = 1'

width: 22'
depth: 12'
height: 8'8"
access: 6'6" - 2'6" - 7'

Figure 5.2 Stage Diagram Drawn to Scale

This last measurement is significant because it limits the size of scenery and set pieces. Obviously, you can't use a set piece or section of scenery if you can't carry it onto the stage.

This diagram and list of important dimensions should be filed in your prompt script.

Some Applications

1. The set designer is on a tight schedule and won't be in town until the second week of rehearsals. The director has planned essential entranceways and windows so that she could start blocking. Now the director asks you to send the set designer information that will allow him to start his plans without actually seeing the stage.

2. You go to a warehouse to pick up set pieces. The furniture dealer offers you one of several rugs that may not be cut. What size will you need? Of course you have that information with you and will not have to make another trip.

3. The set designer of a theater in the round presents his watercolor sketches for the next week's production at staff meeting. You ask how tall the boxy set pieces are. The set designer explains that they are 12 feet tall and that he knows they will fit through the entrances to the tent because he has measured them. You point out that they may fit through the 12½-foot entrances that you have also measured, but since the men who carry them can't very easily hold them a mere six inches off the ground, getting them in and off-stage may be clumsy and therefore slow down the scene changes. You also point out that you will have to raise the microphones that hang at the aisle positions since they are only 10 feet off the ground.

The height of hanging microphones was, in this case, a significant dimension that you should have noted. The demands of a production sometimes determine which dimensions are most significant. If you are doing *Madwoman of Chaillot*, the stage trap dimensions become significant.

Note in the preceding example 3 that both you and the set designer were anticipating problems on the basis of sketches and diagrams rather than waiting for set pieces to be built to see if they worked.

If your theater expects to be in operation for many years, you will want to make sure that many copies of more detailed stage plans are on hand for the use of transient set designers and technical directors (see Figure 5.3).

Circuit Breakers

Check the circuit breaker panel (electric box) at your theater. Are the circuit breakers labeled in some way to show what is on them? If not, write on masking tape or use a tape tool to identify each circuit breaker. Is there a diagram explaining what lines each circuit breaker monitors? If not, make a diagram. It is important that this information be readily available. The diagram should be posted near or on the circuit breaker panel, and you should have a copy in your prompt book.

Take the time to check all the outlets in your theater. A current tester is an inexpensive and handy tool to keep in your kit (e.g., Circuit Master 90-550 Volt, AC & DC; Fordham Mfg. Co. No. 101). You are not expected to repair the outlets, but you should report problems to your producer.

Although you may not be an electrician, you should be comfortable with basic principles of electricity. A source that will give you the fundamentals of electricity in theatrical application is Harvey Sweet's *Handbook of Scenery, Properties, and Lighting*, Volume 2, Chapter 6, "Electricity" (Allyn and Bacon, 1995). Tuck a copy into your kit.

Diagram of Lighting Instruments

Next you will want to make a diagram of the lighting instruments currently in place—type, watt, gel frame size, and condition (see Figure 5.4). Indicate space available and outlets available for plugging in additional instruments (see Figure 5.5).

Plastic templates of various types of instruments are available. You can make your own out of cardboard (see Figure 5.6) to assist in making rapid diagrams of available equipment and its placement in production (see Chapter 11).

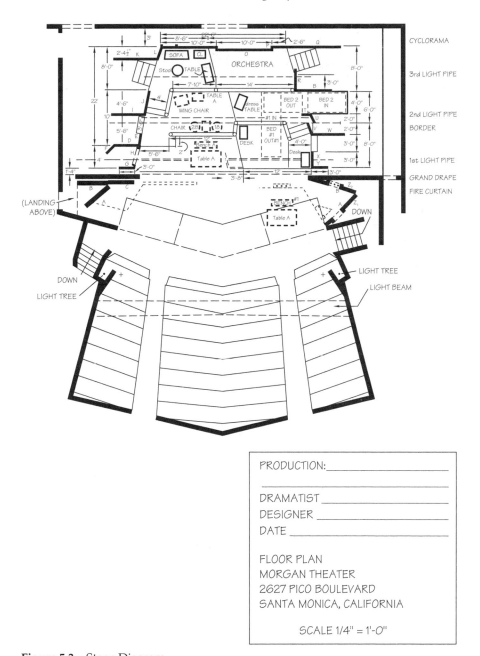

Figure 5.3   Stage Diagram
Courtesy Morgan Theater, Santa Monica, California.

1st pipe

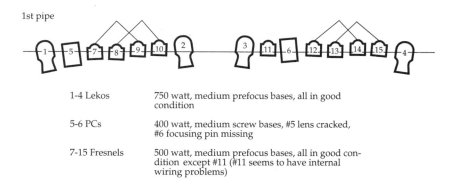

1-4 Lekos	750 watt, medium prefocus bases, all in good condition
5-6 PCs	400 watt, medium screw bases, #5 lens cracked, #6 focusing pin missing
7-15 Fresnels	500 watt, medium prefocus bases, all in good condition except #11 (#11 seems to have internal wiring problems)

Notes: No spare lamps for any instruments on hand!
Only four twofers on hand as indicated.

Ten cables run directly to board.
No ceiling plugging locations.

Figure 5.4   Diagram of Lighting Instruments

While making your diagrams, check on the condition of the lighting equipment (Chapter 11). Is it serviceable or will it need repair? Obviously, if the theater owner has rented your company 60 instruments and 10 are not working, or if a control board doesn't work, this must be brought to the producer's or management's attention. If you discover the limitations of your lighting equipment immediately, you will have time to repair, improvise, rent, or buy additional equipment. Don't wait until the tech rehearsal to find that instruments are out of order.

If the lighting designer and technicians are on hand, checking the equipment is their responsibility (see Chapter 11). But if they are not, as is frequently the case in community theater, you can save the staff and crew a lot of grief by checking out the equipment as soon as possible.

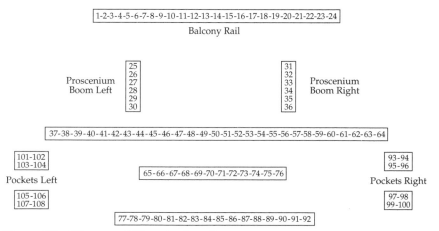

Figure 5.5   Diagram of Plugging Locations

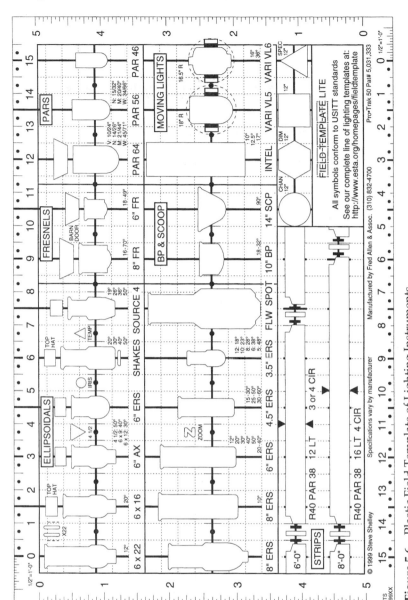

Figure 5.6 Plastic Field Template of Lighting Instruments

Courtesy Steven Louis Shelley, MrTemplate@aol.com, www.fieldtemplate.com.

65

Typical Problems

1. One of the cast members, without asking permission, brings in an electric heater to warm up the dressing room. Soon all the lights and the heater are out. You are called on to restore current. Where, if anywhere, can the electric heater be replugged?
2. The lighting designer has completed her work and left for another production. The director now decides that he needs another lighting effect. The board source line is loaded to capacity, yet another small board will now be needed. Is there another circuit in the building with enough capacity to supply another board?
3. The sound technician can't get the buzzer to work. A lamp is working from the same outlet. Can you help?

Information Packets

If your theater hosts, or has the desire to host, outside productions, you may hope to find on hand a "theater information packet." Or if you are helping to manage your theater, you may be asked to help develop such a packet.

This packet should include measurements of the stage, details of the technical capability, and other information of value to an incoming company.

The purpose of such an information packet is to allow touring companies and other production companies to determine whether or how they can use the theater. It also allows the stage manager and staff of an incoming production to solve many technical problems before ever setting foot in the theater.

Figure 5.7 shows sample information sheets with typical detailed specifications on the capability of the theater for any company that might use it for a production. Along with the physical dimension specifications of the stage would be included some scaled stage diagrams, such as the one shown in Figure 5.3, as well as diagrams of the rest of the theater building and diagrams showing the draw-curtain plan or any other special feature of the theater. Along with the description of electrical capabilities might be a series of electrical diagrams if these show distinctive capabilities. A complete information packet would then go on to describe many of the auxiliary services available from related professionals who are likely to be part of production work in this theater. The auxiliary services described might include these:

The availability of stage crew and help, whether regular theater staff or contracted from local area contacts, as well as standard pay scales for them

HEIGHT:

Floor to weight loading floor is __31__ feet.

The total no. of line sets is __41__ counterweight.
The no. of line sets available for use is __41__.
The no. of lines per set is __5__ on __10__ foot centers on grid.
The pull lines are __5/8__ inch.

The arbors will take from __300__ to __350__ lbs. in weight.

The type of rigging used is __1 - 1 RATIO__.

The length of battens/pipes is __50__ ft., & there are __42__ available.

The distance from curtain line to last set of usable lines is __23__ feet __6__ inches.

The distance from curtain line to first available set of lines is __6__ inches

*ENCLOSED IS A LINE PLOT OF STAGE

The stage floor is hardwood and laid on concrete and will take screws.

The stage floor is not raked.

DESCRIPTION OF DROPS AND LEGS AVAILABLE

Full set of beige -- full set of blacks -- __3 pr. legs, 28 feet__
__high__

__3 borders, 8 feet high -- 1 drop - 28 x 50__

Rigging of house curtain: a. Drop - operates from st. right
                           b. Traveler - operates from st. left

The house curtain is not motorized.

The house switchboard is located on stage right.
Roadshow boards may locate either on stage right or left.

The power available for portable switchboards is __500__ amps., __120__
volts AC. An additional power of __1000__ amps. can be brought in.

The electric service is __3__ wire, __220__ phase - single - __AC__.

HOUSE SWITCHBOARD:

The type of control is auto transformer.
The number of dimmer circuits is __9__.
The number of non-dim circuits is __2__.
The wattage per circuit is __6000__.
The wattage per circuit is __3000__.

A roadshow can play off the houseboard.

(continued)

Theatre: __LINDY OPERA HSE.__   Date of inf.: __March 1, 1965__
City: __LOS ANGELES__   Source of inf.: __HSE. CARPENTER__
Tot. seat. cap.: __1330__   B. off. phone: __WE 7 3500__
Year constr.: __APPROX. 1916__   Owner: __MR. SIDNEY LINDEN__
Address: __5212 WILSHIRE BLVD.__   Manager: __WILLIAM A. McDONALD__

STAGE SPECIFICATIONS

Proscenium height __50__ ft.   Maximum trim height __68__ feet.
Minimum trim height __58__ ft. Width __42__ feet.
There are no unique sight line problems.

Depth: Curtain line to back wall is __24__ feet.
Feet to curtain line is __4__ feet __4__ inches.
The apron is curved with a depth of __7__ feet.
The distance from the center of the stage to the stage right wall is __56__ feet.
The distance from the center of the stage to the stage left wall is __39__ feet.

Describe obstructions, clearance, and/or stacking problems created by any of the following:
Picture screen __NONE__   Radiators __NONE__
Speakers __NONE__   House switchboard __NONE__
Columns or pilasters __NONE__ Legs and borders __NONE__
There is no permanent band shell.
The location of the pinrail is on the floor on stage right.
HEIGHT:
Floor to grid is __59__ feet __3__ inches.
Above grid is __8__ feet.

Figure 5.7 Typical Theater Information Packet Material

LOADING:
The loading door is located on stage left - the rear wall of the stage.
The distance to stage is __48__ feet.
The width of the loading door is __8__ feet.
The height of the loading door is __12__ feet.
The door is truck level and two trucks can unload at one time.
The distance from the loading door to the stage floor is __2__ ft.

A truck can back up to the door.
There are no parking problems.
The truck approach to the loading door is by the street.
*ATTACHED IS A LOCAL STREET MAP WHICH IS MARKED WITH THE LOCATION OF THE THEATRE.

LOCAL TRANSFER COMPANIES

Atlantic Transfer
10053 International Road
Los Angeles, California
776-1870

Local loaders are required. Rates are $25.00 per truck.

ORCHESTRA FACILITIES:
The maximum amount that the orchestra pit will accommodate is __40__.

HEIGHT:
Pit floor to the house floor is __2__ feet __8__ inches.
Pit floor to the stage floor is __6__ feet __3__ inches.
Width from side to side is __41__ feet __6__ inches.
Depth from front to back is __12__ feet __3__ inches.

There are 40 music stands with light on hand.
The piano on hand is a Baldwin - Concert - 9 foot Grand.

There is a rehearsal room - 50 feet x 30 feet - adjoining stage.
The orchestra room is located on stage left.

MUSICIANS:
Minimum requirements for musical shows are as set by local scales for individual types of presentations.
All men must be A. F. of M.
Local scale for performances is as set by local scales for individual types of presentations.

House lighting equipment can play off show switchboard.
A first balcony rail may be hung.
The distance to stage is __48__ feet.
A second balcony rail cannot be hung.

Box booms can be placed in the house.
The distance to stage is __30__ feet.

There is a spot booth and an area for a follow spot(s).
There are 4 power lines available - __30__ amps. - __AC__.
The area will accomodate __4__ follow spots.
The distance to stage is __112__ feet.

The connectors are straight male hubble.

The number of stage floor pockets is __5__ - amps. - __20__ - location 2L - 2R 1 USC.

Houselights are controlled from backstage and light booth.
They are on the dimmer.

The nearest available theatrical equipment rental service is __10__ miles.

SOUND:
The house acoustics are excellent.

A sound system has not been necessary in the past.
Our theatre will permit a roadshow to use its own sound system.
Our theatre has its own sound system which is of monaural type.
The number of mikes is __10__.
The type of mikes is Altec.
The gain is controlled from the aud. booth - auditorium left.
Our theatre has a standby amplifier and it also has a preamplifier.

There is a sound technician available at the theatre.

The roadshow's tape deck can be operated through our system.
The number of inputs - __8__.
The impedance is for high and low impedance mikes.

We have an intercom from the:

a. stage manager to switchbds.
b. stage manager to stage left
c. stage manager to stage right
d. stage manager to fly floor
e. stage manager to follow spots
f. stage manager to front house
g. stage manager to dressing rooms

The stage manager can work from stage right.

Figure 5.7 *Continued*

The availability of wardrobe assistants, costume people, laundry and cleaning facilities, dressing room space and equipment, and sanitary facilities

Information about customary curtain hours and customary audience preferences in attending matinees, weekday evening performances, and so on

Contacts for news and media in the area to ease the publicizing process

Transportation facilities, local and interstate, passenger and freight

Hotel and restaurant services that have proven useful to theater companies

Information on ushers and house managerial services, ticket takers, and so forth

The packet should also include full information on the seating capacity of each section of the theater and a detailed account of parking facilities available.

Some theaters now place their technical information for visiting companies on the Internet. See www.theatreroyal.demon.co.uk.

Suggested Classroom Exercises

1. Have students collaborate to draw an organizational chart for your theater. Include names of faculty and staff working on current or next production. When complete, compare the students' work to the chart on page 52 and discuss the differences.
2. Stop laughing and making jokes about the size of the trunk you would need to hold all of that junk on pages 58–60. Have students individually select 10 items that they think are most useful under rehearsal conditions. Combine their selections into one list.

6

Expediting Auditions and Readings

A verbal agreement isn't worth the paper it's printed on.
—Sam Goldwyn

In auditioning actors for roles in plays, it is desirable to make the actors comfortable and to move them quickly through an interview-audition procedure. In general, two areas are set up, one in which the actors can gather and wait and a second in which the director—and sometimes producer, musical director, choreographer, and other staff members—can interview and audition the performer.

To expedite the procedure, you should ensure that both areas are properly set up. There should be adequate light to read by and comfortable seating. Access to restrooms should be provided for actors who wish to find a mirror and freshen up. If possible, it is a nice touch to set up a coffee/tea table to show hospitality and consideration for those who are trying out.

Since this may be a difficult time for many actors, you should attempt to be a cheerful receptionist. You are usually the first person in the company that the actor is exposed to, and the actor starts to form an opinion of the company by the way you deport yourself. Offer the same warm, friendly welcome that you would want to receive if you were the auditioning actor.

You will want to write down the actors' names as they arrive so that you can audition them on a first come, first served basis.

Working with Actors

You can't make theater without actors. The actor is the central ingredient in making theater happen. Audiences may come to theaters to see the work

My Dance Audition Procedures

At an open dance call, I generally

1. Ask dancers to complete the audition form (see below).
2. Ask for pictures and résumés, which I attach to the audition form.
3. Give each dancer a sticker with a number that matches the number on the audition form. We usually have about 50 dancers at a call and this helps to keep track of them.
4. When the choreographer is ready, I take the dancers into the audition room.
5. I hand the stack of forms to the choreographer.
6. The choreographer will teach the combination to the entire group, reviewing it several times.
7. If there is no piano player to accompany the audition, or if the choreographer prefers a CD or tape, I will run the CD player or tape.
8. Dancers are broken into smaller groups and do the combination for the choreographer. When a cut is made, I get the names of the persons the choreographer wants to keep, and read them aloud. I thank the others for coming and encourage them to audition again.
9. After the dance portion of the audition is complete, I ask all of the dancers to leave the room, to prepare their sheet music in order to to return to the audition room, one at a time, to sing.
10. I escort them into the room, usually in numeric order, to have them sing, usually only 16 bars, for the choreographer, director, and music director.
11. Before they leave, I tell them the callback time, if known.

In general, I try to keep things moving along, try to keep the auditionees as informed as possible about what to expect next, and try to listen to individuals and help them with their specific needs.

> Bob Bones
> Production Stage Manager
> American Musical Theatre of San Jose

Dance Audition Form. Courtesy Bob Bones.

Dance Auditions

Just a few quick notes on things to think about:

Is there room for dancers to warm up before the audition? If they can't have access to the actual audition space, where can they warm up? Is there also a space that will be available for dancers to practice the audition routine once they've learned it and they're waiting to audition?

Who provides a resin box? A first-aid kit with ice packs? Are these readily available at the studio or does your production need to bring them?

Does the producer want a videotape record of the audition, and if so, who provides the equipment, operator, etc.?

Is music live or recorded? Who is responsible for hiring/providing music?

The stage manager can either be outside the audition room (signing in dancers, answering questions about the production and the audition process, etc.) or inside (sorting résumés, running the recorded music, videotaping the dancers, etc.) but I wouldn't recommend trying to do both. I think it's important at any type of audition to be available to the performers as a source of information and encouragement, a face with a name instead of one of the anonymous people behind the table!

> Jill Johnson Gold
> Stage Manager
> SISTERELLA, '97 European Tour

---

of stage managers, directors, and producers, but the only people who can communicate theater magic to audiences, through ideas and emotions, are the actors. They are the only ones who can communicate this by themselves, and, if necessary, they can get along without you. But you can't make theater without the actor.

So, regardless of your personal opinion of individual actors, you have to maintain a healthy respect for the function of the actor. And this healthy respect should be the bedrock of your relationship with cast members. As stage manager, yours is a support function. You are there to assist actors—to help them get more out of rehearsal time and to help them concentrate on their task by having everything so well organized and running so smoothly that there is nothing to distract them from their work.

On the other hand, as the producer's foreman and the director's principal assistant, you are a supervisor of the actors' time and whereabouts. When a stage manager posts a schedule or announces a picture call, she or he expects the actor to be there, just as would a military commander who had given a direct order. When a stage manager has to move backstage to supervise a shift, or for any other reason, cast members are expected to yield the right of way. During performances, cast members are expected not to speak to the stage manager unless they are spoken to (with the exception of informing the stage manager of a fire or some other imminent threat to life or safety or the continuation of the performance). Cast members should know that the stage manager is responsible for the smooth running of the performance, and out of respect for that function, they should do their utmost to cooperate.

So the actor/stage manager relationship should be one of mutual respect and mutual cooperation. As in all human relationships, this may be difficult to codify further. However, in practice, I've found that it works out quite easily. Early in rehearsals, actors realize that you are concerned with their welfare and comfort, that you are anxious to get the show on efficiently, and that you are quite obviously helping them. They see that what you're doing is all for the common goal of a better performance. And so they are willing and anxious to cooperate with you when you exert your authority.

Some comments on the stage manager's relationship with cast members were already made in Chapter 2.

Posting Notes for Readings

During casting calls, most actors will ask "the person with the clipboard" for information. You should be able to refer everyone to the notes you have posted.

If you were an actor showing up for a casting call, what would you like to know about the production?

First, is there a part in it for you? Who's putting this play on? Why? Who's directing? What's the rehearsal schedule like? Where can you get a script? On what pages does the character you're right for appear? What pages will you be asked to read?

Try to anticipate what the actors would like to know and post that information in the lobby or waiting area where actors can read it before filling out audition forms.

Fact Sheet

Coordinate with the producer and publicist to get the basic facts up for the actors: who, what, when, where, and why. If possible, note on the fact sheet where the actors can obtain scripts (see Figure 6.1).

Character Descriptions

How old are the characters? How much do they age during the course of the play? Who played the part on Broadway? How does the author describe the character? How does the director see the character? Many actors do not have time or opportunity to read scripts and study them

```
                              THE EMPEROR COMPANY
                                  December 30

FACT SHEET

What/      A three act play about Nero, notoriously cruel and depraved
           Roman emperor (37 A.D. - 68 A.D.)

Who/       Hermann Gressieker - author
           George White - translator and adapter
           Lou Rifkin - producer
           Charles Rome Smith - director
           Lawrence Stern - production stage manager
           Norman Houle - set designer
           Hellene Heigh - publicist

Where/     Cahuenga Playhouse, 3333 Cahuenga Blvd. West (Barham exit
           of Hollywood Freeway)

When/      Opens February 7, to run on weekends, four week minimum.
           (See posted rehearsal schedule.)

Why/       To present the highly original and well-received German
           playwright to Los Angeles audiences and to showcase local
           talent. This is an Equity production under the Hollywood
           Area Contract.
```

Figure 6.1   Production Fact Sheet for Auditioning Actors

before they come to readings. Sometimes the scripts are simply not available to the actor until 10 minutes before a reading. You can help the actors adjust to this situation by lining up this information from the script and the director and posting much of the information the actors will need (see Figure 6.2).

Equity Paid Parts

Under some contracts, Actors' Equity Association, the union for actors, determines which parts will be paid or not paid. Under other contracts, Equity allows producers to pay chorus members small additional fees to handle small roles. Post the paid parts list if applicable (see Figure 6.3).

Suggested Readings

You may wish to post a list of readings from the play with which the actors may audition. It sometimes expedites casting calls if actors can read in pairs, or even three at a time. Otherwise, you may be called on to read with the actors (see Figure 6.4).

Rehearsal Schedule

If the rehearsal schedule is ready, post it. Otherwise, you might add a paragraph to the fact sheet indicating the anticipated pattern of rehearsals (e.g.,

```
                              THE RIGHT HONORABLE GENTLEMAN

CHARACTER DESCRIPTIONS

Sir Charles Dilke                pp. 1-14, 16-21, 29-43;
     mid 40's, air of distinc-       47-50, 55-67; 77-90.
     tion, natural command,
     enigmatic

Mrs. Ashton Dilke                pp. 1-7, 38-42; 55-57;
     early 30's, kindhearted          83-85.
     busybody, Dilke's sister-
     in-law

Mrs. Emilia Pattison (later      pp. 7-14, 29-40; 81-90.
     Lady Dilke) mature, ele-
     gant, charming, quiet
     integrity & warmth

Mr. Joseph Chamberlain           pp. 10-19, 42-43; 49-54;
     Statesman of Dilke's            77-90.
     stature, at least mid 40's

Mrs. Virginia Crawford (Nia)     pp. 14-40; 50-54; 77-85.
     Vital, restless, intelli-
     gent, waspish, challenging
     manner, 22

Mr. Donald Crawford              pp. 21-27; 81-85.
     Late 40's, stiff, inhi-
     bited, slight Scottish
     accent, formal & pedantic

Sir James Russel                 pp. 32-41; 50-53.
     Distinguished, incisive,
     jurist, dry, mid 50's

Sarah Gray                       pp. 39-44.
     Handsome woman, reserved,
     Mid 30's, a decided cut
     above her station

Mrs. Rossiter (Lila)             pp. 51-56; 81-83.
     Mother of Nia, Maye, &
     Helen.
```

Figure 6.2   Character Descriptions for Auditioning Actors. Note that the character descriptions are either from the script and approved by the director prior to posting or generated by the director.

"We will be rehearsing for four weeks, afternoons and evenings, Monday through Friday" or "We expect to rehearse weeknights from 7:30 to 10:30 P.M.").

Audition Form Format

If preprinted audition forms are not available, you should post a format and examples of the information that the company requires (see "Obtaining Information" later in this chapter).

```
                          SHOW BOAT

       Principals                    Paid Parts


       Gaylord Ravenal               Rubberface
       Julie                         Jake
       Captain Andy                  Guitar Player
       Queenie                       Backwoods Men
       Pete                          Piano Player
       Landlady                      Barker
       Old Lady                      Carrie
       Ellie                         Jim
       Magnolia                      Dancer-Charleston
       Vallon                        Fatima
       Windy                         Mother Superior
       Dahoney King                  Jeb
       Parthy Ann Hawkes
       Joe
       Steve
       Frank
       Kim (child)


    Should a production be sufficiently changed, either by cutting, re-
    writing or re-choreographing, to make questionable the category in
    which a particular part belongs, please consult with Equity immediately
    for a determination.
```

Figure 6.3   Equity Paid Parts Listing

Callback Schedule

If many actors are called back to read for several parts, you may want to set up a schedule so that actors can read in groups, showing how they play to one another. The callback schedule would not normally be posted for actors, as it is not necessary for them to know who else is being considered for the part they want. The schedule will be very helpful to you in managing the callback period efficiently (see Figure 6.5).

With thorough preparation for casting calls, you show cast members from the outset that you are in total command of the situation, anticipating everything.

Accepting Résumés

In the course of casting calls, especially in professional theater, many actors and actresses will submit their résumés. These résumés generally consist of a picture or several pictures in various costumes and poses (composites); written information giving physical measurements, credits in features, TV, and on the stage; and agent's name and phone number (see Figure 6.6).

The purpose of a résumé is to help the director recall and contact the actor after the reading. In a production involving amateur actors, it is wise for a manager to secure information comparable to the résumé coverage

```
                         THE EMPEROR COMPANY
                         December 30

SUGGESTED READINGS

Seneca          monologue I 1-2
                w/Nero III 8-11
                w/Burrus II 9
                w/Nero, Agrippina II 6-8

Nero            w/Actis I 11-18
                w/Poppaea II 10-15
                w/Seneca III 8-11
                w/Seneca, Agrippina II 6-8

Agrippina       w/Nero I 2-4 & 19-21
                w/Seneca, Burrus II 6-8

Burrus          w/Seneca II 9
                w/Seneca, Agrippina I 10-11

Actis           w/Nero I 11-18

Poppaea         w/Nero II 10-15
                w/Nero, Seneca II 16-21

Messenger       w/Seneca, Nero II 25

Paulus          w/Seneca, Nero III 1-7

Thrasea         w/Lucanus, Seneca III 12-14

Lucanus         w/Thrasea, Seneca III 12-14
```

Figure 6.4 Suggested Readings for Auditioning Actors

```
                         THE EMPEROR COMPANY
                         January 4

CALLBACK SCHEDULE

Time   Nero             Actis                Seneca         Poppaea       Paulus
4:00   Nathan Hanek     Betty Ray            Earl Olsen     Liz Victor    Ronald Penny
4:15   John Heyman      Linda Mock                          G. Merriman   Ed Marko
4:30   Barton Carton                                        G. Quentin
4:45   Bill Cannon      Liz Bullard          Br. Matthews   Dol. MacRae
5:00   Glen Colmar      Anita Morrel         Ray Anderson   Jean Scott    Mike Delgado
5:15   Erik Douglas     Darlene Gainsborough John Hammond   A. Shelton    H. Feinberg
5:30   Richard Presby   Manuela Keeney                      Abig. Perry
```

Figure 6.5 Callback Schedule (Not Normally Posted)

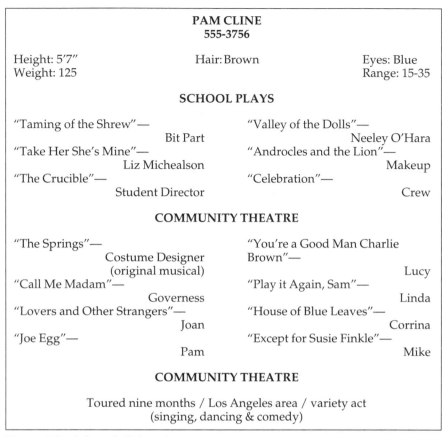

Figure 6.6   A Sample Résumé

and to keep those notes in a convenient form to help the director recall the actors in tryouts.

When you accept a résumé, look it over carefully. For amateur actors, try to secure basic résumé information. For professionals, ask the actor if she or he still has the same agent and if she or he can still be reached at the same numbers. Agents and phone numbers change rapidly, and it is important to make sure that the essential entries are up to date. Be sure to note on the résumé the part for which the actor auditions.

Sometimes the staff will want to look over the actor's résumé (or your comparable notes) before the actor is ushered in to read. This allows the staff to review the actor's background and judge his or her experience level before meeting him or her. In some other theater situations, the actor may be judged solely on appearance and reading, and résumés or preliminary notes are intentionally ignored.

After the show has been cast, don't throw away the résumés or notes. If the résumé picture is an 8" × 10" glossy print, it may be useful to the company publicity person as part of a publicity release or for posting in the lobby. Information on the résumé might be useful to you, the publicity person, or others. Also keep the résumés of those not cast also. You might have to replace a cast member suddenly. When casting your next show, you just might remember someone right for a role by flipping through your collection of résumés.

If you save résumés for future productions, you will want to make some simple evaluation of the actor's ability and code the résumé. A suggested code is: (1) excellent, exciting actor, (2) capable actor, (3) barely competent, (4) no talent; (A) well suited to the part, (B) possible for the part, (C) not suited for the part.

The value of such a code is that in invitational readings for future productions you would not call the 4s to read and would start with the 1s. The letters, along with the names of the roles they read for, might remind you of the actors' physical types.

Controlling Scripts

During the casting call, you are responsible for controlling scripts. If you have not already numbered your scripts, now would be a good time to do so. Jot down the names of the readers and the script numbers as you issue them. As the actors depart the interview area, be sure to reclaim the scripts and cross off their names.

Actors will beg to take scripts home in order to prepare for callbacks. Advise these actors that scripts are needed for auditions and be prepared to point out where actors may obtain duplicate scripts.

Obtaining Information

During auditions, at the first reading, and every time a newcomer joins your cast, crew, or staff, you will want to obtain information that you and other members of your staff can use. It is convenient to gather this information on cards (3" × 5" or 4" × 6") or on standard-sized preprinted information sheets.

The information/audition card may be preprinted (see Figure 6.7), or you may post an explanation of the information you want and the format you want it in, and distribute blank cards (see Figure 6.8). The former method is preferable, as you are more likely to get serviceable results. Whichever approach you use, it is best to check each card as it is completed to ensure that it is legible and that both sides have been completed.

Age range and union affiliation deserve special attention.

```
┌─────────────────────────────────────────────────────────────┐
│                     PLAYLAND THEATRE                          │
│                                                               │
│  AUDITION FORM                DATE _____  # _____       │
│  ADDRESS: _____ AGE: _____ SEX:_____ │
│  NAME: _____ PHONE: _____   │
│           ACTOR ❏      SINGER ❏        DANCER ❏               │
│                 COLOR              VOICE      VOICE           │
│  HT.:____  WT.: ____  HAIR: ____  EYES: ____ TYPE: ____ RANGE: ____│
│  THEATRICAL UNION MEMBERSHIP: _____  │
│  THEATRICAL TRAINING & EXPERIENCE: _____  │
│  _____ │
│  _____ │
│                                                               │
│  NAME & PHONE OF AGENT: _____  │
│  ARE YOU PREPARED TO SING IN THE ENSEMBLE? _____  │
│  SOCIAL SECURITY NO. _____  │
│                                                               │
│     _____ │
│     LAST NAME          FIRST          MIDDLE (Print)          │
│     _____ │
│     Address            City/Zip                              │
│     _____ │
│     Phone Numbers (Home, work, service, other)               │
│     _____ │
│     Equity, SAG, AFTRA, AGVA, SEG, Other                     │
│     _____ │
│     Circle Union Membership                                  │
│     _____ │
│     Agency, Agent          (His phone)                       │
│     _____ │
│     Height, Weight, Color Eyes, Color Hair                   │
│                                                               │
│     RECENT CREDITS:                                          │
│                                                               │
│     STUDIES:                                                 │
│                                                               │
│     CURRENT COMMITMENTS:                                     │
└─────────────────────────────────────────────────────────────┘
```

Figure 6.7   Printed Company Audition Form Cards

Age Range

Some actors do not feel it necessary that you know their ages. Rather than posing the sometimes awkward question of age, ask for the range that they feel they can portray on stage. (You are welcome to your own opinion, but discreetly keep it to yourself.) Or, instead of asking for the age range, you might offer the following multiple choice: (1) child, (2) ingenue, (3) mature. This offends no one (except the "aging ingenue").

Union Affiliation

An actor who is a member of any of the performers' unions (AEA, SAG, AFTRA, or AGVA—discussed in Chapter 18) may be prohibited by the

```
LAST NAME,  FIRST MIDDLE          Recent Credits
(Please print caps)

Address, City, Zip

Phones (Home, Work, Service, Other)

Union membership (SAG, AFTRA,      Studies
AEA, SEG, AGVA, other)

Agency, Agent (his phone)

Height, Weight, Color eyes, Color hair

Social Security Number
                                  Current Commitments

      (front)            FORMAT
```

```
Have you filled out a
card? The information
requested will help
us remember you, cast
you, and reach you.                  (reverse side)
Thank you!
                                  SHOWBOAT Captain Andy
                                  DEATH OF A SALESMAN
                                     Willy
      (front)           SAMPLE    LILI (MGM) Clown
                                  UNTOUCHABLES Mafia member
                                  BREAKING POINT Pencil
FLEEGLE, FRED FIGLEAF                 Salesman

117 ¹/₂ Marrow Bone Drive, LA 90037   Fyodor Lernantovich
                                  Studio (NYC)
555 8763 (home) 555 4588 (days)   Neighborhood Playhouse
555 3000 (serv)                   (Grand Forks, ND)

Equity, SAG, AFTRA                Tape Bob Hope Show
                                  Sept. 2
Talent Ltd., G. Leech (555 7756)  Tour with American
                                  Ballet company starting
6'8", 176 lbs., Grn eyes, Brn hair   Jan. 4
                                  Work afternoons 3-5 PM
492-82-9175
```

Figure 6.8   Posted Model Examples for Audition Information Cards

union from performing in any nonunion production. In auditioning for showcase productions and no-budget, nonunion productions, actors have been known not to state their union affiliation on their audition cards in order to work. It is the producer's responsibility to check, or face union sanctions.

When a preprinted audition form is used, an area can be set aside ("Do not write below this line") for results of questions that the director or casting director will want to ask during interviews (see Figures 6.9 and 6.10).

The information cards or forms should be clipped to the actor's photo or composite. In school theaters, be sure to have the actors write their schedules of classes on their audition forms.

```
                              THE ST. GENESIUS PLAYERS
                              THE ODD COUPLE


C A S T I N G

NAME _____  PHONE_____

ADDRESS _____

HEIGHT _____WEIGHT _____ EYES _____ HAIR _____

AGE RANGE _____

UNION:  AEA   SAG   SEG   AFTRA   AGVA   OTHER: _____
        (circle any to which you have ever belonged)

AGENCY, AGENT, PHONE (IF ANY): _____

ACTING EXPERIENCE:  Use reverse side of this form to list
                    recent credits if you are not submitting
                    a resume.



Do not write below line. _____
------------------------------------------------------------

Felix                    smokes

Oscar                    poker

Speed                    goal

Murray                   schedule

Roy                      SM

Vinnie                   St. G?

Gwendolyn

Cecily
```

Figure 6.9   Full-Length Audition Form

Controlling Forms

The first cast meeting after casting calls and callbacks is frequently a read-through of the script. You should take advantage of a time when all the cast are present by getting the paperwork done. Take a few minutes of cast time to review the cast rules and take care of the required forms. If you fail to get it all done at once, you will have to run after individual cast members to distribute and collect forms, and this can be time consuming.

Plan this paperwork session ahead of time by grouping forms for each actor into a packet. Make sure that you have plenty of pens and pencils on hand. Each packet might include:

Cast keeps:
1. Rehearsal schedule
2. Company rules
3. Cast list (see the following section)

```
┌─────────────────────────────────────────────────────────────┐
│                    WORKSHOP APPLICATION                       │
│                                          TALENT               │
│                                                               │
│  NAME:_____  ACTOR _____        │
│  ADDRESS:_____  DIRECTOR _____       │
│                                  PLAYWRIGHT _____        │
│                                  ST. MANAGER _____        │
│  TELEPHONE NO: _____   DESIGNER _____        │
│  UNION AFFILIATION: _____  TECHNICIAN _____        │
│                                  SINGER _____        │
│     A.E.A. _____  AGVA _____ DANCER _____        │
│                                  CHOREOGRAPHER _____        │
│     SAG _____   C.E. _____ PRODUCER _____        │
│     AFTRA _____   OTHER _____ MUSICIAN _____        │
│                                  OTHER _____        │
│                                                               │
│  PROFESSIONAL BACKGROUND: (LIST ANY ADDITIONAL CREDITS ON     │
│  REVERSE SIDE)                                                 │
│  (RESUME & PICTURE, IF AVAILABLE)                             │
│                                                               │
│  TRAINING: Where and with whom have you studied?              │
│                                                               │
│  CHECK SESSIONS YOU ARE INTERESTED IN ATTENDING:              │
│  _____ LECTURE SESSIONS                                     │
│  _____ WORKSHOP SCENES: Assignments, observations, critiques│
│  _____ DIRECTING CLASS                                      │
│  _____ PRODUCTION:  Panels, Budgeting, Stage Manager, Scenic│
│                       Designer, Lighting, Etc.                │
│          (Please do not write below this line)                │
│  _____  │
│                                                               │
│                                                               │
└─────────────────────────────────────────────────────────────┘
```

Figure 6.10 Model of Workshop Application Form

4. Guides to hotels, restaurants, points of interest (if the cast is from out of town)

You need returned:

5. Biographical data form (see Figure 6.11) (check with your publicity person)
6. Costume size form (see Figure 6.12) (check with your costume designer)
7. Health insurance form (if Equity company—see Figure 6.13)
8. Welfare coverage form (if Equity company)
9. W-4 form (if paid company)
10. Life insurance form (if Equity company)

```
                        BIOGRAPHICAL DATA

        Information requested below will be used for program
        notes and publicity releases. Use reverse side to
        complete comments if space below is not sufficient.
        Thank you.
NAME _____ ROLE _____
Education:
Military service:
Theatrical training:
First stage appearance:
Credits:


Most recent stage:
Most recent film:
Most recent TV:
Current commitments (stage, film, TV):
Family:
Hobbies:
Highlight to date of your career:
Career ambition:
When did you come to Los Angeles? What brought you?




If you wish to add any unusual personal facts or viewpoints
which might aid in publicity, please use reverse side.
```

Figure 6.11   Model of Biographical Data Form

If you have time, print the actor's name on each form before you distribute them. Then make sure that you get back the forms you need. Many actors will want to take them home, insisting that they have the information written down at home and they can copy it if you will just allow them to take the forms home. Don't. You may never see the forms again. Insist that they fill out as much as they can and that you must have all forms back before they get up from the table. Tell them that you will call them at home for the information they can't remember.

"I have my biography at home." "My agent fills these in." "I'm covered by my wife's insurance." "I always forget how many of my husband's children by his first wife I'm supposed to claim." Actors, like most other people, don't like to fill out forms. You must plead, cajole, and remain pleasant.

Have your tailor's tape handy for those who don't remember their costume sizes. Check each returned form on the spot to make sure that it is complete and legible.

```
┌─────────────────────────────────────────────────────────────┐
│                         COSTUMES                            │
│  The costume department needs to know your measurements.    │
│  Please mark them on this sheet and return it to the stage  │
│  manager. Thank you.                                        │
│                                                             │
│  NAME _____  ROLE _____        │
│  HEIGHT ____ ft. ____ inches    WEIGHT ____ lbs.            │
│                                                             │
│                                                             │
│  men only                                                   │
│                            women only                       │
│  jacket size _____                                      │
│                            bust _____                   │
│  shirt _____                                       │
│        (neck) (sleeve)     waist _____                  │
│                                                             │
│  waist _____       waist to floor _____       │
│                                                             │
│  inseam _____       hips _____                 │
│                                                             │
│  shoes _____                                          │
│                                                             │
│  sox _____                                           │
│                                                             │
│  hat _____                                            │
│                                                             │
└─────────────────────────────────────────────────────────────┘
```

Figure 6.12   Model Costume Size Form

Preparing a Cast List

The ability to reach any actor immediately is of prime importance to you. The cast list is an invaluable tool in that function. The list should include the character, full name of the actor who plays the character exactly as that actor wishes the name to appear in the program, address, home phone, cell phone, work or business phone, service number, agent's name, and agent's phone number (see Figure 6.14).

Check for accuracy with each cast member before duplicating.

In rare cases, actors will want to have their home phone and address withheld from all but you. Check this, too, before duplicating and distributing.

There never seems to be enough cast lists. Each cast member wants one so that she or he can contact other cast members. The costume designer needs one. The publicist needs one. The payroll clerk needs one. The program editor needs one. The union insists on one. And as soon as you have given out your last copy, you find that there is still another person who needs one—the assistant director, the assistant stage manager, the doorman, the receptionist, the box office, or the sign painter.

You can't go too far in obtaining extra phone numbers at which you can reach an actor. Ask for any other numbers and e-mail addresses at which he or she can be reached when not at home or at the theater. Note

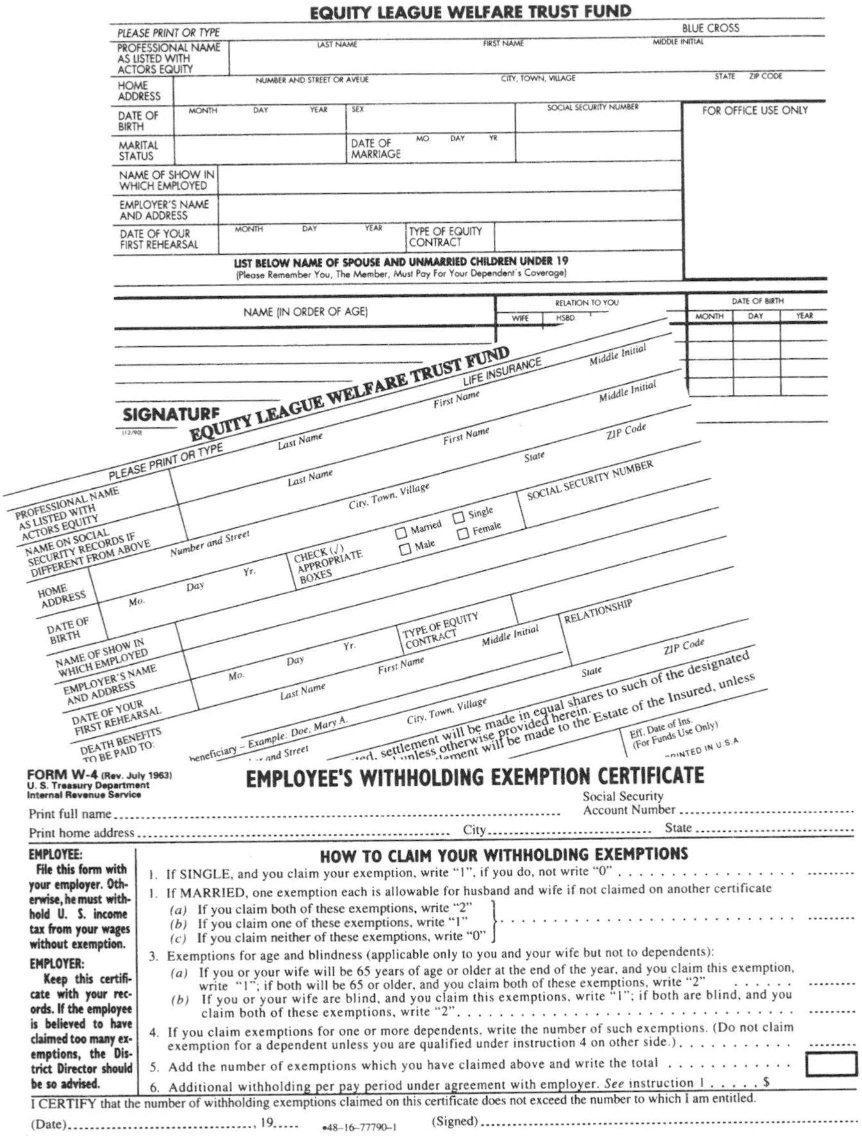

EQUITY LEAGUE WELFARE TRUST FUND

PLEASE PRINT OR TYPE — BLUE CROSS

PROFESSIONAL NAME AS LISTED WITH ACTORS EQUITY — LAST NAME — FIRST NAME — MIDDLE INITIAL

HOME ADDRESS — NUMBER AND STREET OR AVEUE — CITY, TOWN, VILLAGE — STATE — ZIP CODE

DATE OF BIRTH — MONTH — DAY — YEAR — SEX — SOCIAL SECURITY NUMBER — FOR OFFICE USE ONLY

MARITAL STATUS — DATE OF MARRIAGE — MO. — DAY — YR

NAME OF SHOW IN WHICH EMPLOYED

EMPLOYER'S NAME AND ADDRESS

DATE OF YOUR FIRST REHEARSAL — MONTH — DAY — YEAR — TYPE OF EQUITY CONTRACT

LIST BELOW NAME OF SPOUSE AND UNMARRIED CHILDREN UNDER 19
(Please Remember You, The Member, Must Pay For Your Dependent's Coverage)

NAME (IN ORDER OF AGE) — RELATION TO YOU: WIFE — HSBD. — DATE OF BIRTH: MONTH — DAY — YEAR

SIGNATURE

(12/90)

EQUITY LEAGUE WELFARE TRUST FUND

LIFE INSURANCE

PLEASE PRINT OR TYPE

PROFESSIONAL NAME AS LISTED WITH ACTORS EQUITY — Last Name — First Name — Middle Initial

NAME ON SOCIAL SECURITY RECORDS IF DIFFERENT FROM ABOVE — Last Name — First Name — Middle Initial

HOME ADDRESS — Number and Street — City, Town, Village — State — ZIP Code

DATE OF BIRTH — Mo. — Day — Yr. — CHECK (✓) APPROPRIATE BOXES — ☐ Married ☐ Single ☐ Male ☐ Female — SOCIAL SECURITY NUMBER

NAME OF SHOW IN WHICH EMPLOYED

EMPLOYER'S NAME AND ADDRESS

DATE OF YOUR FIRST REHEARSAL — Mo. — Day — Yr. — TYPE OF EQUITY CONTRACT

DEATH BENEFITS TO BE PAID TO: — beneficiary – Example: Doe, Mary A. — Last Name — First Name — Middle Initial — RELATIONSHIP

...and Street — City, Town, Village — State — ZIP Code

...ted, settlement will be made in equal shares to such of the designated ...unless otherwise provided herein. ...ement will be made to the Estate of the Insured, unless

Eff. Date of Ins. (For Funds Use Only)

PRINTED IN U.S.A.

FORM W-4 (Rev. July 1963)
U. S. Treasury Department
Internal Revenue Service

EMPLOYEE'S WITHHOLDING EXEMPTION CERTIFICATE

Print full name .... Social Security Account Number ....

Print home address .... City .... State ....

EMPLOYEE: File this form with your employer. Otherwise, he must withhold U. S. income tax from your wages without exemption.

EMPLOYER: Keep this certificate with your records. If the employee is believed to have claimed too many exemptions, the District Director should be so advised.

HOW TO CLAIM YOUR WITHHOLDING EXEMPTIONS

1. If SINGLE, and you claim your exemption, write "1"; if you do, not write "0" ....
1. If MARRIED, one exemption each is allowable for husband and wife if not claimed on another certificate
   (a) If you claim both of these exemptions, write "2"
   (b) If you claim one of these exemptions, write "1"
   (c) If you claim neither of these exemptions, write "0" ....
3. Exemptions for age and blindness (applicable only to you and your wife but not to dependents):
   (a) If you or your wife will be 65 years of age or older at the end of the year, and you claim this exemption, write "1"; if both will be 65 or older, and you claim both of these exemptions, write "2" ....
   (b) If you or your wife are blind, and you claim this exemptions, write "1"; if both are blind, and you claim both of these exemptions, write "2" ....
4. If you claim exemptions for one or more dependents, write the number of such exemptions. (Do not claim exemption for a dependent unless you are qualified under instruction 4 on other side.) ....
5. Add the number of exemptions which you have claimed above and write the total ....
6. Additional withholding per pay period under agreement with employer. *See* instruction 1 ..... $

I CERTIFY that the number of withholding exemptions claimed on this certificate does not exceed the number to which I am entitled.

(Date) ...., 19.... •48-16-77790-1 (Signed) ....

Figure 6.13 Forms That Professional Cast and Crew Must Complete

these numbers on your copy against the emergency situation when you will have to reach that actor in a hurry.

You will find several uses for a well-designed, complete cast list. One should be posted near your home telephone. Another should be indexed into your prompt script for handy reference during rehearsals. You can use still another copy, with a grid overlay (see Figure 6.15), as a checklist. Every time you have a distribution to make, you can check off each cast member

| THE TORCH-BEARERS | | CAST | | | |
		HOME	WORK	SERVICE	E-MAIL
Mr. Fred Ritter	Albert Alvarez 1058 Bramercy Dr.	753 3691	870 5414 (Jerry Rosen Agcy - 274 5861)	752 7975	alall@zyx.net
Mr. Huxley Hossefrosse	Ben Blahzay 3916 Melrose	232 5756 (William Barnes - 273 0205)	389 7726	none	theblahz@comm.net
Mr Spindler	Charles Corn 12113 Redondo	268 6612 (Ted Cooper - 654 3050)	231 1961	399 7171	corney212@avl.com
Mr. Ralph Twiller	Dave Dumpling 161 S. Berendo	753 3691	870 5414 (Jerry Rosen Agcy - 274 5861)	752 7975	73457@crumpserve.com
Teddy Spearing	Earl Eastman 355 Douglas	753 3691 (GAC - 273 2400)	870 5414	none	earlyman@earlyman.com
Mr Stage Manager	Frank Farley 3607 W. 3rd	732 9444 (Coralie Jr. - 663 1268)	778 3557	none	farfel@comm.net
Mrs. Paula Ritter	Gina Glass 232 S. Serrano	567 6743 (Kurt Frings - 274 8881)	652 7934	334 0101	gglass@avl.com
Mrs. J. Duro Pampinelli	Helen Harvey 1510 S. Vermont	665 1605 (no agent)	none	none	offut59@sac.com
Mrs. Nelly Fell	Ida Isely 2316 McPherson	221 2074 (Kumin-Olenick - 274 7281)	295 1781	752 7975	lstern@ips.net
Miss Flor. McCrickett	Judy Jennings 5716 Aldama Rd.	936 2325 (no agent)	627 4554	none	jjone@comm.net
Mrs. Clara Sheppard	Karen Kirsten 3130 W. 11th	870 5079 (Kendal Agcy - 274 8107)	none	334 0101	karenk@avl.com
Jenny	Louise Lehrer 139 E. 27th	877 2232 (Mishkin - 274 5261)	754 3024	292 1333	landfl@sac.com

Figure 6.14 Cast List for Duplication and Distribution

THE TORCH BEARERS   CAST LIST / Check List

		HOME	WORK	SERVICE	E-MAIL
Mr. Fred Ritter	Albert Alvarez 1058 Bramercy Dr.	753 3691 (J. Rosen Agcy - 274 5861)	870 5414	752 7975	alall@ZYX.net
Mr. Huxley Hossefrosse	Ben Blahzay 3916 Melrose	232 5756 (Wm. Barnes - 273 0205)	389 7726	none	theblahz@comm.net
Mr. Spindler	Charles Corn 1211B Redondo	268 6612 (Ted Cooper - 654 3050)	231 1961	399 7171	corney212@avl.com
Mr. Ralph Twiller	Dave Dumpling 161 S.Berendo	758 0058 (no agent)	292 5352	752 7975	73457@crumpserv.com
Teddy Spearing	Earl Eastman 355 Douglas	665 1052 (GAC - 273 2400)	none	none	earlyman@earlyman.com
Mr. Stage Manager	Frank Farley 3607 W. 3rd	732 9444 (Coralie Jr. - 663 1268)	778 3557	none	farfel@comm.net
Mrs. Paula Ritter	Gina Glass 232 S. Serrano	567 6743 (Kurt Frings - 274 8881)	652 7934	334 0101	gglass@avl.com
Mrs. J. Duro Pampinelli	Helen Harvey 1510 S. Vermont	665 1605 (no agent)	none	none	offut59@sac.com
Mrs. Nelly Fell	Ida Isely 2136 McPherson	221 2074 (Kumin-Olenick - 274 7281)	295 1781	752 7975	lstern@jps.net
Miss Flor. McCrickett	Judy Jennings 5716 Aldama Rd.	936 2325 (no agent)	627 4554	none	jjone@comm.net
Mrs. Clara Sheppard	Karen Kirsten 3130 W. 11th	870 5079 (Kendall Agcy - 274 8107)	none	334 0101	karenk@avl.com
Jenny	Louise Lehrer 139 E. 27th	877 2232 (Mishkin - 274 5261)	754 3024	292 1333	landfl@sac.com

Grid overlay column labels: Contract, 8 x 10 s, W-2, blue x - GHI, AVAIL.-TUES, Program Notes, Picnic, Pick up July 1

Figure 6.15   Duplicated Cast List with Overlay Grid for a Checklist

to ensure that everyone was told about a pickup rehearsal, a cast picnic, or an invitation to see a matinee of another show.

Be sure to store a copy of each cast list for your personal files. This is the only list that has both home phone and home address—information you won't readily have available if you save only a program.

In a musical stock situation with only a one-week rehearsal period, you may not know all the casting until the second day of rehearsals, which is only a few days before the printer needs that information to have programs for opening night. In such a case, it is desirable to run off lists with just the character name so that you can fill in cast members' names on the spot as casting is finalized (see Figure 6.16).

You will also need a complete list of the staff and crew, with their addresses and telephone numbers. A grid overlay on such a list makes a handy coordination form to ensure that you get all schedule changes and other necessary information to every member of the staff and crew.

```
                         SHOW  BOAT

OLD  LADY  ON  LEVEE
QUEENIE                        Bertha  Powell
PARTHY  ANNE  HAWKS
CAPTAIN  ANDY                  Marvin Miller
ELLIE
FRANK                          Dian Barlow
JULIE                          Beverly Alvarez
GAYLORD  RAVENAL               Alan  Gilbert
MAGNOLIA                       Kate Miller
JOE
WINDY
STEVE
PETE
IKE  VALLON                    Lou Boudreau
BACKWOODSMAN
BARKER
FATIMA
DAHOMEY  QUEEN
LANDLADY
ETHEL
MOTHER  SUPERIOR
KIM
JAKE
JIM
MAN  WITH  GUITAR
DOORMAN
MISS  SO-AND-SO
MISS  THINGAMABOB
HEADWAITER
ANNOUNCER
```

Figure 6.16   Production Cast List with Characters in Order of Appearance

Conducting the Deputy Election

At the first meeting of an Equity company, or at the first rehearsal following casting at which the entire cast is present, you should conduct the election of the deputy. The deputy is that cast member who will represent her
or his fellow union cast members in all union business. You should not
serve as deputy.

The union formally mails the official election form to you when your
name is supplied to the union (see Figure 6.17). If you do not receive the
form prior to your first rehearsal, call the nearest Equity office.

Take the time to read the official statement of election policy slowly
and deliberately.

Secret ballots are desirable in large casts. This process slows the election enough to give voters time to think. In small casts, members usually
reach accord in an open discussion of who might best serve. Formality is

Figure 6.17   Deputy Election Letter and Form

To the Equity Company,

When nominating and electing our company's Deputies, please remember that the Principal Deputy represents Principal Actors and Stage Managers; the Chorus Deputy represents Chorus Dancers and Singers. Please consider that:

- the Deputy is our link to the Union;
- the Deputy has the opportunity to gain extensive knowledge about the Contract under which we are working;
- the Deputy should form an amiable working relationship with the Stage Manager to try to solve problems as they arise;
- the Deputy will have direct communication with the appropriate AEA Business Representative;
- the Deputy can be instrumental in protecting all Actors' and Stage Managers' rights and working conditions by communicating directly with Actors' Equity about any possible infractions.

Most Actors and Stage Managers who have become involved in union activity as either Councilors, committee members or Deputies, have discovered that the more we know about our rights and our contracts, the better protected we are and the greater control we have over our working conditions. The Deputy should never have any confrontations with Management. After consulting with the Stage Manager, the Deputy need only communicate with the Union to insure action. This is an important job from which the entire company can benefit.

Our Deputy, once elected, should call the appropriate Equity office and ask for the Business Representative who administers our Contract to establish communication and learn of any concessions granted for this production. Ask to be sent a Deputy kit, if you have not yet received one from the Stage Manager, and ask that the pre-paid postage envelopes be sent to you for weekly reports and for any correspondence with Equity.

The Deputy may call collect.

Your Stage Manager will read the letter on the reverse side prior to the Deputy election, and then conduct election. Please DO NOT sign this election form unless this letter has been read. No one shall be present at the election except those employed under the Equity contract for this production. A Deputy may be elected by voice vote or, if more than one member is nominated, by secret ballot.

We, the undersigned Equity members, who constitute a majority of the cast of the

                                                          Principals
(circle the applicable classification)   Ensemble Singers
                                                          Ensemble Dancers

of the _____ company

under a _____ (type of Equity contract)

located at _____ theatre

under the management of _____

and opening on _____ do hereby elect

_____ as Deputy.

_____   _____

Date of this election: _____   Deputy's local phone: _____

                                               Address (**not** theatre): _____

Courtesy Actors' Equity Association.

not as important as thoughtfulness. Causing cast members to reflect, rather than simply "get it over with," is a matter of tactful persuasion.

Time to conduct this deputy election—and subsequent union meetings, should the need arise—out of paid rehearsal time is guaranteed to union actors in their contracts.

First Cast Meeting or Read-Through

We have all seen trite first-reading scenes in the movies in which the cast sits around a barren, coffee-stained table under a bleak work light. Why must it be this way?

I know one stage manager who brings from home a freshly pressed tablecloth and a bouquet of flowers to place on the first-reading table. It's a nice touch and it starts the cast off with the warm thought that someone went out of the way to make things a little better.

Suggested Classroom Exercise

Discuss the relationship of stage manager and actors in the audition process. What can stage managers do and how can they behave in order to establish an atmosphere of support and encouragement?

7

Budgeting

*A theater requires two good producers: one to produce the play,
and the other to produce the cash.*

—Anonymous

Keeping a record of your expenses is the very least that is expected of you in the area of budgeting. If you pay any money out of your pocket to further a production, whether it be 50¢ for a phone call to an actor who is late or the C.O.D. charge for a prop delivered to the theater, make a record of it, and, if possible, get a written receipt.

You may want to use an expenditures form (see Figure 7.1) and attach your receipts to it. Keep the form in your prompt script so that it is with you when you need it. Periodically turn in the receipts for reimbursement.

In some instances, it is more convenient to set up a petty cash fund, from $50 to $100, depending on needs. When it has been spent, turn over the receipts to the business manager or the box office treasurer, who can advance another $50 to $100, or whatever sum has been arranged and budgeted.

In some companies, a purchase order must be obtained from the business manager before anything can be bought.

In other cases, it may be necessary for you as manager to control funds for the technical director, the costume designer, the property master (see Chapter 10), and other backstage personnel. To make sure that each does not spend beyond the total budgeted for the production, you might need to use a purchase order system: Any staff member must ask for a purchase order *before* buying. You must then check the budget to see if this particular expenditure is within reason, and then approve or disapprove by giving or by denying a purchase order.

The budgeted items for a one-week musical stock production could be, for example, lumber, paint, hardware, fabrics, rigging, electrics, running

```
                          EXPENDITURES
  _____ production of "_____" _____
                                                    dates

  Supplier      Item(s)      Purchased by      Date       Cost

  1

  2

  3

  4

  5

  6

  7

  8

  9

  10

  11

  12

  13


        Page _____ of _____      Prepared by _____

                                      LAWRENCE STERN
                                      PRODUCTION STAGE MANAGER
                                      555-3719
```

Figure 7.1   An Expenditures Record to Keep in the Prompt Script

props, purchase props, tools, and car rental/gas. Figure 7.2 shows the layout of an expenditures record using this example on ledger pages. Many theaters use computer spreadsheet programs to keep track of the budget, so you may very well be working from a computer printout rather than a ledger.

Example

The technical director calls you from the lumber yard to say that the materials required to carry out the scene designer's plans will cost $198. Should you issue a purchase order?

Review the budget for this show and other shows this season.

There's $240 allotted to lumber. But, being familiar with the scene design and the show, you also know that there will be no flying of scenery or actors, or effects that require rigging. So you can add the rigging allocation of $40. You

NAME OF PRODUCTION   *Camelot*

P.O. NO.	$XXX Lumber	$XX PAINT	$XX HD. WARE	$XX FABRICS	$XX RIGGING	$XX ELECT.	$XX RUNNING PROPS	$XX PURCHASE	$XX TOOLS	$XX CAR&TRUCK
500										
501										X.XX
502										XX.XX
503	XXX.XX									
504			xx.xx O.K. PD (circled)					xx.xx		
503										xx.xx (truck)
505										
506						xx.xx	xx.xx O.K. LD (circled)			
507		xx.xx								
508								xx.xx		
509										x.XX
510										
511										.xx
TOTALS	XXX.XX	xx.xx	xx.xx			xx.xx	xx.xx	xx.xx		xx.xx

GRAND TOTAL ($XXX budgeted)
$XXX.XX

Figure 7.2   Ledger Pages Showing Columns for Budgeted Items with Purchase Order Numbers Listed in Left Column

should also be aware of the budget situation for the season: Tools have already cost $30 over the budget because of a lost sabre saw; the last two shows were under budget by $40 and $60, respectively, in lumber, and three of the four coming shows have been staged before in past seasons; therefore, since most of the scenery is stored, they should come in under budget. Sifting these factors, and perhaps some others, while the tech director waits on the phone, you might go ahead and give the purchase order number.

Or you might be under strict orders to clear all overbudget items with the business manager or other higher budget authority. In this case, you might have to ask the scene designer to streamline the design and bring it into line with the budget.

In educational theater, the budget for a single production might have a completely different set of budgeted items (see Figure 7.3). Designers with a level of experience with past college productions can estimate figures at a first production meeting by evaluating whether the current show is more or less demanding than the last. Guest designers and directors and new faculty members are constrained against overspending by others on the staff. The contingency item is normally 10 percent of the overall budget; if not used in one of the categories that is especially needy, contingency money might get diverted into stockpiling items that can be used in future productions of the season or next season. The budget for student productions is not generally made known to the students.

Each department head at our theater is responsible for one section of the budget. As production stage manager, I am responsible for tracking expenses for stagehands, musicians, ushers, theater expenses, and stage manager expenses. The technical director and costume director track their expenses as well as lighting and sound expenses. Our artistic director tracks designer and director expenses. Our finance director keeps track of benefits, health insurance, and workers' comp expenses. We each input figures into separate spreadsheets that link to the master budget [see Figure 7.4].

Bob Bones
Production Stage Manager
American Musical Theatre of San Jose

Figure 7.3 College Single Production Budget Form

Date _____

Ohlone College Drama

Individual Show Budget: Title: _____

Director: _____ Total Budget: _____

Auditions: _____

Show Dates: _____

Rights: _____

Set: _____

Costumes: _____

Props: _____

Lights: _____

Special Effects: _____

Paint: _____

Rentals: _____

Tickets: _____

Contingency: _____   _____

(All consultants, instructors, etc., paid out of separate budgets)   Total

Separate Budget:

Publicity: _____

Publicity Budget Covers   Approval:

All Paper and Ink for: Programs   _____
                       Audition Postcards   Director
                       Show Postcards
                       Posters   _____
                       Art Work   Technical Director
                       Any Photo Work

This budget is prepared at the first production meeting.
No changes can be made outside of a production meeting.

Courtesy Mark E. Nelson, Professor Theatre Studies, Ohlone College.

	A	B	C	D
1	**Show 1**			
2		Rate	Budget	Notes
3	**Total Annual Salaries**			
4	Master Carpenter			
5	Carpenter			
6	Carpenter			
7	Carpenter			
8	Scenic Artist			
9	Scenic Artist			
10	Scenic Artist			
11	Scenic Artist			
12	Carpenter Overhire			
13	Props Overhire			
14	*Subtotal Scene Shop Salaries*			
15				
16	Draper			
17	Cutter			
18	Assistant Cutter			
19	First Hand			
20	First Hand			
21	Stitcher			
22	Stitcher			
23	Stitcher / Overhire			
24	Crafts Master			
25	Crafts Assistant			
26	Shopper			
27	Costume Shop Overhire			
28	*Subtotal Costume Shop Salaries*			
29	**Total Technical Salaries**			
30				
31	Director			
32	Assistant Director			
33	Choreographers			
34	Assistant Choreographers			
35	Musical Directors			
36	Associate Musical Directors			
37	Rehearsal Pianist			
38	Programming			
39	*Subtotal Directors/Chor/MD/Rehearsal Pianist*			
40				
41	Designer/Coordinator — Sets			
42	Designer — Costumes			
43	Designer — Sound			
44	Designer — Makeup			
45	Designer — Lights			
46	Master Elec./Asst. Designer			
47	Asst. Stage Manager (non-AEA)			
48	Prop Master			
49	*Subtotal Designers, Non-Union ASM, ME, Props*			
50				
51	Wig Crew Head			
52	Head Dresser (union)			
53	Dresser (union)			
54	Wardrobe Supervisor			
55	*Subtotal Union Dresser, Wig Crew, Wardrobe*			
56				
57	**Total Designer/Directors**			
58				
59	Ushers			
60	Police			
61	**Total Other Services**			
62				
63	AFM (musicians)			
64	IATSE (stagehands)			
65				
66	Equity Actors			
67	Stage Manager			
68	Asst. Stage Manager			
69				

Figure 7.4   Master Production Budget (Microsoft Excel) for a Union House

Courtesy Bob Bones, Production Stage Manager, American Musical Theatre of San Jose.

(continued)

	A	B	C	D
70	**Total Actor's Equity Salaries**			
71				
72	Non-Union Cast			
73	Non-Union Crew			
74	**Total Non-Union Payroll**			
75				
76	**TOTAL PAYROLL**			
77				
78				
79	*Materials*			
80	Set Materials			
81	Rental Fee			
82	Cartage (rental set to & from SJ)			
83	Cartage (between shop & theatre)			
84	Dry Ice			
85	Video/Projection			
86	Video/Recording (archival)			
87	Video/Rental			
88	Sound (rental)			
89	Lights (rental)			
90	Costumes			
91	Hair/Makeup			
92	Wig Build			
93	Props			
94	Piano Tuning			
95	Stage Manager Supplies			
96	**Total Materials**			
97				
98	Guest Artist Expenses			
99	Scripts & Scores (rental duplication)			
100	Audition Expense			
101	**Total Other Costs**			
102				
103	Theatre Building Rental			
104	Theatre Equipment Rental			
105	**Total Theatre Facility Costs**			
106				
107	**Total Pizza, Tech Mtg. , & Parking**			
108				
109	**Total Contingency**			
110				
111	**Total Material, CPA, Other, Party, & Cont.**			
112				
113	**Benefits**			
114	*Workers' Compensation*			
115	Actor's Equity Association	5.48%		
116	Musical Directors/Choreographers/MD	5.48%		
117	Musicians	3.01%		
118	Total Annual Salaries	5.48%		
119	Technical Salaries	3.01%		
120	Contracted Services/Designers	3.01%		
121	IATSE	3.01%		
122	Ushers	3.01%		
123				
124	Volunteers			
125	**Total Worker's Comp.**			
126				
127	*Union Pension and Welfare*			
128	IATSE (health/welfare)			
129	Dresser (union)			
130	AEA Health			
131	AEA Pension			
132	AFM Pension			
133	**Total Pension and Welfare**			
134				
135	Kaiser (health)			
136	Payroll Tax Expense			
137	Unemployment Insurance			
138	**Total Benefits**			
139				
140	**TOTAL EXPENSES**			

Figure 7.4 *Continued*

Suggested Classroom Exercise

Have students brainstorm the budget items necessary to move your current production to a theater off campus for a short run. Assign a few items to each student, distribute catalogs of theatrical supply houses, and ask students to work together to determine the total cost and the price that would have to be charged for tickets to reach the break-even-point (BEP). Compare the projected cost of tickets off campus to what is being charged on campus for admission. (My sense is that students can endure four years of education without a clue as to how much money is required to make theater happen. The lighting board in a college theater control room, for example, is taken for granted until students know how much it would cost to rent that board for a two-weekend run.)

8

Rehearsal Procedures

*My dear boy, forget about the motivation. Just say the lines and
don't trip over the furniture.*

—Noel Coward

*The center of the stage is where all good actors go when
they die.*

—Anonymous

*The author should keep his mouth shut when his work begins
to speak.*

—Nietzche

Working with the Director during Rehearsal

As the closest assistant to the director, one of your most important functions will be to assist in getting the most productive results out of the time
allotted to each rehearsal. To do this well, it is important to maintain a clear
understanding of the director's function and a working relationship that
will help his or her aims to be carried out smoothly.

The director is responsible for interpreting the playwright's work
through the cast with the help of the staff. It is the director's artistic concept
of the play that the cast, staff, and crew work to obtain.

When casting has been completed and rehearsals are under way, the
director goes about her or his work in phases.

In the first phase, the director ensures that each cast member under-
stands the character to be portrayed. This is accomplished at initial readings and in private discussions between the director and the actor. The
director continues to influence characterization as reflected in line interpretations and business throughout the rehearsal period.

In the second phase, the director blocks—tells the actors where and
how to move on stage and how to handle props.

Next, the director works on pace—the timing of lines and business, of scenes and acts. He or she imparts pace to the play the way an orchestra conductor imparts tempo to a symphony—one scene *presto*, another *moderato.*

In the last phase, the director works on polishing the interaction of characters with sets, with props, and, most important, with one another.

The final quality of the performance is the product of all four phases of the director's work.

(In amateur theater, work sometimes does not go beyond the first two phases by opening night. Work on characterization consists of the actors learning their lines, and blocking means that they don't trip over one another. In professional theater, when a director is unable to progress beyond the first two phases, we call him or her a "traffic cop.")

The stage manager assists the director in two ways. First, she or he helps to expedite the rehearsals so that the director and cast will have as much time as possible to work on pace and interaction. Setting rehearsal furniture, taking blocking notation, and warning actors for their entrances during rehearsals are examples of the duties implied by this function.

Second, the stage manager accepts the responsibility for relieving the director of all concern for the mechanics of production so that the director can concentrate on bringing about an artistic interpretation of the script. Calling all sound and light cues, scheduling crew calls, and informing the director of progress on the sets are examples of the duties implied here.

The stage manager has no voice in the artistic interpretation of the script and must not intrude into this area. When prompting, for instance, he or she must not offer an interpretation of the lines to the actors.

What happens, then, if the stage manager notices during a rehearsal that one actor is addressing a line to a second actor that the playwright obviously intended for a third actor? The mistake is repeated at the next rehearsal. Still, the actors and director miss the obvious.

The stage manager should make a note in the prompt script and call the error to the attention of the director after the rehearsal and out of earshot of the cast. Let the director take remedial action.

Sometimes the stage manager observes very basic mistakes in direction. For example, focus is drawn away from an actress's important lines by an actor moving upstage of her during her speech. The stage manager observes that the director is oblivious or condones this at rehearsal after rehearsal. What should the stage manager do?

The stage manager calls such items to the director's attention, privately and tactfully.

Now let's take it to extremes. The stage manager notices during rehearsals that the director is demanding a light, comedy tone from an actress in a speech that simply won't work that way. It throws her fellow cast members off and it ruins the whole impact of the scene. What does the stage manager do?

[From a small college] We got a new director (head of theatre arts department). She has one of those organic work processes; you never know anything until the last possible moment. It is quite frustrating for a tyro stage manager like myself, not to mention the design team and many of our acting students. She's not really a people person, and has a hard time communicating her ideas to the designers. She has an abrasive and demanding nature. During rehearsals, the actors are obliged to stand around until she figures out what she wants to do. Often she will preface a rehearsal with this statement: "Okay, get ready for me to lose my temper." She does. She'll single out actors and make derogatory statements about them. The show will be reblocked right up until opening night. I don't mind erasing until I have Carpal Tunnel Syndrome, but I worry about how last-minute changes affect the quality of the show. How do I deal with a director of this nature? How do I tell her that her attitude is very negative and decreases morale?

> Name withheld at request of writer
> Name of college also withheld

[Working with difficult people can sometimes be the hardest part of stage management.

1. Understand that you cannot change another person's personality or behaviors. Do not label. Do not blame. Do not accuse. Ask questions privately, not within earshot of cast or crew. Do not add to conflict. Remain calm when all about you are stamping their feet.

2. Focus on how the director's behaviors have an impact on your work. Analyze. Separate your perceptions of negative personality traits from the behaviors that affect your work. Remain professional. Do what you need to do to meet stage management objectives.

3. Use preproduction staff meetings and postproduction critique meetings to ask questions (e.g.,"How many rehearsals prior to opening night should a no-more-changes-in-blocking deadline be set in order to obtain a polished performance?" "Would a no-more-changes-in blocking deadline have led to a more polished performance?" "Should that deadline be moved up in our next production schedule?").

4. Set limits for yourself and announce "I-messages"(e.g., "I have a low threshold for conflict. I will walk in the event of temper outbursts, regardless of source").

5. Decide whether you wish to continue working with that director. Negotiate conditions under which you will continue, and come to a clear understanding with that individual.]

The stage manager should judge with great care whether to discuss the matter confidentially with the director. I advise great caution until you get to know and understand the director. Certainly the stage manager should be extremely proficient in his or her own area before offering a director advice in another.

Although the stage manager does not participate in the creative interpretation of the script, he or she does make a conscientious effort to identify and understand the director's interpretation so that he or she can retain it, if called upon to do so, in keeping the show in hand during a long run (Chapter 16) or blocking replacements and rehearsing understudies (see the end of Chapter 16). Again, in these last mentioned duties, it is the director's intent that the stage manager strives to retain; the stage manager does not impose his or her own artistic interpretation.

Preset Diagrams

As soon as the scene designer decides where the sets and set pieces are to be located, you should make a diagram that will allow you to place those sets (or indications of sets) and set pieces (or rehearsal substitutes) exactly where they should be (see Figure 8.1).

As frequently as placement changes in the course of rehearsals, you must update your diagrams.

When it is decided which props will be *discovered* (found on the set at the rise of the curtain), you should add these props to your diagram with exacting specifications on just how the props are to be set (e. g., the label on a bottle should face downstage; the envelope is to be placed under the telephone with the address up and the flap open and pointing downstage).

The purpose of the preset diagram is to allow you to make a visual inspection prior to every rehearsal and performance. You must ensure that every part of the set, all set pieces, and all props are in exactly the position that the cast expects to find them. This ritual is one of your most sacred duties.

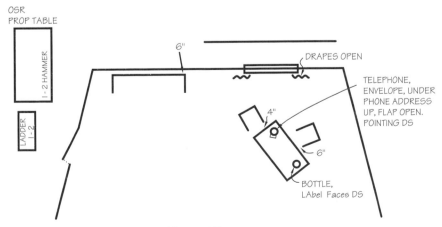

Figure 8.1   Preset Diagram of Set and Props

The preset diagram differs from a diagram of the stage (Chapter 5) in that it includes indications of sets and props, and it need not be drawn to scale. The preset diagram may be the same as a scene shift diagram (Chapter 12), but the shift diagrams are placed in the crew area to help brief the crew, whereas preset diagrams are placed in your prompt script.

Examples

1. The property person is late. You know where everything goes from your diagram. You set the props in her (his) absence and rehearsal is not delayed.
2. The crew, in setting for Act II, forgets to move a table on stage. During the intermission you check your diagram for Act II, realize that the table is not in place, and remind the crew.
3. An actor omits the business of closing the drapes on the set in Act II. Checking your diagram for Act III you realize that the drapes are supposed to be discovered closed. You make the adjustment.

Actors become very dependent psychologically on the exact placement of set pieces and props. Their timing for business is dependent on this placement. Adjusting to misplacement puts a strain on them, and sometimes it throws them off completely.

Your preset diagram should extend to the wings and include all stacked set pieces and props that are offstage. You must check their presence just as carefully as the units on stage.

Example

A ladder and hammer, used as a set piece and prop in Scene 2, are borrowed for practical use in the shop and not returned. The items are not preset for Scene 1. If the crew waits until their cue for the Scene 1-2 fast change to discover that the props are missing, the change will be delayed. Your inspection of the offstage sets and props avoids this type of incident.

Rehearsals Away from Your Stage

When stage time is not available for rehearsals and scenes must be rehearsed in other areas, preset diagrams, drawn to scale, allow you to lay out the exact dimensions of the scene using measuring tape and masking tape and/or spare rehearsal furniture to indicate flats and doors. Physical barricades used to indicate flats are better than tape. Actors tend to move closer to the taped lines or even step over them. They later feel cramped when they get onto the actual set. Your care in setting up the makeshift rehearsal area saves the time and energy of the cast in reblocking on the actual set.

Your Rehearsal Call

Usually you should arrive in the rehearsal area 30 to 40 minutes prior to the rehearsal call, depending on how much work must be done to ready the area.

Besides arranging sets and props according to your present diagram, you should check on working conditions. Sweep the stage and dust the rehearsal furniture, if necessary, and make whatever improvements you can in ventilation, temperature, and lighting.

Also prepare a work area for yourself and the director. Usually you will place a desk with two chairs in front of the apron. (Some directors prefer to use a music stand to hold their script as they remain standing during rehearsals.) Is there adequate room for your prompt script, the director's script, scratch paper, pencils, and refreshments? Ensure that there is satisfactory lighting so that you can follow your scripts comfortably.

Now, is everything ready to start rehearsal at the minute it is called? Or will the cast have to stand around 15 minutes waiting and/or adjusting things and not really rehearsing? Just 15 minutes of prerehearsal work by you can save two or three hours of cast time at every rehearsal. These hours saved and devoted to the quality of the final production are one of your very valuable contributions to the production process.

Rehearsal Duties

Try to anticipate the entire course of the rehearsal and have all working materials at hand so that you can be stationary or at the director's side throughout. As the director's closest assistant, you must be able to devote your full attention to the rehearsal because it is your busiest and most demanding work period. You have many duties and a few run concurrently:

Calling all sound and light cues and special effects, pinpointing cues
Spiking set pieces
Prompting
Warning
Taking blocking notation
Maintaining order
Timing of rehearsals and performances

Calling and Pinpointing Cues

From the very first rehearsal, you should call every light, sound, and special-effects cue. You should do it with such regularity and accuracy that no cast member ever fears for a second that you will miss a cue during the production.

> I use those fluorescent self-stick dots in my prompt script as I work in a very dim corner during performances. They show up nicely in my blue light.
>
> Patty Kilpatric
> Stage Manager
> Charles Town, WV

No matter how many times the director reruns the same scene, you always call the cues.

At first, you go by the script. You ring the phone at the place indicated by the script and the place where you inserted your light pencil rough cue (discussed in Chapter 3). But during rehearsals, you discuss the exact pinpointing of the cue with the director. Perhaps the director wants the phone to ring two lines prior, and the actors to allow it to ring twice in order to heighten suspense as to which of the actors will answer the phone. Or the director decides that she or he doesn't want the first phone ring to come at the end of the actor's line, but three words from the end so that the actor can cross to the phone on the last words of his line. Now the cue is specific. You should caret the exact point in your script. Later, just prior to the technical rehearsal, or during it, you will mark the exact cue with bold marking pen.

It is handy for you to have a bell/buzzer device in your kit (see Chapter 5) to provide some basic rehearsal sound effects. If you don't, simply call out, "Phone," "Doorbell," "Auto horn," or whatever sound is needed. Similarly, you should call all lighting effects to which the actors must react. You call "Curtain" and/or "Lights" at the beginning and end of every act. You will also call the beginning, and sometimes the end, of all special effects: "Fog rolls in," "Vase rises from bookcase," "Rain begins," "Rain ends."

Call all cues *resolutely,* letting the cast know that you know your business and are self-assured.

Spiking Set Pieces

It is very important to the actors' movement on stage that set pieces be in exactly the same place at every rehearsal and performance. To ensure this, you not only check your preset diagrams but you also *spike* the set pieces; that is, you mark their position on the stage floor. Then, if moved accidentally or intentionally, the set pieces can be returned to exactly the same location.

Spiking is usually done with masking tape placed on the stage at the upstage end of the set piece, thus out of sight of the audience.

Spike your set pieces as early in the rehearsal process as practical.

When many scenes are to play in the same area, it becomes necessary to code the spike marks—to write on the masking tape which set piece plays there during which scene. Next to one tape marked "II-2 table" there might be another tape marked "III-7 chair."

Frequently, shifts must be made so fast that stagehands do not have time to read the tapes. In these cases, the tapes should be color-coded, painted a certain color for each scene.

If the changes are to be made in blackouts, it may be helpful to paint the spike marks with luminous paint. The stage lighting will usually "heat up" the luminous paint so that it will glow during blackouts. If you are using luminous paint in areas where it is not hit by stage lights, you can heat it up by shining a spot or sunlamp on it at close range for a few minutes prior to performance. (Be sure to add "preheating" to your checklist; see Chapter 14.)

Prompting

Prompting procedure is determined by the director. You should ask the director privately, prior to rehearsals, how he or she wants the cast prompted. How close are the actors to be held to the lines in the script? Letter-perfect? Or may they paraphrase as long as they get the sense of the line? How are the actors to call for lines? When and how are you to review lines with actors? Ask the director to brief the cast at the outset of rehearsals on just what he or she expects in the prompting process.

The few words on the subject might go like this: "Our stage manager has been instructed to hold you very close to the script. If you deliver a line and our stage manager calls out the correct one, repeat the line as he gives it, without breaking character, and carry on. Do not argue about changing the line. See me before or after rehearsals about any possible line changes. Our stage manager will also approach you during breaks and after rehearsals to cite lines or cues that were missed. Please do not argue. Simply repeat out loud the line cited and then say, 'Thank you.' Call for lines by saying 'line,' and in no other way."

Some directors insist that the cast be held letter-perfect to the script, particularly if the playwright's reputation is great. They allow their casts greater latitude with the works of lesser-known playwrights. Some directors feel that they must update plays and encourage their cast members to experiment with and modernize the dialogue.

Certain directors insist that the stage manager throw the exact line whenever an actor hesitates or paraphrases, as well as when an actor calls for a line. Others want lines thrown only when the actor calls for them or when the cast jumps out of sequence. But they want all errors in lines brought to the attention of the cast during breaks or after rehearsals.

Some directors want cast members to say "line" when asking for a line. Others want them to snap their fingers but otherwise to remain in character. Some directors do not want their actors to call for lines at all. Some set a date in the rehearsal schedule after which actors are not to call for lines. Many directors resent any other remarks that actors throw when calling for lines, such as, "Oh, I always forget that one."

Talk it over with your director. If she or he does not give specific instructions to the cast explaining the prompting interaction expected, start out in the way you feel is best, and apply her or his criticism of your prompting technique as you go along.

To prompt efficiently, read the script to yourself, mouthing the words as the actors recite them. That way you are right there with them. Actors appreciate getting their lines immediately after they call for them. If actors and the director have to wait while you search for the line, then you are delaying the rehearsal.

When you prompt, give the actor the line in a clear, resolute, but emotionless tone of voice. Do not interpret the actor's line for him or her.

If line changes are made, be sure to note them in your prompt script. Prompt the new lines as if they were the old lines.

As you prompt, lightly pencil in a caret in the margin to indicate every line that was delivered improperly. Use a code to indicate the type of error, such as:

C—called for line
P—paraphrased
BB—bobbled
L—late (cite cue to actor)
PR—pronunciation
J—jumped cue
H—handle—added extra word not in script prior to line
S—sequence, jumped out of

Use any code that works for you.

At the next break or after rehearsal, go to each actor, point out the missed line, and ask the actor to read it aloud. It is not necessary to say why you marked the line unless you are asked. Then erase the caret and code (see Figure 8.2).

Most professional actors are grateful for this service. If you should meet with resentment ("That's exactly what I said," "I know I missed it; you don't have to tell me"), say, "Thank you," politely, and walk away. Try it again at the next rehearsal and see how the actor accepts your help more graciously. When the actors are convinced that you are trying to help them, they are appreciative.

If there is an intentional pause prior to or during a line, you should mark your script with an inverted caret ($\wedge$) at the pause point so that you are reminded not to prompt there (and don't panic on opening night).

Sometimes it is convenient to write out line cites during rehearsal so that you can hand each actor a list of lines that need to be reviewed. This

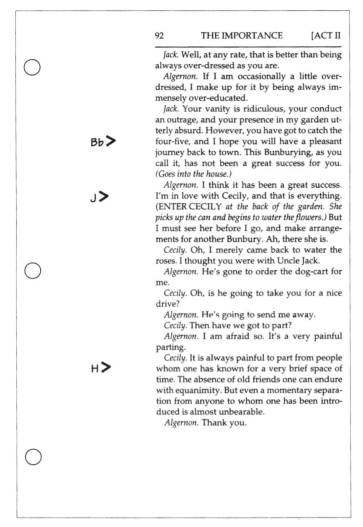

92   THE IMPORTANCE   [ACT II

Jack. Well, at any rate, that is better than being always over-dressed as you are.

Algernon. If I am occasionally a little over-dressed, I make up for it by being always immensely over-educated.

Jack. Your vanity is ridiculous, your conduct an outrage, and your presence in my garden utterly absurd. However, you have got to catch the four-five, and I hope you will have a pleasant journey back to town. This Bunburying, as you call it, has not been a great success for you. *(Goes into the house.)*

Algernon. I think it has been a great success. I'm in love with Cecily, and that is everything. (ENTER CECILY *at the back of the garden. She picks up the can and begins to water the flowers.)* But I must see her before I go, and make arrangements for another Bunbury. Ah, there she is.

Cecily. Oh, I merely came back to water the roses. I thought you were with Uncle Jack.

Algernon. He's gone to order the dog-cart for me.

Cecily. Oh, is he going to take you for a nice drive?

Algernon. He's going to send me away.

Cecily. Then have we got to part?

Algernon. I am afraid so. It's a very painful parting.

Cecily. It is always painful to part from people whom one has known for a very brief space of time. The absence of old friends one can endure with equanimity. But even a momentary separation from anyone to whom one has been introduced is almost unbearable.

Algernon. Thank you.

Figure 8.2 Prompting Cites, Lightly Penciled on Inside Script Margin

allows you to dismiss the cast faster after rehearsal, rather than hold them while you flip through pages of the script. If the director habitually holds the cast after rehearsals to review notes with them, you might use that same time to cite lines, doing it as unobtrusively as possible, and not interfering with the director's notes.

Getting up on lines is basic to any production. You helped establish deadlines for line memorization in making up the master calendar and rehearsal schedule. Now, how can you help the actors meet those deadlines? Are you willing to run lines with them before or after rehearsals? Can you arrange extra prerehearsal sessions for cast members at which they can help each other by running lines? Can you assign a gopher to run lines with an actor who is offstage?

Start prompting with gusto just as soon as cast members are willing to put down their scripts. Let the cast know that you mean to help them get up on their lines quickly and accurately. It is easier to start working hard than to start leniently and then apply pressure after the cast has gotten into sloppy habits.

If you can make every actor feel that you are earnestly trying to help rather than criticize, your prompting technique is good.

Prompting during a performance is a matter of the director's policy. Once a production has opened, it is generally considered very unprofessional to prompt, and actors are expected to ad-lib their way out of any situation.

Warning

During rehearsals, actors may wander out of the rehearsal area. If they leave, they must always check out with the stage manager to say where they are going ("I'm going to get this sewn up in costumes," "We're running lines in the lobby"). They should also check in with the stage manager when they return (see "Entrances and Exits" in Chapter 3).

You must think ahead. Which scene will the director work on next? You must warn wandering actors to be ready to appear. Waiting for an actor to be summoned so that a rehearsal can continue wastes a lot of time. If you observe your entrance warns (see Chapter 3 and Figure 3.10), you can avoid such delays. If an actor is on the premises and rehearsal is delayed while waiting for that actor to appear, the fault is yours.

Sometimes an actor will be summoned only to find that the director wishes to rerun the scene prior to her or his entrance. It is better that a single actor be inconvenienced than that several be hung up by her or his absence. When you work at mounting a few plays with the same director, you will develop a sixth sense as to whether the director will press on or rerun.

If possible, don't leave your post to summon a wandering actor. Send a gopher or another actor.

During performances you are not responsible for warning actors for individual entrances, but you are responsible for warning the crew about impending shifts and the orchestra about musical cues, as necessary. (See "Actors and Their Entrance Cues" in Chapter 3 for a discussion of exceptions.)

Taking Blocking Notation

Recording the movement of the actors helps to expedite rehearsals. With a written record of where they move on their lines, you are able to remind them when they forget. You will also use this notation to block in replacements and conduct understudy rehearsals (see Chapter 16).

Normally you simply observe the initial blocking that the director gives the actors. Do not start to take blocking notations until the blocking starts to jell. There are several systems for making such notations.

Method I

The stage is divided as shown in Figure 8.3. Blocking notations using this method might read:

XDR—The actor crosses to the down right area of the stage.
XLC—The actor crosses to the left center area of the stage.

Method II (for theater-in-the round)

The stage is divided as shown in Figure 8.4. The stage is thought of as a clock, with the orchestra pit at 12 o'clock, and then divided into four concentric circles lettered from the audience to the center of the stage.

For a large stage:

UR	URC	UC	ULC	UL
R	RC	C	LC	L
DR	DRC	DC	DLC	DL

C - Center of the stage

D - Down (toward the audience)

U - Up (away from the audience)

R - Right (actor's right facing the audience)

L - Left (actor's left facing the audience)

For a small stage:

UR	UC	UL
R	C	L
DR	DC	DL

Figure 8.3   Divisions of Proscenium Stage for Blocking Notation

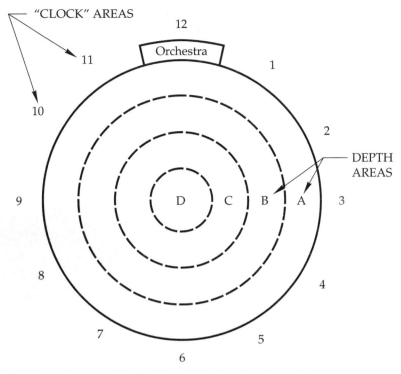

Figure 8.4   Divisions of Round Stage for Blocking Notation

Blocking notations might read as follows:

> X3B—The actor crosses to the second ring at 3 o'clock.
> X11.A—The actor crosses to the first ring at 11 o'clock.

Method III

All notations are made, regardless of the shape of the stage, with reference to the destination of the actor and the number of steps she or he takes in the direction of that destination. Blocking notations might read:

> X door 2—The actor takes two steps toward the door.
> X Pat 5—The actor crosses five steps toward Pat, another character.

With this type of notation, it is not possible to understand from reading a single entry where on stage the actor is located. This disadvantage should be countered by using extensive "French-scene" diagrams (described in a later section).

Method IV (combinations)

Prior methods are combined. Blocking notations might read:

X DR door—The actor crosses to the down right door.
X2 DR door—The actor takes two steps toward the down right door.
X2 DR—The actor takes two steps toward the down right area.
X3B door—The actor crosses to the door in the 3B area.
X2 3B door—The actor takes two steps toward the 3B door.

The best method is the method that works best for you.

Most often the actors move on their lines; that is, they cross while delivering a line of dialogue. They frequently start to move at the beginning of the line and stop moving with the last word of it. So when you make a blocking notation adjacent to an actor's line, it automatically indicates that the actor is moving on the line.

If an actor is blocked to move on another actor's line—not usually the case—this must be indicated. For these instances, and for the purpose of "French-scene" diagrams, it is convenient to have a symbol for each actor:

C—Constance
I—Irene
G—George

Now, if George moves on Irene's line:

Irene: One or two? G XDR *table*

(On Irene's line, George crosses down right to the table.)

Or if two or more actors move at the same time:

Constance: I won't insist. XDL; I XDR; G XULC

(On Constance's line, she crosses down left, Irene crosses down right, and George crosses up left center.)

What if the actor moves before or after his or her line but not on another actor's line? Use carets:

Constance: ∧ I won't insist. XDL

This indicates that Constance starts her cross prior to her line and finishes it with the end of her line.

Constance: ∧∧ I won't insist. XDL

These two carets indicate that Constance begins and ends her cross prior to her line, but not on another actor's line.

Constance: I won't ∧ insist. ∧ XDL

Constance starts her cross with the word indicated and completes the cross after the line.

>   *Constance:* I won't insist ∧∧ XDL.

Constance begins and ends her cross after her line.

Blocking notation is not an exact science. Some stage managers find that they can remember where and when an actor moves without precise notation. Others rely very heavily on notation and longhand notes (see Figure 8.5).

After you have observed the first few rough blocking rehearsals, you will start to make your notations, realizing that the blocking is not yet set

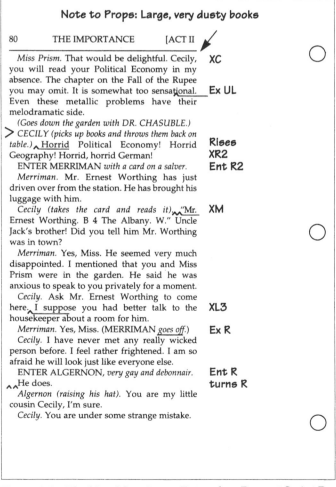

Figure 8.5   Blocking Notation as Entered on Prompt Script Page

(permanent). It is best to take notation in light pencil. If you do not care to erase, you can make changes in columns at the side of the original blocking.

Constance: I won't insist. XDL/XULC/XRC

Using columns may be advantageous. When a director wants to go back to an earlier blocking, you will be able to tell the actors how they used to move.

After a few rehearsals when the same blocking is repeated, it is safe to assume that the blocking is set. A director may still change all or part of the blocking after this point, but it is set insofar as the director expects the actors to repeat their movement unless he or she changes it. The time when this happens varies with the director's technique. Some directors rough block at home, using diagrams of the stage and tokens for actors. They bring in their own notation of projected blocking and start early rehearsals with very firm blocking. Other directors allow cast members to drift at will as they recite their lines, and then try to arrange the drifting, sometimes called *organic blocking.*

I punch holes on the right side of my blocking sheets so they are facing the text page (right side of my book). I write the blocking on the sheets with numbers that correspond to numbers that I write on the text page where a specific action occurs. When the action is changed to a different line, I find it easier to move the number than to rewrite the blocking notation. Props are usually noted on the blocking sheets opposite the first page of each scene. [See Figure 8.6.] If there are tables with many props, I will also draw a close-up picture of just the table so that each prop can be labeled and positioned precisely.

Most musicals that I have done use 4" numbers on the DS edge of the stage to help with spacing for the dancers. By placing these numbers on my blocking sheets, I can be very specific about where the choreographer has placed each dancer. [See Figure 8.7.]

Cari Norton
AEA Free-Lance Stage Manager

When you feel that the blocking is set, you should start to prompt on blocking.

Example A

An actor says: "I know I was supposed to move on that line but I've forgotten where."

You: "Your cross is down left."

Example B

A director says to an actor: "You're not supposed to be there when Sam enters."

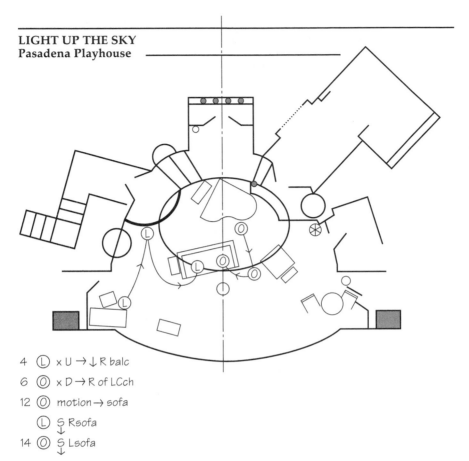

LIGHT UP THE SKY
Pasadena Playhouse

4 Ⓛ x U → ↓ R balc

6 Ⓞ x D → R of LCch

12 Ⓞ motion → sofa

    Ⓛ S↓ Rsofa

14 Ⓞ S↓ Lsofa

Figure 8.6 Computer-Generated Blocking Diagram with Blocking Notation for *Light Up the Sky,* Pasadena Playhouse. Cari Norton uses MacDraft to draw her blocking diagrams and a plastic furniture template (1/8" scale) to add furniture pieces.

Courtesy Cari Norton, AEA freelance stage manager.

You advise the director (not the actor): "He missed his cross down left three lines back on 'Hark, here comes the king.'"

In general, in the prompting of blocking, you should advise the *director* rather than the actors.

If you observe actors not following their blocking, you should whisper to the director without interrupting the flow of the scene. Let directors decide if they want to stop and bring the error to the actor's attention, or if they want you to call the error to the actor's attention later, during a break or after the rehearsal, or if they want you to change your blocking notation in order to take advantage of what the actor has done instinctively.

DESERT SONG
MTSC
I-3, II-5 General Birabeau's House

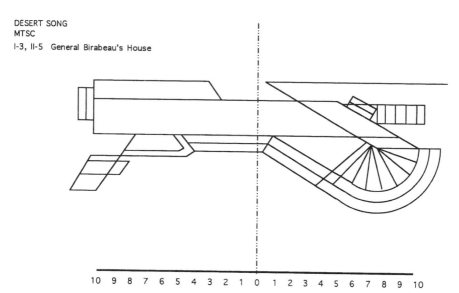

10 9 8 7 6 5 4 3 2 1 0 1 2 3 4 5 6 7 8 9 10

Figure 8.7 Computer-Generated Blocking Diagram for Musical *Desert Song,* Music Theatre of Southern California, San Gabriel.

Courtesy Cari Norton, AEA freelance stage manager.

Actors frequently take their crosses on the line following their cross line. The cross line triggers their memory too late. But they get where they are supposed to be in time not to upset the overall effect of the scene. This error can usually be corrected by calling the actor's attention to it after the scene is over. If you place a lightly penciled caret in the margin with an appropriate symbol, this will remind you of what the actor did wrong.

Constance: I won't insist. XDL < LX

After you have brought the late cross to the actor's attention, during the break or after rehearsal, erase the caret and symbol.

Production notes

While taking blocking notation, you should make production notes (I use the upper-right corner of my prompt book page) on (1) blocking that will require special lighting and (2) light and sound cues that will be dependent on blocking.

Example A

The director decides that an actor will sit on the apron and recite a poem with the curtain closed to cover a scene change. You realize that this will call for at least one additional lighting instrument that was not in the lighting designer's original plans. You make a note. After the rehearsal, you tell the lighting designer and you change your light plot. You also place new cues in your prompt script.

Example B

The director decides that the nurse will rise and cross to a table to examine a knife before she hears a bell that summons her offstage. Formerly, the cue for the bell was the doctor's line to the nurse. You realize that the cue for the bell is now a visual one rather than an oral one, so you make this change in your prompt script immediately.

French-scene diagrams

A *French scene* is that part of a scene or an act in which the number of characters is constant. Within a scene there may be many French scenes. Every time a character enters or exits, a new French scene is begun (named from the conventional scene designations in classical French drama).

The director usually starts or resumes rehearsing from the beginning of a French scene. You may find it quite helpful to make small diagrams of the position of the cast at the beginning of each French scene (see Figure 8.8).

If the director says, "Let's take it from the top of page 83 where Fran enters," the cast members will probably not remember where they are supposed to be for Fran's entrance. By reviewing your blocking notation just prior to Fran's entrance, you may eventually be able to determine where they are, but it will take time. But if you have made a diagram, you can say immediately (from Figure 8.8), "Al is seated on the couch facing down left, Ralph is looking out the window, and Alice is standing down right center facing down left."

As there are often many French scenes in every act, you can expedite your diagramming with a cardboard template of the set and set pieces (see Figure 8.8). At the top of every promptbook page on which a character enters or exits, you simply copy your scene diagram. Jotting in the positions of the cast takes very little effort.

Maintaining Order

A director should never have to ask for quiet working conditions that will allow him or her and the cast to concentrate on their work. You should be aware of any noise or other disruptions and try to remedy the situation.

Try personal contact. Approach the noisy offender and explain, eyeball to eyeball, that rehearsals require silence from those who are not on stage, that it is a matter of courtesy.

Do not hesitate to shout, "Quiet, PLEASE!" if personal contact fails.

Some people have greater tolerance of noise levels than others. If you can read Christopher Fry during a rock concert, but your director gets shell

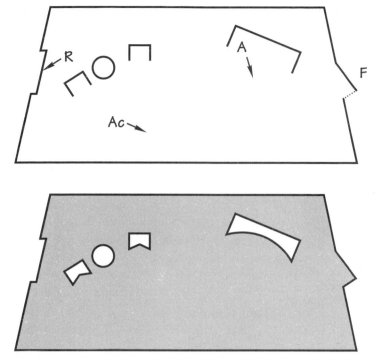

Figure 8.8   "French-Scene" Cardboard Template and Scene Diagram

shock from seats squeaking, try to sympathize with his or her problem and hold the cast down to the level the director can tolerate.

Giving Rehearsal, Publicity, and Costume Calls

The last official voice that every actor should hear as she or he leaves a rehearsal is yours, giving the next call, whether that call is for a rehearsal, publicity meeting with a TV interviewer, costume call at a supply house across town, or conference with the producer.

It should be standard procedure that every actor check out, after rehearsal or performance, with the stage manager. This might simply mean a cheerful "Good night," to which you might answer with an equally informal "See you at ten tomorrow." That informal "ten tomorrow" is an order to appear at 10 o'clock sharp.

It is not enough to publish, post, and distribute rehearsal schedules. You must give the calls in person, face to face. You must then mentally or physically check off each cast member; if anyone left early and failed to check out with you, you must phone that individual to give the call.

If you are working with a large cast, divided into principals, chorus, and dancers, or other major groups, you may wish to use a special callboard.

The term *callboard* has come to mean a bulletin board where any information, including the next call, can be brought to the attention of the cast. *Special callboard* is used here to mean a board display with only the next call (see Figure 8.9). Rather than placing it on the general callboard, it is more effective to place the special callboard by itself near the exit through which the cast must leave.

The special callboard form can be covered with plastic, glass, or even a plastic film wrap so that the blanks can be filled in with crayon and then erased with a rag.

When photo calls are scheduled in the rehearsal area—whether for publicity, cast souvenirs, or the theater scrapbook—it is often helpful to post a picture schedule (see Figure 8.10).

The publicity person usually decides who is to appear in the pictures. But to save time in posing the shots, you might want to preselect emotional peak scenes from the script. During the call you can then throw a line

---

Your Call For

TUES. July 14
(DATE)

		TIME	PLACE
PRINCIPALS			
	Frank *	10:00	TENT
	JuliE *	10:30	Music Room
	RavenaL	10:30	Costume Shop
	All Others	10:30	Tent
SINGING ENSEMBLE			
	BOYS	Off	
	GIRLS	11:00	Chorus Room
DANCING ENSEMBLE			
	BOYS	11:00	Costume Shop
	GIRLS	11:00	Chorus Room
LOCAL CHORUS			
	BOYS	5:30	Costume Shop
	GIRLS	5:30	Costume Shop
*SPECIAL APPOINTMENTS			
Frank	Publicity Lunch	12:00	Florentine Room
Julie	Hairdresser	6:00	Claire's 140 W-2nd

Figure 8.9   Special Callboard Format, for Next Upcoming Calls

```
                          PICTURE CALL

Thursday night after performance pictures will be taken. Please remain in
costume and change for subsequent shots.

  1. Entire Cast (curtain call order) and crew.

  2. III-2:   "So I'll say goodnight. . ." - Arlene, Jonas, Terry

  3. III-1:   ". . . because I'm going to get married." - Arlene, Sandy,
              Rita, Larry

  4. III-1:   "My arms, my lips. . ." - Larry, Rita, Sandy

  5.  II-3:   "I'm going to be frank with you, Pa." - Jonas, Dave, JoAnne

  6.  II-3:   "We going to be here that long?" - Dave, JoAnne, Terry

  7.  II-1:   "I want to go to a hotel." - Jonas, Arlene

  8.  II-1:   "He don't look like no Cary Grant to me." - Dee, Sandy, Norma,
              Jonas, Rita

  9.   I-3:   "Then start going out on dates again." - Arlene, Jonas

 10.   I-2:   "Stop trying to fix me up with all your friends." -
              Shirley-May, Jonas, Terry

 11.   I-2:   "Rosalind, do me a favor." - Terry, Vicky, Jonas, JoAnne

 12.   I-2:   "Rosalind, you know my brother Jerry." - Vicky, Jonas, Terry

 13.   I-1:   "I'm in trouble now, Ma." - Arlene, Rita

 14.   I-1:   "Will you get dressed and go to school." - Arlene, Rita, Sandy
```

Figure 8.10   Picture Call Schedule

before the emotional peak and have the cast pick it up in character. If someone shouts "Freeze" when they come to the peak line, this process will usually result in an interesting tableau.

It is often necessary for the photographer to tighten the shot by moving
the actors closer to one another than they normally appear in that sequence.
But reposing and rerunning is still quicker than deciding in front of the
camera just what poses are appropriate.

If the picture call follows a run-through, dress rehearsal, or performance, it is desirable to start with poses selected from the last scene of the
last act and work backward so that cast members are saved an unnecessary
costume change.

Posting a picture call and picture schedule well in advance allows cast
members to plan for the session in terms of shaving, hairstyle, makeup,
costumes, and time.

Posting the Running Order

The *running order* is a list, in production sequence, of the scenes, giving the
place of the scene, the cast members in the scene, the songs or dance numbers (if any) in that scene, and special cue lines (see Figure 8.11). You

```
                    T A K E    M E    A L O N G

                         RUNNING ORDER

                            ACT I

I-1   OUTSIDE MILLER HOME

      Townspeople
         "Fire Machine"

      Fire Chief, Nat, Essie, Art, Tommy, Mildred
         "Oh, Please"

      Lilly
         reprise: "Oh, Please"

I-2   MACOMBER HOUSE

      Richard, Muriel
         "I Would Die"

      Macomber

I-3   CARBARN

      Sid, Voices
         "Sid, Ol' Kid"

I-4   STREET (Played In Aisle)

      Art, Sid

I-5   MILLER HOME

      Essie, Lilly, Tommy, Mildred, Nat, Richard, Macomber
         "Staying Young"

      Art, Sid
         "I Get Embarrassed"
         "We're Home"
         "Take Me Along"

I-6   PICNIC

      Sid, Carter, McDonald, Nat
         "For Sweet Charity"
```

Figure 8.11   Running Order on a Large Board, Easily Legible

should post it on the first day of rehearsal or as soon thereafter as possible, and update it as necessary.

The function of the running order is to remind cast members of when they appear next. Why is this necessary? Shouldn't every cast member know when he or she appears next?

Sometimes it is very confusing. In a one-week rehearsal for a musical stock show, the chorus may have rehearsed their songs in a chorus room and rehearsed their dances in a rehearsal hall. Many will not have gone through the show in production sequence until the "put together," possibly the day before dress rehearsal, and only two days before opening night. So, as the chorus members dash from the stage to the dressing room, they need to have some easily accessible reference to answer the questions "What do I do next?" and "Which of my eight costumes do I change into?"

In the rewrite phase of a new musical, the chorus might come in for half-hour call to find that the running order has been drastically changed. The finale will be sung as the opening number, the show will be done as a flashback, and the principals will reprise the finale at the final curtain with the chorus humming the bridge from the wings. Then, the next night at half-hour call, the chorus learns that the finale will be sung at the second act curtain and that they will reprise their Act I, Scene 2 hit song as the finale. Their actual performance sequence will vary from day to day. So, in addition to briefings from the staff, they need a written running order that they can refer to in haste.

The running order should be BIG!—possibly two feet wide by three feet tall—and carefully lettered so that it is easy to read. It should be well-lighted and placed along the path from the stage to the dressing rooms so that cast members don't have to detour to read it. Position it in the same place from the time it is posted until closing night, so that cast members don't have to search for it.

If there is a blackout within a scene to denote time lapse (called a *false blackout*), this should be noted on the running order so that cast members will be forewarned not to enter on that blackout for the following scene. A song or line that occurs after the time lapse blackout should be listed so that cast members will have an accurate cue for their entrance blackout.

All reprises should be carefully designated as reprises so that there is no confusion as to whether the song or the reprise is the cue. This is a particular problem when the song and the reprise occur within the same scene.

To make the entries on your running order immediately discernible, write your song titles in one color or style of script (e.g., letters underlined), the names of the scenes in a second color or style (e.g., large capitals), the cast members involved in a third (e.g., small capitals), and special notes about cue lines and blackouts in still another (e.g., cursive script). A work of art is not your goal, but any scheme that will help cast members decipher the running order quickly is helpful.

You must call all revisions to the attention of the cast and discuss with them the problems incurred by changes.

Typed copies of the running order should be placed in the crew area and on the callboard. You are very definitely responsible for alerting all crew members (props, lights, scene changes, costumes, etc.) to changes. The crew is not expected to decipher and apply a revised running order without a briefing from you and your immediate close supervision.

When changes in the production sequence are made, the running order should not be done over, but revisions should be cited with a bold marking pen so that cast members can pick out the changes without studying the whole running order.

Summer stock running orders rarely parallel the New York productions as reflected in published scripts, so the running order must be coordinated with the staff before it is posted.

I never had to prompt performers between acts, but I did need to post a running order. The biggest difference between circus and theatre is that in theatre, at no point would an actor ever walk in and say, "Gee, I don't feel like playing that one scene today; let's skip it." But in circus, if a performer is not feeling well or is injured, the stage manager has to encourage him/her NOT to do an act. It is an onerous task, as these professionals want to go on no matter what. But in a show where serious injuries and even death are definite and consistent possibilities, running orders can change on a daily basis, depending on the well-being of performers.

> Bradley Spinelli
> Stage Manager
> New Pickle Circus

Timing of Rehearsals and Performances

You should carefully time each scene, and sometimes even critical parts of scenes. The purpose of timing during rehearsals is to let the director know what the total playing time is and to let the box office and house manager know what time the show will be out and what time to expect intermissions. The purpose of timing during performances is to keep track of the pace of each scene and act.

Using a stopwatch is desirable, but an ordinary watch with a sweep second hand can be used.

Start to time scenes just as soon in rehearsal as the scenes are run without interruption. At the end of each rehearsal, advise the director of the running times. Tell him or her not only how long the scenes took but also how long it took last time they were run, and the shortest time in which they were run.

As soon as every scene in the play has been timed once, give the director some projection of the total running time.

During the run, time each scene at every performance. You will find that running time of each scene varies from performance to performance. Sometimes it's audience response; sometimes it's actors who are not picking up their lines or are adding pauses; sometimes a bit of business will vary in time. There are many reasons for differences in the timing of scenes. If the director is "with the show" (attending performances regularly or even periodically), judgment as to why the times vary may be left to her or him. If the director has left the show, or if the show is on the road, then it is your responsibility to evaluate the running times and take appropriate action (see Chapter 16).

If you index a weekly time chart (see Figure 8.12) into your prompt script, you will easily be able to make the necessary comparisons and have the information readily available to your staff.

In most theater situations you will be responsible for the timing of blackouts and intermissions. You must direct the blackouts and the backstage aspects of the intermissions just as carefully as the director directs the scenes. Some of the factors involved in a blackout or intermission are changing sets, striking and/or setting of props, changing position of actors, changes in costumes, patching the lighting board, and re-gelling instruments (see Chapter 11).

During a blackout, audience attention wanders. Perhaps the first 10 seconds of a blackout are consumed in applause and/or mental reaction to what has just happened. After that, coughing, fidgeting, and conversations indicate that the audience is no longer involved with the scene that is past. The longer the audience is left in darkness, the harder it is for the actors in the following scene to regain the audience's attention, emotional focus, and/or intellectual concern.

WEEKLY TIME CHART

PRODUCTION __The Bunny__   WEEK OF __Oct. 10__

	Tues Dress	Wed Dress	Thurs opening	Fri	Sat early	Sat late	Sun
Announced Curtain	8:00	8:00	8:30	8:30	8:00	10:30	8:30
Actual Curtain	8:06	8:14	8:41	8:35	8:04	10:31	8:36
I - 1	8:14 / 8	8:22 / 8	8:41 / 7	8:43 / 8	8:12 / 8	10:40 / 9	8:45 / 9
Blackout	8:14 / :30	8:38 / :16	8:48 / :25	8:43 / :20	8:12 / :20	10:40 / :20	8:45 / :20
I - 2	8:29 / 15	8:39 / 17	9:03 / 15	8:58 / 15	8:27 / 15	10:54 / 14	9:00 / 15
Blackout	8:30 / :35	8:39 / :30	9:04 / :30	8:59 / :30	8:28 / :30	10:55 / :30	9:01 / :30
I - 3	8:47 / 17	8:55 / 16	9:19 / 15	9:14 / 15	8:44 / 16	11:10 / 15	9:16 / 15
Intermission	9:09 / 22	9:07 / 12	9:30 / 11	9:25 / 11	8:53 / 9	11:20 / 10	9:26 / 10
II - 1	9:25 / 16	9:23 / 16	9:46 / 16	9:42 / 17	9:10 / 17	11:36 / 16	9:42 / 16
Blackout	9:26 / :48	9:24 / :45	9:47 / :40	9:43 / :35	9:11 / :35	11:37 / :35	9:43 / :30
II - 2	9:37 / 11	9:34 / 10	9:56 / 9	9:52 / 9	9:20 / 9	11:46 / 9	9:52 / 9
Blackout	9:37 / :25	9:34 / :25	9:56 / :25	9:53 / :30	9:20 / :25	11:46 / :25	9:52 / :25
II - 3	9:57 / 20	9:53 / 19	10:14 / 18	10:11 / 18	9:39 / 19	12:04 / 18	10:10 / 18
Total Running Time	1:27	1:26	1:20	1:22	1:24	1:21	1:22

Figure 8.12   Chart Record of Running Time

So it is very important that you organize the proceedings during blackouts to make them as short as possible. Some directors insist that no blackouts be longer than 20 seconds. During the technical rehearsal and subsequent dress rehearsals, you must ask to run, rerun, and, if necessary, choreograph blackouts until you and the director are satisfied that they are run in minimum time.

During the rehearsals you should also time certain sound effects and special effects to figure out the length for your plots.

Example

You realize during a rehearsal that an alarm bell sound effect must last long enough to cover an actor's business of opening a safe, ransacking it, and escaping through a window, and it must also last long enough to cover the entrance of two other characters, their reaction, and the closing of the curtain. How long should a tape of that alarm bell effect be? During the rehearsals, you carefully time the business and either make a production note in your script or add this timing to your sound plot. Then at the sound session you are prepared to say, "We will need at least three minutes of the alarm bell on tape."

Keeping Track of Rehearsals

Rehearsal Log

The rehearsal log is a very brief diary of what happened or failed to happen at rehearsals. You should always be able to answer the question "How did we come to this state of affairs?" with specifics. It is not always possible to remember the specifics unless you keep notes. It is convenient to tab your log into your prompt script.

Entries in the rehearsal log should include date, cast members who were late or absent, cast changes, the scene or scenes that were blocked or run, the number of times these scenes were run, delays and causes of delays in rehearsals, failure to run a scheduled scene, and any significant occurrence out of the ordinary—for example, an accident, failure to meet a deadline, or mechanical failure of equipment (see Figure 8.13).

If you have the opportunity to help critique a production, your rehearsal log will be an invaluable asset (see Chapter 19).

Rehearsal Reports

In some companies the producer or top management may require a daily written report from the stage manager. This report usually includes the same information that you keep in your log, but in a more formal format (see Figures 8.14 and 8.15). If you were to keep a copy of this report, you would not have to keep a log, because the same purpose would be served.

Note that in the rehearsal report, under the heading "Engaged/Dismissed," you are expected to indicate those cast members who joined or

```
                          REHEARSAL LOG

Sunday, May 28       - Read through script (Mike, Will, Jackie
                       out).

Monday, May 29       - Read through again, made a few revisions
                       (Jackie still out).

Friday, June 2       - Blocked Act I to p. 17.

Saturday, June 3     - Started 15 minutes late. (Dick claimed
                       shooting wound up late.) Blocked
                       remainder of Act I.

Sunday, June 4       - Jackie, Dick only - script changes.

Monday, June 5       - Jackie, Dick only - blocked their scenes
                       in Act II.

Tuesday, June 6      - Billy only. Worked him through all
                       blocking as Eric's replacement.

Wednesday, June 7    - Ran Act I twice. Sound session after
                       rehearsal. (Steve was late but no delay
                       in rehearsal.)

Thursday, June 8     - Blocked Act II (except Jackie, Dick
                       scenes.)

Friday, June 9       - Attempted to integrate sound but
                       amplifier went out. Ran Act II twice.

Saturday, June 10    - First runthrough, integrated sound cues.

Sunday, June 11      - Polished Act I, ran five times.

Tuesday, June 13     - Ran Act II twice. Dick, Pandora out so
                       rehearsal suffered; did not run Dick-
                       Jackie scenes (Dick was shooting,
                       Pandora's husband in auto accident.)
```

Figure 8.13   Rehearsal Log with Typical Entries

left the company. The payroll department and Equity must be notified in these cases.

In some companies the stage manager is also required to submit a report to Equity (see Figure 8.16).

Accident Prevention and Reports

In *The 776 Stupidest Things Ever Said,* Ross and Kathryn Petras cite the U.S. Occupational Safety and Health Administration for the following: "Hazards are one of the main causes of accidents." Did you laugh? If you did, you are probably not an experienced stage manager. Despite the intrinsic humor of that statement, stage managers have had too many sad experiences with hazards and accidents to find *any* mention of them humorous (see Figure 8.17).

```
                                    COMPANY    J. Gill

              STAGE MANAGER's REHEARSAL REPORT FORM

   PLACE:   Loft                DATE:   Aug. 13
  ──────────────────────────────────────────────────────
                              │ Rehearsal started:  7:30
                              │
          CALL:   7:30         │ Lunch/Dinner break: ──
                              │
          SCENES:   I-4        │ Rehearsal   resumed: ──
                              │
                  II-2        │ Rehearsal ended:   10:00
                              │
                              │ Rehearsal time:   2:30
                              │
                              │ Overtime (if any): ──
                              │─────────────────────────
                              │ Expenses:
                              │
                              │       ──
                              │
                              │
                              │─────────────────────────
   Engaged/Dismissed:          │ Injuries:
                              │ Dinah left early—
          ──                  │             see report
                              │
                              │
                              │─────────────────────────
   Absent/Excused:             │ Late:
   AL—still out sick           │
                              │       ──
                              │
  ──────────────────────────────────────────────────────
   Remarks:   Good work done on both scenes despite
        Al's absence.—Dinah did well before she left.


                      Lawrence Stern
                      ─────────────────
                       Stage Manager
```

Figure 8.14   Rehearsal Report Form

My first experience with a theater accident occurred in an Equity production of *Enter Laughing* at the Players Ring Gallery in Los Angeles. It was staged in the round for the first time since its Broadway opening. Carl Reiner sat in at a rehearsal to give director Harvey Korman some tips on the staging.

I had helped the technical director and scene designer place a heavy wrought-iron gate used as a set piece in the actors' entrance to the stage. It was not to be moved throughout the production. In the blackout preceding the cemetery scene, sound effects of crickets and a creaking gate were

AMERICAN MUSICAL THEATRE OF SAN JOSE
Stage Manager Rehearsal Report

Show:_____   Date:_____

Scheduled Start Time:_____   Break:_____

Lunch/Dinner Break:_____   Break:_____

End Time:_____   Break:_____

Total Rehearsal Hours:_____

Set Notes:	
Costume & Hair Notes:	
Prop Notes:	
Sound & Light Notes:	
General Notes (plus injuries, illness):	

Figure 8.15   Rehearsal Report Form Used at American Musical Theatre of San Jose
Courtesy Bob Bones, Production Stage Manager, San Jose.

STAGE MANAGER'S WEEKLY REPORT

Location: _____   Week Ending: _____

Name of Theatre: _____

Violations by Actor

  1. List the name of the Actor.

  2. Type of violation (lateness for half-hour, altering
      direction, etc.)

  3. Indicate in column 1 if sufficient explanation given
      so that violation should be considered excused (E
      for excused, U for unexcused)

  4. Has the Actor been spoken to about this type of
      violation before? Indicate in column 2
      (R for repeated, 1 for the first time, 2 for second
      time, etc.)

NAME	VIOLATION	COLUMN 1 2

Violations by Manager

  1. List only violations by Manager which he has not
      corrected after being informed by you, the Deputy or
      Equity.

                    Signed: _____
                            Stage Manager

7/29/68 Rev. 4/72   USE REVERSE SIDE FOR REMARKS   PO-5

Figure 8.16   Report Form to Actor's Equity

heard. As the lights came up on the scene, a single spot hit the gate and the two actors. It would appear to the audience that they had just opened the gate, but the gate never moved. Because the gate was not to function at all, we reasoned that there was no need to secure it. This heavy gate simply leaned in the entrance area. There was plenty of room to enter and exit the stage without touching the gate (as was done in all of the other scenes of the play). Following a dress rehearsal, an actor on the way out of the theater left the dressing room and came into the theater through that entrance. The actor somehow managed to knock over the gate and injured an ankle. The wound required stitches, and the actor did the run of the show wearing a bandage.

The actor felt personally to blame for the accident and did not blame the stage manager, technical director, or producer. The theater was not sued.

Civic's Season in Red Ink Because of Accidents

Varsity, The Stage Daily, Feb. 1994

Favorable reviews and large audiences would have resulted in a profitable season for the city-owned Civic Theatre—had it not been for accidents. *A Chorus Line, South Pacific, the Mikado, Guys and Dolls,* and *An Evening with Sondheim,* during the past season, built audiences and profits beyond expectations of previous seasons. But the season was plagued with costly accidents.

Disaster struck on opening night of *South Pacific* when an actress exiting the stage was struck by moving scenery resulting in the fracture of her arm. The performance was cancelled and tickets refunded. During a performance of *The Mikado,* a wrench fell from the grid above the stage. The union cast invoked workplace safety rules which resulted in cancelling a performance. An additional performance was scheduled to accommodate season subscribers. Ticket holders were also offered seats to remaining shows. The third and most serious accident was the collapse of a flat during *Guys and Dolls* injuring two chorus members. Litigation is pending in this incident.

The Civic Theatre hosts national touring productions of opera and ballet and is also the home of the Civic Symphony. Because of the heavy use of the facility, the theater "loads in" each show, techs, and dress rehearses it in less than one week. Management of the Civic Theatre claims that increased efforts are being made to prevent accidents.

Performing Arts — Former Israeli Foreign Minister Falls from Platform

Los Angeles Messenger, Nov. 1993

Abba Eban, former Israeli Foreign Minister, is suing the San Mateo Performing Arts Center for injuries sustained when he fell from a platform following a speech.

On January 7, Eban, 78, spoke to a full auditorium from a platform, according to a lawsuit filed Friday. When he finished his speech, he turned to exit and fell from the platform breaking his hip.

Representatives of the Performing Arts Center describe the platform as "a professional 8-inch platform that was 8 feet by 8 feet with a nonskid surface and white safety border. In the past it had been used by several other speakers, including President Jimmy Carter.

Mr. Eban's suit for unspecified damages names the Peninsula Speakers Series, the San Mateo Union High School District on whose property the center sits, and San Mateo County. The suit claims that Eban was "exposed to serious risk of injury due to uneven surfaces and a dangerous drop on the surface of said stage." It accuses the defendants of negligence.

Eban, a resident of Tel Aviv, is living in New York on a temporary teaching assignment. He was Israel's first permanent representative to the United Nations, served as Israeli ambassador to the United States from 1950 to 1959, and served as foreign minister from 1966 to 1974. He later became foreign policy spokesperson for Israel's Labor Party.

Figure 8.17 Accidents Can Happen Anytime, Anywhere—and Result in Injury, Pain, Lawsuits, and Financial Problems

In retrospect, that gate should have been secured. As stage manager, I should have inspected it the first time it was placed in the entrance. I should have made the judgment that although it was a heavy piece, it still needed to be secured. I should have either advised the technical director to secure it or nailed it to the wall myself with the help of plumbers' tape. This was one of my first Equity productions, and I blame the accident on my inexperience.

So trite, but so true: An ounce of prevention is worth a pound of cure.

Whenever the stage manager is involved in an accident, there is a question about the degree of his or her responsibility. So here's my rule: Take the time to inspect for hazards. Adopt the attitude that anything that can possibly go wrong probably will. Pretend that an earthquake is about to happen. If you make the stage and backstage area more safe than they need to be, no harm can come of it, and, hopefully, no harm will come to your cast and crew.

Here are a few backstage horror stories from stage managers who have some suggestions to pass on. Put yourself in their shoes and try to gain from their experiences.

I was in tech for a production of *Funny Girl* at Long Beach Civic Light Opera and going into a scene change for the first time. The actors and technicians had been talked through the change and it seemed that it would be a simple thing to execute. Unfortunately, as I called the rail cue that would bring in a heavy drop with a pipe weighting the bottom, one of my cast members walked downstage, right under the incoming drop. The pipe hit the actress on the top of her head.

Three people could have theoretically stopped this accident from happening: the actress, the flyman, and me. But as stage manager, it is wholly my fault that it happened. I had a view of the stage, and could have stopped the incoming drop if I had seen her move into its path. Instead I was preparing for the upcoming cues and not watching as closely as I could have. The actress was okay—I was a mess!

Accidents that you aren't directly involved with are more frustrating and discouraging. For instance, on tour there are new dressers, stagehands and new backstage traffic patterns every week. Inevitably someone will run into someone else and be injured. The stage manager is the person who will hear about it from the injured party, often in the heat of the moment of pain and fear (and usually as you're calling the hardest part of the show!). It is up to you to talk to the people involved and make sure that it won't happen again. Tact, patience, and the realization that this is not a personal attack are all important.

Anything you can do to prevent accidents will be to your advantage. Remember, if someone gets hurt, YOU have to fill out the paperwork.

Jill Johnson
Stage Manager
Long Beach Civic Light Opera
[see her résumé, p. 325]

It was the day of our first preview for the first show of our season. As usual we had only 15 hours of tech rehearsal on a major musical with a set we had built. Early in the afternoon I had a strange feeling that we were not ready to do this show.

We did a dress rehearsal that afternoon and only got about one-third of the way through the show, As we broke for dinner, I told the cast to be careful that night. "It's only a preview. Don't panic."

The show began and we were doing fairly well. For the first time we were getting through scenes and shifts without stopping.

The final moment of Act I involved two actors, one carrying the other, crossing down center, and stepping onto a stage elevator that lowered from the stage into the orchestra pit. I called the cue for the elevator to go down. Then I heard a bang. On my TV monitor I saw the two actors fall into the trap where the elevator was supposed to be. I believe I yelled for the operator of the elevator to stop, and then I threw off my headset and ran out on stage. One of the actors was in the orchestra pit, and one was lying on stage. The one in the pit seemed okay, but was shaken. The actor on stage was crying and bleeding from a foot and a leg.

We got someone to call 911 and then checked to see how serious the injuries were. Unfortunately, the elevator was located downstage of the curtain. We could not bring it in to cover what was going on. So 2,800 people watched.

We decided to clear the house.

An ambulance took the two actors to the hospital. The actor who had been bleeding had no bones broken but had bad cuts on the foot and leg, and some internal injuries to the leg. (There is still some litigation pending on this case so I cannot go into much more detail.)

I was never really questioned or blamed for this incident. I know that I am not directly responsible for what occurred. It turned out to be a freak mechanical failure. But I still feel some responsibility. Why didn't I speak up about my instinct earlier in the day and tell the producer that we were not ready?

I felt that my crew and I did everything possible to help once the accident occurred. We dealt quickly and calmly with a bad situation so neither the cast nor the audience ran screaming from the theater.

There was a cast meeting after the injured left for the hospital. I told the cast and crew to call my office the next day so that I could tell them how the injured were doing and what the plans for the show would be. I believe the most important thing to do is to let everyone know that you do care about them as people. *The show does not need to go on no matter what happens.*

We had a counselor available for a couple of days after the accident to help anyone who was traumatized by the incident or anyone who just needed to talk. We delayed opening for three days until technical problems were worked out and we all felt more comfortable.

If nothing else, this incident reinforced in my mind how important it is to put safety first.

Safety awareness must start from the beginning of the production. Ask questions. Speak up if something concerns you. Trust your instincts.

(continued)

Further suggestions: When an accident occurs, make sure you call the actor's emergency contact, which you should have on file. Also, if the actor is a member of Equity, call Equity and report the incident. Fill out an accident report and workers' comp claim form. Make sure the injured parties have the theater company's name, address, and phone number to take with them to the hospital. If possible, have someone from the theater staff go with the injured person.

Finally, you should have a well-equipped first-aid box nearby during rehearsals and performance. Contents should include instant ice packs, ace bandages, Band-Aids, and ointments. You, as stage manager, or someone on your staff should be trained in CPR and first aid. It is not that expensive or time consuming to become certified, and any theater company should be happy to have someone with those skills on staff.

Bob Bones
Production Stage Manager
San Jose Civic Light Opera

Just when you think you've made a show accident-proof, something will happen completely out of the blue just to keep you on your toes. At the end of the Thenardier Inn scene in *Les Miserables,* the staging calls for Madame Thenardier to jump on top of her husband, who is leaning over a table downstage center. At the same point, the turntable begins to revolve to clear the scene to go directly into the next one. One afternoon, she jumped, the downstage table legs gave way, and both actors were pitched downstage as the turntable started to turn. The actor playing Thenardier was able to hang on to the stage and ride the revolve offstage. But Madame Thenardier went completely over and into the pit! I was calling the show from offstage right, saw the whole thing happen, and was powerless to stop it.

The worst thing about an incident like this is trying to keep the show going while trying to find out about the possibly injured. The audience had obviously seen the actress fall. Some of the cast were aware of what had happened, and some weren't. A major scene shift was in progress on stage, and the musicians had to keep playing as the actress in the pit struggled to disentangle herself from the drum set. I was in headset communication with the conductor; he might have advised me that it was not possible to continue music-wise. The production stage manager was at my side to make the decision to stop the show. An assistant stage manager ran to the pit to see how the actress was; understudies and wardrobe were alerted to the possibility of a quick cast change, and first-aid equipment was standing by. The actress was bruised and shaken but wanted to continue, and on her next entrance she got a terrific ovation from the audience!

In that case we were really lucky that everyone was relatively unharmed. But we were prepared to deal with any scenario. I guess the lesson to be learned here is to prepare for the worst—the best thing that can happen is that you never need to use your emergency plans.

Keeping your cool and thinking ahead are the best things to do. If you stay calm then both the company and the audience will follow your lead. Always remember that it's theater, not brain surgery. People and safety are more important than the next scene change.

Accident prevention is an ongoing, important, and often frustrating job. As stage manager, everything is ultimately your responsibility, and it is your job to insure the safety of your company to the best of your ability. This can range from asking an assistant to edge the stage with glow tape (and then checking that it is done) to stopping a rehearsal or show in mid-scene due to some imminent disaster that only you can see.

The easiest way to insure that your company is prepared is to talk to them briefly about safety on your first day in the theater. While on tour we meet on stage before our first sound check in any new theater to point out to the cast any changes in the set-up, potential dangers offstage, and where the first aid kits and ice packs are located. On *Les Miz*, we also set times for every new cast member to walk on the turntable and climb on the barricades before going into a run-through so there are as few surprises as possible. Even if the show is playing just one venue, make sure that everyone who is going to be on stage or in the wings has the chance to walk around in the light and learn the layout before plunging them into show conditions. Glow tape, offstage clip lights, and white tape are your friends. Use them liberally.

Jill Johnson
Stage Manager
Les Miserables National Tour
[see Jill's résumé, p. 325]

[Please notice Jill's professional attitude. "We were prepared to deal with any scenario." When you call "Places, please," will you be able to say what Jill said?]

You must always be alert to situations that might cause accidents: set construction materials left on stage or backstage, materials left perched precariously on ladders and on flats, nails and boards protruding upstage of flats that might tear actors' costumes or skin, wires not secured on which to trip, sharp edges on corners in dark areas backstage, and so on. The list is endless.

Check flying cables, whether or not you have immediate plans to use them, to be sure they will hold under strain. Twist the cables open to check the condition of the inside. If they are rotten, replace them.

It takes constant vigilance to prevent carelessness and inconsideration from turning into serious accidents. You should encourage all members of the staff, cast, and crew to report unsafe conditions to you, and you should take immediate steps to correct them.

Large or long-established theaters are generally covered by accident insurance as a form of protection against suit by actors or patrons for accidents that occur on the theater premises. Most insurance companies want

About a year ago an attorney asked me to be an expert witness in a theater accident case. The crux of the matter was that during a first technical rehearsal for a community theater production on a college campus, one of the actors fell off a platform while trying to exit the stage in a blackout. As a result of the fall he injured his arm and was unable to continue with his career as a house painter. The university paid his initial medical bills, but he wanted compensation for therapy and lost income. The university said that they were not responsible for his accident and would not pay.

When I was brought into the case, I found out that the actors had never been shown the set without the stage lights on. Also, there were no running lights or glow tape to illuminate the edges of the set to help the actors see the edges.

In my testimony I said that as a professional stage manager, it is my responsibility to make sure that the cast and crew are safe at all times, and I must do whatever needs to be done to assure their safety. In this case, either the technical director or stage manager should have gone over the set prior to the first technical rehearsal to make sure that the set was safe for the actors to work on, under all conditions. Or, if something was not ready, the cast should have been warned. In this case, if it was known that there were no running lights or glow tape, then the cast should never have been allowed to attempt to exit the stage in the dark. I also said that the cast looks to the stage manager as the one person who is looking out for them and if he or she does not perceive that there is a problem, then the cast, who have a lot on their minds, will trust that everything is okay. This is why, in this case, the actors still exited the stage even though they could not see where they were going.

A few weeks later, I learned that the injured party won his case and received additional money to pay medical bills and make up some of his lost wages.

Being involved in this case gave me a chance to evaluate my own thoughts on safety. Going into the case I looked for information in textbooks and Equity rulebooks about who is responsible for safety and what are considered safe conditions on stage or backstage. Unfortunately, I found very little on the subject.

My own experience, training, and instincts tell me that as the stage manager, I am the person responsible for the safety of all people on and backstage. Logically I know that I cannot keep an eye on everyone all of the time *or* be responsible for a decision someone may make that results in an accident. But it doesn't mean I don't try. I am fortunate in that I hire the other stage managers as well as part of the crew. So I try to hire people who share my desire to do the best show possible as safely as possible. Also, I believe that "we" set an example for everyone else and if "we" remain calm and in control, others will follow suit. I believe I need to learn everything possible about all aspects of a show so that I can anticipate any problems and deal with anything unexpected, calmly.

Bob Bones
Production Stage Manager
San Jose Civic Light Opera

to have the same information about any accident that occurs (see Figure 8.18). If your theater does have such insurance, make sure that you have accident report forms on hand.

In the event of an accident, whether or not your theater has insurance, obtain all the information required (see Figure 8.18) and write a brief narrative of what happened. Ask the individual involved to write his or her own brief narrative, and have him or her sign it.

EMPLOYER		
1. FIRM NAME	1A. POLICY NUMBER	
2. MAILING ADDRESS (Please include city, Zip)	2A. PHONE NUMBER	
3. LOCATION IF DIFFERENT FROM MAIL ADDRESS		
4. NATURE OF BUSINESS e.g., painting contractor, wholesale grocer, sawmill, hotel, etc.	5. State Unemployment Insurance Acct. No.	

EMPLOYEE		
6. NAME	7. DATE OF BIRTH / / Month Day Year	
8. HOME ADDRESS (number and street, city, Zip)	8A. PHONE NUMBER	
9. SEX ☐ Male ☐ Female	10. OCCUPATION (Regular job title, not specific activity at time of injury)	11. SOCIAL SECURITY NUMBER
12. DEPARTMENT IN WHICH REGULARLY EMPLOYED	12A. DATE OF HIRE / / Month Day Year	
13. HOURS USUALLY WORKED EMPLOYEE WORKS ____ HOURS PER DAY FOR ____ DAYS PER WEEK	13A. WEEKLY HOURS	13B. Under what class code of your policy were wages assigned?
14. GROSS WAGES/SALARY EMPLOYEE EARNS $ _____ PER ☐ HOUR ☐ DAY ☐ WEEK ☐ EVERY TWO WEEKS ☐ MONTH ☐ OTHER _____		

INJURY OR ILLNESS		
15. WHERE DID ACCIDENT OR EXPOSURE OCCUR? (number and street, city)	15A. COUNTY	15B. ON EMPLOYERS PREMISES? ☐ YES ☐ NO
16. WHAT WAS EMPLOYEE DOING WHEN INJURED? (Please be specific. Identify tools, equipment or material the employee was using.)		
17. HOW DID THE ACCIDENT OR EXPOSURE OCCUR? (Please describe fully the events that resulted in injury or occupational disease. Tell what happened and how it happened. Please use separate sheet if necessary.)		
18. OBJECT OR SUBSTANCE THAT DIRECTLY INJURED EMPLOYEE e.g., the machine employee struck against or which struck him. the vapor or poison inhaled or swallowed; the chemical that irritated his skin; in cases of strains, the thing he was lifting, pulling, etc.		
19A. DESCRIBE THE INJURY OR ILLNESS e.g., cut, strain, fracture, skin rash, etc.	19B. PART OF BODY AFFECTED e.g., back, left wrist, right eye, etc.	
20. NAME AND ADDRESS OF PHYSICIAN		
21. IF HOSPITALIZED, NAME AND ADDRESS OF HOSPITAL		
22. DATE OF INJURY OR ILLNESS / / Month Day Year	23. TIME OF DAY ____ a.m. ____ p.m.	24. Did employee lose at least one full day's work after the injury? ☐ Yes, date last worked _____ ☐ No
25. HAS EMPLOYEE RETURNED TO WORK? ☐ Yes, date returned _____ ☐ No, still off work		☐ Yes, date _____ ☐ No

Completed by (type or print)	Signature	Title	Date

Form 5020 (Rev. 4)
January 1983

FILING OF THIS REPORT IS NOT AN ADMISSION OF LIABILITY

Figure 8.18   Accident Report Form

No matter how many copies of the accident form are required by the insurance company, make one additional copy for your files.

Keeping a Do-List

A *do-list* is a self-kept list of things that you need to do. It is usually kept on your clipboard, but might just as practically be attached to the inside front cover of your prompt script (see Figure 8.19). Anyone who has ever made out a shopping list can write one, and anyone who has ever made out a shopping list will appreciate the necessity for one.

Your do-list should always be with you. Whenever staff, crew, or cast tell you anything that requires an action on your part, you should make a note of it. Any change of schedule should be noted so that you can figure out the consequences and deal with them. You will also want to note information that must be relayed to other staff members. Do not trust your memory. There are simply too many things to be done.

Writing something on your list implies that you will take care of it or see that it is taken care of. It is reassuring to a director to see you make a note when he or she asks for something.

Take time at the end of each day to review your list and to assess what must be done first tomorrow and what can be delegated to others.

Keep a special area for notes for the director. In doing so, you will be functioning not only as the director's assistant but as the director's secretary. When the director promises to do something—bring in a prop, contact a scene designer with whom he or she has worked in the past, write a letter of introduction for a cast member who will be going to New York—jot down a note for him or her. After rehearsal, present your notes with tact. Obviously, if the director does not appreciate this, discontinue. You'll find most directors grateful.

Your book helped me to survive my first summer stock experience, but unfortunately you did not touch one area which is fast becoming the difference between the "men and boys" in stage management: coffee. I found that the making of a good pot of java brings the same respect as calling cues on time. It's a way of getting ahead in this business. The choices are difficult: Coffee-mate vs. Cremora; Sweet 'N Low or Sweet 10 or Equal or Sugar Twin or Necta Sweet. Remember, most coffee machines must be cleaned once a week. A solution of vinegar and water works wonders.

Gary L. Schaffer
Assistant Stage Manager
Pittsburgh Ballet Company
Pittsburgh, PA

[It's a good idea to have some tea and herb tea on hand as well.]

Wednesday

1. Touch up staples reflecting lights

2. weight bottom of flaps swinging in draft

3. Call Norman on plans for ramp

4. Get sack of wheat paste

5. tell Nick he won't be needed Friday night

6. Call photographer for schedule

   <u>remind Chuck:</u>
   1. mortar & pestle
   2. Bring in III revisions
   3. Call Ray 7:00 PM

Figure 8.19   Manager's Daily Do-List and Reminder Checklist

Avoiding Rehearsal Problems

I'll take a few paragraphs here to throw in a little philosophy—the Gospel according to Stern—very little and not too deep:

My "Discipline of the Theater" theory is an oversimplification and can be stated very briefly: The play exists *only* on stage when the curtain is up. Prior to performance, the play exists *only* in the mind of the director, and *everyone* works to realize his or her concept.

In reality, this theory never quite works. Still, I feel that it is the premise on which everyone should work, and it is a premise that serves stage managers well in deciding what their words and deeds should be.

Play production is a process of compromise. From the first casting audition, the director may find that an actor brings forth an aspect of characterization that is superior to her or his original concept. Or, she or he may find that no actor really lives up to that concept, so the best available actor is cast. Either way, the original concept is changed. Compromise.

During rehearsals the director attempts to bring forth from the cast his or her concept. Actors experiment in early rehearsals and present the director with their concepts. Further compromise.

The scene designer talks to the director to understand the director's concept of the play and then supports the director by designing a set that will put the director's concept on the stage. It is the same with the costume designer, the lighting designer, the sound designer, and all of the other creative people concerned with the production. In reality, there are further compromises as the designers try to turn the director's inspired or approved concepts into reality.

The stage manager is concerned with this process because the inevitable compromises are sometimes preceded by confrontations that disrupt rehearsals or preproduction work and/or demoralize cast members.

Producer/Director Conflicts

Sometimes problems arise between the producer and the director. In theory, the producer is responsible for obtaining the materials and personnel to make the play happen. He or she generally hires or selects the director. Thereafter, the producer is supposed to work to realize the director's concept along with everyone else. But the producer hires the director and can usually fire the director. In commercial theater, the producer is concerned with possible loss of great amounts of money if the director's concept does not pay off. In theory, the producer should discuss and evaluate the director's concept before hiring her or him; once the producer has hired the director, he or she should go with the director.

In practice, however, the producer feels that his or her powers should allow him or her to influence the director, not only as to general concepts but also with respect to specifics. So there are many incidents of producers directing over the director's shoulder—pulling strings in casting, changing designs that the director and designers have agreed upon, demanding that changes in the director's realm be made up to the very last minute, and so on.

Even if the producers do not subscribe to my oversimplified theory, they should honor some ethics of supervision:

1. The authority of any supervisor should not be diminished before his or her subordinates.
2. A person can follow the dictates of only one supervisor.

Translated into theater practice, this means that a director and producer should never discuss their differences of opinion in front of cast members, staff, or crew. Once their differences have been ironed out, all resulting changes should be announced by the director. They should not be prefaced with any disclaimers, such as, "I don't feel this way, but due to circumstances beyond my control . . . ." If the director can't say firmly, "I have decided that . . . , "then she or he should firmly announce, "I have quit and it's up to the producer to provide another director."

As stage manager, if you should observe that producer/director conflicts during rehearsals are demoralizing cast members or disrupting rehearsals or work calls, you should call the director and producer aside and tactfully request that their disputes be resolved in private. It's psychologically hard to back down in public, but significantly easier to listen to reason and to change one's mind in private.

Theater is not a democratic process in which the producer and director debate and then resolve their differences by a vote of the cast.

It is always preferable to anticipate such problems and to discuss problem-solving procedures at early staff meetings before they erupt into rehearsal delays.

Playwright at Work

What happens when the playwright is present? The play still exists in only one place prior to the curtain's rise—in the director's mind. I know this sounds improbable, and I've never met a playwright who could accept it. But once the playwright commits her or his work to paper and the producer turns it over to the director, the play is a concept in the director's mind.

Of course, some changes can and should be made as the playwright and director see the play come to life. But the playwright should go through the director privately to work on changes and should not communicate directly with the cast. The director should also suggest changes to the playwright privately.

I have seen playwrights angrily interrupt rehearsals because an actor paraphrased a line. I have seen casts thoroughly demoralized by director/playwright conflicts during rehearsals. If you are going into any production in which the playwright will be allowed in the rehearsal area, discuss in advance with the director, playwright, and producer what procedures will be used to resolve disputes, and particularly *where* disputes will be handled—in private and outside the rehearsal area, I hope.

I have the greatest respect for playwrights. None of us could work without their words and ideas. But I believe that if they cannot accept the principles discussed here, they should write novels or greeting cards, or direct their own plays.

[Here's another rule that I would like to see accepted by playwrights. I put it in brackets because I know that this is a book on stage management and not on playwriting or directing: Every director should have the right to cut 5 percent of a playwright's lines without negotiation. There isn't a play by William Shakespeare, Eugene O'Neill, Arthur Miller, Tennessee Williams, or Neil Simon that could not survive a 5 percent cut easily. It's hard for playwrights to see this.

[I find that inexperienced playwrights become emotionally involved—in love!—with their every word, article, and comma. Directors bring a different perspective to a script. Experienced directors know instinctively when action is bogging down in verbiage, when a scene is not playing. They don't need to wait for audience reaction to know.

[When it comes to discussions or arguments between playwright and director, the playwright can always rationalize every syllable that he or she has committed to paper. "It reveals character." "It'll get a laugh." "It advances the plot." "It foreshadows." The playwright knows all the good writing craft reasons why every word is immortal. The director knows only that those immortal words don't play.

[If the playwright doesn't trust the director enough with his or her baby to allow the director to change the diapers, he or she ought to find another director.

[But this is not a book on directing or playwriting, and stage managers do not make rules for the relationship between directors and playwrights; they only make things run smoothly by getting an understanding of what the rules are, and ensuring that everyone knows them.

[Sometimes actors approach a playwright to ask if they are giving the playwright the interpretation of the role he or she wants. Actually the actors are looking for reassurance or seeking praise. The playwright launches into a discussion of characterization, completely confusing the actor, not only by giving specifics that conflict with the director's but also by talking an entirely different language. Playwrights should have a stock of supportive generalizations to offer insecure actors: "I really appreciate all the hard work you are putting into this production." "I really admire the way you take direction." "I'm very well pleased with the way the director is interpreting my work and the way the cast is supporting her interpretation."

[The best time for the playwright to clarify his or her intent is when he or she is writing the play. If it isn't in the script, he or she shouldn't expect his or her presence at rehearsals to put it on the stage. If he or she must have contact with the cast, the playwright may give extensive notes at an early reading. But when the director and cast are in blocking, pacing, and polishing rehearsals, all further changes and clarifications should be discussed between the playwright and the director privately, and then any agreed-upon changes should issue from the director.]

Change Procedures

A "no more changes" deadline should be established at an early staff meeting. Additionally, playwrights should understand that the later changes are made in rehearsals, the less chance there is for a polished performance.

Stage managers who are new to their work or are working with a new company should raise the issue of change procedures at the very first production meeting to arrive at an understanding among director, producer, and playwright. Tell them that you or your fellow stage managers have had bad experiences in the past and that you want to prevent future problems by getting procedures spelled out in advance. If the playwright, producer, and director can't agree, or if you can't live by their agreement, find another job.

Suggested Classroom Exercise

Arrange for one student to shadow a stage manager during three consecutive blocking rehearsals, preferably at a community or professional theater. Have the student report observations of what the stage manager did before, during, and afer rehearsal.

9

Keeping the Cast
on Time

*Take care of the minutes and the hours will take care
of themselves.*

—Chesterfield

The best way to predict the future is to invent it.

—Alan Kay

You are (of course) personally so punctual that it is hard for you to understand those who are late. Your mental clock is 10 minutes ahead of real time. You always feel that if you are not 10 minutes early for an appointment, you're late. You know that you are being paid to think ahead. You plan ahead with master calendars and schedules. You work ahead of others, arriving at the theater before the staff and cast to open up and prepare for rehearsals and performances. You are never late. With that kind of orientation, and with punctuality so deeply infused into the fiber of your being, you find it difficult to comprehend how an actor can possibly show up 22 minutes late for a rehearsal. Yet it happens.

When an actor does arrive late, the rehearsal should not come to a halt while that actor is questioned. You should tell the late actor what page of the script you are on, or the scene if you are off book, and ask the tardy actor to take her or his place. He or she should be advised not to apologize, but simply to get to work. If the individual is not in the scene, you should tell her or him which scene will be worked on next, and ask him or her to go over lines until needed.

Under no circumstances should you allow other cast members to sit around to wait for a late actor. Urge your director to do the scene that was scheduled. Either throw the missing actor's lines or have another cast member or understudy read the part. Make use of the time as best you can. Perhaps the director will allow you to check your visual display of characters and select a sequence that can be rehearsed without the missing actor.

If there is only one actor present on time, regardless of the minimum number needed to do a scene, start working with that one actor. It is important to the play, to the on-time actors, and to the late actors that work be in progress from the minute that the rehearsal was called!

At the end of the rehearsal period, discuss tardiness with the late actor, privately. First, especially in a professional situation, you should turn to your log in the presence of the actor and write the number of minutes that he or she was late, ask the reason for the tardiness, and write it also. Then ask him or her to sign the log. In any case, confront the actor politely with the facts and ask if the rehearsal schedule was clear and if he or she understood what time he or she was expected. Ask the individual if there is anything you can do to help overcome the cause of the tardiness. Then ask if he or she needs to be called prior to the next rehearsal. If necessary, review the importance of rehearsal time, the fact that 22 minutes of tardiness represents over two hours of lost rehearsal time in terms of complete cast interaction, that not only the tardy actor but all the other actors in the scene suffer, and ultimately the quality of the play suffers. Stress the positive factors—that early arrival at rehearsals allows the actor to review lines and to run lines with other actors, that the director is going for the kind of polished performance that needs every possible minute of rehearsal time, and that since this is also the tardy actor's goal, you know that you can count on future cooperation. In short, make it absolutely clear that you care and that it is important to you that actors be on time.

In professional theaters, steps may be taken against habitually tardy actors through their union, but in both union and nonunion situations, you should try to educate and stress the positive rather than threaten and punish.

Directors should not have to discuss tardiness with actors. They should be able to rely on you in this matter.

Sign-In Sheets

As early as dress rehearsals, sign-in sheets should be posted (see Figure 9.1). Cast members should be reminded to initial in, until they get into the habit. Initialing prevents actors from placing a check mark in the wrong block. If they initial the wrong block, the error can be traced. Alternate lines of the sign-in sheet can be set up in different colors or in different indention patterns; this makes it easier to find the correct space to initial.

The sign-in sheet saves you work. It allows you to see if the cast is there by looking in only one place. If anyone has not initialed in by half-hour call, you must check the dressing rooms. Then you must phone those who are late.

Placement of the sign-in sheet on the callboard ensures that cast members will be close enough to the callboard to read any urgent new information that has been posted.

Please <u>Initial</u> In !

ALBATROSS

SIGN IN

	TUE	WED	THUR	FRI	SAT	SUN
Frank Aletter						
Jenny Gillespie						
Pauline Meyers						
Lee Meriwether						
James R. Sweeney						
James B. Sikking						
Marge Redmond						
Paul Bryar						
Kathleen Freeman						
Dick Ramos						
Ellen Webb						

Figure 9.1   Sign-In Sheet for Cast Members

If you have a cast of 2, you may elect not to post a sign-in sheet. If you have a cast of 100, you may elect to turn the sign-in sheet over to a gate man or stage door guard and have that individual check in the cast. You would still check with that individual for tardiness.

Calling any actor who has failed to sign in by half-hour call (see the following section, "The Calls") is an important responsibility. Nothing should get in the way of your carrying out that duty.

Examples

1. During a three-month run, the home of a habitually late actor was frequently called. His wife always answered the phone and told the stage manager that the actor had left for the theater. When the actor arrived, the stage manager explained that he had called his home. The actor complained that the stage manager was needlessly alarming his wife, who would worry about traffic accidents until he called her to reassure her that he'd arrived safely. The stage manager's complaint that he was late and the actor's complaint that the stage manager was needlessly worrying his wife were frequently voiced—until the evening that the stage manager called and woke him up!

2. On opening night of a musical, five principals and the director were late for half-hour call. None responded to the stage manager's phone calls. The stage manager assumed that they were on their way. At 15-minute call, they were still not there. The stage manager alerted the house manager and the

producer. Then a chorus member remembered that one of the principals had mentioned that they were going out to dinner before the show. The restaurant was called. They had been there and left—35 minutes ago. At 5-minute call, they had still not arrived. Now the producer and the house manager were pacing the lobby. An audience of 1,400 waited, completely unaware that they were missing quite a drama. At curtain time, there were still no principals and no word from them. The producer's guidance was, "Stay calm," but he was clearly upset. How could such a thing happen? Why hadn't they called? The stage manager was numb.

At 7 minutes past curtain, the principals and director arrived. Blocked road, train accident, waited to clear road, hemmed in by other cars, no way out, no phone or house visible to horizon.

At 13 minutes past curtain time, the overture began.

And that was the night that one of the bit players who lived next door to the theater overslept and missed his one line. The stage manager had failed to call him.

In a situation of complete pandemonium, don't fail to carry out your basic duties!

During the run of any production, if an actor is late for half-hour call, she or he should be reminded that the half hour prior to performance is meant to be used by the actor to get into costume, makeup, and character and to relax in order to store up energy for the performance.

Actors sometimes argue the necessity of being at the theater one-half hour prior to curtain. They claim that they can get into costume, makeup, and character in 7½ minutes, they can relax at home, and they have plenty of energy. Then too, they don't like to wait backstage because it's musty, crowded, and so on.

Regardless of such arguments, you should continue to expect punctuality. Call every time the actor is late and use whatever methods you can to convince the actor to be at the theater for half-hour call.

Should an actor who drives for 45 minutes to get to the theater still have the same call as other cast members? Should you call that actor's home 45 minutes prior to curtain to assure yourself that the actor is on the way? What if that same actor does not appear until 15 minutes into the first act?

Should another actor who does not appear until the third act be granted a late call? Should an actress who puts on her makeup and costume at home to avoid using the overcrowded dressing room be allowed to sign in after half-hour call?

These are but a few of the practical questions that will come up. To answer them, you must ask yourself: Can I help ensure that this actor will get to the theater on time? Can I ensure that the cast will not be rushed in putting on makeup, getting into costume, and getting into character? Can I assure myself that I will have adequate time to call actors and still carry out my other precurtain duties?

If an actor is ever granted a late call, the call should coincide with a period of time that you have free to check on his or her arrival.

The Calls

Calls—announcements of the time to the curtain—are given in order to alert cast members to how much time they have before the play begins. The traditional calls are:

> Half hour, please.
> Fifteen minutes, please.
> Five minutes, please.
> Places, please.

The first three calls are given 30, 15, and 5 minutes prior to the announced curtain time. The "places" call is given after the house manager has turned the house over to you and when you are ready to run the show. Notice that "please" is a part of the call. Don't omit it.

It is traditional that all cast members acknowledge your calls with a cheery "Thank you." If cast members are unaware of this custom, you might bring it to their attention.

In some cases, the curtain will be delayed—last-minute rush at the box office, bad weather, traffic and parking problems, late arrival of theater parties, and the like. The house manager might ask you to hold the curtain for 5, 10, or 15 minutes. You should relay these holds to the cast with an additional call of "Five-minute hold, please." If possible, you should explain to the cast the reason for the delay.

At intermissions, the calls are "Five minutes, please," and "Places, please."

Do not rely on a one-way speaker system from your work area to the dressing rooms to give the calls. You not only run the risk of mechanical failure but you also lose that bit of contact with the cast.

A two-way communications system is only slightly better because mechanical failure is immediately noticeable and cast members have a chance to respond. A face-to-face exchange is much better.

Only if it is absolutely impossible for you to give the calls should you assign this duty to an assistant or call-person. But this is not a task that should be delegated. This is one of your more important duties.

If you cannot greet and chat with each cast member as that cast member arrives at the theater, you have all too little contact. The call itself is not sufficient. There has to be a little dialogue between you and cast members. The subtext is, "Are you all right? Can you give a good performance tonight? Are you overtired? Did you get too sunburned? Did you have too much to drink? Do you have a stomachache?"

There is very little that you can do to relieve the pains and suffering of the acting condition. But hot coffee, a few aspirins, and some kind words can go a long way in boosting cast morale to performance level. If you are effective, you can make just a few words and a friendly, sympathetic smile serve as a mental rubdown.

Under normal conditions you are not expected to give calls or warns for individual actor entrances once the act has begun. Actors are expected to listen for their cues in the wings or, if available, on dressing room monitors. There are exceptions, however.

Example

A big-name personality who had played the same role in hundreds of theaters-in-the-round across the country had become so indifferent to the script and local variations in blocking that he had to be led out of his dressing room by the hand, pointed down the correct aisle, and pushed on cue. He also had to be retrieved as he exited, whenever and wherever he chose, and led back to his dressing room, as he could never remember where the dressing room was. The stage manager assigned the big name a "seeing-eye gopher."

Many opera singers have done their roles 3 or 4 times, some as many as 50 or 60 times, in a variety of theaters. They may get the different productions confused. So, ASMs are expected to cue entrances. Standing beside the singers, ASMs give both visual and verbal cues. Sometimes during rehearsals, a singer will not like the cue where the director wants it. The singer will say, "The director told me to go here." I have always told my assistants to reply, "Thank you; however, the director did not pass that on to me, so I must call it as is." The director will advise both singer and ASM if the entrance was not as intended. Opera stage managers also give 5-minute entrance warns ("Ms. Smith, to stage left, please." "Children's chorus to stage right.").

> David Grindle
> Production Stage Manager
> The Atlanta Opera

[David recommends *The Da Capo Opera Manual* by Nicholas Ivor Martin, Da Capo Press (1997), for those interested in opera production.]

If you are a new stage manager, do not worry about gaining the respect of the actors. Just assume that you already have it. You do have it by virtue of your title, and you will earn it by virtue of your work. Respect is reciprocal. The more you give, the more you can count on getting back. As soon as the actors realize that you respect them, you will gain their utmost cooperation.

Suggested Classroom Exercise

Discuss your theater's policy with respect to the tardiness of an actor or actress. Would the curtain be delayed? How long? Would an understudy be readied? At what point? Would the stage manager or someone else go on holding book? Would the performance be cancelled?

10

Department Management and Property Management

The quickest way to do many things is to do only one thing at a time.

—Anonymous

The Stage Manager as Supervisor

Stage managers are called on to work with, coordinate the efforts of, and/ or supervise many theater workers—the builders on the "premises of illusion": set designers, lighting designers, technical directors, master carpenters, lighting technicians, crew members, costume designers, property masters, and others.

To do this, stage managers must first be knowledgeable about their work. They must understand the technical aspects of making theater. This they gain through observation and study.

Next, they must understand their personal relationship to coworkers. As stage managers move from theater to theater, from educational to community to professional levels, they find the titles and relationships of the builders changing frequently. At one theater the set designer is the technical director. At another there is no technical director, and the stage manager and set designer work together in supervising the construction and painting of sets. At still another there are both a resident scene designer and resident technical director, and the latter supervises both the stage manager and the master carpenter.

Despite the wide range of job titles and descriptions and the deviations in the chain of command, stage managers quickly find out who does what and who reports to whom by observation and through conversations with the staff (see Chapter 5).

150

Once she or he determines which of the staff are directly responsible to her or him, the stage manager exerts control over their work. She or he acts as the foreman for the producer or management, coordinating staff work through the master calendar and the schedules she or he distributes. The stage manager personally oversees staff work as necessary.

Getting along with subordinates and managing their work is an art form in itself. Stage management is certainly a proving ground for this art. Here are a few simple recommendations for supervising subordinates:

1. Take time to give your instructions with great clarity, making sure that you are understood, or that the director's or producer's intention, which you are passing on, is understood.
2. Give instructions in bite-size portions. Don't give a gopher 20 things to do. Give one, and when it's finished, then give the next.
3. Don't give an individual more work than you feel confident he or she can accomplish. If you anticipate that he or she will need more labor or more time than immediately available, explain that you only expect that a start be made on the work.
4. Deliver instruction with calmness and self-confidence.
5. Follow up on the work you assign, checking on problems and reviving interest in projects as necessary by showing your interest and appreciation. Reemphasize goals when the enthusiasm of your subordinates is flagging.
6. Whenever you assign work, remember that the responsibility for its completion remains with you.

Additional comments on getting along with others and supervising department heads can be found in Chapter 2.

Supervision of Department Heads

In the course of your work you are likely to be supervising the property manager, but you may also be asked to supervise a few other department heads—sometimes the costumer and sometimes the technical director.

If so, during the rehearsal period you will want to see that the department heads (1) are working, (2) are on schedule, and (3) have not run into any "insurmountable" problems.

1. Department heads and their assistants don't usually punch clocks. But if they are not there to do the work, the production will not be able to open on time. You informally make the rounds to see if the staff is at work. It may occasionally mean rousing a late sleeper or providing transportation for someone with an unreliable auto. When you make the rounds, chat about progress on the current production.

2. Falling behind on the schedule sometimes means that a department will need more staff. Can you send over an assistant, some apprentices, or your gopher to help the shop wire on the ornamental grapes that light up? Or will you have to approach the business manager because the costumer insists on another union costume technician at union wages in order to accomplish the costume work on time?
3. Problem solving is frequently the same as listening well. If every department head feels able to express herself or himself to you, she or he will air "insurmountable" problems. In doing so, the department head will usually come up with the solution. If you should observe that the department heads themselves are largely the cause of their own problems, keep this to yourself and praise their solutions.

By asking questions ("What if ... ?" "What would happen if ... ?") rather than imposing solutions ("You should ... ") or placing blame ("You should have ... "), you tactfully get department heads to feel that they are in command of the situation, and the commander usually works harder than the person who is merely following orders.

In supervision, tact can usually get it done.

Property Management and You

Regardless of theater level, the function of the property person remains the same—to get the props. Your usual function is to supervise. To do this, you should know all aspects of property management.

In union theaters the property person is paid for services. In community, educational, showcase, and children's theater the property person is usually an unpaid volunteer. Some people do not consider working on props particularly exciting or glamorous. It calls for someone who is methodical and persistent.

Finding and motivating a competent property person is a problem that plagues many theaters. Sometimes when a property person cannot be found, you find yourself either working as property person or retaining overall responsibility for props and dividing the prop work among the staff and cast.

Whether supervising or doing it yourself, you should appreciate the importance of having props available for rehearsals.

If actors can hold a prop with one hand and their script with the other, the props ought to be in place, even before the actors put down their scripts. Having props in hand helps them to memorize their lines. Using props early in the rehearsal period allows the cast and director to experiment and to develop suitable business. This is highly desirable, as it may add immeasurably to the quality of the production.

Conversely, not having props on time leads to serious problems.

Examples

1. Scenes may have to be reblocked because an actor did not allow enough room for his imagined sword.
2. The leading lady sneezes through opening night because of the bouquet. The wadded-up newspaper used as a rehearsal prop did not affect her allergies.

Property Person's Checklist

To help determine the extent of the property person's responsibilities, you might review the following:

Before Rehearsals

Before rehearsals will the property person

1. Be responsible for hand properties?
2. Be responsible for set pieces? Which ones?
3. Be responsible for obtaining transportation to pick up and return all props?
4. Coordinate with the director, scene designer, and producer to ensure appropriate props?
5. Ensure that set pieces arrive on time for the take-in?
6. Obtain hand props as soon as possible in order to give actors maximum rehearsal time to work with them?
7. Provide temporary rehearsal props for unusual or costly props that cannot be obtained until later in the rehearsal period?
8. Give a written receipt to lenders of props and set pieces? Note on both the original and copy the condition of the prop and the intended date of return?
9. Coordinate with the producer, through the stage manager, prior to rental of expensive props?
10. Be able to give _____ hours per week for _____ weeks to this work?
11. Need assistance (an assistant property master)?
12. Report to the stage manager any difficulties that he or she encounters in sufficient time to avert a last-minute rush?

During Rehearsals

During rehearsals will the property person

1. Attend rehearsals to make notes of additional props, where and how props are used, which actors use them, and from which entrance they come on stage?

2. Bring in large boxes and label them by act or scene as necessary in order to store the props?

3. Set props for each scene 15 minutes before rehearsal is scheduled?

4. Lock up or otherwise secure all props after rehearsals?

5. Draw maps of prop tables and post them on or above the prop tables offstage to ensure quick, accurate checks of all props prior to rehearsals and performances?

6. Make maps of locations of props in each scene so that he or she can change or supervise changes of props between scenes?

7. Draw diagrams on stage surfaces (tables, bars, mantels, etc.) to indicate exact placement of props?

Prior to Performance

Prior to the performance will the property person

1. Check presence and condition of all props, and report to the stage manager (usually 45 minutes prior to performance)?

2. Replace expendable items (water in pitcher, tea in booze bottles, telegram that gets crumpled, etc.) prior to each performance?

During Performance

During the performance will the property person

1. Change properties on the stage between acts as needed?

%$# icebag! All through rehearsal it was used empty. At dress, she (actress) filled it with ice. Why? I'll never know. It dribbled all over the stage, her, others. It was old and worn. Newspaper would have puffed it up fine. (A doctor once told me *never disrupt the body temp of an actor under hot lights,* unless in pain.) So, old ice bags, activated, are a NO NO.

> Billy Carr Creamer
> Associate Director
> Amarillo Little Theater
> Amarillo Civic Center
> Amarillo, TX

[The general lesson is that all props must be used at the earliest possible rehearsal just as they are to be used on opening night.]

Simply put eight drops of yellow food color, three drops of red, and one drop of green into whatever bottle one is using, add water and you have perfect whiskey. (This process eliminates the bubbles that you get when using instant tea.)

William J. Buckley, III
Stage Manager
Woodstock Playhouse
Woodstock, NY

[Be sure to clean the bottle thoroughly first!!!]

After Performance

After the performance will the property person

1. Check for return of all props to the property tables?
2. Store props between performances, providing secure storage for expensive props?

After Production

After the production will the property person

1. Clean or repair borrowed items to ensure goodwill for future borrowing?
2. Obtain receipts for return of items borrowed, give notes of thanks, and thank contributors personally?
3. Be financially responsible for all lost props?
4. Keep a list of sources, and the types of props that can be borrowed from each, as an aid to future productions?
5. Write a critique of his or her experience, emphasizing problem areas, in order to help the next property master?

Although it is desirable, it is not necessary that the property person do everything reflected in the questions here. Rather than review the preceding list with the property person, you might want to give her or him just a few items at a time, or as much responsibility as you feel she or he can accept at one time. A new property person might accept more and more responsibility gradually but might balk if presented with the whole range. It is necessary, however, that you and the property person come to a clear understanding of her or his exact duties.

Property Forms

The two forms "Borrowed Items" and "Acknowledgment of Borrowed Items (Returned)" can be used by the property person to control props (see Figures 10.1 and 10.2). When she or he picks up a prop, the property master fills out the "Acknowledgment" form and gives it to the lender. She or he then notes on the "Borrowed Items" form the program credit line that is expected and other information. When the property master returns the prop, she or he picks up the "Acknowledgment" form.

Receipt forms, found in most stationery stores, can be used in place of these two forms (see Figure 10.3). One receipt and a copy are made out for

```
                          BORROWED ITEMS
    _____ production of "_____" _____
                                                      dates

   Item(s) Borrowed | Date Received | Borrowed From* | Date (to be) Returned

1  _____

2  _____

3  _____

4  _____

5  _____

6  _____

7  _____

8  _____

9  _____

10 _____

11 _____

12 _____

13 _____

* include company name, address, phone no., extension, and personal contact!

        Page _____ of _____       Prepared by _____

                                       LAWRENCE STERN
                                       Production Stage Manager
                                       555-3719
```

Figure 10.1   Property Master's Control Form and Record of Borrowed Items

```
        ACKNOWLEDGMENT OF BORROWED ITEMS (RETURNED)


The following items, loaned to the _____ production

of "_____" were returned on _____
                                              date
by _____ in satisfactory condition:
1.
2.
3.
4.
5.
6.
7.
8.
9.
10.
11.
12.
13.
14.
15.
                              Received by:
                                name_____

LAWRENCE STERN                  position _____
Production Stage Manager
555-3719                        company _____
```

Figure 10.2   Acknowledgment Form for Borrowed Items

each borrowed prop. The copy is issued to the lender and retrieved when the prop is returned. The original is kept by the property master.

In some cases it is easier to use the prop plot (Figure 3.9) as a control form. If many copies of the prop plot can be duplicated, then they can be posted on prop storage boxes, placed on prop tables, and even given to cast and staff as reminders of the props they have pledged to bring in. Figure 10.4 shows the prop table preset for Act I of *Rigoletto.*

The cost of all props that must be purchased by the theater should be carefully recorded on the property person's expense sheet (see Figure 7.1). For bookkeeping purposes, the property person might be asked to record expendable and permanent items on separate sheets.

Program credits and/or complimentary tickets are sometimes given for the use of props. It is important to check the producer's or management's policy and coordinate with the program editor. In some cases, the lender definitely does not want a program credit. Be sure to clear this with the lender.

As soon as props are used in the rehearsals, you should remind the cast to cooperate with the property person by returning all props to the prop

Great American Theater
Date___ **Nov, 24** ___   No.**3873**
Receiver Of **Shiker Bar Furnishings Inc.**
Address **1038 Bluedale Road**
1 finished bar, 2 bar stools $___
For   **3" scatch upstage end**

HOW PAID	BALANCE DUE	to be returned Jan. 11, P.M. by us.
5X 820 Rediform		By *Eric Spelvin, PM*

Great American Theater
Date___ **Nov, 24** ___   No.**3873**
Receiver Of **Shiker Bar Furnishings Inc.**
Address **1038 Bluedale Road**
1 finished bar, 2 bar stools $___
For   **3" scatch upstage end**

HOW PAID	BALANCE DUE	to be returned Jan. 11, P.M. by us.
	Rediform	By *Eric Spelvin, PM*

Figure 10.3 Receipt Form Acknowledgment for a Borrowed Item. The original is kept by the property master and duplicate is issued to the lender. Both copies should specify the date of return and the condition of the prop.

tables when they are carried offstage as part of the actor's business. Otherwise, the property person finds herself or himself searching the dressing rooms and even the pockets of costumes.

As a safety factor, the stage manager is usually responsible for, and must carefully supervise, the firing of blanks, even though the weapon is a prop (see Figures 10.5 and 10.6).

When the property person is also responsible for specific set pieces—those that will be bought, borrowed, or rented, as opposed to those that will be constructed—you must make absolutely certain that all staff members know which set pieces they are responsible for.

Figure 10.4 Prop Table Preset, Act I, *Rigoletto*. At the Atlanta Opera, the property master carries out the running moves but the ASM supervises. Both keep an eye on the clock. "Water Spritz" refers to the spraying, by a props person, of a fine mist to add moisture to the air, which opera singers appreciate.

Rigoletto
Prop Table Preset—ACT I
Approximate Running time: 00:53:00

STAGE RIGHT	STAGE LEFT
Scene 1	*Scene 1*
19 Gold goblets (Chorus: G. Jordan, A. Kauffman, G. Jones, K. Barnes, V. Clark, M. Cleghorn, D. Haggerty, K. Lee, G. Sterchi, E. Drew, D. Davis, J. Clark, K. Foster, M. Jaye, J. Young, D. Martin, B. Larkin, J. Jones (2))	7 Pieces of ladies undergarments (M. Durham, T. Allen)—FROM COSTUMES
2 Large pitchers (K. Barnes, W. Siede)	
1 Silver hairbrush (N. Paul)	
1 Large red fabric (M. Durham, T. Allen)	
1 Large feather fan (C. Burns)	
4 Combat swords with sheaths and belts (belts labeled: J. Young, D. Davis, B. Larkin, D. Martin)	
1 Jester's Bauble (Potter)	
1 Deck of tarot cards (K. Rosquist)	
2 Bunches of practical white grapes (M. Jaye, S. Mayer)	
1 Cane (P. Haynie)	
2 Daggers—combat (McMillan, J. Clark)	
1 Pair gloves (P. Haynie)—FROM COSTUMES	
1 Hat (P. Haynie)—FROM COSTUMES	
1 Necklace (L. Wood)	
1 Bracelet (K. Rosquist)	
1 Jester's shoulder bag (Potter)	*Scene 2*
1 Ring of keys (Potter)	1 Sword w/ curved guard (Bell)
1 Locket (Potter)	1 Hairbrush (James)
1 Knife inside bag (Potter)	1 Electric candle on small black stand (James)
	1 Gag labeled GILDA (Delligatti)
Scene 2	1 Length of rope (Delligatti)
1 Coin purse (Villa)	1 Gag labeled GIOVANNI (James)
6 Torches (C. Hawkins, G. Sterchi, S. Mize, C. Hooper, G. Williamson, L. Compton)	1 Length of rope (James)
1 Blindfold (Morrissey)	
1 Wine Skin (P. Haynie)	
1 Key on Ribbon (McMillan)	
1 Ladder (V. Robertson)	
1 Knife—must be combat knife (McMillan)	
1 Mask—says THOMAS POTTER inside (G. Williamson)	**RUNNING MOVES:**
	48:00 min.—Give candle to James at top of SL stairs.
RUNNING MOVES:	*50:00 min.*—Receive candle from Delligatti top of SL stairs. Give gag (GILDA) & rope.
41:00 min.—Light torch. Give torch to McMillan.	
46:00 min.—Receive and extinguish torch from McMillan.	*NOTES:* Scene 1 and 2 props should be set at top of show. Scene 1 is 14:00 min. Scene 2 is 39:00 min.
47:00 min.—Light 6 torches and give to choristers (C. Hawkins, G. Sterchi, S. Mize, C. Hooper, G. Williamson, L. Compton)	
57:00 min.—Receive and extinguish 6 torches from choristers.	
	CHANGEOVER from I-1 to I-2:
CHANGEOVER from I-1 to I-2: 5 minutes	**5 minutes**
INTERMISSION SHIFT from I to II:	**INTERMISSION SHIFT from I to II: 20**
20 minutes	**minutes**
WATER SPRITZ	**WATER SPRITZ**

Courtesy Sean M. Griffin, ASM, The Atlanta Opera.

Figure 10.5   Equity's Theatrical Firearms Questionnaire

**Theatrical Firearms Questionnaire
for Productions That Utilize Firearms**

If your production utilizes theatrical firearms, please complete this questionnaire and return it to your Equity Business Representative as soon as possible. (Note: For long running productions, this form must be filled out every six (6) months.)

Dear Stage Manager:

The Producer has obligated itself under the Collective Bargaining Agreement with Actors' Equity Association to provide a safe place of employment. Pursuant to Equity's right to check the Producer's compliance with that provision of the Collective Bargaining Agreement, we have devised the following checklist for you to use to see if the Producer is undertaking minimally prudent safeguards when firearms are used in a production.

Name of Show	Contract: (e.g., Production B&T, National LORT, Stock, LOA, Mini, etc.
Name of Theatre	Number in Cast
Date Stage Manager	Date Deputy

1. *Firearms Rehearsals.* It is essential to insure the Actors safety. Please confirm whether such rehearsals have taken place. if, for any reason, it is not possible to hold such rehearsals, Actors' Equity Association must be notified immediately.
2. *Identify all Firearms.* Please identify make or model, caliber, and load used.
   a) Are rehearsals to check firearms angles held regularly? Weekly? Daily? Each performance?
   b) Are the Blanks Crimped or Wadded?
   c) Have the firearms been recently certified? If so, when?
   d) How often are firearms cleaned? Wet Cleaning? Dry Cleaning?
   e) Who is in charge of the firearms and where are they stored?
   f) Is the ammunition stored separately? If so, where?
3. *Use in Production.* Please identify how the firearms are used. Include the number of shots in each scene and the activity of the Actors.

Act/Scene   Number of Shots   Activity of Actors

4. If any Actor experiences any adverse effects from the use of firearms during the run of the production, please notify the Actors' Equity Association immediately. Possible adverse effects include: Powder Burns, Errant Particle (e.g., a piece of casting which is propelled from the gun when fired) and Eardrum Problems. Also, please insure any injury is reported to Workers Compensation.
5. *Miscellaneous.* Please provide any other information you feel would be helpful. (Attach additional pages, if necessary)

cc. Deputy

Courtesy Actors' Equity Association.

Figure 10.6 Safety Tips for Use of Firearms

PLEASE POST IF FIREARMS ARE USED IN PRODUCTION

SAFETY TIPS FOR USE OF FIREARMS

Use simulated or dummy weapons whenever possible.

- Treat all guns as if they are loaded and deadly.
- Unless you are actually performing or rehearsing, all firearms must be secured by the property master.
- The property master or armorer should carefully train you in the safe use of any firearm you must handle. Be honest if you have no knowledge about guns. Do not overstate your qualifications.
- Never engage in horseplay with any firearms or other weapons. Do not let others handle the gun for any reason.
- All loading of firearms must be done by the property master, armorer, or experienced persons working under their direct supervision.
- Never point a firearm at anyone, including yourself. Always cheat the shot by aiming to the right or left of the target character. If asked to point and shoot directly at a living target, consult with the property master or armorer for the prescribed safety procedures.
- If you are the intended target of a gunshot, make sure that the person firing at you has followed all these safety procedures.
- If you are required to wear exploding blood squibs, make sure there is a bullet proof vest or other solid protection between you and the blast pack.
- Use protective shields for all off stage cast within close proximity to any shots fired.
- Check the firearm every time you take possession of it. Before each use, make sure that gun has been test-fired off stage and then ask to test-fire it yourself. Watch the prop master check the cylinders and barrel to be sure no foreign object or dummy bullet has become lodged inside.
- Blanks are extremely dangerous. Even though they do not fire bullets out of the gun barrel, they still have a powerful blast that can maim or kill.
- If the director or property master shouts, "Put the gun down," place the piece gently on the ground with the barrel pointing in a safe direction and step back quickly.
- Never attempt to adjust, modify or repair a firearm yourself. If a weapon jams or malfunctions, corrections shall be made only by a qualified person.
- When a scene is completed, the firearms shall be unloaded by the property master. All weapons must be cleaned, checked and inventoried after each performance.
- Live ammunition may not be brought into the theatre.
- If you are in a production where shots are to be fired and there is no qualified property master, go to the nearest phone and call Actors' Equity. A union representative will make sure proper precautions are followed.
- State and federal safety laws must be honored at all times.

This announcement must be posted on callboard when firearms are used in a production involving Equity members. Courtesy Actors' Equity Association.

About the snow: we use paper. I don't know what the exact origin of the material is. We buy it as "confetti." I suspect it may be the base material for colored confetti. It is very hard to find plain white confetti. It is also flame retardant. It sells for about \$7/lb. We have about 150 pounds sitting in the wings at the top of every show (of which we recuperate probably 98% during cleanup). The traction on "snow" is surprisingly good, especially after being in the dancers' sweaty hands. We've had one dancer slide and fall during a performance, so far. I'm not sure whether that was caused by the "snow" or by something else like transpiration on stage. There aren't really any precautions dancers can take when they're going full out. We keep the wings downstage of the first portal and upstage of the last portal as wide as possible so that dancers can maintain a straight line until they slow down.

> Johan Henckens
> Technical Director
> *The Hard Nut*
> Mark Morris Dance Group
> New York, New York

[This unusual prop has a spectacular effect, but consequences of its use must be considered by both dancers and stage crew. See Figure 10.7.]

Figure 10.7 Snow Scene from *The Hard Nut* (ballet). How do you think this spectacular effect was created?

Photo by Catherine Ashmore, Mark Morris Dance Group, New York, New York.

Suggested Classroom Exercise

Assign a student or students to work props at your theater or at a community theater. Ask the individual(s) to evaluate the checklist on page 153 to see how it relates to the reality of prop work.

11

Lighting, Sound, and Cueing Equipment

Technology improves things so fast, that by the time we can afford the best, there's something better.

—Anonymous

Are you ready for opening night in terms of lights? The process of getting ready started long prior to opening night. It started when you first became familiar with the circuit breaker capacities, the lighting equipment, and the plugging locations of your theater (described in Chapter 5). Prior to rehearsals you analyzed the script, made lists of the problems (Chapter 3), and drew tentative light pencil lines in your prompt script so that you could call light, sound, and special-effect cues during rehearsals (Chapter 3). Throughout rehearsals you have coordinated with the lighting designer, sound designer, and special-effects people (see Chapter 8, "Production Notes").

Prior to opening night curtain, as well as prior to the curtain at every performance, a check should be made of all light, sound, cueing, scene shift, and special-effect equipment. If your lighting designer, sound designer, scene designer, and technical director are on hand, they may want to conduct these checks, and you need only ensure that the work was carried out. However, after opening night, some of these people may not be around, and the responsibility for carrying out the checks will become your responsibility even if the actual checks are carried out by other crew members (see Chapter 14, Figure 14.1).

Conducting the Light Check

To conduct the light check, you normally ask the master electrician, lighting technician, or board operator to bring all of the instruments used in the

One should *never* bring all of the instruments "to full." Instead, bring them to a glow for a few minutes in order to warm the filaments gradually as a way of reducing burnouts.

Anonymous Reader

(As an incandescent lamp ages, the tungsten boils off the filament. It does so unevenly, causing a weak spot to develop on the filament. The most common failure mode is when the filament breaks at this weak spot when the lamp is first turned on and receives the full in-rush current.

This anonymous reader is right by stating that lamp life is extended by turning the lamp on in a dimmed mode, therefore avoiding the full in-rush current and reducing the tungsten evaporation. However, the filament could still fail when full power is restored.)

The author is right in stating that by turning the lamp on at full power (stressing it) during the light check, you will weed out the weak lamps, thus reducing the likelihood of a lamp failing during the performance.

William Gregory
GE Lighting

show "to full." You then inspect the instruments to make sure that all are working correctly. You must also see that the instruments are properly focused. To do this, bring up one unit or area of the stage at a time and check the effect against your focus charts or area lighting diagrams (see Figure 11.4, later in this chapter). Then you check the focus of each special-effect lighting instrument.

If gel frames are changed in the course of the show for special-effect lighting, you must make an inspection to be sure that the correct gel is set for Act I. (For instance, one spot may be used to produce both a bright sunlight effect that floods a window in Act I and a moonlight effect at the same window in Act III by changing a gel frame during an intermission. As part of your light check, your inspection should determine that the correct gel is in place for Act I.)

The complete inspection of lights must be finished early enough to allow time to correct problems without delaying the entrance of the audience. How long would it take you to bring in the ladder, set it up, trace a short in a cable, repair the short, and strike the ladder? That amount of time should be allowed between the light check and the opening of the house. Yes, it means an early call for you and the lighting technician at every single performance.

Do you have on hand spare lamps ("bottles") of the appropriate base type and wattage for your instruments? Do you have on hand appropriate repair parts and tools?

Here are a few examples of mishaps that properly conducted light checks would have avoided:

Example A

On Sunday mornings a small theater in Hollywood was used by a religious sect for meetings. During one meeting a screen was hung to show a movie—from the yokes of two instruments set for a performance that night. The stage manager later supervised the light check and found all of the instruments to be working. But he did not check focus against his area lighting diagram or focus chart. Result: An actor who was to give his final monologue illuminated by a single spot delivered his speech in virtual darkness while a nearby table was lit beautifully. The actor could not move into the light without mounting the table.

Example B

In another incident the light check was habitually late, conducted after the audience was in. The stage manager peeked through the curtains (extremely unprofessional) from his work area backstage to check the anti-pros, even though he could not replace burned-out lamps at this point without working over the heads of the audience. Then he checked instruments behind the curtains. Finding that one instrument on the first pipe was not working, he hurriedly brought in a ladder, checked the instrument by cross-plugging, and concluded that there was a short in the cable. Quickly he replaced it with a spare cable and called "places." Unfortunately the play began with a coronation parade of the cast from the rear of the house. As they approached the proscenium, the curtain was to open, revealing the throne. The stage manager cued the curtain. It opened two feet and stopped!

In his haste, the stage manager had run the replacement cable through the curtain rope. Subsequent repair had to be done in full view of the audience while the coronation parade looked on.

Example C

The house lights dimmed, an actor delivered the first line of the script, and the director's voice came from the back of the theater: "We don't have any lights. Check out the problem and let's back it up and start again."

The stage manager had not only forgotten to perform the light check but he had also failed to ensure that the dimmers were on. The house, on a separate dimmer, went out all right, but when the board operator brought up the first light cue, there was no light. The first actor to speak was to start in darkness, taking his cue from a sound effect. When the lights failed to come up, the actor continued, assuming that the lights were late. So the director had to stop the show from the back of the house.

Embroider this on your sampler: An ounce of leisurely inspection prior to the opening of the house is worth tons of rushed repair.

In addition to conducting a thorough light check prior to half-hour call, you must check each lighting effect immediately after you give the cue.

This is also true of each sound, special-effect, and scenic cue. (This will be discussed again in Chapter 14.)

If you are fortunate enough to be working in a booth in back of the audience, you will have a good view of every effect. But if you are in the wings, you must arrange for a view, resorting to peepholes, mirrors, or TV monitors, if necessary.

If the cue is not immediately followed by the anticipated effect, you must be programmed as follows:

1. Don't panic.
2. Did the technician recognize and execute the cue you gave?
3. Is there a mechanical failure?
4. Is there anything you can do to alleviate this problem? If yes, do it. If not, restrain yourself.

This, too, is true for sound, special-effect, and scenic cues. In the case of a mechanical lighting problem that cannot be immediately corrected, the most important principle to remember is the most basic and obvious one: The audience must see the actors.

Example
You give a cue to bring up an area. The area comes up slowly to full and a lamp blows. What should you do? Answer: Give the actors any light you can, short of shining your flashlight at them from the wings. You might bring up adjacent areas in the hopes that the actors will find some of it or gain from the spill. You might throw on the work light. At last resort you might even have to bring up the house lights. If and when the actors have enough light to continue the scene, then see how to remedy the problem.

The continuance of the play takes precedence over the quality of the lighting.

Preparation of the Lighting Cue Sheet

A lighting designer who has been with the production from its inception, has studied the script, and has worked with the producer, director, and other designers will prepare the lighting cue sheet (see Figure 11.1) or supervise the board operator in preparation prior to the technical rehearsal, and will work with the board operator to refine the cue sheet during the technical rehearsal. In working with the lighting designer, you would offer your list of lighting problems (Figure 3.6) that you made in your analysis of the script (see Chapter 3) to check against the lighting director's list, early in the production process. You would also bring to the lighting designer your rehearsal notes that affect lighting (see Chapter 8, "Production Notes"). In some cases, if the lighting is controlled by a man-

CUE	PRESET	FUNCTION																												V_1	V_2	V_3	V_4
☐																																		
COUNT ○	1	2	3	4	5	6	7	8	9	10	11	12	13	14	15	16	17	18	19	20	21	22	23	24	A	B	C	D	E	F				

CUE	PRESET	FUNCTION																												V_1	V_2	V_3	V_4
☐																																		
COUNT ○	1	2	3	4	5	6	7	8	9	10	11	12	13	14	15	16	17	18	19	20	21	22	23	24	A	B	C	D	E	F				

CUE	PRESET	FUNCTION																												V_1	V_2	V_3	V_4
☐																																		
COUNT ○	1	2	3	4	5	6	7	8	9	10	11	12	13	14	15	16	17	18	19	20	21	22	23	24	A	B	C	D	E	F				

CUE	PRESET	FUNCTION																												V_1	V_2	V_3	V_4
☐																																		
COUNT ○	1	2	3	4	5	6	7	8	9	10	11	12	13	14	15	16	17	18	19	20	21	22	23	24	A	B	C	D	E	F				

CUE	PRESET	FUNCTION																												V_1	V_2	V_3	V_4
☐																																		
COUNT ○	1	2	3	4	5	6	7	8	9	10	11	12	13	14	15	16	17	18	19	20	21	22	23	24	A	B	C	D	E	F				

CUE	PRESET	FUNCTION																												V_1	V_2	V_3	V_4
☐																																		
COUNT ○	1	2	3	4	5	6	7	8	9	10	11	12	13	14	15	16	17	18	19	20	21	22	23	24	A	B	C	D	E	F				

Figure 11.1 Lighting Cue Sheet for a Two-Scene Preset Control Board. Compare this form to Figure 3.6. Cue sheet forms that reflect the capabilities of modern boards can usually be obtained from the manufacturer.

ual board, the board operator would write out the cue sheet, hopefully roughed out prior to the tech.

Some operators like to work from 3" × 5" cards. Those who favor the cards say that it is so much easier to insert cues. If you work from cue sheets, in order to insert a cue, you have to cut the sheet and add another full sheet, then paste the partial sheets to full sheets. Those who oppose use of 3" × 5" cards say that they can get out of order too easily. A good compromise is to use 3" × 5" cards until dress rehearsal and then write out the sheets prior to opening night.

In a union theater the board operater is usually the master electrician, a member of the International Alliance of Theatrical and Stage Employees (IATSE).

In a nonunion theater, the board person is sometimes referred to as a lighting technician, light operator, electrician, light tech, or light board operator. Sometimes the community theater stage manager is asked to serve as board operator, but this is not desirable. You should give the cues (see Chapter 14) but should not handle the equipment. You need to be free to observe the results of all cues and you need to be able to react to the unexpected, as well as emergencies, without being tied to a specific piece of equipment.

The board person needs to know which channels to work for which cue, which direction, how far, and how fast. The lighting cue sheet gives the board person this information.

Some Commonly Used Terms

Bump up	Up as fast as possible; opposite of a blackout.
Fade up on a 5 count	Cue is brought in on a 5 count.
Cross-fade	Two cues are simultaneous, one coming in, one going out.
Lag fade	Start first cue, take second as soon as the first is perceptible.
Fade out (7)	Take cue on a count of 7.
Imperceptible fade (20)	Take cue so slowly that the change in effect is not noticeable.
Blackout	Take out as fast as possible, with 0 count on computer board or blackout switch on manual board.

Re-Gelling Plans/Instrument Schedule

You've just finished your light check. You found one lamp out in an instrument and one gel in a special-effects instrument so faded that it needs to be replaced. So you or an electrician climbs up the ladder to remove the old lamp, finds out what size it is, climbs down the ladder, finds a replacement lamp, climbs back up the ladder to put it in, then climbs up the ladder to get the gel frame from the light instrument, climbs down the ladder, holds the gel frame over the gel sheet, cuts out the new gel, and climbs up the ladder to replace the frame. Right?

Wrong. You completed your re-gelling plan/lighting schedule at the beginning of the season and you know the watts, base types, and gel sizes of every one of the 267 instruments without climbing the ladder to find out. Your re-gelling plan/lighting schedule is indexed into your prompt script (see Figure 11.2). And you have gel patterns (see Figure 11.3) so that you don't need the gel frame as a pattern. You can take your replacement gel and lamp up the ladder the first time and save yourself a trip.

INST#	TYPE	AREA PLAYED	HANG POSN	lamp watt type base	GEL SIZE	GEL COLOR	PLGNG	DIMMER

page ____ of ____ pages

RE-GELLING PLAN / LIGHTING SCHEDULE

Figure 11.2   Format for Re-Gelling Plan/Lighting Schedule

The main purpose of the re-gelling plan is to enable the lighting designer to tell the lighting technicians what color gels to put into what instruments. This form will expedite the turnover between shows. So you want to be sure that the form is on hand and filled in up to date.

You are usually responsible for supervising re-gelling for productions that run longer than the life of the gels, so it is desirable that you review the form with the lighting designer.

Gel Patterns

Gel patterns may be made of cardboard (see Figure 11.3). They are cut to the size of the gel frames used in your instruments. If you have spare gel

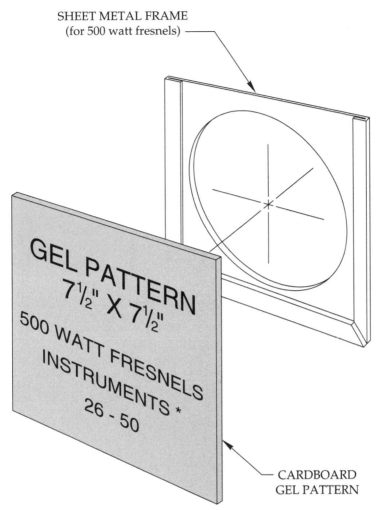

SHEET METAL FRAME
(for 500 watt fresnels)

GEL PATTERN
7½" X 7½"
500 WATT FRESNELS
INSTRUMENTS *
26 - 50

CARDBOARD
GEL PATTERN

Figure 11.3   Gel Pattern Template with Complete Labeling

frames on hand for all the different sizes used in your instruments, you can use the spares as patterns. The advantage of cardboard patterns is that you can easily write on them the numbers of the instruments that take the size. The cardboard patterns are also easier to handle.

In some theaters, cutting boards are premarked with the gel sizes commonly used. In still other theaters, gels are precut and filed in folders so that they don't curl.

Area Lighting Diagrams

The area lighting diagram or focus chart (see Figure 11.4) shows the areas on the stage where the instruments are focused. It may be expanded with notes and diagrams to remind you where certain focusing is critical—for example, the lighting designer wants an instrument shuttered so that the light is exactly on a door frame and there is no spill on adjacent flats.

In re-gelling instruments, or during other work near instruments, technicians sometimes accidentally jar the instruments out of focus.

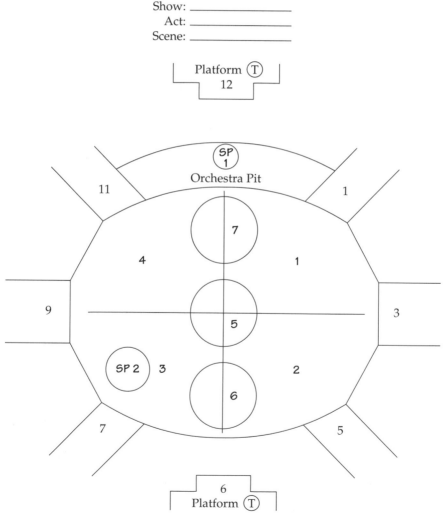

Figure 11.4   Area Lighting Diagram for Round Stage

Sometimes an instrument is not tightened sufficiently when initially focused and slips over a period of time. The area lighting diagram helps you prevent such occurrences from affecting the lighting quality in a performance.

The lighting designer usually makes a complex area lighting diagram for her or his own purposes. You can use the lighting designer's or copy the important aspects of it. But for the sake of your familiarity with the lighting design, it is better if you make your own and then review it with the lighting designer.

Control Boards

From candlelights to gas footlights, to electric bulbs, to dimmers, to control boards, to computerized control boards—the advances in technology of the theater come faster and faster. If the stage manager who retired when this book was first published were to return to a modern control booth, he or she would look around and say, "Where are the dimmer handles?" The long banks of dimmer handles that were either in the control booth or in the wings are gone. Instead, there are one or two CRTs (cathode ray tubes) and one or two control consoles that are not much larger than typewriters. Instead of two lighting technicians pulling on large resistance dimmer handles, one technician can execute a difficult cue with just the touch of a single button.

More than 30 companies in the United States manufacture a wide range of lighting control systems. Stage managers should be familiar with the technology.

To get a quick grasp of all systems, see Figure 11.5, "Lighting System Product Chain." It shows that the control console or board sends a signal to a dimmer that sends a measured amount of electricity to a luminaire (lighting instrument). Simple, isn't it?

I reap the benefits of the technology every time I call a show. Knowing that cue counts will be consistent, that you can "go to" any cue in a matter of seconds, and relying on disks rather than lost or out of order Q-sheets are a few of the many assets associated with computer boards from a stage manager's point of view. It also makes it a little less nerve-wracking when a substitute electrician comes in to know that all they have to do is push a button and not deal with a manual preset board or a flurry of patches.

Jill Johnson
Production Stage Manager
Long Beach Civic Light Opera
Long Beach, CA

LIGHTING SYSTEM PRODUCT CHAIN™

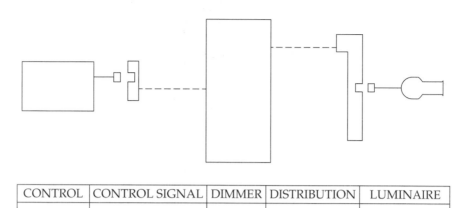

CONTROL	CONTROL SIGNAL	DIMMER	DISTRIBUTION	LUMINAIRE

Figure 11.5   Lighting System Product Chain. *Luminaire* is another word for lighting instrument or lighting unit.

Courtesy Steve Norman and Strand Lighting (www.strandlight.com).

Types of Control Boards

The types of control consoles vary. Generally they can be classified as manual, manual with memory, memory with manual, midrange memory, and high-capability (or high end or flagship) products.

Selecting the Right Control Board

Stage managers should understand the variety of boards available today (see Figures 11.6 and 11.7). If you make yourself knowledgable about control-room equipment, you make yourself more valuable to your theater's management team. Is your current control board ideal for your theater and/or the next production that you will mount? If your theater's management team is thinking of selecting a system or upgrading the current system, what factors would you want to bring to the attention of producer, lighting designer, and/or technical director that might influence their decisions?

    1. *Number of dimmers:* How many dimmers do you have in your theater now? You need a control system that will be able to handle your present dimmers plus any expansion that you foresee. Twenty-four dimmers should make it worthwhile and advantageous to move up from manual to memory-assisted, but this number is not written in stone.

    2. *Compatibility of dimmers:* Dimmers have protocols (or speak languages). The control console must have the same protocol as the dimmers

Figure 11.6 ETC's Microvision FX, a small board, is used to control 96 dimmers in the Black Box Theatre at Santa Clara University's Department of Theatre and Dance. David Sword, Production Manager, finds the board meets all demands placed on it by flexible staging possibilities. David is a graduate of Yale School of Drama and served on its faculty.

Courtesy David Sword and Santa Clara University Department of Theatre and Dance.

in order to speak to the dimmers. If your dimmers were purchased in the 1970s or earlier, it's possible that expensive interface equipment may be necessary in order to use those dimmers. Replacement of dimmers may be a cost factor in addition to the cost of the control system.

3. *Complexity of shows you produce:* If your theater is a community theater that does single-set light comedies with an occasional drama or musical, your needs are different from those of a theater that hosts touring musicals and rock concerts. If you repeat shows annually, this is an important factor. Some community theaters repeat the same Easter and Christmas shows every year. Wouldn't it be handy to store all the lighting information on a computer disk and restore it after a year, instantly?

4. *Personnel:* If your lighting designer, lighting technician, and stage manager are long term with your theater, they can be trained to use complex equipment effectively. If your personnel are new with every show, they have to be trained in use of equipment with every show. Will you be able to train them to use the equipment effectively?

5. *Cost:* When funding the upgrading of your lighting control, do not underestimate the cost of installation. It may be as great as the cost of the control equipment. Some systems require specially cooled, separate rooms

Figure 11.7   Light Operators Wendy Edmonds and Dale Intorf Use the Electronic Theatre Controls Insight 2X at the Mountain Community Theater in Ben Lomond, California. A grant from the Cultural Council of Santa Cruz County helped to obtain the equipment.

Courtesy Wendy Edmonds, Dale Intorf, and the Mountain Community Theater (www.mct-shows.com).

(usually adjacent to the control booth) for the dimmer banks. Will rewiring be required from dimmers to luminaires?

6. *Manufacturer/Distributor support:* Most manufacturers and distributors offer a one-year warranty. But the extent of their support beyond the warranty is a very important factor. Many distributors and manufacturers have display rooms where they can introduce you to the equipment and hold training sessions.

When comparison shopping, besides checking the specifications on Figure 11.8, it's a good idea to get a feeling for the equipment by actually using it. Ask the manufacturer/distributor for the name of a satisfied customer near you; then visit and talk.

Will the salesperson come to your theater to help you evaluate your needs? Is the equipment user-friendly? Is the manual easy to understand and follow? Is a customer service representative or sales representative available to answer questions by phone?

In the worst of emergency situations, would the distributor or manufacturer provide a loaner to replace down equipment?

7. *Speed:* Steve Norman of Strand Lighting points out that speed of use is a very important factor. How fast can the job of lighting design be done

Figure 11.8 Control Board Comparison Chart. These are some of the features you will want to assess when considering the purchase of a new control board.

FEATURES:	High-Capability	Mid-Range Memory	Memory with Manual	Manual with Memory	Manua
	P3000C EX+	P2000C Plus	Scene Master 60 XLC Plus	Status 24/48	Pack Master 24
Dimmers	1536	400	512	512	24
Channels	1000	400	60	48	24
Cues	447	390	200	120	2 Scene
Submasters	24	24	60	24	None
Bump Buttons	12	12	20	24	24
Time Faders	8	4	3	2	2
Maximum X/Y Fade Rates	999.9 Sec.	999.9 Sec.	999.9 Sec.	999.9 Sec.	120 Sec.
Fade Progress Indicators	Yes	Yes	Yes	Yes	Yes
Grand Master	No	No	Yes	Yes	Yes
Blackout Switch	No	No	Yes	Yes	Yes
Independent Master	No	No	No	No	Yes
Blind Record	Yes	Yes	Yes	Yes	n/a
Memory Lockout	Partial	No	No	Yes	n/a
Softpatch	Yes	Yes	Yes	Yes	n/a
Number of Shows	1	1	1	1	n/a
Proportional	No	No	No	No	n/a
Storage	3 1/2" Disk	3 1/2" Disk	3 1/2" Disk	EEPROM Card	None
0-10 VDC Analog	No	No	No	No	Yes
Strand SMX	No	No	No	No	No
AMX 192	Optional	Optional	Optional	Optional	No
Colortran MUX	Yes	Yes	Yes	Yes	No
DMX-512 (USITT Standard)	Yes	Yes	Yes	Yes	No
Kleigl K-96	No	No	No	No	No
Analog Input Switches	10 to 42	Up to 32	Up to 32	No	No
Effects Package					None
Number of Chases	Up to 99	Up to 99	Up to 99	Up to 24	n/a
Steps per Effect	Up to 99	Up to 99	Up to 99	Up to 48	n/a
Level Control	Yes	Yes	Yes	Yes	n/a
Rate Control	Yes	Yes	Yes	Yes	n/a
Sound Trigger	No	No	No	No	n/a
Proportional Steps	Yes	Yes	Yes	Yes	n/a
Accessories					
Printer	Yes	Yes	Yes	No	No
Display	2 Color CRT	1 Color CRT	1 Color CRT	LCD Display	No
Remote Monitor	Yes	Yes	Yes	No	n/a
Hand-Held Remote	Yes	Yes	Yes	No	No
Software Version	5.3	5.2	4.1	1.32	n/a

Courtesy of Colortran, Inc. (Colortran is now a division of NSI Corporation www.nsicorp.com.)

People who work at the theater come and go and generally have no experience. That is usually the case with our lighting operators. Therefore, it's imperative to have a system that is simple and quick to learn. Even as computerized as it is, with 56 preset scenes, I find that the people who are smart enough to use it, do not. They prefer to play with the lighting system. They like to push, flip and turn knobs during the production. I guess this creates a sense of being irreplaceable. Unfortunately, this approach increases the potential for inconsistency and mistakes during production.

Dale Williams
President, Board of Directors
Amarillo Little Theater
Amarillo, TX

on the equipment? Some equipment, usually high end, is designed from the point of view of both the lighting technician and the lighting designer.

Control Board Capabilities

The general capabilities and components of a lighting control system are listed in Figure 11.8. This chart was provided by Colortran, Inc., but the intent of this chapter is not to promote or compare products of various manufacturers. The intent of this chart is to inspire knowledgeable comparison shopping. Highlight the items that are critical to your needs when you compare the boards available to you.

Dimmers (Maximum)

The dimmer is the actual power device that controls one luminaire (but may control two or three using "twofers" or "threefers," depending on the capacity of the dimmer).

Channels

Each channel may have from one to many dimmers assigned to it and controls their level of intensity.

Cues (Maximum)

Each cue may control the intensity of one to all of the channels available—a single lighting look.

Submasters (Maximum)

Submasters allow the operator to group channels within a scene or cue.

Bump Buttons

Bump buttons are momentary buttons that bring the lights on a channel to instant full or preprogrammed intensity.

Time Faders

Time faders control the rate of fade. They are programmable to do the time counting for the operator.

Maximum X/Y Fade Rate

The maximum X/Y fade rate is the number of seconds over which a fade takes place.

Fade Progress Indicator

The fade progress indicator gives visual indication at the control board of fade that the operator may or may not be able to see on stage.

Grand Master

The grand master controls the overall intensity of all light levels.

Blackout Switch

The blackout switch provides instant blackout of all luminaires.

Independent Master

The independent master allows a particular channel or channels to be assigned to this fader for operation independent from group or scene masters. It controls any channels assigned to an "independent" status.

Blind Record

The blind record allows the operator to create a cue without actually changing the lighting on stage. It is sometimes called preview. You can also change a cue without seeing it.

Memory Lockout

Memory lockout makes it impossible to change cues while the equipment is in the show run mode.

Softpatch

Softpatch allows the assignment of dimmers to channels with the touch of buttons, as opposed to a hard patch.

Number of shows   Number of soft patches per show
Proportional   Dimmers can be patched to channels at a maximum level

Storage

Memory boards store information on disk, tape, or memory modules.

Output (Protocol)

Protocol is the language with which control boards communicate to dimmers.

0–10VDC   Basic analog protocol (one wire per dimmer from control)
Strand SMX   Strand Lighting's protocol, digital
AMX 192   Analog multiplexed
Colortran MUX   Colortran's protocol, digital
DMX 512   USITT's digital standard for the industry
Kleigl K–96   Kleigl's digital protocol

Analog Input Switches

Analog input switches are user-programmable switches that can cause a variety of actions to occur at the touch of a switch—also called *macros*.

Analog Input Channels

Analog input channels allow input from manual console to computer/memory console that has no manual slider control of channels.

Effects Package

Chase gives you the ability to do special-effects lighting with a single cue, such as having lightning flashes go from stage left to stage right. But this effect could be achieved without the built-in chase capability. So chase is an example of "bells and whistles" that may be available on the high end of lighting control boards. Do you need it? If you're the lighting designer for a touring rock group and want to include marquee-like lighting effects, I'm sure you do. If you need it, then you would want to consider the number of chases, steps per effect, level control (overall intensity of chase), rate control (speed of sequencing), sound trigger (allows board to respond to sound cues such as drum beats), and proportional steps (different levels of intensity for steps).

Accessories

Printer interface

The printer interface allows the control board to print out lighting data on an optional printer.

Display

Do you need to see your data in color, or will monochrome suffice? Some boards have LED displays, which may suffice but may be augmented with a monitor (CRT).

Remote monitor

The remote monitor allows the lighting designer or technician to access data from the audience, the stage, or the wings.

Hand-held remote

The hand-held remote allows for the input of cues as well as changes of cue or design from the audience, stage, or wings. It is especially useful for bringing up lights during focusing.

Software version

Some memory boards have updated their control programs since they initially went on the market. The software version number designates the latest program being used with the equipment.

Musical Instrument Digital Interface (MIDI)

Computers already have the ability to reproduce sound and play instruments, solo or in unison, record and edit music in the same way that word processors process words, and communicate with light boards. In terms of theater application, this means that sound and light cues can now be integrated into one program. Sound effects that were digitally stored on CDs can just as easily be stored on any computer memory device.

Some of the major manufacturers in the musical keyboard/computer industry agreed on a protocol called Musical Instrument Digital Interface (MIDI), which allows computers to communicate with a variety of instruments and synthesizers, just the way that DX512 allows control boards to communicate with a variety of dimmers. Some control boards are already MIDI compatible, which means that light and sound cues can be controlled through the same board.

Cost

The cost you pay is not the same as the basic advertised cost of equipment. Be sure to evaluate what optional capabilities and peripherals will cost, plus the cost of installation and any necessary rewiring. Is there already sufficient power available for the system you want to put in? Many dimmer banks contain fans that make noise. It's therefore desirable to place them in a room separate from stage and control booth. In some climates, banks of dimmers may even require additional cooling. Also, control boards, like computers, may require precautions against static electricity, such as static mats and ground lines. For outdoor theaters, how easily can the board be moved indoors for secure storage and protection against the elements? Factor in all related costs, down to additional locks, if necessary.

Audio Equipment

The purpose of audio equipment is to allow every member of the audience to hear every actor as if that actor were but a few feet away, the way we hear normal conversation. All music and every sound effect must also be heard clearly and at appropriate volume. If you are working in a 100-seat theater with only three rows of seats, you do not need microphones for the actors. You might need limited equipment for music and sound effects. If the acoustics of your theater are excellent (think ancient Roman theaters), and the actors can project, you do not need microphones. However, the acoustical problems inherent in the design of large theaters, as well as the complexities of balancing music and sound effects with actors' voices, make audio equipment essential.

The stage manager has limited responsibilities with regard to sound, but should understand some basics. The closer microphones are to lips and speakers are to ears, the fewer problems there are in sound systems. Think telephones for a moment: You might get a call from Hong Kong and hear the voice as if the speaker were right next to you. Note that the microphone is within inches of your lips and the speaker is pressed against your ear. As soon as you switch to speaker phone, you hear distortion. Sound people joke that they would love to surgically implant microphones in the noses of actors.

Microphones

Two types of microphones are dynamic and condenser. *Dynamic* mikes produce electronic data when sound causes a diaphragm to vibrate. They are generally more durable than condenser mikes. *Condenser* mikes use an electric field within the microphone to change sound waves into electronic data. When sound disturbs the electric field, a signal is generated. Condenser mikes are more sensitive and accurate, but less convenient to use because they require a power source (with some exceptions).

Microphones are designed for specific uses and placement. Lavaliere mikes attach to clothing. Wireless mikes produce a radio signal that's transmitted offstage to a receiver and relayed to the mixer. Floor mikes are designed to pick up both the sound of voices/instruments and the sound that bounces off the floor. Some microphones are even designed with modular components that allow the user to select the best configuration for the application.

Mixers

The mixer (audio control console) is the heart of the audio system (see Figures 11.9). Its function is to combine multiple sources into one or two outputs while controlling the level on all sources. Besides controlling which input device sounds will go to which output devices, it also allows sound designers to mix or layer sound effects. In a musical, it allows the sound operator to balance singers with the orchestra so that the singers are not drowned out. Some of the names in mixers are Mackie, Soundcraft, Spirit, and Yamaha (see Figures 11.10 and 11.11). For web addresses of these and other sound equipment manufacturers, see Appendix D.

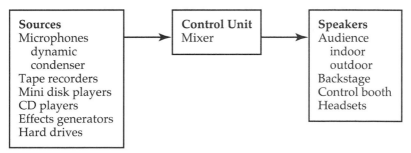

Figure 11.9 Audio Chain. Sources allow voice, music, and sound effects to enter the system as electronic data. The mixer switches, processes, and distributes the data. The speakers deliver the data to the audience by converting electronic data into sound. Auxiliary devices (pre-amps, amplifiers, equalizers) protect the system, carry the data, and help process the data. Auxiliary devices have been omitted from this diagram to keep it simple.

Figure 11.10   The Mackie SR24/4 Mixer Meets the Needs of the Mountain Community Theater in Ben Lomond, California. Sound designer Steve Edmonds works in a booth at the back of the house. He hears the actors the same way the audience in the last row hears them.

Courtesy Steve Edmonds and the Mountain Community Theater (www.mct-shows.com).

Speakers

The function of speakers is to convert electrical signals coming from the mixer via an amplifier into sound waves, usually done by vibrating a paper cone. Speakers may be designed to handle a specific range of frequencies. Selection of the size/power of a speaker and determination of placement are dependent on the acoustics of the room or auditorium; the acoustics are related to the size and shape of the room as well as the amount of sound-absorbing and reflecting materials in and/or on the walls, seats, and occupants.

Computers Used in Sound

Sound effects may now be edited by computer and stored on hard drives for immediate access and play. Recording or "burning" a sound effect onto a hard drive may take considerably more time than the playing time of the effect. Once placed in memory, however, the effect can be edited and cued

	SR24.4 VLZ PRO	SR32.4 VLZ PRO
Total channels	24	32
Buses	4	4
Mono channels	20	28
Stereo channels	2	2
Mic preamps XDR™	20 XDR™	28 XDR™
EQ (mono chs.)	3-band swept mid +low cut	3-band swept mid +low cut
EQ (stereo chs.)	4-band	4-band
Aux sends/ch.	6	6
Aux returns	4	4
Sub outputs	8	8
Channel inserts	20	28
Faders	60mm	60mm
Width	31.00"	39.25"

Figure 11.11   Mixer Comparison Chart: Mackie Models SR 24.4 and SR 32.4. The number of channels limits the number of microphones and input devices that can be used at once. A theater that produces musicals with wireless microphones for singers would need more channels than a theater that produces nonmusical plays.

Courtesy Mackie Designs, Inc. (www.mackie.com).

instantly (see Figure 11.12). Level Control Systems, in Sierra Madre, California, is one of the designers of sound systems that use computer software and hardware. For further information, go to www.lcsaudio.com.

Sound Effects

A wide range of sound effects are now available on CDs in collections of one to one hundred compact disks. They are available at many theatrical supply houses. Some of the providers are Sound Ideas, SFX, BBC Library, Hollywood Edge, and Digifects Library. Costs of sound-effect collections have come down to the point where many theaters can maintain a library to meet most of their needs. Some sound effects can be downloaded directly from the Internet. See Appendix D for a list of sound effect websites. Sound designers are still called on to design or locate effects that cannot be found in libraries. When all else fails, a sound designer can contact the Theatre Sound Mailing List (www.brooklyn.com/theatre-sound) to seek the help of other sound designers in locating or creating a sound effect.

Figure 11.12   Sound Designer Garth Hemphill at American Conservatory Theater, San Francisco, Uses Level Control Systems' RIF-108 Remote Fader Pack for the Supernova Computer Audio Control System. Setting up the sound designer's table in the house during tech rehearsals (1) allows the sound designer to hear sound as the audience will hear it and (2) allows the director to be in immediate contact.

Courtesy Garth Hemphill (www.glhdesign.com) and ACT San Francisco (www.act-sfbay.org).

Backstage Communications/Cueing Equipment

In equipment used to cue lights, sound, special effects, and other backstage personnel, there are two choices: voice communication or signaling lights. They may be used together in some cases. Some of the names in backstage communications are Clear-Com, Electronic Theatre Controls (ETC), Motorola, and Telex (see Appendix D).

In voice communication, the choices are wired and wireless. Wired beltpacks (see Figure 11.13) require jack plates or mike cables. Wireless units are more expensive and may be prone to interference.

Signaling lights used in ETC's Cue Light Controller system use jumbo LEDs with more than 100 individual LEDs contained in one lamp so as to prevent burnout that might disrupt a performance. A portable panel is available so that cues may be given from the house during tech and dress rehearsals. Theatre Projects Consultants is working with theater builders, producers, and stage managers to improve the design and utility of both the Cue Light Controller system and the Worklight Master Controller system (which regulates work lights, house lights, and blue running lights throughout a theater). For contact information of manufacturers of this equipment, see Chapter 18 and Appendix D.

Figure 11.13   Clear-Com Wired Intercom. The Belt Pack model RS-501 is connected with standard microphone cable. Theaters may be prewired with jack plates on the wall for intercom, or stand-alone microphone cables can be used to connect the belt packs with each other and the intercom main station/system power supply. Wireless models are also available. Sean McCullough, Theater Manager at Cabrillo College Visual and Performing Arts Department, has used several of Clear-Com's models over the years.

Courtesy Sean McCullough, Cabrillo College Visual and Performing Arts Division, and Clear-Com Intercom Systems (www.clearcom.com).

One Terrific Internet Source of Sound Information

The Theatre Sound Mailing List (www.brooklyn.com/theatre-sound) allows all persons interested in theater sound to exchange information very rapidly. You can read about "bugs" in specific equipment and how to overcome them, recommendations of certain equipment for specific applications, needs for sound effects with immediate response as to where to get or how to make that effect, and job openings. Kudos to Jim Bay for maintaining this site, which brings together sound designers, sound board operators, sound instructors, students of sound, and sound equipment manufacturers and distributors—over 600 people in 17 countries!

Worldwide there are hundreds of companies that manufacture audio equipment that will meet or exceed the needs of your theater, from control boards to microphones to speakers to backstage communications. Via the Internet, you have access to many of them. For a complete list of U.S. manufacturers, go to www.esta.org.

Sound Strategies

1. In becoming acquainted with your theater (see Chapter 5), clarify with the producer, director, technical director, sound designer, and sound board operator your responsibilities with regard to sound. (Will you distribute and collect microphones? Will you be responsible for replacing batteries in wireless mikes? If an actor's mike becomes inoperative during performance, who replaces it during intermission?) Inventory the theater's sound equipment. (Do you know where the manuals and/or warranties are? [Some manuals may be downloaded from www.mackie.com.] Do you know where equipment goes to be repaired?)
2. *Before* tech rehearsal, discuss the numbering of cues with the sound designer (see Chapter 14, page 212). If the sound designer was not aboard at the beginning of the rehearsal process, do not wait until the tech to review with the sound designer your initial sound plot (list of sound problems—see Figure 3.7) and your rehearsal notes that pertain to sound.
3. Do not talk to the sound designer or board operator while the producer, director, or cast members are talking to (yelling at) them. It's a pet peeve of sound designers.
4. If you want to increase your understanding of theater sound, the following two books are recommended: *Guide to Sound Systems for Worship* (Yamaha) and John Eargle's *Sound System Design Reference Manual* (which may be downloaded free from www.jblpro.com/pub/technote/ssdm_99.pdf).

Keeping Current

Developments in the technology of the theater come faster every year. The important thing is that stage managers keep current. In Chapter 18, in "Guides to Goods and Services," you will find several methods of plugging into the latest in lighting instruments, color media, control boards, audio equipment, and backstage communications. It's always exciting to find and apply technology that makes theater production easier.

Suggested Classroom Exercise

Lead students on an inspection of the light, sound, and cueing equipment in your theater. Discuss the age of the equipment and whether newer equipment would merit the cost in terms of the quality of future productions.

12

Supervision of Shifts

All things come to him who waits, but they come sooner if he goes out to see what's wrong.

—Anonymous

When working in the round, find a way to coordinate a stage crew of 15 in making scene shifts, striking an average of 5 props and 11 set pieces and setting as many—in 30 seconds—in the dark—every 12 minutes—for 1 hour and 35 minutes—for a total of 14 shifts. This is the type of a logistical problem that can make stage managers lose sleep and eat aspirins.

Shift Plot Charts

A shift plot chart (see Figure 12.1) is a device that will help you in planning and supervising scene shifts. Although this technique (and this example) is primarily applicable to productions in the round, it may also be used for complex shifts in any theater. The chart may be posted in the scene dock and prop area so that the crew can use it as a self-briefing aid.

Notice that the top row lists the scenes, the second row lists the cue that precedes the shift, and each row beneath describes an individual crew member's responsibility in each shift.

Make your shift plot chart BIG so that it is easily readable. Allow 2½" high by 3" wide rectangles for each separate entry. This allows you to make corrections conveniently by posting halves of 3" × 5" notecards over entries that must be changed.

Notice that each entry gives the following information (for an "in the round" production):

TAKE ME ALONG - ACT II	II - 1 BARROOM	II - 1 BALLET	II - 2 & 3 MILLER HOME
WARN CUE	PRESET	HE READS BOOK IN BED. THUS SPAKE ZARA-THUSTRA BLACKOUT	BALLET ENDS... BLACKOUT
GEORGE RAY IATSE 1	↓7 (4:00) STRIKE PIANO SET BIRDCAGE (12) SET BLKBOX (9) ↑7	1ST ↓5 ~~SET DESK (2:00)~~ STRIKE PIANO (W. BILL) ↑5	1ST ↓1 SET DESK (2:00) STRIKE FOGPOT (3) 1↑
DENNIS IATSE 2	↓7 SET BAR (10:00) STRIKE PORCH (7) ↑7 W/HAROLD	1ST ↓11 STRIKE BAR W/ HAROLD ↑$11	1ST ↓5 SET PORCH (5:00) W/HAL ↑7
HAROLD IATSE 3	↓7 10:00 SET BAR (W DENNIS) STRIKE PORCH (7) ↑7 W/DENNIS	2ND ↓11 STRIKE BAR W/ DENNIS 11↑	2ND ↓5 SET PORCH (5:00) W/DENNIS ↑7
BILL C.	↓7 W/MIKE SET PIANO & STOOL STRIKE CHAIR (2:00) TO RCH HALL	2ND ↓5 STRIKE PIANO W/GEORGE 5↑	3RD ↓7 SET WINDOW ST. (6:00) STRIKE CHAIR ↑&1
MIKE	↓7 (1:00) SET 2 CHAIRS STRIKE TABLE (3) TO RCH HALL	1ST ↓1 STRIKE TABLE ↑1	3RD ↓11 SET TABLE (11:30) & CHAIR ↑7
WALLY	GATE TENT	2ND ↓1 STRIKE 2 CHAIRS ↑1	~~2ND ↓11~~ ~~SET CHAIR (11:00)~~ ~~↑11~~ FLYMAN DROP BKT.
WAYNE	GUARD / INSIDE TENT	SET DRY ICE IN BUCKET (9:00)	3RD ↓11 SET STEPS (11:00) ↑11

Figure 12.1   Shift Plot Chart for Several Crew Members

1. Aisle traveled to reach the stage (e.g., 1st down *11;* the number 11 means the aisle at 11 o'clock if the stage is compared to the face of a clock with the orchestra pit at 12 o'clock).
2. Order number on which to travel (e.g., *1st* down 11; if a crew member is preceded by two others, she or he is "3rd down aisle"). Controlling order helps you to choreograph the change.
3. Set piece or prop carried on and location it is to be placed (e.g., "Set table at 11:00"). The location designator is not an exact one, but is used to refresh the runner's memory when used in conjunction with "before and after" diagrams. (See Figures 12.5 and 12.6.)

II - 4 BEDROOM	II - 5 & 6 BEACH	II - 7 & 8 MILLER HOME	AFTER PERFORMANCE
"STAYING YOUNG" reprise BLACKOUT	HELLO, OPERATOR PHONE LIGHT OUT	SCRUMPTIOUS SHORT: 9:00 REPRISE BLACKOUT	WHEN AUDIENCE OUT
2ND ↓1 (2:00) STRIKE DESK W/WAYNE ↑1	3RD ↓1 SET LOG CTR. ↑7	1ST ↓1 SET DESK (2:00) WITH JOHN ↑1	STRIKE LAMP (4:30) UNPLUG
2ND ↓7 SET PLATFORM W/HAROLD (ctr.) ↑5	1ST ↓11 STRIKE PLAT. W/HAL ↑7	1ST ↓5 STRIKE LOG W/HAL ↑7 DURING SCENE MOVE TROLLEY INTO POSIT.	STRIKE LAMP (11:30) UNPLUG
3RD ↓7 SET PLATFORM W/DENNIS ↑5	1ST ↓3 SET PLATFORM W/DENNIS ↑7	2ND ↓5 STRIKE LOG ↑5 HAVE TROLLEY TO POSITION	STRIKE PLUG (11:30)
4TH ↓7 SET BED OPER. W/MIKE STRIKE F.PLACE ↑7	2ND ↓7 SET FIREPLACE (9:00) ↑11	2ND ↓5 SET WINDOW SEAT (6:00) ↑5 PULL TROLLEY	
1ST ↓7 SET BED W/ BILL COOK ↑7	1ST ↓11 (11:30) SET TABLE (11:00) & CHAIR ↑7 AFTER WINDOW SEAT IN	↓11 STRIKE F.PLACE (9:00) PULL ↑11 TROLLEY	UNPLUG (11:30)
4TH ↓1 STRIKE LOG ↑1	3RD ↓11 (11:00) SET STEPS ↑11	↓11 SET LAMP (11:00) PLUG IN ← STRIKE TABLE (11) ↑11	
1ST ↓1 STRIKE CHAIR ↑1	3RD ↓7 SET 6:00 LWR. RAIL W/HAL ↑7	↓11 SET SMLL. PLG. STRIKE CHAIR ↑11	

Figure 12.1 *(Continued)*

4. Set piece or props to be struck, and destination if other than the scene dock and prop area (e.g., "Leave at top of aisle 11 for use in Sc. 5").
5. Aisle to exit.
6. Order to exit is designated rarely—when more than one large set piece must move up the same aisle, or when fast-traveling light pieces must precede slow-moving heavy pieces to expedite the shift.
7. If more than one crew member handles a single set piece, the names of the other crew members working on that unit are listed so that

each crew member knows with whom she or he is to work (e.g., "with Roy").

8. If errors were made at any performance, you may put special cautions in an entry rectangle (e.g., "Watch out for hanging mike hit on opening night"). Other cautions might concern a false blackout or the rapid succession of two cues (e.g., "Hustle back to prop table for next shift").

Normally you wait until the take-in (see next section) to make up the chart because you must know definitely and exactly where the set pieces will play. Since the chart takes so much time to make, it is advisable to lay it out in advance, filling in the first column (crew members), the top row (scenes), and the second row (cues) well in advance of the take-in.

At the take-in, you see all the set pieces on stage for the first time. You should handle each piece. How much does it weigh? Should more than one person be assigned to carry it? Can it be picked up easily or should handles be added? Should wheels be built onto it or can it be moved on a dolly? Can it be carried in some other way than intended—upside down, sideways? Should it be cut in two, carried down in sections, and fastened together during the shift? Does it have sharp protruding edges that might be a safety hazard?

At the take-in, you also make changes in your scene diagrams to indicate the exact placement of each set piece as determined by the set designer. There may be still more changes during the dress rehearsal, and you must continue to update your diagrams and call changes to the attention of the crew via the chart.

Immediately following the take-in you should be ready to make your chart. The best way to do this is by using cutouts of paper for the set pieces. Actually move the paper set pieces as you calculate who should move what and when. It is a fairly complex problem and errors are easy to make.

When there is time and money to allow for a crew rehearsal, all of the errors may be worked out by repeating shifts until they are "greased." (Also see "Crew Briefing" later in this chapter.) But, as often happens, when crew rehearsal and dress rehearsal are simultaneous and the producer must justifiably use all available time for the cast and orchestra, which the audience will see and hear, rather than for the crew, which the audience should not see or hear, shifts must be corrected and "greased" by debriefing—that awkward process of trying to talk through what happened and visualize what changes should be made. The shift plot chart and the scene diagrams are invaluable in this process.

What sometimes happens in a union situation is that after Act I and part of Act II have consumed the entire dress rehearsal call, the producer opts to finish the rehearsal by putting the cast and orchestra on overtime; but the union crew members are sent home in order to save money. You then carry out the remaining shifts with any hands available, and find yourself in the unenviable position of running some of the shifts with actual personnel involved for the first time on opening night—briefing union crew members during the scene for their moves at the end of the scene. Can you imagine the pressured chaos? The preciseness and accuracy of your shift plot chart are really significant factors in running those "no rehearsal" shifts.

The chart should be posted prior to the first crew rehearsal, and each member of the crew should jot down her or his moves from the chart to avoid checking the chart between each scene shift. This can save a lot of walking if she or he has two consecutive moves up and down an aisle that is 180 degrees away from the aisle leading to the scene dock.

If you wish, you can issue each crew member a complete strike/set order (see Figure 12.2). This order would take the place of the individual crew member's notes and theoretically make it unnecessary to post the shift plot chart. Unfortunately, this type of strike/set order gets lost or left

			TAKE ME ALONG
SET/STRIKE ORDER for George Spelvin (IATSE 1)			
ACT SCENE CUE	ENTER	SET/STRIKE/DO	EXIT
Preset		Set desk 2:00 Lay trolley track.	
I-2 "Oh, Please" reprise!!!!! blackout	First down one	Set porch rail 3:00 Strike desk 2:00 with Wayne	Up One
I-3 "I wish we still belonged to England." blackout	Second down Five	Set Lamp 4:30 PLUG IT IN!!!!!!!!!!!! Strike porch rail (to rehearsal hall, not scene dock)	Up One

Figure 12.2 A Strike/Set Order with Typical Entries

in other clothing. Then the crew member has to have some reference from which to copy. So you still need the chart.

Take-In

Coordinating with the scene designer and technical director, you share in supervision of the take-in. The *take-in* is a procedure in which all the set pieces and scenery are brought from storage, the shop, and the scene dock and set up on stage for the first time. This allows the scene designer, technical director, and you to assess your progress and problems in turning the scene designer's sketches into illusion.

Your responsibility is to get enough hands out to move the scenery quickly so that the take-in can be completed as soon as possible without wearing out the participants. As usual, many hands make light work.

Your work during the take-in has been described earlier as part of your preparation for making the shift plot chart (Figure 12.1). Again, you must personally handle all the set pieces and scenery so that you know what problems your crew members will encounter.

Crew Briefing

Generally, you brief the whole crew prior to their first rehearsal.

1. Introduce crew members to one another and explain that you expect them to work as a team.
2. Cite general problems.
   a. Audience moving during blackouts.
   b. Hitting mikes with set pieces.
   c. Too much talking among crew during scenes, thus distracting audience.
   d. Necessity of crew members staying out of tent or backstage area during scenes.
   e. Necessity of having all props, set pieces, and scenery in the scene dock prior to the show, during intermissions, and after the show so that everything is out of sight of the audience and not a safety hazard.
3. Explain clock system (for round theater) or stage areas if necessary, set diagrams, and shift plot chart.
4. Review safety rules.
   a. Don't run.
   b. Pointed set pieces should be moved base first so as not to spear audience members.
5. Review dress and behavior expected of crew.
   a. Don't mingle with audience.

b. Don't call attention to self.

A handout to the crew is helpful in passing on important points that you've learned from experience (see Figure 12.3).

Scene Dock

The scene dock is the area in which sets and props are stored while waiting to be placed on stage (see Figure 12.4).

```
                        ATTENTION CREW

1. Shake hands with your new crew members. The crew is a team. Everyone
   must know everyone else — and be able to depend on him.

2. Think of the stage as a clock. The orchestra pit is at 12 o'clock.
   Aisles 1, 3, 5, 7, 9, and 11 are relative — one o'clock, three
   o'clock, etc.

3. The shift plot chart and diagrams of "before and after" positions of
   all props, set pieces and scenery are located above and on the prop
   table. Study them at your conv. If you don't understand, ask the SM,
   George Spelvin, or IATSE crew chief, Nate Spelvin, to explain it to
   you.

4. Follow these rules PLEASE!
   A. Don't run.
   B. Crouch at the bottom of aisles behind sight lines anticipating
      the blackout noiselessly.
   C. Watch out for audience moving on blackouts.
   D. Don't hit hanging mikes with tall units.
   E. Stay out of the tent when not doing your thing.
   F. Stash all props and units in scene dock prior to intermission
      and after show so that audience can't trip over them.
   G. Move pointed  units base first so as not to stab audience
      members.
   H. Don't mingle with audience during intermission.
   I. Don't call attention to yourself.
   J. No talking or noise while you work or wait.
   K. Report any accident to the SM.

5. Please wear black polo shirts and black full length pants. Black
   tennis shoes and sox are available (free) from the costume mistress.

6. Maintain a clear aisle of 2' in front of the prop table. Don't set
   any units on that area painted yellow.

7. Report any damage to any prop or unit to the property master or crew
   chief as soon as practical.

8. Check each night for red markings on the shift plot chart. Changes
   in your strike/set duties are indicated by the entire rectangle out-
   lined in red. Study the change and discuss it with the crew chief.
   Red X's indicate errors made; red cautions advise you how to prevent
   repetitions of the error.

9. You are expected to check in with the gate man at 7:45 pm SHARP!
   Don't be late. In case of emergency, call the theater, 555 3558, and
   leave a message with the box office.
```

Figure 12.3   Handout of Instructions to Crew

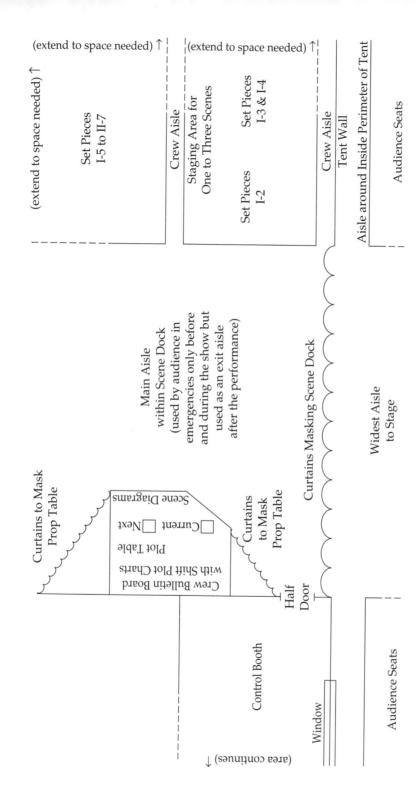

Figure 12.4 Scene Dock Layout

During the first crew rehearsal you should delegate the responsibility for arranging the scene dock. Perhaps the crew chief or a particularly alert crew member can do it. Depending on the space inside the scene dock, the arrangement of scenery and set pieces must be controlled so that everything is accessible when needed. If a crew member needs a set piece that is blocked by other units, she or he must climb over the other units and unnecessarily expend time and energy. The person placed in charge of arranging the scene dock should supervise the placement of returning sets just as carefully as you supervise their placement on stage.

Here are the factors to consider in designing your scene dock:

1. The main aisle within the scene dock should not be wider than the widest aisle down to the stage, but just as wide.
2. The width of the set piece staging areas should be just slightly less than the widest aisle.
3. The smaller aisles within the scene dock should be just wide enough for crew members to stand in.
4. Lines delineating the set piece storage areas should be painted on the ground.
5. Curtains masking the scene dock should open to the width of the widest aisle to the stage.
6. The scene dock should be as close as possible to the control booth so that the stage manager and the crew chief can communicate rapidly.
7. Set pieces for Act I, Scene 1 may be stored outside the tent and then brought into the main aisle of the scene dock if there are to be rehearsals on stage. Otherwise, they may be preset for the next performance after the audience departs.
8. Depending on the size and number of set pieces, they may have to be stored as far away as the shop or other storage areas and then rotated into the scene dock during scenes.
9. The scene dock should be covered in case of rain.

Shift Inspection

During the shift, you or your assistant should be on stage to supervise. If possible, do not assign yourself anything to carry in the shift. Keep your hands free to cope with emergencies. Attach your flashlight to your belt. Follow the crew onto the stage. Stay out from under their feet and watch carefully what they do. Check the placement of scenery, set pieces, and props. Make sure that every item from the previous scene is struck. Check that all actors who are to be discovered are in place. Check that all crew members have left the stage. For a round theater production, signal the booth, usually by blinking your flashlight from the stage, that you are ready for light and sound. Dash offstage or up the aisle as the scene commences. You should be the last person to leave the stage before the performance resumes.

Do you think you can do all of that in less than 30 seconds? Practice.

Scene Shift Diagrams

Diagrams of every scene can help if there are many scene shifts and many crew members. These diagrams are a visual aid that will help prepare crew members for their journeys down and up the aisles in a theater in the round (see Figures 12.5 and 12.6) or offstage to the scene dock. These sketches allow crew members to check their next move and refresh their memories as to the exact location and specifications for the placement of props, set pieces, and scenery.

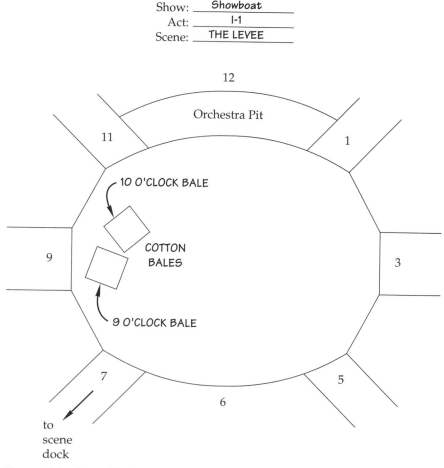

Show: _____Showboat_____
Act: _____I-1_____
Scene: _____THE LEVEE_____

Figure 12.5 Scene Shift Diagram: First Scene

Show: _____Showboat_____
Act: _____I-2_____
Scene: ___THE KITCHEN___

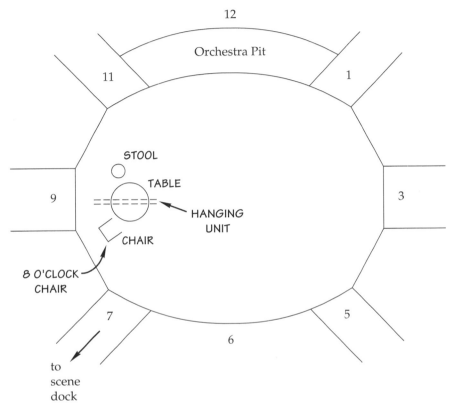

Figure 12.6 Scene Shift Diagram: Second Scene

Post these diagrams in the crew areas so that only two at a time are visible. Rotating your diagrams in "current" and "next" positions, rather than posting all of the diagrams at once, avoids confusion.

Let's look at an example. The following discussion refers to a theater-in-the-round production of *Showboat*—Act I, Sc. 1, The Levee (Figure 12.5), and Act I, Sc. 2, The Kitchen (Figure 12.6).

The shift from Scene 1 to Scene 2 calls for the dropping of the hanging unit, the striking of two cotton bales, and the setting of a stool, table, and chair—not considering props. How will you assign your crew to accomplish this one shift? Study the diagrams for a moment.

Here are some considerations:

1. If there is an experienced flyman on the crew, she or he should drop the hanging piece.

2. Since the table is large, two men should be assigned to it and it should move down aisle 7, the widest aisle and the aisle closest to the scene dock, thus eliminating carrying the table around the outside perimeter of the theater.
3. It is generally most efficient for one crew member to both strike and set a piece. But in this situation, since there are so few set pieces to be moved, there will be hands available to do the change more efficiently by having one crew member strike only and one crew member set only.
4. Usually the fewer crew members used for a scene the better, as they have a tendency to run into one another in the dark.

In this case, a stool is to play where a cotton bale is now set. If one crew member is assigned to set the stool and strike the cotton bale, she or he has to do the following: (1) run the stool down the aisle, (2) set it down, (3) pick up the cotton bale and move it aside, (4) pick up the stool and put it in place, (5) pick up the cotton bale and run it up the aisle. Yes, the move could be made this way, but evaluate the time and noise factors.

Or, you might have two crew members take care of the previously cited units, with an empty-handed striker going first to pick up the cotton bale ahead of the crew member who sets the piece that goes in its place. The striker might creep halfway down the aisle prior to the blackout and have the bale well offstage by the time the setter got her or his piece down to the stage.

Or, you may have the chair setter, not the crew member carrying the stool, place the chair at 8 o'clock and strike the 9 o'clock bale, to be followed by the crew member who places the stool. (Note that it is the 9 o'clock bale, not the 10 o'clock bale, that is blocking the placement of the stool. A set piece is designated as the "X" o'clock set piece according to its most easily discernible, if not exact, clock position. Finer designations, such as the "9:35 cotton bale," just don't seem to work.)

To stay neat and professional I would never suggest shining a flashlight from the stage in the round to cue the booth. Too many customers can see the effort. Find a way to cue that is hidden from the audience.

Leonard Auerbach
Associate Professor, Department of Theatre Arts
State University of New York at Stony Brook

[A green gelled flashlight might be a bit less conspicuous. Or, if you can afford high tech, how about a voice-activated FM transmitter headset? Any other suggestions are welcome.]

By now you can see that this simple-looking scene change needs thorough evaluation if it is to be done efficiently. These are the kinds of details that you will work out with diagrams and paper cutout set units as you make your shift plot chart.

You must also cope with the movement of cast members. If at the end of I-1, the lights faded on two cast members standing next to the cotton bales, and if in I-2, two different cast members are discovered seated on the stool and chair, then there is the additional consideration of four traveling cast members during the blackout.

The general practice is to specify certain aisles or wing exits for cast exits whenever possible. For entrances, cast members usually follow crew members down the other aisles. During rehearsals you may remind the director to channel cast via aisles reserved for cast exits. When this is not possible for any special reason, you should note it and accommodate unusual cast exits in planning your scene shifts.

It is practical to select the narrower aisles for cast exits, as they are less convenient for moving large set pieces. Also consider the location of tent poles or other major fixtures in the aisles.

The importance of remembering exit blocking should be stressed to the cast. Obviously, a cast member who dashes up a darkened aisle in a rush to make a quick change, only to find herself or himself blocked, does not need to be told twice.

Audience Caution

Members of the audience are usually cautioned in the program to remain seated during blackouts. In many theaters-in-the-round, the caution is repeated on the public address system prior to the performance. This responsibility usually rests with the house manager.

Distribution of Scene Diagrams

As soon as the scene designer has completed his or her design, scene diagrams should be made. Haste in this matter should take precedence over accuracy. In the course of building the set pieces and scenery there may be many changes. When the units are gathered all together on stage for the first time at the take-in and the scene designer sees what the set really looks like, as compared to the original perspective sketches, there are likely to be more changes, both in number and arrangement of units.

Yet if you wait until the take-in to make your diagrams, you might find yourself quite rushed. It is much more expedient to make corrections on diagrams with a bold marking pen than to wait for perfect initial copies.

Diagrams can be used at staff meetings to help everyone understand the sets for the coming production. The scene designer, technical director, master carpenter, property person, stage manager, and assistant stage manager should all be issued a complete set. The producer's secretary tucks still another set into his or her files for coming seasons when the show might be repeated.

The property person uses her or his copies for preset diagrams of props.

The stage manager and the assistant stage manager use their copies to help work out their shift plot chart. They note the cast members discovered in each scene and the special-effects lighting that is initiated during rehearsals.

The technical director and the master carpenter use their diagrams to augment perspective sketches and line drawings to understand where units are to play.

The making of the diagrams is normally a responsibility of the scene designer (but they have been developed with the director's and your views in mind). You merely see to it that the diagrams are duplicated and distributed.

Upkeep of Sets

After opening night you are responsible for upkeep and minor emergency repair of scenery, set pieces, and lighting equipment. You are not expected to reupholster a couch or overhaul a dimmer, but you are expected to patch, shore up, glue together, and generally keep the set fit for the eyes of the audience and the comfort and safety of the cast.

You must always have the tools on hand to carry out this function. Check to see that you have access to appropriate tools.

In the absence of a staff technical director, you might find yourself responsible for the theater's tools. If so:

1. Provide a secure, locked area for storage. Disappearance and theft can thus be considerably reduced. Temporarily, the trunk of a car can serve for tool storage if there is no lockable space in the theater building.
2. No matter how small your tool collection is, it is desirable to make a tool board on which each tool is mounted and outlined or silhouetted. This allows you to determine easily which tools are not in place. It is also convenient since you can always expect to find your tools in the very same place (see Figures 12.7 and 12.8).
3. Painting all of your tools one color can also help to deter loss as there is no possible confusion as to whose tools they are.

Figure 12.7 A Well-Designed Tool Board. Note that orange paint was used to draw pictures of the tools on the pegboard wall. This allows student crews to return tools to the same place every time, and ensures that needed tools are where they are supposed to be. It also allows Production Manager David Sword of Santa Clara University's Department of Theatre and Dance to see if any tools have not been returned at the end of a work call.

Courtesy David Sword and Santa Clara University Department of Theatre and Dance.

Example

When transient crews come in to work, they sometimes walk off with tools, thinking that the tools are theirs. At an all-girls school the tools were painted pink on the theory that no self-respecting transient male would steal a pink tool.

In nonprofessional companies where the actors are called on to help build and paint scenery, you can save the company money by closely supervising the cleanup after work calls. This ensures that tools are returned, brushes properly cleaned, and paint cans tightly closed.

Close supervision in the proper use of tools can also prevent damage to the tools and to the users.

You should keep on hand small quantities of the paints used on the set so that you can do touch-up work without having to buy fresh paint that matches the original. Sometimes this merely means having the wisdom to save nearly empty cans of paint until the close of the production. Date your paint cans.

Figure 12.8   Well-Organized Tool Cabinets. Anya Finke, Assistant Theater Manager, Cabrillo College Visual and Performing Arts Division, points to the staple guns shelf in a series of tool storage cabinets. The signs on the inside and outside of the cabinets allow student crew members to find equipment without opening all cabinets and replace equipment so that it can be found next time it's needed. Well-labeled locking cabinets are a good alternative to open tool boards when greater security is needed.

Courtesy Anya Finke and Cabrillo College Visual and Performing Arts Division.

Suggested Classroom Exercise

Using the scene shift charts (Figures 12.5 and 12.6), have the class plan the shift and write on a chalkboard in the format shown in Figure 12.1 what each member of a seven-person crew would do during the shift.

13

Running the
Technical Rehearsal

The only place where a person answers the phone and never gets
a wrong number is the theater.

—Anonymous

The purpose of the technical rehearsal is to make a final confirmation and integration of all light and sound cues, special effects, scene changes, and curtain pulling. Every mechanical effect that should happen during the performance should happen at the technical rehearsal, and just the way it is to happen in performance.

It is during the "tech" that you will probably move from the director's side to your work area, usually in the wings, but possibly in a booth behind the audience.

Traditionally, the tech is the time when actors stand around, holding positions while lights are refocused, or endlessly repeating cue lines until sound cues are tightened and sound levels are set. It is usually a rehearsal at which overtime runs long and tempers run short. It need not be so.

The actors, who have rehearsed for weeks, meet the crew, who have possibly never rehearsed. The cast is impatient. They want to do their thing. They can't understand why the director, technical director, and stage manager are now giving their complete attention to the minutiae of mechanical matters that are totally insignificant compared to their performances. So think the actors. They can't understand why the crew can't get things right the first time.

You can most effectively shorten and sweeten the tech by holding a separate crew, and crew only, rehearsal of all the cues and scene changes prior to the tech—sometimes called a *paper tech*. Many of the problems of the tech can then be ironed out in advance. The crew will be able to do the work involved in smoothing out cues without the cast looking on.

The real purpose of the technical rehearsal should be coordination and integration of light, sound, special effects, and scene changes, not the initial attempt at each. The tech should *not* be used to finish the design or devise the effects. If this distinction can be kept in mind—and if time, money, and union rules will allow you to hold a separate crew-only rehearsal prior to the tech—you will be doing a great service to the director, producer, and play by supervising that separate crew rehearsal.

If this is not possible, your burden increases with respect to planning the tech, anticipating problems, and briefing crew members.

The perfect tech is one in which the actors can have the benefits of a run-through while all technical aspects are polished as the play is in progress, or during breaks and intermissions.

This calls for good communications. If the director can talk to you, as well as the technical director, lighting designer, costume designer, and other staff members without noisily interrupting the tech, it will go more smoothly.

Sometimes the seating arrangement of the staff can help. If staff members who do not absolutely have to be backstage will sit in the audience in the row in front of the director, she or he can simply lean forward to whisper comments. All staff members should have paper and pencil. You should provide them with adequate light so that they can take notes.

Since you have moved to your work area, be it backstage or booth, the director must be able to talk to you without running or shouting. You should try to set up whatever communications are necessary.

Many theaters do not have adequate communications. Sometimes you can improvise. Two prop phones in working order, sound wire, and a battery can be hooked up to give you some link. Of course, headsets would be an improvement.

You will usually need to talk to the lighting board technician, the sound technician, follow spot operator, curtain puller, and others during the tech and during performances (see Chapter 11). Ideally, you should be able to talk to them via headsets. You should also be able to speak to the dressing rooms and the green room without leaving your work area. (A P.A. system that would allow you to reach the entire audience from your work area in case of an emergency, monitor equipment enabling cast to hear the performance in the dressing rooms and green room, and a phone would round out most of your communications needs.) In our age of technology, it is surprising that theater communications have been so neglected that these amenities are usually lacking or inadequate.

When planning for and scheduling your tech rehearsal, plan to give the staff, cast, and crew as much time as possible to work together. Any business other than the prime function of the tech should be relegated to other rehearsals. Directors should accept the fact that the tech is not the time to reblock or polish acting performances.

Cast members should be warned well in advance that they must expect to work late and that they must stay through to the end of the rehearsal.

There is a tendency for the crew to be concerned with their personal comforts and accommodations during the tech. Yes, it is important that the technician on the follow spot have a light in order to follow book. Yes, she or he should have a comfortable chair, since she or he has to sit there throughout the performance. Maybe she or he needs a pillow, too. And it would be desirable to run a phone line to her or him so that the two of you can talk to one another. But the period of the tech is not the time to take care of these things. They should be seen to before or after, but not while a cast of 20 and staff of 10 are waiting to rehearse.

Communications, lighting, seating, and other crew necessities and comforts should be anticipated and arranged. If these things cannot be worked out at a separate crew rehearsal, give your crew an early call for the tech and take care of these things before the cast and staff arrive (see Chapters 11 and 12).

It is a good practice for you to run the tech by yourself, giving all cues to cast and crew as if it were opening night. If the show can be run as a run-through, do so, stopping only when technical problems make it impossible to go on. In the case of a very heavy technical show, you may wish to skip from technical effect to technical effect instead of running through. In either case, it is important that you have all of your cues clearly marked in your prompt script and all supporting paperwork—scene shift diagrams, shift plot charts (see Chapter 12), light tech's lighting sheet (see Chapter 11), and so forth—distributed and reviewed with those concerned prior to the tech.

In some cases, you may start your tech rehearsal as a run-through and then, seeing that you are falling behind, skip through the remainder of the show from tech effect to tech effect.

There is no such thing as a cue-to-cue technical rehearsal in opera. The ASMs and volunteers, who have been told in advance not to wear white or black, "walk lights." The cue-to-cue is done with them, and not the cast. The "walk lights" call precedes the technical rehearsal. During the technical rehearsals the lighting designer will smooth out the lighting cues as the show goes along.

David Grindle
Production Stage Manager
The Atlanta Opera

If time permits, it is desirable to schedule two technical rehearsals as a safety factor.

The technical rehearsal is one of the biggest tests of your ability, for it is the one single rehearsal where you can save the cast and staff the greatest amount of time and energy.

Few fledgling stage managers have the good sense to rig a fail-safe cue light—two bulbs at the receiving end of the cable so that if one blows the other will probably still function.

> Leonard Auerbach
> Associate Professor, Department of Theatre Arts
> State University of New York at Stony Brook

Suggested Classroom Exercise

Ask one student to shadow a stage manager during a technical rehearsal and report to the class what the SM did, what problems arose, and how those problems were overcome.

14

Running the Show

There are three kinds of people in the world—those who make things happen, those who watch things happen, and those who say, "What happened?"

—Anonymous

Now comes the easy part—the production phase.

The director tells you that it's all yours. There's an audience out there. All you have to do is run the show. You have some long-range responsibilities (see Chapter 16), but your basic functions should now be firmly under control.

An interesting difference between new and experienced stage managers is that the new stage manager thinks of running the show as the most difficult and most demanding part of the job, whereas the experienced stage manager thinks of it as the most relaxing part. Perhaps the reason is that the experienced stage manager has built up work habits that make her or him so thoroughly prepared for the production phase that she or he just sits back during performances to watch that preparation pay off.

Checklists

Precurtain, intermission, and postproduction checklists will help you remember all the little things you must do. These checklists should be placed into your prompt script facing the first page of dialogue and following the last page of dialogue of each act.

A good approach is to think of someone replacing you immediately. Write out your list as if you were telling someone else what to do. List the items in the sequence in which you perform them. Don't be afraid to be too detailed (see Figures 14.1 and 14.2).

```
                        Precurtain Checklist

7 P.M.    turn on air conditioning
Dusk      turn on marquee
7:30      check crew present, call late ones
          conduct light, sound check (incl. bell, buzzer)
          unlock props, place on prop tables
          unlock stage door, sweep alley, empty butt cans
          unlock dressing rooms, turn on lights, check paper
          supplies
7:55      final check of stage: sweep it, all set pieces in
          place, all discovered props in place, set hands of
          clock (UR) to 3:45 and check wound
          check all set pieces and props in correct positions
          backstage, ready for changes
          turn off work light, masking tape over switch
          bring in curtain warmers, house lights, cue start
          of taped music
          turn house over to house manager
8:00      give half hour call, check sign-in sheet (post
          new one on Wednesdays), chat with cast, close
          curtain to green room
8:05      call late actors
8:15      turn on stage monitor, give 15 minute call,
          check monitor working in dressing rooms
8:25      give 5 minute call, blink marquee lights
8:30      await house manager's signal to call places (or
          give hold to cast) - call places
```

Figure 14.1   Detailed Precurtain Checklist and Schedule

Leave space between entries so that you can make last-minute additions in sequence.

When you arrive at the theater, open your prompt script to your checklist and mentally check off each entry as you accomplish it. That way, when you call "places," there won't be that aggravating question in the back of your mind: "What have I forgotten?"

In stock companies where you do a new show every week or two weeks, each day may bring both a rehearsal and a performance. Instead of prerehearsal and precurtain checklists, you will want to write out daily checklists covering your procedure for each day.

Your checklists, even if geared to a specific production rather than a season of plays, would be good material to pass on to the person who succeeds you.

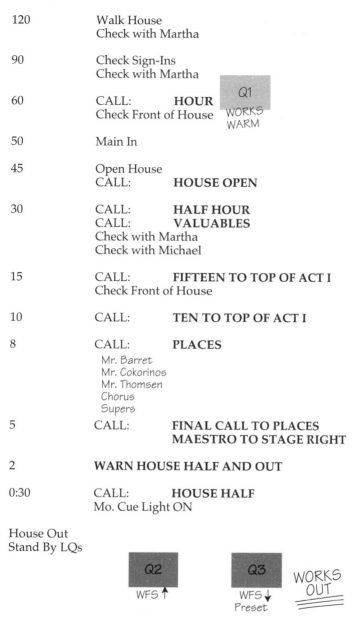

120	Walk House Check with Martha
90	Check Sign-Ins Check with Martha
60	CALL: **HOUR** *Q1 WORKS WARM* Check Front of House
50	Main In
45	Open House CALL: **HOUSE OPEN**
30	CALL: **HALF HOUR** CALL: **VALUABLES** Check with Martha Check with Michael
15	CALL: **FIFTEEN TO TOP OF ACT I** Check Front of House
10	CALL: **TEN TO TOP OF ACT I**
8	CALL: **PLACES** Mr. Barret Mr. Cokorinos Mr. Thomsen Chorus Supers
5	CALL: **FINAL CALL TO PLACES** **MAESTRO TO STAGE RIGHT**
2	**WARN HOUSE HALF AND OUT**
0:30	CALL: **HOUSE HALF** Mo. Cue Light ON

House Out
Stand By LQs

Q2 WFS ↑   *Q3* WFS ↓ Preset   *WORKS OUT*

Figure 14.2 *Cosi Fan Tutte* Preshow Checklist/Calls. "Main in" is curtain closed. "Valuables call" allows cast members to store watches, wallets, and other valuables in large freezer bags that are kept in a secure place. Post-it notes are used for cues in the checklists, libretto, and score. Light cues are in green; places cues are in blue.

Courtesy David Grindle, PSM, The Atlanta Opera.

A few items on your checklists deserve special comment.

Sweeping the stage, including the backstage walkways between the dressing rooms and the stage, is your responsibility. You may assign this task to someone, but you must make sure that it's done. Following the sweeping, you should inspect for nails, screws, stage pegs, splinters, loose edges of rugs, or any other hazards. Only when you are willing to walk barefoot across the stage is the stage ready for the cast.

You must check off on an overlay or on a tear-off sheet or some other device. That way, if interrupted, you have a record of what you have not yet done.

Leonard Auerbach
Associate Professor, Department of Theatre Arts
State University of New York at Stony Brook

Besides checking to make sure that the worklight is off prior to curtain, you should check that it is on when needed, and that it is on as fast as possible in order to expedite scene changes and to enable the cast to leave the stage safely (see Chapter 12). Remember that the bright stage lights will leave the cast temporarily blinded and that they will need the worklight in order not to trip over set pieces on their way out. Even if the worklight is controlled by a separate switch, and not through the dimmer board, place the cue for it in your prompt script as if it were any other lighting effect. Call for it in the same manner that you cue all other effects.

Giving Cues

To run the show, you must signal or cue lights, sound, special effects (Chapter 11), and curtain, and thus coordinate these elements with the action of the play, making them happen at precisely the right time.

Your light pencil lines that identify cues (see Chapter 3) allow you to call the cues during rehearsals when you pinpoint them with the guidance of the director (see Chapter 8). During the technical rehearsal, or just prior to it (Chapter 13), you confirm the final cues. In your prompt script with bold marking pen lines, number the light cues and letter the sound cues (see Figure 14.3). Now you are ready to give the cues to the lighting technicians, master electrician, sound technicians, curtain puller, and special-effects people.

Following your script through performance, just as you did at rehearsals, you give the cues clearly, firmly, and with certainty. If you do not feel clear, firm, and certain, pretend. The new stage manager can be compared to a person just learning to drive a car; she or he is afraid to step on the gas pedal. The experienced stage manager, on the other hand, gives her or his cues with the authority of a marine drill sergeant, but in a whisper.

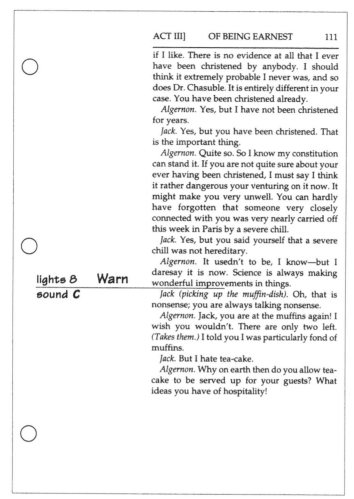

ACT III]   OF BEING EARNEST   111

if I like. There is no evidence at all that I ever have been christened by anybody. I should think it extremely probable I never was, and so does Dr. Chasuble. It is entirely different in your case. You have been christened already.

Algernon. Yes, but I have not been christened for years.

Jack. Yes, but you have been christened. That is the important thing.

Algernon. Quite so. So I know my constitution can stand it. If you are not quite sure about your ever having been christened, I must say I think it rather dangerous your venturing on it now. It might make you very unwell. You can hardly have forgotten that someone very closely connected with you was very nearly carried off this week in Paris by a severe chill.

Jack. Yes, but you said yourself that a severe chill was not hereditary.

Algernon. It usedn't to be, I know—but I daresay it is now. Science is always making wonderful improvements in things.

Jack (picking up the muffin-dish). Oh, that is nonsense; you are always talking nonsense.

Algernon. Jack, you are at the muffins again! I wish you wouldn't. There are only two left. *(Takes them.)* I told you I was particularly fond of muffins.

Jack. But I hate tea-cake.

Algernon. Why on earth then do you allow tea-cake to be served up for your guests? What ideas you have of hospitality!

lights 8   **Warn**
sound C

Figure 14.3   Final Cues and Warns Confirmed in Script with Bold Marking Pen

Generally the cues are "Warn," "Standby," and "Go." The warn part of the cue is usually accompanied by the cue number so that the technician will know which cue it is that he or she is to execute: "Warn sound C."

If there are sound and light cues in the same general area, you need to clarify your warn: "Warn lights number eight, sound cue C."

The warn is usually given one and a half to two minutes before the cue is to be executed. This is usually a half page to a full page before the cue.

The warn should be given in enough time for the technicians to reach their equipment for the cue, check the cue on their plot or cue sheet, and give their total attention to executing the cue. If a cue requires extensive preparation—the changing of reels on or cassettes in a tape recorder—then you might wish to write a separate tech cue into your prompt script on the

I mark cues in my prompt script when they come up during rehearsals, but I don't number cues until they are given to me by designers. Occasionally we might have time for a paper tech prior to the first tech and the numbering can occur then. Otherwise it's done at the tech. I will number rail cues on my own since I am the one generating that cue sheet, but I do wait until just before tech to create that cue sheet so that it does not have to be continuously updated during the rehearsal period. Too many changes can happen during rehearsals. Although I follow any system the lighting designer uses, I let it be known that I prefer that Act I start with 1 and Act 2 start with 200. If there are added cues, they are usually point cues (37.1) because lettered cues don't go into most computer boards. I like the sound cues to be lettered (A for the cue, A1 for level change, Ax for the out cue) and I will usually request that of the sound designer. If there are projection cues or another set of cue numbers is needed for something else, I like to start with 500 or a number past any of the electrics cues.

I usually sit right next to the lighting designer at the tech table, and when a new cue or effect is being built I hear it on the headset. The designer will double check with me that I heard the number and got the correct placement. If cues have been done as work notes outside of tech time I will meet with a designer just before the tech rehearsal and get any notes of added or deleted cues at that time.

Cari Norton
AEA Freelance Stage Manager

page prior to the warn (or immediately following the previous cue), to remind the technician to do this

The standby portion of the cue should precede the go by 5 to 10 seconds, giving the technicians enough time to place their hands in position, flex their muscles, and rivet their eyes and ears on you to await the go. Sometimes the verbal standby is accompanied or replaced by raising the hand.

The go can be given verbally or by lowering the hand.

The exact nature of your cues will depend on the communications equipment backstage, your proximity to your technicians, and their ability to see you and watch their equipment at the same time.

If several cues occur in a fast sequence and there is no time to warn in between them, you will warn and give standby for the series. Then give only your go, or signal for go, once for the whole series. If it is an extremely intricate series of cues, it is possible that you will want to rehearse it carefully, so that the technicians can get a feeling for the timing or rhythm of the series.

Again, all cues—warn, standby, and go—must be given clearly, firmly, and with certainty. Calling cues is another of your sacred duties, a *sine qua*

One of my pet peeves—only a strong personal preference—is the necessity of using "Standby" in calling cues. Once the warnings are spaced correctly in good tech rehearsals, the next order should be "Cue 48 . . . Go." The reiteration of the cue number should serve as a sufficient standby. There is much less room for misunderstanding.

Leonard Auerbach
Associate Professor, Department of Theatre Arts
State University of New York at Stony Brook

When calling a show I use just a "Stand By" and "Go." If there has been a really long time between cues I might also give an early "Warn." (I will usually ask the operator if he or she would like one.) On really busy shows I find there is sometimes no need for the "Stand by" for electrics because there isn't even time for the operator to take his or her finger away from the board. On the national tour of *Show Boat*, I gave stand-bys to the rail and deck, but not to electrics.

Cari Norton
AEA Freelance Stage Manager

[Rather than observing tradition, many stage managers discuss the cueing sequence with their light and sound board operators and use the sequence that they mutually agree will work most effectively.]

non. You must be able to coordinate lights, sound, special effects, and curtain, and you do it by cueing.

Don't avoid this responsibility, and don't delegate it. Even if the light and sound technicians can see and hear the cues and follow book just as well as you can, it is still your job.

Check the result of each cue that you give immediately. If you don't get what you expected, don't panic. Check it out calmly. The tendency is to reach over the technician's shoulder and pull a handle or throw a switch. But keep firmly in mind that the audience is much less aware of gradual changes than abrupt ones. Bringing in the correct effect slowly is usually more desirable than immediate correction of an improper effect.

Mistakes occur in every line of work. Don't allow an error on your part to prevent you from executing all subsequent cues correctly. Don't allow errors to compound. Calm down, compose yourself, and get the next cue right.

Musical Cues

In musical comedy, opera, and ballet it is often necessary that the stage manager read music and take light cues from a note in the score rather than from a word in the script.

In such cases the stage manager has a copy of the score and marks the cues in the score, spacing "Warn," "Standby," and "Go" as described earlier with respect to the time needed to alert the technicians. The stage manager might write a cue for herself or himself in the prompt script to go to the score for the next cue, including the page number of the score. Or the stage manager might place the score pages on which there are cues in the prompt script.

If you do not read music, tell your director and don't attempt to fake it. With the director's help you can sometimes get around your deficiency by using a stopwatch. Rather than listening for a note, you would time how far into the music that note occurs and then take the cue from the stopwatch. If there is a fast series of cues from subsequent notes, you would substitute mental counts for listening to notes. Sometimes you can look for concurrent cast movement rather than notes from which to take your cues. These are all cumbersome methods, and learning to read music is preferable—and usually a prerequisite for stage management jobs in opera and ballet (see Figure 14.4).

Equipment for Cueing

Should you use verbal and hand signals, or should you use a hand-held blinker light? Or should you wire in sets of red and green lights with buttons at the stage manager's desk so that you can communicate with your technicians? Or should you wear TV-type headsets so that you can talk to, and listen to, your technicians? (See Chapter 11 for more about cueing equipment.)

There is no best system. It's a question of what will work best for your theater. Expensive headsets won't improve the quality of your performance any more than will closed circuit TV in the dressing rooms so that offstage actors can watch the performance. More important than your cueing equipment is your consistency in using the system of cues described here.

Timing Curtain Calls

You must learn to exercise your best judgment in timing the curtain call. You should insist on ample rehearsal of the curtain call so that it will be as professional as the rest of the play.

The director usually determines the curtain call order and the effect he or she wants to create in the process of having the actors acknowledge the audience's applause.

In some cases the producer or the management will have a policy on calls for every play performed in that theater. The policy may be, for instance, that the cast form a single line, in order of appearance, left to right. The policy may be that they should take only one bow, regardless of the

Figure 14.4 Last Page of Score for *Samson et Dalilah*. Notes given by the director prior to rehearsals are written on the score. During rehearsals and tech, the PSM adds transparent Post-it notes to indicate placement and actual cue. At the top ("SR fast to full"), the director wanted the stage right fan, which was blowing the curtains in Dalilah's apartment, to go to full speed quickly. The Post-it note ("Fans to 10") was the actual cue.

Courtesy David Grindle, PSM, The Atlanta Opera.

audience response. This very professional or institutional form of curtain call is hard on the actors' egos, since the stars are not individually acknowledged by the audience, but it usually results in the house lights coming up while the audience clamors for more. This is quite desirable compared to the call where the applause dwindles as the cast takes its last bow.

The design of the call will vary with the taste of directors and producers, ranging from the absolutely simple, as just discussed, to the complexly choreographed. I once saw a fancy curtain call add zest to an overwritten and dull last act of a musical, thus arousing some applause, but that was a highly unusual situation.

Often the planning of the curtain call is left for the very last moment and then done in haste. You can help by making a careful diagram of the call order as set by the director, and by posting this diagram on the call board (see Figure 14.5).

The timing or running of the call is another of your sacred duties. You must decide how often to bring up the lights and how long to hold them up. Judgment in this matter can come only from experience. You will quickly learn to sense how long and hard the audience will applaud. It is your good judgment that avoids the curtain closing to waning applause.

You should crank the curtain call cues into the lighting plot and rehearse these cues along with all the others. It is disturbing to endure a long blackout following the final scene while the crew discovers that they must repatch before they can bring up the stage lights for the call. It is even more disturbing to see the house lights come up for the curtain call rather than the stage lights. We have all seen such incidents mar otherwise technically perfect productions.

When there is no curtain and the call is conducted with lights only, a cast member should be designated the "call leader" and given the respon-

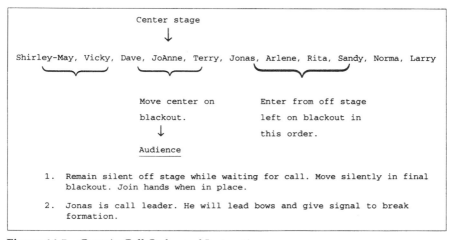

Figure 14.5   Curtain Call Order and Instructions

sibility of signaling the cast when to break their call formation and leave the stage. This will prevent a straggling exit that is discernible in the blackout. It also prevents cast members from breaking too early and being caught out of position when the lights come up.

Questions sometimes arise as to whether an actor is to appear in the curtain call and whether he or she must be in costume and makeup. Yes, he or she is just as obligated to appear in the call as he or she was to appear in the play.

"I have such a small part that the audience won't miss me." "I have a date after the show tonight and I don't want to keep her waiting while I get out of makeup." "I die in the first act and I don't want to hang around for two acts." There are many excuses, but no good ones. It is best for you to include a rule on curtain-call participation in the company rules (Chapter 4) and carefully explain to the cast what is expected.

Walking the Curtain

Sometime during rehearsals you should have the curtain pulled while you watch from the audience to see how it comes together. If there are no gaps when it is closed, there may be no need to have it walked. But if crew is available, it is always safer to have someone walk the curtain—walk out of sight behind the curtain to ensure that it closes smoothly and completely.

Some of the familiar incidents you are guarding against by having the curtain walked are these:

Examples
1. The person on the rope hits a snag and thinks the curtain is closed. The actors are hung, waiting for the curtain to close completely.
2. An actor accidentally jostles a set piece, moving it past the curtain line. The curtain drags the set piece and finally overturns it.

Access to the Control Booth

Only authorized personnel should be allowed in the control booth. Tampering with, or unintentional playing with, sound or lighting equipment by unauthorized personnel could detrimentally affect the running of your show. It is best to post a sign, and enforce it: "No admission" or "Authorized personnel only."

Is the director authorized? It's hard for a stage manager to tell the director to stay out, especially if the stage manager has not discussed this possibility with the director prior to opening night. There is the tendency for the director to want to talk to someone during the performance, someone who will understand his or her anguish, someone who will confirm that all of the actors are not doing what he or she told them to do. Worst of all, the director wants to give last-minute notes or make just a little change in some cue or effect.

If you and the director have done your work properly, there is absolutely no reason for the director to be in the booth before, during, or after the performance. Make this clear in advance—that his or her presence would be a distraction. The same goes for cast members. Put this item in your company rules—you don't want anyone in the booth unless she or he is there to report a fire!

(Parenthetically, I don't feel that directors should give notes to cast members during intermissions. It's sometimes hard to convince a director that the urgent things she or he wants to say to the cast are not going to make that much difference in the second act. It's very hard to limit my comments about the director's behavior. I have to remind myself that this book is about stage management and not directing. From the stage manager's point of view, there is very little you can do to keep the director out of the backstage area during intermissions. You should discuss this behavior with the director in advance—such as, "I hope you're not the kind of director who comes backstage at intermissions. I've found in the past that this seems to upset cast members more than anything else.")

Suggested Classroom Exercise

Ask students to work together to write a precurtain checklist for the current or upcoming show in your theater. When complete, compare it to the one shown in Figure 14.1.

15

Working with the House Manager

Never confuse the seating capacity of your theater with the sitting capacity of your audience.

—Anonymous

The function of the house manager is to ensure the audience's safety and comfort prior to a performance, during intermissions, and after the performance. You must understand the house manager's function and coordinate with her or him in the total effort of assisting the audience to see the production.

Normally, the most important item in your coordination is deciding how the house manager can notify you that the audience is ready to see the production. Will the house manager call you on a backstage phone or intercom and say, "It's all yours"? Or will you run the show at a prearranged time unless the house manager tells you otherwise? How might she or he tell you otherwise? Should you synchronize your watches?

There must be a very definite understanding between you and the house manager. It seems so obvious and yet it is frequently overlooked. How often does the audience return to its seats to find a scene in progress? How often does an audience return to its seats to wait several minutes before the curtain goes up? The audience resents being rushed or having to wait, and the actors resent playing to a moving audience. But it does happen and will continue to happen if you fail to coordinate with the house manager.

In large commercial theaters, house managers belong to their own union: the Association of Theatrical Press Agents and Managers (ATPAM), 165 West 46th Street, New York, NY, 10036, phone (212) 719-3666, fax (212) 302-1585. In a small company, the house manager may be one of the actors, and may have several other duties in addition to house managing and acting.

In some theaters the house manager is in charge of the whole theater plant, box office staff, ushers, custodial staff, and so on. He or she turns the house over to the stage manager for the period of the play only, and resumes total responsibility during intermissions and after the final curtain.

In a small theater the house manager may double as usher, custodian, and assistant director. Halfway through the first act he or she may turn all of his or her responsibilities over to the stage manager and depart the premises.

In a showcase theater there might be a different house manager every night of the run, and it might be your responsibility to brief each new house manager. The following discussion of a house manager's duties was written for a showcase theater.

Duties of the House Manager

The house manager acts as the producer's or sponsoring management's representative in greeting and seating the audience. He or she should be well dressed, well mannered, and wear a badge or ribbon to indicate his or her position. The house manager:

1. Obtains the reservation lists from the reservation clerk and brings them to the theater. This enables him or her to handle future reservations at the theater as well as the reservations for the evening's performance.
2. Arrives at the theater 45 minutes prior to the curtain. He or she ensures that both the sidewalk in front of the theater and the lobby are clean.
3. Checks the condition of the seats and the audience area. Ensures that all fire exits can be opened easily and that alleys beyond them are not blocked.
4. Answers the phones.
5. Greets and seats arriving audience, especially VIPs, and places reserved signs on front row seats for Meryl Streep, Mike Nichols, and such.
6. Prevents the audience from bringing food and lighted cigarettes into the theater.
7. Handles reservations problems: people arriving on the wrong night, overbooked audiences, and so forth. Holds people without reservations until all those with reservations have been seated. Helps people in wheelchairs to find the most convenient aisle space from which to watch the performance. Is alert to other disabilities among audience members and tries to assist if possible.
8. Watches for causes of audience delay—rain, traffic congestion, severe parking problems, and so on—and if he or she senses that

the audience will be late, asks the stage manager to give the cast a five-minute hold.

9. When the audience is seated, he or she closes the back doors, walks to the stage door, and tells the stage manager that he or she may "Take the show."

10. After the curtain rises he or she returns to the lobby and seats people who arrive late, cautioning them that the curtain is up and asking them to be as silent as possible. (He or she tries to fill the house tightly from the front so that empty seats will be at the back for late arrivals.)

11. During the acts he or she again checks the sidewalks and lobby so that the audience will find these areas clean when they emerge from the theater during intermissions and after the show.

12. Finds time during acts to sit for a few minutes in the audience to check the temperature in the theater and to observe any audience distractions.

13. At intermissions he or she opens the back doors and outside doors to ventilate the theater. (Body heat and the lighting equipment may make the theater quite warm by the end of each act.)

14. Directs the audience to the rest rooms and the telephone. Ensures that the rest rooms are clean and serviceable.

15. Makes any necessary announcements to the audience:
    a. "No smoking." (He or she speaks to those individuals who haven't read the posted signs and those who don't wish to comply.)
    b. Announces any unusually long delays in the curtain.
    c. "Lights on in car parked outside, license number EMR 223."
    d. "Is there a doctor in the house?"
    e. Announces fire and other emergencies (see Figure 15.4). No stage manager should simply yell "Fire!" Calm words should precede that word. (The house manager knows exactly what to do to evacuate the theater. He or she knows the numbers to call for fire, police, and ambulance, and always carries a cell phone. Also see Figure 15.1.)
    f. Announces any cast changes and omissions in the program.

16. Times the intermissions and blinks the outside lights and/or strikes chimes in the lobby and/or announces, "Curtain going up," to bring the audience back in. Closes the back doors and the street doors at the end of the intermissions. Does not wait 10 minutes to bring the audience back in, but starts them coming back after 8 minutes so that they are seated and ready to go when 10 minutes have elapsed.

17. If there are doctors on call in the audience, he or she takes their names and seat locations and summons them if they should get a call during the performance.

(*Varsity, the Stage Daily*, August, 2000)

PROP BURSTS INTO FLAMES AS PLAY REACHES HIGHLIGHT

Murfreesboro, Tenn., Aug. 15—Just as Mark Antony was about to deliver his "Friends, Romans, countrymen" speech in praise of Julius Caesar he was left speechless when a fire out on the stage of the Anders Theater during a Rebel Theat pany performance of the Sh ean play last night.

The blaze ignited a 1511 foam and fiberglass but u which dominated the Jap stage throughout the pla veloped the stage props the rest of the seventee ater before the eyes of tators.

Stage Manager re nounced what spectators ss... knew, that there was a fire, and asked patrons to leave as quietly as possible. More than a thousand spectators occupying three-fourths of the theater building managed to file out without panic. Shortly afterward four fire rigs arrived to quench the blaze, although stagehands and actors had already acted to douse the flames.

(*Varsity, the Stage Daily*, February, 2001)

FIRE DEPT HALTS SHOW

After a thirty minute delay, during which debris was removed and further precautions were taken against the outbreak of any other fire, patrons were permitted to re-enter the theater, still smoke-filled, and the play continued with Chuck Kitting as Antony resuming his eulogy of Caesar. Most of the audience waited out the firefighting efforts and returned to watch the end of the play. The biggest ovation of the evening went to five members of the Murfreesboro Fire Department as they marched out with full equipment shortly before the play was ready to resume.

FLAMES CALL OFF LIVING THEATER

(*Los Angeles Messenger*, February, 2001)

Performances of Living Theater at USC cancelled this after fir ola...

Figure 15.1   Onstage Fire Can Threaten Your Production Anytime, Anywhere

18. Answers questions of the departing audience, notes their complaints and suggestions, and passes them on to the producer.
19. Coordinates with the stage manager in securing the theater when everyone has left. Pushes up the seats and searches for lost items. Before leaving the theater he or she must conduct a sniff test (fire inspection) of every row in the audience and every room and cranny of the theater and dressing rooms to ensure that no burning cigarettes have been left anywhere.
20. Returns the reservation lists to the reservations clerk.

Problems frequently occur when you come to your job from one theater and the house manager comes from another. You have different expectations of one another based on different past experiences.

Talk it out. Give it a dry run. Anticipate problems together. What will you each do if it rains torrents on opening night? Who will roll out the heavy-duty mats in the lobby? Who will put down the planks in the gulley at the actors' entrance? How will the house manager tell you from out front that the rain has delayed the audience and that she or he wants you to hold the curtain an additional five minutes? Since there's no cloakroom, where can the audience store raincoats and umbrellas? Does the house manager lock up the theater? Do you? Or do you both share or alternate shut-down procedures? If you share or alternate, do you both know exactly what is to be done?

Anticipate emergencies together. Review what you each will do in the event of fire, civil disorder, earthquake, flood, heart attacks among the audience, animals in the audience, incredibly loud noises emanating from places unknown (see Figure 15.2), and hysterical patrons begging to be let out.

[Los Angeles *Bugle*, **2001**]

LETTERS

Nuisance Noises

We recently attended the visiting St. Louis Opera Company's performance of "Aida" at the Municipal Opera Pavilion on December 5. In the middle of the opera we were severely distracted by pulsating drumbeats and musical sounds which seemed to come from the ceiling of the auditorium, as if they emanated from the restaurant upstairs. It was impossible for us to get a clear hearing of the last part of the opera. In order to be sure that the vibrations from above were not somehow imaginary, we turned to a neighbor for confirmation, "Good grief!" he said, "I've been fighting it since the second act." We wrote a strong complaint after the performance, but never received any acknowledc very poor taste on the part ment to permit conflicting this to be audible to patrons formances.

Morris and Art Faye
Northeast Cucamong

Danny Bongo, public relations director for the Pavilion, admits there was no theater employee directly responsible for checking on such intrusive sounds beyond the first few minutes after the performance is under way. "Until somebody gives us the word," he said, "we have no way to be aware there's a problem." However, on December 5, a verbal complaint was made to a guard and, according to Bongo, the sound of the dance band was "totally sealed off" as a result by the end of the opera. Bongo denies that anybody involved received any written protest. But a similar complaint appeared in the Bugle's review of "La Gioconda" as performed by the St. Louis company during the same month here.
—The Editor

Figure 15.2   Plan Ahead to Handle Emergencies and Surprise Interruptions

During my prep week, I always find the evacuation routes, fire extinguishers, first-aid, and emergency supplies, but fortunately I have never had to use them. I also always make sure that I have a public address microphone, communications with the house manager, and prepared announcements in case an audience needs to be evacuated. I guess I have been very fortunate. In my nine years as an Equity stage manager, I have never had a fire.

Cari Norton
Stage Manager

[See Figures 15.3, 15.4, and 15.5.]

Blood-Borne Pathogens

In the 1980s, the theater world became aware of the dangers of blood-borne pathogens—disease-causing microorganisms that are present in human blood, including hepatitis B virus and human immunodeficiency virus (HIV). In any accidents in a theater that involve the spill of blood, vomit, urine, or feces, safety in cleanup has become an issue for which the theater staff must plan. Who will do what and when? Will the necessary equipment be available?

In a large theater complex or university, it is usually the security staff that is given responsibility for cleanup. In smaller theater situations, the house manager may be delegated the responsibility for the whole building by the producer. The stage manager may find that he or she has some responsibility in the absence of others so assigned. What happens if there is a hazardous situation during rehearsals, or backstage, or in the dressing rooms during performance? The stage manager should know where he or

---

EVACUATION ANNOUNCEMENT

"May I have your attention please? Please, may I have your attention? A situation that is not immediately threatening requires us to evacuate the building at this time. We ask that you please walk to the nearest exit. The ushers will be available to assist you and will direct you to a safe gathering point. Thank you for your cooperation."
(Repeat as necessary.)

Figure 15.3   Emergency Evacuation Announcement Used at the American Musical Theatre of San Jose (California). The stage manager has a bullhorn stage right in case the power goes out and he cannot communicate via his public address microphone.

Courtesy Bob Bones, Production Stage Manager, American Musical Theatre of San Jose.

HOUSE ANNOUNCEMENT

Casting Change

Ladies and Gentlemen. May I have your attention please. Welcome to _____ . In this evening's performance, the role of _____ , usually played by _____ , will be played by _____ . Thank you and enjoy the show.

Technical Problem

(Brief stop)
Ladies and Gentlemen. May I have your attention please. We are currently experiencing some technical difficulties on stage. Please bear with us and the performance will continue in just a moment. Thank you for your patience.

(Intermission)
Ladies and Gentlemen. May I have your attention please. We are currently experiencing some technical difficulties on stage. At this time we will take an early intermission. Please feel free to leave your seats, and we will ring the lobby chimes as soon as we are ready to continue the performance. Thank you for your patience.

Possible Fire:

Ladies and Gentlemen. May I have your attention please. We have been notified of a possible fire somewhere in our building. For your safety, and the safety of those around you, we are going to evacuate the theatre until the fire department tells us it is safe to resume the performance. Please stand and calmly exit to the exit door nearest you. Please notify an usher if assistance is needed. Move away from the building to a safe distance, and we will notify you when it is safe to return to your seats. Thank you.

Noticeable Fire:

Ladies and Gentlemen. At this time we need to ask you to exit the theatre building. For your safety, and the safety of those around you, please stand and calmly exit to the exit door nearest you. Once again, please stand and calmly exit to the exit door nearest you. Move away from the building to a safe distance, and we will notify you when it is safe to return to your seats. Thank you.

Earthquake:

Ladies and Gentlemen. Please crouch down as low as you can in your seat and cover your head with your hands. We are experiencing a small earthquake and it will be over shortly. DO NOT ATTEMPT TO LEAVE YOUR SEATS AT THIS TIME. Actors, please exit the stage into the wings. Once again, crouch down low in your seats and cover your head with your hands. Please remain calm and remain in your seats.

Figure 15.4 Emergency Announcements. Cari Norton finds that many theaters now have evacuation announcements posted in the control booth. In case they don't, however, Norton has her own.

Courtesy Cari Norton, Stage Manager.

**EVACUATION PROCEDURES
FOR THE CENTER FOR THE PERFORMING ARTS**

In the case of an emergency requiring the evacuation of the building, a decision made by the police, events coordinator, CLO manager on duty and the stage manager, the following steps are to be taken backstage to evacuate.

1. The Stage Manager will stop the performance, if it has not already stopped, and through the microphone backstage that goes into the house system, go on stage and direct the audience as to what to do. If power is out, the stage manager will use the bullhorn that is located stage right.
2. The Stage right ASM and the IA steward on the call will make sure that everyone on stage, on the rail, in the immediate backstage rooms stage right, and the loading dock area are evacuated.
3. The Stage left ASM will go upstairs and make sure the dressing rooms are evacuated.
4. The orchestra conductor will make sure the pit and lower level-rooms are evacuated.
5. The security guard will stay at the stage door to make sure people exiting that way do so safely and quickly.
6. The Stage managers, steward, and orchestra conductor should then meet the security guard at the backstage door and let the others know that backstage is evacuated. Then go to the meeting place outside the building on the Park Ave. side.

Figure 15.5 Evacuation Procedures Used by the American Musical Theatre of San Jose (California). See Chapter 18, "Police, Fire, and Municipal Regulations," for additional information.

Courtesy American Musical Theatre of San Jose.

she can find the cleanup kit or biohazard station (see Figure 15.6) and the instructions on how to dispose of the hazard (see Figure 15.7).

It is highly recommended that the stage manager ensure that the blood-borne pathogens cleanup kit be kept next to the first-aid kit and that instructions for use be placed in the kit as well as on the bulletin board. Cast and crew should be told in an early briefing that they are to report any potentially infectious material to the stage manager rather than attempting to dispose of it themselves, especially without proper equipment and instruction.

California law, effective July 30, 1999, states that if an employer (read producer) designates an employee (read stage manager) to be responsible for implementation of first aid/blood-borne pathogen control, then the employer must provide training. Whether you have or have not been designated, it is desirable that you voluntarily seek training. Any first-aid emergency involving blood spill must be considered a blood-borne pathogen emergency. If you need further information try the federal Occupational Safety and Health Administration (OSHA) of U.S. Department of Labor (www.osha.gov) or your state OSHA website (in California: www.dir.ca.gov/DOSH/BloodborneFAQ.html).

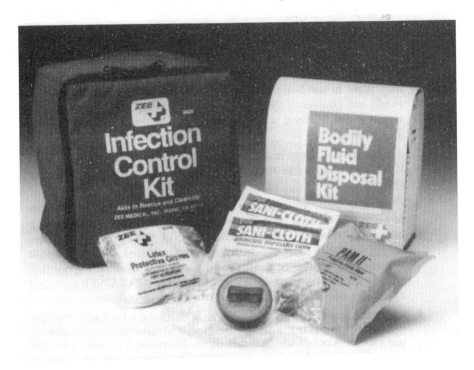

Figure 15.6 A Blood-Borne Pathogen Kit

Courtesy Zee Medical, Inc., Irvine, California (www.lifeessentialsbyzee.com).

Rotating Duty Rosters

When there is no staff house manager and the cast must carry out the custodial duties, you may find it desirable to prepare a rotating duty roster (see Figure 15.8).

Example

In a showcase theater situation where there was no budget for cleanup and maintenance of the theater, the cast was called to a discussion by the artistic director (one of the actors). They were asked how to solve the cleanup problem. All agreed that they were the only ones who could solve the problem, that they did not want to levy a tax to pay a custodian, and that their chief concern was an equitable distribution of the work. The artistic director then asked the stage manager (also an actor in the group) to set up a rotating duty roster.

The rosters were not posted in the dressing rooms or on the callboard, since cast members did not want their friends who visited after performance to see that they were expected to do chores. Instead, each cast member was given a copy of the roster. The stage manager supervised and carried out his chores.

Cast members were given the option of carrying out their assignments 15 minutes prior to or after the performance. By doing one chore before and one after the performance, they could work on chores every two nights.

1. **For Liquid or Wet Blood, Use the Kit Provided**

   1. First, put on a pair of rubber gloves. If you have a large spill, use a pair of heavy utility rubber gloves. If using disposable rubber gloves, you may want to use two pair in case of a small hole or tear. Wear face shield and goggles. If there is a chance of getting blood on your clothing or a chance blood may penetrate your clothing, wear disposable Tyvek coveralls.

   2. Spread the absorbent beads that are found in the white pouch in the Kit or use floor dry to absorb the liquid. Pick up with a dust pan or shovel.

   3. Dispose of the absorbent in the WHITE BAG and tie it closed. Dispose of all materials used such as gloves, towels and any of the clean-up materials in the RED, INFECTIOUS WASTE BAG provided. If there are no needles or sharp objects that are contaminated, you may deposit the bags in the compactor. If there are sharp objects, including needles, etc., these must be disposed of in the SHARPS CONTAINER provided in the clean-up kit.

   4. Clean the area with a germicidal cleaner that is provided with the kits or that are located in the designated First Aid stations. If not available, use a solution of household bleach diluted between 1:10 and 1:100 with water. Clean-up of equipment is covered in the section titled Cleaning Up of Contaminated Equipment. A WORD OF CAUTION: HANDLE INFECTIOUS MATERIALS AS LITTLE AS POSSIBLE.

2. **Dry Blood Clean-Up**

   When cleaning up dry blood, follow the same procedures as for liquid clean-up AND wear face shield with eye protection or a dust mask and goggles to prevent ingesting dust through eyes, nose or mouth. Do not breathe any dust or get dust into any body cavity.

   Equipment clean-up is covered in a following section.

3. **Clean-Up of Vomit, Urine, and Feces**

   Put on a pair of rubber gloves.

   Cover liquid with floor dry compound. Allow liquid to be soaked up into the compound. Sweep into a dustpan and dispose of in a plastic bag. Tie bag securely and place in compactor.

   Clean area with disinfectant or diluted bleach solution.

4. **Cleaning Contaminated Equipment**

   Dispose of contaminated rubber gloves, coveralls and face masks in the manner stated in Section 1.

Figure 15.7 One of Several Pages of a "Safety Procedures" Bulletin. Disclaimer: "The Santa Clara Convention Center is not in the business of providing advice or counsel regarding this or any other safety procedures. Accordingly, no warranty as to its adequacy or completeness is made."

Courtesy R. D. "Ray" Anderson, Director of Security, Santa Clara Convention Center.

ROSTER

	Thursday	Friday	Saturday	Sunday	Thursday	Friday	Saturday	Sunday
Albert Alvarez	A	B	C	D	E	F	G	H
Ben Blahzay	B	C	D	E	F	G	H	I
Charles Corn	C	D	E	F	G	H	I	J
Dave Dumpling	D	E	F	G	H	I	J	K
Earl Eastman	E	F	G	H	I	J	K	L
Frank Farley	F	G	H	I	J	K	L	A
Gina Glass	G	H	I	J	K	L	A	B
Helen Harvey	H	I	J	K	L	A	B	C
Ida Isely	I	J	K	L	A	B	C	D
Judy Jennings	J	K	L	A	B	C	D	E
Karen Kirsten	K	L	A	B	C	D	E	F
Louise Lehrer	L	A	B	C	D	E	F	G

A Sweep front sidewalk
B Strain sand in all four cans in lobby; move 2 outside
C Sweep/mop lobby
D Put all seats up; sweep/mop audience area
E Clean men's room
F Clean ladies' room
G Clean dressing room tables
H Sweep dressing rooms
I Clean Green Room
J Empty all waste baskets: rest rooms, dressing rooms, Green Room (trash can behind theater)
K Resupply all paper to dressing rooms, rest rooms from supply cupboard
L Dust lobby furniture, straighten

Figure 15.8 A Rotating Duty Roster

By inviting the cast to participate in solving the problem, the artistic director gained their cooperation. If he had simply ordered the roster posted, it might not have worked as well as it did. A few minutes of group consultation in advance can prevent a great deal of individual dissent later.

The stage manager also might take pains to explain where the cleanup materials are kept, how a mop wringer is used, and the importance of putting things back where they were found and reporting shortages of materials. (It was discovered, in the previous example, that a 30-year-old actor did not know how to use a mop! He had never used one. The stage manager demonstrated and the actor caught on. Unfortunately, he became much more skilled at mopping than acting.)

Not all duty rosters need be of the rotating type if the cast is willing to distribute chores in another way. Again, a group talk session in advance will help in the voluntary tapping of labor.

VIP Lists

A showcase theater's purpose is to attract to its audience producers, directors, agents, and other very important people (VIPs) who can hire the cast members for roles in movies, television, industrial shows, live theater, and other paying jobs. Community, educational, and commercial theaters may function as showcases, even though it is not their primary purpose.

If the cast members know which VIPs have seen their performance, they can follow up the impression they've made by sending résumés and phoning for interviews. They can ask agents who have attended to represent them on the basis of their performance.

So it is desirable that the cast know which VIPs have been in the audience. Posting a VIP list on the callboard is the easiest way to let the cast know (see Figure 15.9). Posting such a list is not a mandatory function of the stage manager. Anyone who takes the time to check with the box office,

```
ONE FLEW OVER THE CUCKOO'S NEST

VIP LIST

Dale Wasserman        author
Charles Faber         critic - Citizen News
John Houser           critic - Herald Examiner
Phillip Scheuer       critic - L.A. Times
Jimmy Powers          critic - Hollywood Reporter
Dale Olsen            critic - Variety
Robert Lewine         agent V.P.     C.M.A.
Milton Lewis          manager
Lurene Tuttle         actress
Jim Lister            cast. dir. Stalmaster-Lister Rawhide
                      Gunsmoke
Boris Kaplan          producer
Gene Banks            casting ABC
Betty Garret          actress
King Donovan          actor-director
Meyer Mishkin         agent Mishkin Agency
Hy Sieger             agent Park-Citron Agency
Norman Pincas         producer
David Graham          agent
Bob Raison            agent Ralson-Branden Agency
Harold Swoverland     agent Swoverland Agency
Eddie Foy, Jr.        casting Columbia Screen Gems (I Dream
                      of Jeannie)
Jack Donaldson        agent Donaldson Agency
Bob Bowser            casting Universal
Bob Shapiro           agent William Morris
Naomi Hirshhorn       producer legit
George Pal            producer MGM
Dick Lyons            producer MGM
Al Trescony           casting MGM
Meryl Abeles          Desilu 20th
Dick Berg             producer Chrysler
Bert Kennedy          director MGM writer
Dale Garrick          agent Garrick Agency
```

Figure 15.9   Portion of VIP List for the Callboard of a Showcase Theater

house manager, producer, and director might make such a list. But it is one of the extra items that would demonstrate your interest in the welfare of the cast and the reputation of the theater.

Suggested Classroom Exercise

Have the class brainstorm the duties of the house manager for your theater. When arranged in chronological order, compare their list to the one on pages 222 to 224.

16

Keeping the Show in Hand

The dictionary is the only place where success comes before work.
—Anonymous

The most difficult problem in a long-running production is keeping the quality of each performance as good as it was on opening night. If the director remains with the show, in attendance regularly and in communication with the cast, it is his or her burden. But if he or she says to you on opening night, "It's all yours," and means it, then you have your work cut out for you. It is your basic responsibility to retain the director's artistic intent (see Chapter 8). It would be good practice for all directors in every theater environment to remind cast members that the stage manager will "give notes" after opening night.

Long-Run "Improvements"

In a short run there isn't much of a problem. But as the actors feel more at ease in their roles, especially if the show runs for two weeks or more without the director's presence, "improvements" set in.

Here are some examples of the things that happen in extended runs:

1. *New business:* An actor sometimes feels "hung up" during the lines of fellow actors. During rehearsals and the first few performances, he was busy thinking of coming lines and business, but with his newfound ease and self-assurance, he begins to feel that he is not doing enough. So he invents new business that he feels is appropriate to his character. He removes his shoe and darns a hole in his red sock with green yarn that he removes from his eyeglass case.

Or it just happens by accident. He trips on the set and hits his head on the door frame, severely shaking the flat, and the audience laughs, so at the next performance. . . .

2. *New lines:* A late entrance prompts two actors to ad-lib some lines while awaiting the late-comer. At the next performance the ad-lib lines are repeated on the entrance, and at the next performance the entering actor waits for the ad-lib lines.

Or, an actor throws in an ad-lib line on impulse and gets a laugh, so at the next performance. . . .

3. *Pauses:* The actor now senses that his big moment is being missed by the audience because he doesn't have focus. So he decides he needs a dramatic pause, big enough to drive a truck through. It just seems that long. Actually, his new dramatic pauses and those of his fellow actors only add up to one and a half minutes on your time sheet for the scene—of yawning and coughing in the audience.

4. *Handles:* Suddenly every other line in the script has as preface a new expletive ("Well"), an exclamation ("Wow"), or direct address ("You"). The actors start to make themselves "comfortable" with the playwright's lines. The crispness is gone, the pace is down, but each actor knows in his or her heart that the single word she or he has added is right, just the way the character would say it.

So you observe and listen carefully, and each time you hear new lines, handles, or pauses, or observe new business, you make a caret in your prompt script at the place where it occurred and note the new addition carefully. After the performance you bring the changes and improvements to the attention of the actors, privately. (Important: In matters of acting performances, directors give notes to the whole cast, but stage managers counsel individual actors privately.)

And that's when you hear wondrous things from the actors in justification and rationalization:

"I've grown in the part."

"It got a laugh."

"It just happened by accident but the audience bought it, so why not keep it?"

"I'm experimenting. Don't want to get into a rut."

"Got to keep that magic, spontaneous, first-time quality so I decided to do it for the first time without warning him so he'd give me a response I could play off of, but the dumdum just gave me the same tired line reading he's always been giving me."

Etcetera ad nauseum.

What do you do in the face of such static? You bring as much friendly persuasion as you can to the situation. You remind the actor of the traditional discipline of the theater—that changes in lines, pace, the interpretation of lines, and the inclusion of business are all strictly the prerogative of the director. In the absence of the director, they are now the stage man-ager's prerogative, and you do not approve the changes and improve-ments the actor wishes to make.

You may or may not go on to explain your reasons for the undesirabil-ity of the change or improvement.

Perhaps you will point out that an actor's reputation for self-discipline is more important in the long run than the change or improvement she or he feels is so important.

You might even point out that historically the worst performances of the best actors have occurred when they undertook to direct themselves.

You might also console the actor by explaining that the decision not to accept her or his changes and improvements does not in any way diminish your respect for the actor's excellent taste, inventive genius, great experi-ence despite her or his youth, sagacious artistic judgment, and her or his manifestly sincere desire to improve the production. But cut it!

Finally, you simply do not argue about it. Your authority extends only as far as your persuasive influence in this matter. Never make the actor feel that she or he must apologize or even agree with you. If she or he gives you static after you have counseled her or him, simply leave her or him with a pleasant, "Why don't you give it some thought?"

You cannot control absolutely an actor's performance. You cannot run out on the stage and twist the actor's arm. Ultimately the actor must realize what you already know—that in live theater, the stage belongs to the actors, not the director or the stage manager. On the other hand, a produc-tion is a delicate balance of many performers' efforts, and any actor's rep-utation can suffer if she or he persists in upsetting it. For the really recalcitrant, the ultimate threat would be replacement with an understudy or a new actor, but this would be an administrative decision.

Cast Morale

Sometimes the gloom in the air at half-hour call following a bad review is enough to make any stage manager feel that a comedy could not possibly be performed that evening, or that the tragedy about to be enacted on stage is nothing compared to the one backstage.

Here's how you handle the situation:

1. Don't overreact.
2. Get it out in the open.
3. Don't act elated when others are depressed.
4. Keep your own personal morale high.

It's never quite as bad as you imagine it will be before you get to the theater. Actors and actresses have a way of buoying up their own morale when they get together. Never feel that you must become court jester or psychiatrist backstage. This is not the time for a good show biz anecdote. Don't overreact.

Get it out in the open. A casual, "Rough break, Sam," to an actor who has been devastated by bad reviews might get it out from the sulking level to the verbal level and allow the actor to vent his choicest invective about the reviewers. But keep it casual. Show the actor that you don't attach too great importance to it.

Don't be elated when others are depressed. You should be sympathetic enough with the plight of a demoralized cast not to want to appear to be celebrating their disaster.

Keep your own personal morale high. Your morale is dependent on the fact that you are doing a difficult job very well. Continue to do your job very well. Let the cast know, by your deportment, that it is business as usual tonight, that you expect everyone to be on time and to acknowledge their calls cheerfully, regardless of the reviews.

Second-performance slump and "down" performances are other situations of which you should be aware.

The second performance of a run has a tendency to be a poor one. The cast, emotionally up for the opening night, experiences a letdown. The sense of urgency that attended opening night is gone. The second performance seems to be less important. Part of the challenge is missing. They know they can do it because they did it last night. And now they know how good they are. Didn't all of their friends tell them? So the cast relaxes, and the performance quality slips.

Sometimes you are simply not aware of the causes of a down performance. You observe the results. The first scene drags, the audience is unresponsive, and during the intermission it's very quiet in the dressing rooms. The cast is listless.

There is no one best way to respond to second performance slump or other down performances. You must judge from your past experience how best to handle the situation. Do you give a pep talk to the cast during the intermission? Do you ask them for the old pizazz? Do you individually enlist the help of the old hands in the cast and ask them to pick up the pace? Have you developed the kind of rapport with the cast during rehearsals or on the tour thus far that enables you to give them the football coach's "You guys are letting me down" routine?

If you think that you can be effective in fighting down performances, then you should try to do so. But you must not feel that it is an obligation. Simply make sure that you do not contribute to poor cast morale.

Blocking Replacements and Rehearsing Understudies

Traditionally, as the closest assistant to the director, you are presumed to have the duty of blocking in replacements and rehearsing understudies. In reality, you rarely get to perform these duties. Sometimes the director wants to do it herself or himself. Sometimes other staff members step in. Sometimes there is simply no need to block replacements or rehearse understudies.

Of course, you should be ready and able to do it since you have the blocking notations in your prompt script.

Rehearsing understudies or replacements is unlike original direction in that you should attempt to prepare the understudy or replacement to fit into the already mounted play. In most cases, replacements and understudies have the opportunity to observe the cast and take their own blocking notation during a rehearsal or performance.

If working with an Equity company, you should review the rules concerning understudies with the producer. Some contracts require that understudies be present at the theater, while other contracts require that the understudies simply be on call. Stage managers are not allowed to work as understudies. Assistant stage managers may act or understudy, depending on the contract. If unsure, check with your Equity office.

You should append the names and phone numbers of potential replacements and understudies to your cast list so that you are able to reach them when the need arises. Since you never can tell when you will need a replacement, it is a good idea to keep the résumés submitted during auditions along with your notes of evaluation.

Before the final performance of a production of Wagner's "The Flying Dutchman" in Richmond, VA, for which I was an Assistant Stage Manager, we received a call at the theatre 75 minutes before curtain that the tenor singing the role of Erik was undergoing emergency surgery at a local hospital. The cover [understudy] for the role was also cast as the Steersman, and needed to sing that part in the show as well. When called to the production office, the cover admitted that he knew the music, but had never had a staging and didn't know the blocking. Any hopes of teaching him the blocking, in less than an hour, for a major role like Erik were out of the question.

We realized that it was possible for him to sing his on-stage role as well as sing the part of Erik from the pit, since, fortunately, both characters were never on stage at the same time. The head of the company then turned to me and said, "You fit the costume. You walk the part." So, I went to costumes and wigs, spent Act I reviewing the blocking and then went on stage, without script, to essentially mime the role of Erik for his appearances in the last two acts. At the end of the evening, the singer and I received a standing ovation in our tandem bow. So my paying attention in rehearsal paid off.

David Grindle
Production Stage Manager
The Atlanta Opera

Upkeep of Sets and Costumes

On the very mundane level, the stage manager of a long-run production becomes responsible for the upkeep of the sets and costumes.

Every member of the cast should be encouraged to report to the stage manager any part of a set piece or set that is becoming worn or unserviceable. This might range from a door that is sticking, to a hole in a flat, to a loose cable backstage.

The stage manager should try to stay ahead of the cast by inspecting sets, set pieces, and costumes periodically and carrying out minor repairs before the cast members notice the need.

The stage manager is also responsible for seeing to it that costumes are laundered when necessary and repaired if necessary (see Figure 16.1).

Suggested Classroom Exercise

Plan inspection of the set of your current production to cite those things that would need upkeep if the play were to run for an extended period.

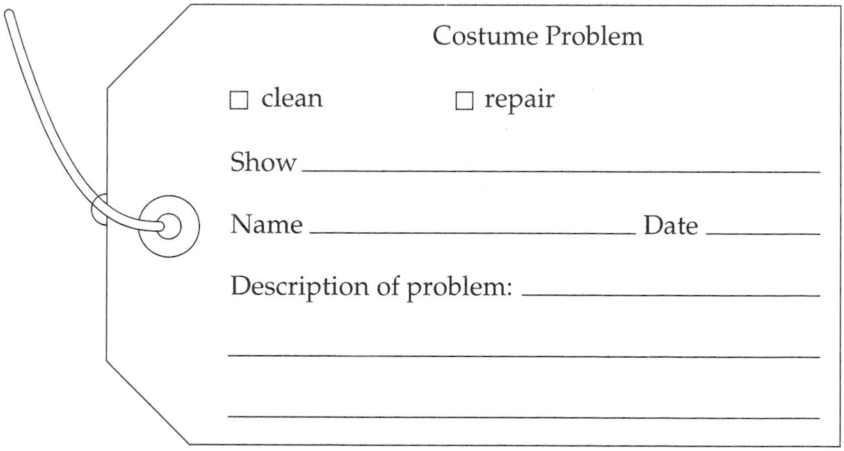

Figure 16.1 Costume Tag. Tags with eyelets, and preferably wire ties, are available in stationery stores. When you have a large cast, it is important that you get the right costumes back to the right actor. Tags should be left in the dressing rooms and actors should be informed via company rules when and where they are to turn in costumes for cleaning or repair.

17

Closing and Moving/Touring

Someone is always doing what someone else said could not be done.

—Anonymous

When the show has completed its run, it is time to strike—tear down the sets and return or store the props and costumes. It is usually desirable to clean the stage area as soon as possible after the last performance.

In union companies the close of the show is announced two weeks in advance by a closing notice signed by the producer and posted on the callboard.

Strike Plan

To accomplish the strike efficiently, write out and distribute a strike plan. This plan lets each person involved know what is expected of him or her (see Figure 17.1). You should coordinate the plan with all concerned department heads.

Will the actors be involved in the strike or only the crew? In a union theater situation, cast members do not participate in the strike. In educational, community, and showcase theater, they usually do.

If you are working in a union situation, your strike plan will be very brief. It will advise the union crew of their call. Along with the producer, business manager, or production manager, you will want to evaluate the amount of time required and review the applicable union rules and pay scales to determine whether the strike can most economically be carried out during a night call following the final curtain, or delayed for a future date, even possibly the day that the next set is to be brought in. You will

THE TORCH-BEARERS

STRIKE NIGHT PARTY*
Sunday, June 14
11 PM — 1 AM

<u>General</u>
1. Strike can be completed in less than 2 hrs. with the cooperation of all.
2. Please bring hammer and/or crowbar <u>plus at least one large corrugated paper box suitable for packing.</u>
3. Please change out of costume and make-up and into work clothes as soon as possible.
4. Urging final night guests to leave as soon as possible will expedite.
5. Remove your own personal costumes, make-up, and props, to your cars as soon as possible to facilitate cleaning of dressing rooms.
6. Stay off the stage unless specifically assigned there because of falling flats and flying hardware, tools, & crew members. (Use side doors to go between dressing rooms and aud.)
7. Upon completion of assigned tasks, see stage manager.

<u>Assignments</u>
Crew: Dick, John, Fred, Barry (others):
   A.   Strike front rows of chairs in aud.
   B.   Bring in stairs, garbage cans, place in aud. near DSL.
   C.   Remove sconces, place in one box; all furn. in aud. near DSR.
   D.   Remove all portable lighting equip. to storage room, rear aud.
   E.   Remove all flats, braces, rigging to aud. near DSL.
   F.   <u>When stage strike complete</u>, replace curtains, move furniture to patio.
   G.   Dick will be in charge of further refining crew assignments.
Doug:
   A.   Oversee removal of all items from stage.
   B.   Supervise replacement of curtains front and rear.
Len & Hoke, Brett & Ben:
   A.   Form 2 teams to work in aud. near DSL area to accept flats, rigging, stage pieces from crew.
   B.   Remove hardware & break down to smallest desirable parts.
   C.   Store all hardware in box.
   D.   Remove all parts to patio & store as directed.
   E.   Bring screw driver and/or pliers; work gloves desirable to avoid splinters.
Karl:
   A.   Turn on patio lights.
   B.   Organize patio area for quick future removal of all materials.
   C.   Show Len, Hoke, Brett, Ben where & how to store flats & materials.
   D.   When all materials stored, instruct crew to bring out furniture and supervise placement.
Jeanne, Barbara, Margaret, Evelyn, Marlene, Beatriz:
   A.   Clean Dressing rooms.
   B.   Store costumes to be ret.
Harvey and <u>Bandy</u>: *See me for prop forms*
   A.   Pack all props in boxes.
   B.   List contents of box on outside.
   C.   Insure with completed forms that we will know what goes where & to whom on Tuesday, June 16th when furniture & props will be returned.

If you anticipate any strike night problems please see me.
Thank you all in advance for the swift, pleasant strike.

Figure 17.1   Strike Plan Handout

want to evaluate availability of storage space, storage cost, and trucking costs.

It is wise to review the strike plan with the union crew before finalizing it.

If the staff technical director is responsible for strike supervision, the stage manager will work for him or her as directed.

In a nonunion situation, it is usually best to accomplish the strike as soon after the final curtain as possible. Tools and transportation should be well planned so that your cast, staff, and crew will have everything on hand that they need to accomplish the strike. Be sure that you have enough bags and boxes to get all of the props and costumes properly packed and out of the theater, and enough back seats, trucks, and trunk space to accommodate all of the set pieces, scenery, props, and costumes. Cleaning implements should be in plentiful supply, too, so that the theater can be left clean for the next production.

Most cast members actually enjoy the strike if they know what is expected of them. There is usually a letdown that follows the closing performance, which is buffered when the cast members continue working together for the brief period of the strike. There is a sense of urgency, team play, and accomplishment present at the strike that makes it quite enjoyable.

During the strike don't tie yourself down with repetitive manual tasks. You should be free to observe and supervise. You should also delegate supervising authority to others, particularly when there is more than one area. Can an actor be put in charge of the shop area while you are on stage? Can one supervise an even smaller area, like a loading dock? Actors who suddenly remember long-lost hernias and war wounds at the mention of the strike have been known to do vast amounts of work when named supervisor.

You must be especially aware of safety problems during the strike, and take time to caution everyone about the most basic of potential dangers: Watch where you step; don't step on nails and tools; don't fall into the pit; don't use power tools that you have not operated before until you have been instructed in their use; look above for falling scenery and tools.

Start the strike with a safety lecture and caution workers when you see dangerous practices.

The strike may well be the last chore that cast members see you do. Try to make a good final impression by carrying out the strike with the same calm and meticulous organization with which you managed the rest of the production.

Changeover Schedule

In cases where the theater will not have a dark night between two consecutive productions, it is necessary to prepare a changeover schedule. This schedule is actually a combination of strike plan, set-up plan, and rehearsal schedule that aids in smoothing out the transition from one production to another. It tells who has use of the stage space during the critical hours of transition. It coordinates the personnel of the outgoing production, the incoming production, and the house staff (see Figure 17.2).

Before posting it, you should coordinate the schedule with the producer, business manager, production manager, and staffs of the incoming and outgoing productions.

During the changeover you must be on hand to supervise the on-the-spot adjustments that become necessary.

Examples

1. When construction takes longer than anticipated, and it frequently does, you must keep the master carpenter from coming to blows with the choreographer of the incoming show who expected those all-important ramps to be in place at the beginning of the rehearsal period and not left for last.

2. You must be forearmed with the authority to make decisions as to whether 10 members of a union will be paid for an additional four-hour call because their services are required for 15 additional minutes (when the union requires a four-hour minimum pay period). Discuss contingencies with the producer. Find out what authority you have to commit her or his money.

Send all personnel concerned a copy of the changeover schedule and post copies on the callboard, in the shop, and in the crew lounge area.

```
                    JOHNNY MATHIS/U2 ELEVATION
Friday       July 15      8 AM to noon       Electrics
                          1-5 PM             Carpentry
                                             Props
                                             Electrics

Saturday     July 16      Open

Sunday       July 17      1-6 PM             Sound
                          8 PM               Half hour
                          8:30               Curtain MATHIS show
                          end performance    Begin strike

Monday       July 18      12:00-3 AM         Strike/set
                          3-6 AM             Full Orchestra
                                             Dress rehearsal
                          6 AM to 12 noon    As needed
                          1-6 PM             Technical cleanup
                                             (no performers)
                          8 PM               Half hour
                          8:30               Curtain U2 ELEVATION
```

Figure 17.2 Changeover Schedule between Two Productions

Moving the Show

All moves are alike and all moves are different. They require coordination of staff, crew, and cast in moving the cast, crew, and equipment.

> You are moving your production from one theater to another. Your lease ran out but your advance sales are great so you have to find another house.
>
> You tried out in Azusa and now you're opening in West Covina.
>
> You are on a national tour, either via train and/or plane to major cities, or by truck and bus to the hinterlands.
>
> Your children's play is traveling to all the elementary school auditoriums in town.
>
> Your industrial show will tour 38 cities in two and a half months.

In any of these situations, here are some of the steps you will want to take:

1. Prepare and distribute an itinerary.
2. Caution the cast/crew on travel deportment.
3. "Mother-hen" the cast on the road.
4. Supervise the load-in, setup, strike, and load-out.
5. Pave the way with letters to business agents, host theater owners, and so on. Request the host theater's info packet (see Chapter 5).

Itineraries

The first thing you need is an itinerary, whether you are moving across the street or across the nation (see Figures 17.3 and 17.4). What day are you making the move? What time? What is your destination? What's the new address (with zip code)? What's the new phone number (with area code)? What is the rehearsal and performance schedule during the period?

Planning the itinerary is not necessarily your responsibility, but you should contribute. Think through the moves in advance. Has enough time been allotted for setups? Try to anticipate problems. Have all of the union rules been considered (e.g., union casts may not travel on their day off)?

It is your responsibility to make sure that every member of the cast and crew has a copy of the itinerary—perhaps two or three for family and friends who will wish to write or phone while the show is on the road.

Touring Agreement

Caution the cast and crew about deportment expected on the road (see Figure 17.5). You are expected to be a model for the rest of the company. You must advise the company members if things get out of hand. In the absence of a regular company manager on the road, you may be expected to do some "mother-henning." You should tactfully remind cast members that

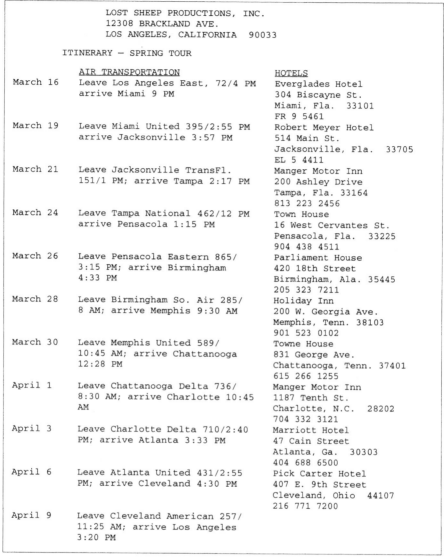

```
              LOST SHEEP PRODUCTIONS, INC.
              12308 BRACKLAND AVE.
              LOS ANGELES, CALIFORNIA  90033

           ITINERARY — SPRING TOUR

              AIR TRANSPORTATION                HOTELS
March 16      Leave Los Angeles East, 72/4 PM   Everglades Hotel
              arrive Miami 9 PM                 304 Biscayne St.
                                                Miami, Fla.  33101
                                                FR 9 5461
March 19      Leave Miami United 395/2:55 PM    Robert Meyer Hotel
              arrive Jacksonville 3:57 PM       514 Main St.
                                                Jacksonville, Fla.  33705
                                                EL 5 4411
March 21      Leave Jacksonville TransFl.       Manger Motor Inn
              151/1 PM; arrive Tampa 2:17 PM    200 Ashley Drive
                                                Tampa, Fla. 33164
                                                813 223 2456
March 24      Leave Tampa National 462/12 PM    Town House
              arrive Pensacola 1:15 PM          16 West Cervantes St.
                                                Pensacola, Fla.  33225
                                                904 438 4511
March 26      Leave Pensacola Eastern 865/      Parliament House
              3:15 PM; arrive Birmingham        420 18th Street
              4:33 PM                           Birmingham, Ala. 35445
                                                205 323 7211
March 28      Leave Birmingham So. Air 285/     Holiday Inn
              8 AM; arrive Memphis 9:30 AM      200 W. Georgia Ave.
                                                Memphis, Tenn. 38103
                                                901 523 0102
March 30      Leave Memphis United 589/         Towne House
              10:45 AM; arrive Chattanooga      831 George Ave.
              12:28 PM                          Chattanooga, Tenn. 37401
                                                615 266 1255
April 1       Leave Chattanooga Delta 736/      Manger Motor Inn
              8:30 AM; arrive Charlotte 10:45   1187 Tenth St.
              AM                                Charlotte, N.C.  28202
                                                704 332 3121
April 3       Leave Charlotte Delta 710/2:40    Marriott Hotel
              PM; arrive Atlanta 3:33 PM        47 Cain Street
                                                Atlanta, Ga.  30303
                                                404 688 6500
April 6       Leave Atlanta United 431/2:55     Pick Carter Hotel
              PM; arrive Cleveland 4:30 PM      407 E. 9th Street
                                                Cleveland, Ohio  44107
                                                216 771 7200
April 9       Leave Cleveland American 257/
              11:25 AM; arrive Los Angeles
              3:20 PM
```

Figure 17.3 Itinerary for a Touring Company

their health, as it affects their performances, is the first concern of the management, and it is for that reason that you are cautioning them to watch their health.

The most common occurrence for touring companies is simply making too much whoopee once out of town, resulting in reduced energy levels that bring down the quality of performances. You can't always prevent such things, but you can caution. If tactful influence fails and an actor's performance suffers as a result of his or her offstage activities, you must inform the producer or the management.

DATE	LEAVE	ARRIVE	HOTEL	PLACE OF ENGAGEMENT OR REHEARSAL	TIME CONCERT	TIME RHSL	CALL NEXT DAY	NOTES
BURT BACHARACH				NOVEMBER			ITINERARY	
THUR. NOV. 19	NO GROUP	TRAVEL	NONE	ATM RECORDS 1416 N. LABREA LOS ANGELES STAGE #1-555-2711	NONE	7 PM	NONE	PARK IN BACK LOT
FRI. NOV. 20	NO GROUP	TRAVEL	NONE SOUND PSL HOLIDAY INN HYLAND ST. 555-3714	LONG BEACH ARENA 270 E. LAKESIDE LONG BEACH CALIF.	8:30 PM	4 PM	NONE	BE AT AIRPORT 1 HR. BEFORE DEPARTURE
SAT. NOV. 21	PERSONNEL AUTO TO TERMINAL #116 (LA)	ARRIVE 1:30 PM SALT LAKE BUS & LIMO	HILTON 200 W. SIXTH SALT LAKE	SPECIAL EVENTS CTR. UNIV OF UTAH 619-555-3719 SALT LAKE CITY	8:00 PM	5 PM	11/22 9 AM	NOON CKOUT. TRVL. W/SAL MONTE TO HOUSTON 11/22
SUN. NOV. 22	SLT. LAKE WAL 5 11:00 LAS VEGAS NAT 2 2:30	L. VEGAS 11:00 HOUSTON 6:50	CHECK RIVIERA HOTEL THEN TO HOUSTON & SAME HOTEL		NONE	NONE	NONE	MERCER McCUNE
SUN. NOV. 22	SLT. LAKE WEST. A.L. 4:10 @ 1:31	DENVER 2:58 555-7010	SHERATON 777 PARK McCUNE & CAR	NOTE: WAIT IN COFFEE SHOP FOR MERCER	NONE	NONE	PUNCH NONE	BURNS

Figure 17.4   Itinerary for a Touring Musical Show

Serving as assistant lighting director on national tours of *Tommy* and *Company*, I loaded in the lighting rig with union crews, focused the show, called the cues for up to six follow spots, then struck it all and moved on to the next venue. I work closely with stage managers throughout the production process. From the SM I expect a preliminary production calendar, contact sheet, and rehearsal reports (if there's any information pertinent to lighting). Once the show has been teched and the tour begins, I give the stage manager (1) followspot cue/track sheets, (2) light cue list, (3) focus charts, and (4) magic/cheat sheet. I keep a production notebook in the lighting road box which has all the plots, paperwork and advance information which is sent to the theater prior to our arrival.

A good SM knows whether a special is off focus, or if the actor forgot the blocking, and has the initiative to remedy the situation. The best SMs know their shows inside and out, and really watch what's happening on stage every night, becoming both director and lighting designer once the show has opened.

Ben Kato
Assistant Lighting Designer
Jeffrey Finn Productions

Overseeing the Arrival

The packing, padding, and care of sets, props, costumes, and technical equipment concern every department head. You coordinate with them in planning every move. You are the overseer of the move.

```
TO:  LOST SHEEP PRODUCTIONS, INC.
     12308 Brackland Ave.
     Los Angeles, California  90033

Gentlemen

It is my understanding that all personnel employed by, and
who will travel with, the Lost Sheep road company must agree
to the following:

That while we are in the employ of Lost Sheep Productions,
Inc., we will conduct ourselves in a manner that will not
bring any adverse criticism to Lost Sheep Productions or its
clients.

That our manner of dress will be businesslike, neat, and in
good taste, particularly when traveling.

That we will travel with the group as assigned and ask for no
changes or deviations from travel schedules and itineraries.
All travel departures are final and no changes can be made
except by Lost Sheep Productions or representatives who have
been instructed that the only change that can be made is a
change for the entire group. The reason for this is that
changes affect price and budget and will not be allowed.

It is our understanding that we are on a job and a business
trip and not on a paid vacation. The show and any rehearsals
are to take first consideration in any planning of extracur-
ricular activities.

That when technical rehearsals are called, all personnel in-
volved are expected to put the same effort into them as into
the performances.

That all personnel will be prompt at any and all calls for
fittings, rehearsals, or performances as called by the stage
manager.

                        AGREED TO:_____
                                        (name)

                             DATE:_____
```

Figure 17.5   Touring Agreement for Cast and Staff

It is particularly important that set diagrams be accurate and that all
flats be marked with accurate butting guides so that crews who have never
seen the assembled set can put it together with ease.

On arrival at a new location you first go to the theater. You inspect the
premises to ensure that your setup plans are workable (see Chapter 5,
"Information Packets"). You assign dressing rooms and make sure that
they are in serviceable condition. You supervise the setup and check your
personal equipment. You greet the new crew members who will run the
show and review the running order, lighting sheet, sound plot, and shift
plot chart with them (see Chapter 12).

One thing that was of great importance to our company was mail! Always get a list of forwarding addresses for the tour, and make sure that you get the correct delivery addresses for the theatre. If you only have an office address, mail won't be accessible on weekends, or the office may be in another building entirely and you'll never know it's there. Leave a list of addresses with each theatre so if mail gets there after you've left, they can forward it. If they won't do that, make sure they will return it to sender. Mail is very important to you when you're on the road. You don't want a letter from your husband sitting on a desk in Wilmington when you're in Boston wondering why he hasn't written.

> Jill Johnson
> ASM, City of Angels
> Shubert Theatre, Los Angeles

On the tour I was responsible for making sure that all luggage was on and off buses/carousels/luggage carts. I tipped all porters, bellhops, and bus drivers each time we moved into a city, and I coordinated color coding and tagging all bags so that they were delivered to the correct hotels. Hopefully there's a company manager as well, which we had. But he wasn't always with us on travel days and the bulk of travel duties fell on the SMs. I was also in charge of Equity breaks and food stops.

> Jill Johnson
> ASM, City of Angels
> Shubert Theatre, Los Angeles

On the McCartney concert tour they were forcing the crews not to eat meat while the show was in the venue. Everything was soy and tofu, and we were not allowed to bring our own food. It was very disturbing to a lot of people.

> Sean P. Crandall
> Local Crew Member
> Paul McCartney Concert Tour

[Does the tour management have the right to impose dietary rules on the crew? Are the rules made clear to the crew prior to their being hired?]

Before leaving the theater, post your local address and phone number on the callboard so that it is available in an emergency for the management of the theater and the local crew members.

You should then check with the cast to ensure that their hotel accommodations are satisfactory.

Advance Letters

In very large companies there are sometimes advance people who go to a new location ahead of the company to prepare for their arrival. Sometimes an assistant stage manager may be dispatched in advance. But in many cases the problems of a traveling company can be anticipated and smoothed out via letter (see Figure 17.6 and Chapter 5, "Information Packets," and also Figure 5.7). Letters requesting specific support (to hotels for accommodations, to business agents of unions for local personnel, to host theater owners, etc.) are usually sent out over the signature of the producer or company management. You can contribute to these letters by letting management know what problems you anticipate or encounter—for example, difficulty of hotels cashing checks for cast members on paydays, unavailability of an elevator during a load-in, and so on.

Calling a special staff meeting to brainstorm a move or series of moves can save time and money on the road.

For the stage manager who travels and needs to focus a show quickly and efficiently, I have found that it is most helpful to grid the stage by dividing it into squares with numbers across the foots and up the center line. That way positions and hot spots can be identified and recreated with great precision. The only additional information needed is shutter information and gel color.

Leonard Auerbach
Associate Professor, Department of Theatre Arts
State University of New York at Stony Brook

```
            LOST SHEEP PRODUCTIONS, INC.
            12308 BRACKLAND AVE.
            LOS ANGELES, CALIFORNIA   90033

Mr. Victor M. Otorino
General Manager
The Chechonovitz Civic Light Opera
2020 Himmelfarb Drive
Chechonovitz, California

Dear Mr. Otorino,

On November 18, 2001, we will be setting up the Lost Sheep
production of THE MAGNIFICENT EIGHT. Our truck should arrive
on Thursday at 11 AM.

We would appreciate it if you would take the necessary mea-
sures to clear any alley or passageway to allow our truck ac-
cess to your loading dock at that time. Because of a very
tight schedule, it is essential that our truck be allowed to
unload immediately upon arrival and if elevators are in-
volved, that a man be placed on duty on a freight elevator
for our use at the time above until we have finished carrying
in our equipment.

Our stage manager will be Mr. Lawrence Stern. Anything he
asks of you will be in the name of Lost Sheep Productions and
your cooperation will be appreciated.

We would like your house electrician, when we unload, to an-
swer any questions of our technical crew. Mr. Chris Pa-
padapoulos will be our carpenter. We will be carrying all of
our own stage draperies, lights, PA system, and projection
equipment.

We will be coming in on a yellow card and we will be employ-
ing union stagehands. Our carpenter will be in touch with
your local business agent concerning calls for local men to
assist us.

We will need a grand piano, tuned to 440 pitch, piano bench,
and a 12' x 12' rug for the musicians at stage right.

Thank you for your cooperation. We look forward to working
with you in your facility.

                          Sincerely,

                          Sid Rosenwald

                          SID ROSENWALD
                          Executive Producer
```

Figure 17.6   Advance Letter to Host Theater Manager

Suggested Classroom Exercise

Brainstorm a strike plan for a current production and put it in chronological order. Compare it to the strike plan shown in Figure 17.1.

18

Organizing Information

*All plays are problem plays, the problem being to get
the play produced.*

—Anonymous

The world is in the midst of an information explosion. The availability of
books, magazines, newspapers, radio and TV broadcasts, microfilm,
photocopies, and computer printouts is almost overwhelming. As the
amount of information available to every stage manager increases, she or
he must decide on how to organize it so that she or he can make use of
it.

Local Theater

You might want to start your personal acquisition of theater information
by sending a postcard to every live theater in town, asking to be placed on
the theater's mailing lists. Write to commercial, educational, showcase,
community, and children's theaters. You will soon receive information in
the mail about who's doing what, and you will receive more complete and
accurate information than you can find in your newspaper.

Go to the theater as often as you can. Make notes in your programs as
to outstanding acting and technical credits. Save your programs.

Newspapers and Magazines

Read local newspapers and national magazines regularly. Making a scrapbook of theater information is the easiest way of keeping abreast of live theater (see Figure 18.1).

(*Varsity, The Stage Daily,*
May, 2001)

**LEGIT TECH MEN
CONVENE IN L.A.**

The United Institute for Theater
Technology will hold its nint^
conference at the Los A^
today through Thu^
287 professio^
nected v^
ten^
Th
Total
will be
and less
week. Rig
Between R
and the Left
panel chairec
fessor from No.
tomorrow morni
The next sessio,
noon, is "New Tech
computers in theatres
be discussed. Wednesc
tour the Music Center b
"Building Codes and Sig
sion at Ahmanson Theatre
noon session will be "Prope
ery," conducted at L.A. City .
"Electronics in the Theatre'
"Techniques of the Thrust Static
be subjects of the final meetings ,
Thursday at the Hilton.

(*Varsity, The Stage Daily,*
December, 2000)

BROADWAY OPENINGS

Last of the Red Hot Lovers

New York, December 29—Neil
Simon does it again in this new
comedy, which opened last
night at the O'Neill Theater to a

(*Los Angeles Messenger,*
February, 2001)

**NEW THEATER GROUP
IN EAST CUCAMONGA**

Northeast Cucamonga—A new community theatrical group is forming
here to bring back the flavor of the
straw hat summer theater circuit to
this bustling area, long destitute of
its former theatrical ornament, the
Greater Cucamonga Thespians' Theater Playhouse and Operatic Pavilion,
now dark.

The Cucamonga Caperers, a group
composed of theatrical people formerly active in Anaheim and Azusa, is
under the leadership of Fred Freedley,
stage director, George Geomble, scenic designer, Louis Lumber, music director, and Archie Arkwright, legal
and business advisor. The non-profit
organization will provide talented locals with an outlet for their creative
energies, and visiting stage favorites
with a chance to show their stuff to
a summer audience.

Four plays are yet to be selected
as kickoff items to get the group moving, the first due to open in late May
or early June of this year.

(*Los Angeles Bugle,*
January, 2001)

STAGE NEWS

**Top Billing for Computer in
"Tommy"**

If you want information about
the production of the rock op-
ra "Tommy," now playing at
: Roxy Theater as directed by
/ Rosen and starring Teddy
hers in the title role, then
the stage manager.
'hat's that? The stage man-
^ys. Well, why not? Stage
^nds are in a pretty good
^nd know what's going
^you say, directors are
better one—except
^r where some very
^re's recording the
director would
is stage man-
^.
^annel com-
^nager Dan
^rammed
^dy. All
^r rush-
^oride
^sis-
^gs
^

^d by
^ true mar-
^nd technical art
^cacy of handling is
^ou don't upstage your
^ors. And we have just the
man to do the delicate handling:
our audio-visual programmer-
director, Jim McKie.

Figure 18.1 Likely Items for a Manager's Scrapbook

Clip local reviews of plays. Note the technical credits. You may soon
discover, for instance, that just a handful of people are getting all the good
lighting reviews. Even if you have never worked with these people, you
will start to know who they are.

You will also be able to determine trends. What type of plays are being
done by the many community theaters in your area? What types of plays
are the educational theaters doing? The showcase theaters? The commercial theaters? The experimental theaters? By reading nationally published
reviews of Broadway and off-Broadway openings, you can learn to anticipate which of these plays will later be done by certain local theaters.

Which local producers do consistently good work? By judging the type
of plays they do and the quality of their work, which producers would you
prefer to work for? Which could you learn the most from? The largest, most
plush plant in town may not be doing the kind of work with which you

would want to associate yourself. By going to the theater and reading reviews, you can discover the theaters in which you would most like to work.

Also, clip articles on all aspects of production and reviews of new books about theater.

A subscription to one or more of the trade papers might provide you with good current information.

Trade Papers

Back Stage
770 Broadway
New York, NY 10003-9595
(646) 654-5700
www.backstage.com

*Back Stage West, The Performing Arts
  Weekly*
5055 Wilshire Blvd., 6th Floor
Los Angeles, CA 90036-6103
(323) 525-2225
fax: (323) 525-2226
www.backstagewest.com

Hollywood Reporter
5055 Wilshire Blvd., #600
Los Angeles, CA 90036-4396
(323) 525-2000
fax: (323) 525-2377
e-mail:
   mailbox@hollywoodreporter.com
www.hollywoodreporter.com

Variety
Los Angeles Office
5700 Wilshire Blvd., Suite 120
Los Angeles, CA 90036-5804
(323) 857-6600
fax: (323) 857-0494
www.variety.com

Variety
New York Office
245 West 17th Street
New York, NY 10011-5383
(212) 337-7002
fax: (212) 337-6975
www.variety.com

Magazines

TDR (The Drama Review)
MIT Press
5 Cambridge Center
Cambridge, MA 02142-1493
(617) 253-2889
fax: (617) 577-1545
e-mail: journals-orders@mit.edu
www.mitpress.mit.edu

Dramatics
2343 Auburn Avenue
Cincinnati, OH 45219-2819
(513) 421-3900
fax: (513) 421-7077
e-mail: lckelley@etassoc.org
www.etassoc.org

Entertainment Design
P.O. Box 470
Mount Morris, IL 61054-0470
(800) 827-0315
   or
32 West 18th Street
New York, NY 10011-4612
(212) 229-2965
fax: (212) 229-2084
(800) 827-0315
www.etecnyc.net

Lighting Dimensions
32 West 18th Street
New York, NY 10011-4612
(212) 229-2965
fax: (212) 229-2084
(800) 827-0315
ldsubs@intertec.com

Magazines (continued)

Plays
120 Boylston Street
Boston, MA 02116-4615
(617) 423-3157
fax: (617) 423-2168
www.channel1.com/plays

Plays and Players
Mineco Designs Ltd.
Northway House
1379 High Road
London N20 9LP England
44-181-343-8515
fax: 44-181-446-1410

The Technical Brief

Theater
Yale University, School of Drama
Yale Repertory Theatre
222 York Street, Yale Station
New Haven, CT 06511-4804
(203) 432-9664
www.yale.edu/drama/
    publications

Ulrich's International Periodicals Directory (1999) lists 450 international publications devoted to theater. It is available at many libraries. (The directory is published annually by Cahners Business Information, 121 Chanlon Road, New Providence, NJ 07974-1541, [800] 346-6049.)

Guides to Goods and Services

A fast reference that you will want to index into your prompt script is the theatrical supply listings from the yellow pages of the local phone directory. You might enclose the listings in a mylar sheet protector for convenience.

Where can you get lighting supplies in a hurry? Where can you send someone to repair a damaged wig? Who has Max Factor pancake makeup in 7A on hand? Get the answers fast. Use your yellow pages.

How many times have you driven to a supply house only to find on arrival that they don't have what you need in stock? Call ahead.

Entertainment Design (www.etecnyc.net) publishes an annual Industry Resources Special Issue that lists many of the manufacturers and services that support live theater. In England, *Contacts* (www.spotlightcd.com/spotpubs/pub7.html) lists suppliers and services.

You are only a mouse click away from names, addresses, and websites of suppliers at the following web addresses:

ESTA (Entertainment Service and
    Technology Association)
Princeton University Theatrical
    Supplies
University of Virginia

www.esta.org

http://webware.princeton.edu/
    theater/VENDORS.HTM
www.people.virginia.edu/~rlk3p/
    desource/links/LinkList.html

World's Greatest Lighting
　Manufacturers
(Lighting Internet Service)

www.lighting-inc.com/
manufacture1.html

Here's a sampling of manufacturers:

Altman Stage Lighting Company,
　Inc.
57 Alexander Street
Yonkers, NY 10701-2714
(914) 476-7987
(212) 569-7777
fax: (914) 963-7304
e-mail: rleonard@altmanltg.com
www.altmanltg.com

Apogee Sound, Inc.
2180 S. McDowell Blvd. Ext.
Petaluma, CA 94954-6902
(707) 778-8887

BASH Theatrical Lighting, Inc.
3401 Dell Avenue
North Bergen, NJ 07047-2348
(201) 863-3300
fax: (201) 279-9265

Clear-Com Intercom Systems
4065 Hollis Street
Emeryville, CA 94608-3505
(510) 496-6666
fax: (510) 496-6699
e-mail: sales@clearcom.com
www.clearcom.com

Colortran-Leviton Controls
　Division
20497 SW Teton Avenue
Tualatin, OR 97062-8812
(503) 404-5500
fax: (503) 404-5600
(800) 576-6060
fax: (800) 576-6080
e-mail: info@nsicorp.com
www.colortran.com

Dudley Theatrical
3401 Indiana Avenue
Winston-Salem, NC 27105-3403
(336) 722-3255
fax: (336) 722-4641
e-mail: sales@dudleytheatrical.com
www.dudleytheatrical.com

Eastern Acoustic Works
One Main Street
Whitinsville, MA 01588-2238
(508) 234-6158
fax: (508) 234-8251
www.eaw.com

Eastern Costume Company
7243 Coldwater Canyon Avenue
North Hollywood, CA 91605-4204
(818) 982-3611
fax: (818) 982-1905
e-mail:
　cust.serv.@easterncostume.com
www.easterncostume.com

Electrol Engineering, Inc.
500-A Bynum Road
Forest Hill, MD 21050-3051
(410) 638-9300
fax: (410) 638-2878
e-mail: dimmers@electrol.net
www.electrol.net

Electronic Theatre Controls, Inc.
3030 Laura Lane
Middleton, WI 53562-1754
(608) 831-4116
fax: (608) 836-1736
(800) 688-4116
e-mail: mail@etcconnect.com
www.etcconnect.com

High End Systems, Inc.
2217 West Braker Lane
Austin, TX 78758-4031
(512) 836-2242
fax: (512) 837-5290
e-mail: info@highend.com
www.highend.com

Kliegl Bros.
5 Aerial Way
Syosset, NY 11791-5502
(516) 937-3900
fax: (516) 937-6042

Level Control Systems
130 East Montecito Avenue, #236
Sierra Madre, CA 91024
(626) 836-0446
fax: (626) 836-4883
e-mail: info@lcsaudio.com
www.lcsaudio.com

Mackie Designs, Inc.
16220 Wood-Red Road, NE
Woodinville, WA 98072-9061
(425) 487-4333
fax: (425) 487-4337
(800) 258-6883
e-mail: sales@mackie.com
www.mackie.com

Martin Professional, Inc.
3015 Greene Street
Hollywood, FL 33020-1038
(954) 927-3005
fax: (954) 929-6405
fax: (888) 298-4776
e-mail: martin@martinpro.com
www.martin.dk

Musson Theatrical TV Film
890 Walsh Avenue
Santa Clara, CA 95050-2640
(800) THEATER
(408) 986-0210
fax: (408) 986-9552
e-mail: bob@musson.com
www.musson.com

The Phoebus Co., Inc.
2800 Third Street
San Francisco, CA 94107-3502
(415) 550-1177
fax: (415) 550-2655
e-mail: lighting@phoebus.com
www.phoebus.com

Rosco Laboratories, Inc.
52 Harbor View Avenue
Stamford, CT 06902-5914
(203) 708-8900
fax: (203) 708-8919
(800) 767-2669
e-mail: info@rosco.com
www.rosco.com

Strand Lighting
18111 South Santa Fe Avenue
Rancho Dominguez, CA 90221-5573
(310) 637-7500
(310) 632-5519
(800) 733-0564
sales@strandlight.com
www.strandlight.com

Strong Entertainment Lighting
4350 McKinley Street
Omaha, NE 68112-1643
(402) 453-4444
fax: (402) 453-7238
(800) 424-1215
e-mail: jack.schmidt@btn-inc.com
www.strongint.com

Tomcat USA, Inc.
2160 Commerce Drive
Midland, TX 79703-7504
(915) 694-7070
fax: (915) 689-3805
e-mail: info@tomcatusa.com
www.tomcatglobal.com

See *The New York Theatrical Source Book* or *The Contact Book* for further selections.

Studying a few catalogs will help to make you aware of the industry that is ready to back up the theater. It will help you keep abreast of new products. What do you know about quartz lights? Black light? Foam scenery? Solid-state communications equipment?

Request samples, swatches, and gel books. Services and demonstrations are sometimes available from manufacturers who wish to promote their products. Can you get lighting equipment sales representatives to come out to your theater to help you analyze the problem of augmenting your lighting equipment for a particularly heavy show? Can he or she help you with the know-how to create special effects?

Before you buy, compare products carefully. Not all the factors about a product are stated in brochures. You will want to evaluate cost, durability, repair costs, availability of spare parts, capability of the product, ease of cleaning, ease of repairing or replacing worn parts, proximity to a repair facility, ease in use, unique advantages, and peculiar disadvantages.

Contact File

Use 3" × 5" or 4" × 6" note cards to assemble information: names, street addresses, e-mail addresses, websites, and phone numbers of people who may be helpful to you in your theater work (see Figure 18.2). Keep cards for actors, producers, directors, designers, technicians, costume designers, suppliers of equipment, sources of props, unions, and others. You will want to alphabetize your cards, and you might even want to use some sort of code—various color cards or flags—to help you pull information quickly. A durable metal or wooden box used to be essential for holding the cards, but today's stage manager can carry an electronic organizer or a personal digital assistant (PDA), which begin at around $100.

You may be able to help in casting by keeping tabs on the various fine actors that you discover in plays that you see. Write a card for each actor whose work impresses you. Get his or her address and phone number, as well as his or her agent's name and number. Go out of your way to see the actor in the next play that he or she does.

Books

You should have available a few books on theater that can recharge your intellectual batteries—the type of book that you can read more than once and still find interesting and helpful. These might be considered your "clothesline" books, giving you the basic information that will allow you to assimilate other information, pinning it up on the "clothesline" in your mind.

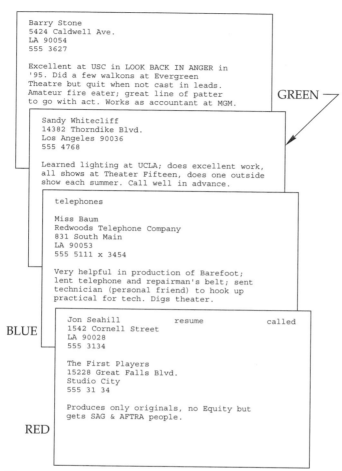

```
Barry Stone
5424 Caldwell Ave.
LA 90054
555 3627

Excellent at USC in LOOK BACK IN ANGER in
'95. Did a few walkons at Evergreen
Theatre but quit when not cast in leads.
Amateur fire eater; great line of patter
to go with act. Works as accountant at MGM.
```

GREEN

```
Sandy Whitecliff
14382 Thorndike Blvd.
Los Angeles 90036
555 4768

Learned lighting at UCLA; does excellent work,
all shows at Theater Fifteen, does one outside
show each summer. Call well in advance.
```

```
telephones

Miss Baum
Redwoods Telephone Company
831 South Main
LA 90053
555 5111 x 3454

Very helpful in production of Barefoot;
lent telephone and repairman's belt; sent
technician (personal friend) to hook up
practical for tech. Digs theater.
```

BLUE

```
Jon Seahill                resume              called
1542 Cornell Street
LA 90028
555 3134

The First Players
15228 Great Falls Blvd.
Studio City
555 31 34

Produces only originals, no Equity but
gets SAG & AFTRA people.
```

RED

Figure 18.2   White, Actors; Green, Technicians; Blue, Suppliers; Red, Producers

What seven books would you take with you to another planet if you expected to establish a live theater there? Perhaps the seven books listed in Figure 18.3 would be a good start for your own personal library. It is better to know seven books well than to own a huge collection of books with uncut pages.

Extensive bibliographies for every theater arts subject can be found in your local library.

In addition, if you are interested in a program of directed reading, many graduate schools of theater arts publish graduate reading lists. Contact the university nearest you. Or you may wish to add your name to the mailing lists of the several publishers who specialize in books on theater arts.

"What Seven Books Would I Take to Another Planet if I Expected to Establish a Live Theater There?"
(a small, prejudiced, but useful selection)

ACTING

Actors on Acting
Cole, Toby, and Helen Krich Chinoy
Crown, distributed by Random House, 1995

DIRECTING

Directors on Directing
Cole, Toby, and Helen Krich Chinoy
Macmillan, distributed by Prentice-Hall, 1990

MAKEUP/COSTUMING

Stage Makeup
Corson, Richard, and James Glavan
Allyn and Bacon, 9th ed., 2000

The Costume Technician's Handbook
Ingham, Rosemary, and Liz Covey
Heinemann, 1992

SCENE DESIGN/SET CONSTRUCTION/LIGHTING

Scene Design and Stage Lighting
Parker, W. Oren, and Harvey K. Smith
Holt, Rinehart & Winston, 7th ed., 1996

HISTORY

History of the Theatre
Brockett, Oscar G., and Franklin J. Hildy
Allyn and Bacon, 8th ed., 1998

PLAYWRITING

Playwriting: How to Write for the Theater
Bernard Grebanier
Barnes & Noble, a division of Harper & Row, 1979

Figure 18.3   Seven Titles to Start a Theater Library

Postcards sent to the following publishers will bring you the latest information about new books on theater as well as lists and mail order prices of hardcover and paperback editions of interest to you.

Allyn & Bacon, Inc.
75 Arlington Street, Suite 300
Boston, MA 02116
(617) 848-6000
www.ablongman.com

Cornell University Press
Sage House
512 East State Street
Ithaca, NY 14850-4499
(607) 277-2338
www.cornellpress.cornell.edu

The Drama Bookshop
723 Seventh Avenue, Floor 2
New York, NY 10019-6856
(212) 944-0595
(800) 322-0595
www.playbill.com/cgi-bin/plb/
    dramabooks?cmd=search

Drama Publishers
260 Fifth Avenue
NewYork, NY 10001
(212) 725-5377
fax: (212) 725-8506
e-mail:
    info@quitespecificmedia.com
www.quitespecificmedia.com

The Fireside Theater
Member Service Center
6550 E. 30th Street
P.O. Box 6375
Indianapolis, IN 46206-6375
(800) 688-4442

Indiana University Press
601 North Morton Street
Bloomington, IN 47404-3797
(812) 855-4203
fax: (812) 855-7931
credit card orders: (800) 842-6796

The Internet Theatre Bookshop
e-mail: info@stageplays.com
www.stageplays.com

University of Miami Press
P.O. Box 4836
Hampden Station
Baltimore, MD 21211-0836
(410) 516-6952

Keeping Current with the Technology of Theater

Here are five suggestions for keeping abreast of the incredible technology that is now available.

1. *Join USITT:*

> The United States Institute for Theatre Technology
> 6443 Ridings Road
> Syracuse, NY 13206-1111
> (315) 463-6463

The USITT studies the technology of theater and disseminates information about theater equipment, production materials, and production techniques. Membership is encouraged from theater planners, owners, clients, architects, engineers, and designers; city officials, builders, administrators, and managers; educators, writers, critics, playwrights, performers, and directors; designers and makers of stage scenery, lighting, machinery, furnishings and equipment; and designers and technicians in all theater disciplines.

The USITT arranges meetings, programs, discussions, tours, and demonstrations. It also publishes a magazine, *Theatre Design and Technology*, in addition to a newsletter, *Sightlines*, newsletter supplements, a membership directory, an annual report, as well as regional newsletters and reports.

An annual Conference and Stage Expo is held to further promote an exchange of information between outstanding professionals and theater people who share concerns and who can help you solve professional problems. The conference is attended by thousands.

Membership benefits include discounts on publications, New York hotels, and car rentals.

Beyond this, the USITT annually honors individuals, services, innovations, and publications that have made outstanding contributions to the performing arts.

It was the USITT that brought about the use of a standard protocol for communication between control boards and dimmers (DMX 512). Most U.S. manufacturers of theater lighting equipment now provide for the protocol even if they feel that their own is more effective. This allows a theater to use a control board manufactured by one company with dimmers made by another.

2. *Subscribe to Entertainment Design:*

> *Entertainment Design*
> (subscriptions)
> P.O. Box 470
> Mount Morris, IL 61054-0470
> (800) 827-0315
> from outside US: (815) 734-1116

Entertainment Design is published by Intertec Publishing Corporation, whose editorial and advertising offices are at 32 West 18th Street, New York, NY 10011-4612, (212) 229-2965, fax: (212) 229-2084. This magazine features articles on new theater technology and novel theater applications of technology developed for architectural and other purposes. Much of the new technology is reflected in advertisements. The January issue annually features a "Technical Literature Guide" that lists product brochures, catalogs, specification sheets, newsletters, and other descriptive materials available from companies that manufacture, distribute, and provide services for theater. Products include lighting equipment, scenic materials, costumes, special effects, and more. Among the many services are flameproofing and rigging. The June issue features an annual directory of many companies that manufacture, distribute, and provide services for the theater.

3. Attend the annual LDI trade show:

> Lighting Dimensions International
> (contact: Mike Doolittle)
> 32 West 18th Street
> New York, NY 10001
> (212) 229-2965
> fax: (212) 229-2084
> www.etecnyc.net

Lighting Dimensions International (LDI) is an international trade show of lighting, sound, and special effects for clubs, concerts, theater, television, and films. It has become the *de facto* tech products trade show of the entertainment industry. There are booths where you can try out new equipment, as well as workshops, exhibits, and other events. Many manufacturers, both domestic and foreign, introduce their new products at this show. The show is held in the fall. Visit their website for schedule and registration information.

4. Browse the World Wide Web (WWW):

Here are just a very few of the companies that have pages out in cyberspace. Appendix D has an expanded list.

Barbizon	www.barbizon.com
Chimera	www.chimeralighting.com
Dove Systems	www.dovesystems.com
Eastern Accoustic Works	www.eaw.com
Electronic Theatre Controls, Inc	www.etcconnect.com
High End Systems	www.highend.com
Intertec Publishing	www.etecnyc.net
(for information about LDI and TCI)	
Iridion	www.vari-lite.com
Premier	www.premier-lighting.com
Strong	www.strongint.com
Tomcat	www.tomcatusa.com

5. Research software that can be applied to stage management:

From word processing to spreadsheet programs to databases, there are many software programs now available that can be applied to theatermaking and stage management.

Office computers are another boon for stage managers in a number of ways. Forms that change only in names/dates rather than format can be stored and called up for each show, rewrites can be done (and redone!) in a matter of minutes with a script on disc, and home computers offer the option of doing work at home instead of chaining yourself to the office. Fax machines are equally helpful in terms of timesaving devices—contracts to agents, measurements to New York costume houses, and set drawings to tech directors can be sent in seconds and answers return as fast. E-mail is wonderful! I now e-mail all my reports to the office as well as to most of my designers. I come home to find at least two messages every night from designers with questions and attachments of sound breakdowns, wardrobe plots, etc. Actually, I don't know if I should be so happy that all that work finds me at home, but it does make things easier!

Jill Gold
Stage Manager
Pasadena Playhouse

Computer-Aided Design and Drafting (CADD)

Computer programs used by draftspeople and engineers, called computer-aided design and drafting (CADD), can also help scene and lighting designers. In addition to increasing accuracy in the drafting of sets, CADD programs allow you to make changes very quickly, store drawings, and create a library of drawings that can be recalled and reused. In selecting a printing device, consider dot matrix, laser, and plotters. The better the quality of your output, generally, the higher the cost of the printer. As in the selection of light boards, it's important to talk to people who have used the programs and equipment, and then shop around. An increasing pool of people are qualified to apply CADD and other computer programs to the challenges of theater production. See *TCI*, April 1996, pages 50–51, for an article on computer-generated scenic design.

An intriguing application of CADD programs is in the area of costume design. Patternmaker is a full-featured garment design program for the PC with both DOS and Windows versions. Software runs on any PC with Windows 3.1 or better, to support most commonly available digitizers, printers, and plotters up to 72" in width. As with CADD scene design, the aquisition of a satisfactory printer is a major concern since the best application of the software is to produce a clear pattern. A free demo of Patternmaker may be downloaded from the Internet at www.patternmaker.com. At this website you may also join an online discussion group.

Police, Fire, and Municipal Regulations

You should be aware that there are police regulations, fire laws, and municipal codes that may control the operations of all theaters, if and when applied (see Figure 18.4).

These regulations vary with each city and within cities, depending on the size of the theater. They are generally written in the form of ordinances and sections of the city code. The ordinances and codes are available in the offices of city administrators concerned, and in public libraries. Unfortunately, not all regulations pertaining to live theater are neatly grouped together. They may be found under such diverse headings as "Rules Governing Cafe Entertainment and Shows," "Assemblage Occupancies," "Safety to Life Requirements," and others. Figures 18.5 and 18.6 show samples of fire plots that are filed with the local fire department.

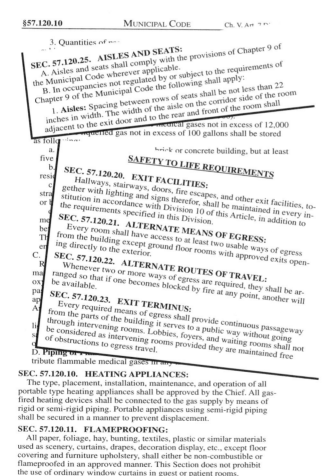

§57.120.10   MUNICIPAL CODE   Ch. V. Art 7 D

3. Quantities of n

SEC. 57.120.25. AISLES AND SEATS:
A. Aisles and seats shall comply with the provisions of Chapter 9 of the Municipal Code wherever applicable.
B. In occupancies not regulated by or subject to the requirements of Chapter 9 of the Municipal Code the following shall apply:
1. **Aisles:** Spacing between rows of seats shall be not less than 22 inches in width. The width of the aisle on the corridor side of the room adjacent to the exit door and to the rear and front of the room shall

medical gases not in excess of 12,000
liquefied gas not in excess of 100 gallons shall be stored as follo

brick or concrete building, but at least

SAFETY TO LIFE REQUIREMENTS

SEC. 57.120.20. EXIT FACILITIES:
Hallways, stairways, doors, fire escapes, and other exit facilities, together with lighting and signs therefor, shall be maintained in every institution in accordance with Division 10 of this Article, in addition to the requirements specified in this Division.

SEC. 57.120.21. ALTERNATE MEANS OF EGRESS:
Every room shall have access to at least two usable ways of egress from the building except ground floor rooms with approved exits opening directly to the exterior.

SEC. 57.120.22. ALTERNATE ROUTES OF TRAVEL:
Whenever two or more ways of egress are required, they shall be arranged so that if one becomes blocked by fire at any point, another will be available.

SEC. 57.120.23. EXIT TERMINUS:
Every required means of egress shall provide continuous passageway from the parts of the building it serves to a public way without going through intervening rooms. Lobbies, foyers, and waiting rooms shall not be considered as intervening rooms provided they are maintained free of obstructions to egress travel.

D. Piping

tribute flammable medical gases in any

SEC. 57.120.10. HEATING APPLIANCES:
The type, placement, installation, maintenance, and operation of all portable type heating appliances shall be approved by the Chief. All gas-fired heating devices shall be connected to the gas supply by means of rigid or semi-rigid piping. Portable appliances using semi-rigid piping shall be secured in a manner to prevent displacement.

SEC. 57.120.11. FLAMEPROOFING:
All paper, foliage, hay, bunting, textiles, plastic or similar materials used as scenery, curtains, drapes, decoration display, etc., except floor covering and furniture upholstery, shall either be non-combustible or flameproofed in an approved manner. This Section does not prohibit the use of ordinary window curtains in guest or patient rooms.

Figure 18.4 Typical Theater Safety Regulations

728 West Peachtree St   Phone 404.881.8801
Atlanta GA 30308   Fax: 404.881.1711

The Atlanta Opera

Fax

To:	Captain Nathaniel Grissom	From:	David Grindle, Production Stage Manager
Fax:	404-853-7093	Pages:	1
Phone:	404-853-7062	Date:	07/17/00
Re:	Live Flame in Cosi fan tutte	CC:	Sarah Wikle

☐ Urgent   ☐ For Review   ☐ Please Comment   ☐ Please Reply   ☐ Please Recycle

Captain Grissom-

I wanted to advise you as to our plans for use of live flame for the upcoming Atlanta Opera production of *Cosi fan tutte* at the Fox Theatre.

In the final scene of the opera (approximate 3 hours after the show starts) we are planning to use six (6) tikki torches (the backyard Kmart type) and 2 candleabra. The tikki torches will be brought on and placed in fixed spots on the set and then lit. The candleabra will be carried lit by two chorus men. One man per candleabra.

The burn time for these items will be approximately 20 minutes for tikki's and 10 minutes for the candles.

As we have not yet staged the final scene, I do not have a precise plot to fax you. Once I have that, I will get it to you.

The following is a list of rehearsal dates and times when the live flame is scheduled to be used on stage. The times are for the complete rehearsal, the actual use of flame will occur sometime during the time frame indicated.

Friday, June 2 7p-10p	Thursday, June 8 8p performance
Sunday, June 4 7:30p-10:30p	Saturday, June 10 7:30p performance
Monday, June 5 7p-10:30p	Sunday, June 11 3p performance

Tuesday, June 6 7p-10:30p (there will be an invited audience at this rehearsal)

Figure 18.5   Notice to Fire Department of Intended Use of Fire. Dates and times of both rehearsals and performances are given. All persons who handle fire receive careful instruction and precaution.

Courtesy David Grindle, PSM, The Atlanta Opera.

Experts are usually available to assist theater owners and producers who may call to request inspections of their facilities, or submit plans for approval. The stage manager does not normally do this.

Occasionally, whether requested or not, fire marshals inspect theaters just prior to the opening of new productions to check fireproofing, exits, smoking signs, and and so on. Theaters have been closed and performances postponed as a result of such inspections (see Figure 18.7).

The Atlanta Opera
MACBETH
Fire and Pyro Plot

Act I Scene II

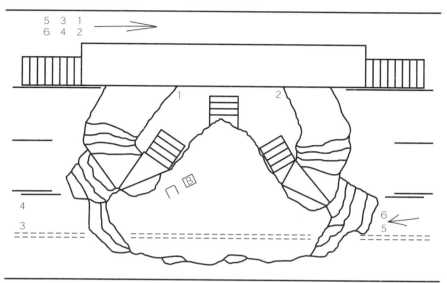

	Live Flame	*F/x*
Top of Scene	Brazier lit (see map for placement) (B)	No Pyro, Fog, or Dry Ice in this scene
6:00	Flash paper thrown on Brazier by Lady Macbeth	
9:30	Brazier extinguished and struck DL by chorus men (T. Tunnell and G. Jones)	
23:00	6 torches carried on by Supers from SR to SL (Brown, Seide, Chrestensen, Coyle, Haynie, Smith)	
27:30	Torches extinguished by supers using dead man switch built into torch	

Figure 18.6   Fire Plot, MACBETH, Act I, Scene II. Fire and special effects are listed on this plot, which is submitted along with notification (see Figure 18.5).

Courtesy David Grindle, PSM, The Atlanta Opera.

I have a very close relationship with the Atlanta Fire Department. We discuss any new regulations. New fire marshals who visit the theatre are always impressed at how well prepared we are, mostly because we started by going to the AFD many years ago to ask them what they require. We also try to keep them abreast through casual conversation of new theater technologies. Before opening night, I fax a list of the use of fire to the fire chief. The most important thing is that I hide nothing from him. If a fire marshal shows up five minutes before curtain and wants a demostration of everything we are using—its ignition, its extinguishing—I do it and hold the show.

> Dave Grindle
> Production Stage Manager
> The Atlanta Opera

(*Los Angeles Bugle,* July, 2000)

STAGE NEWS TODAY

*

The Awareness Theater, recently closed by the fire marshall, has relocated temporarily at the Psychiatry Center Auditorium at the UCLA Medical Center where Bella Harpman is directing two one-acts by Harry Rose on Friday and Sunday nights. The plays are "Big Sol" about an aging convict who fantasizes about the blonde he murdered so effectively that he has his cellmate seeing things, and also "One Time Charlie" which deals w an opium addict who drops peddling dope on horseba

Mrs. Harpman say versity will reinstate ness Theater, starti other members of ' Students' Guild r while the thea duction on c cal Center after ovation c theater

(*Los Angeles Messenger,* February, 2001)

USC LIVING THEATER CALLED OFF

Performances of the Living Theater Saturday night and tonight were canceled at USC following apparent violations of fire safety regulations.

Police called a tactical alert on the campus Friday evening after learning that fire safety laws had been violated and that too many persons were occupying the r-sized stage at once in on of regulations.

 rsity executive di- university rela- aid that the per- nce had been can- because the theater nd staff were "inade-   to assure that the ssary compliance with   safety codes and audi- nce safety would be carried out in accordance with municipal regulations."

Refund information is available by telephone at the following numbers: 555-7834, 555-6093, 555-8427.

(Varsity; The Stage Daily February, 2001)

FIRE DEPT HALTS SHOW OF LIVING THEATER

Performances of Living Theater at USC were cancelled this weekend after fire safety code violations were alleged by fire marshals. A tactical alert was called by police Friday after notification that fire safety codes were apparently being ignored and that too many people were being allowed on stage. Refunds were made available.

Figure 18.7   A Theater in Violation of Safety Laws Can Be Closed Down

You should review public safety requirements with the staff of your theater. The entire staff should take the time to review plans for emergencies.

Frequently in small theaters, scene designers and technical directors build into the audience, covering exit lights and no-smoking signs, and blocking exit aisles with scenery. You should prevent this by calling their attention to the rules.

If you are involved in opening a show in a building that has been newly converted into a theater, ask the producer or management if local regulations have been checked. The number of people allowed in the building, the number of off-street parking spaces necessary, and even the amount of lavatory space are all the subjects of city regulations.

If you are working in an Equity company and feel that the producer is failing to comply with regulations, thus endangering public safety, and you have discussed it with him or her, then take the issue to your union and let the union take up the issue with the producer.

If you are in a nonunion theater situation and can't convince your management or producer to make the theater safe, quit. Then call for fire, police, and building code inspections as a concerned citizen.

People die in theaters as the result of negligence—failure to know and obey the law. As a stage manager, the lives of your cast, crew, and audience may depend on your knowledge and application of the law.

Getting to Know the Unions

"You can't join Equity until you have a job in an Equity company, and you can't get a job in an Equity company until you are a member of Equity." This seeming paradox is often quoted but quite misleading. As soon as you can convince an Equity producer or director that you should be his or her stage manager, the doors of the union will open to you. Equity is not one of the closed unions where nepotism reigns or where "blood is thicker than talent."

If it is your intent to become an Equity stage manager, don't wait for an Equity job to get acquainted with the union. Try to understand the benefits and disadvantages of union membership. Go out of your way to meet a union stage manager. Engage her or him in conversation about her or his work and union. If you live in a city with an Equity office, visit it and get to know the people in the office. The union office is not a placement service, but the union staff is in a good position to know what producers are anticipating productions or casting. Bulletin boards in the union offices frequently display information useful to stage managers. Sometimes the union has available handouts, such as lists of union-approved theaters where you might apply for work.

Figure 18.8 Definition of the Duties of a Stage Manager

DEFINITION OF THE DUTIES OF A STAGE MANAGER

A stage manager under Actors' Equity Contract is, or shall be obligated to perform at least the following duties for the Production to which s/he is engaged, and by performing them is hereby defined as the Stage Manager:

1. Shall be responsible for the calling of all rehearsals, whether before or after opening.
2. Shall assemble and maintain the Prompt Book which is defined as the accurate playing text and stage business, together with such cue sheets, plots, daily records, etc., as are necessary for the actual technical and artistic operation of the production.
3. Shall work with the Director and the heads of all other departments, during rehearsal and after opening, schedule rehearsal and outside calls in accordance with Equity regulations.
4. Assume active responsibility for the form and discipline of rehearsal and performance, and be the executive instrument on the technical running of *each* performance.
5. Maintain the artistic intentions of the Director and the Producer after opening, to the best of his/her ability, including calling correctional rehearsals of the company when necessary and preparation of the Understudies, Replacements, Extras and Supers, when and if the Director and/or the Producer declines this prerogative. Therefore, if an Actor finds himself/herself unable to satisfactorily work out an artistic difference of opinion with the Stage Manager regarding the intentions of the Director and Producer, the Actor has the option of seeking clarification from the Director or Producer.
6. Keep such records as are necessary to advise the Producer on matters of attendance, time, health benefits or other matters relating to the rights of Equity members. *The Stage Manager and Assistant Stage Managers are prohibited from the making of payrolls or any distribution of salaries.*
7. Maintain discipline as provided in the Equity Constitution, By-Laws and Rules where required, appealable in every case to Equity.
8. Stage Manager duties do not include shifting scenery, running lights or operating the Box Office, etc.
9. The Council shall have the power from time to time to define the meaning of the words "Stage manager" and may alter, change or modify the meaning of Stage Manager as herein above defined.
10. The Stage Manager and Assistant Stage Managers are prohibited from handling contracts, having riders signed or initialed, or any other function which normally comes under the duties of the General Manager or Company Manager.
11. The Stage Manager and Assistant Stage Managers are prohibited from participating in the ordering of food for the company.
12. The Stage Manager and Assistant Stage Managers are prohibited from signing the closing notice of the company or the individual notice of any Actor's termination.

Courtesy Actors' Equity Association.

Figure 18.9   Equity's Responsibilities of the Actor. Note the references to the stage manager.

RESPONSIBILITIES OF THE ACTOR

Equity requires management to meet all of its responsibilities under its contract with Equity. In turn, members have certain professional responsibilities to the producer, to the production and to fellow Equity members. **All Equity members must:**

- Be on time for all rehearsals and half-hour calls;

- Notify the Stage Manager as soon as possible, and certainly before half-hour, if you are ill or unable to reach the theatre on time;

- Remember that, even though places for each act will be called, you alone are responsible for all of your entrance cues;

- Observe all reasonable rules of management not in conflict with Equity rules;

- Cooperate with the Stage Manager and Assistant Stage Managers, Dance Captain and Fight Captain;

- Take proper care of and make no unauthorized changes in your costumes, props or makeup;

- Maintain your performance as directed;

- Appear at curtain calls in complete costume and make-up;

- Go to your Deputy in cases of disagreement. If a disagreement cannot be resolved by the authorities backstage, refer it to the appropriate Equity Business Representative.

Your Stage Manager is obligated to report violations to Equity and Equity will, when necessary, call before a Membership Relations Committee any member who violates these rules.

Discipline is a sign of professionalism. Maintain a professional attitude at all times.

Office of the Executive Director

Courtesy Actors' Equity Association.

An Equity card is what one should strive towards, not start with. We recommend that stage managers (and actors) get as much experience as they can before accepting an Equity contract. An Actors' Equity Association card does not guarantee you work. This is attested to by the high unemployment of both actors and stage managers in our union. There are from one to three stage managers in any given production, as compared to whatever the number in the cast. So jobs are even harder for a stage manager than an actor. Stage managers limit their experience possibilities by getting their Equity card because they cannot work non-Equity once they join the union. Experience is the only way for a stage manager to perfect his/her craft. I recommend that a stage manager get as much experience as possible before accepting a job as an Equity stage manager. I cannot stress enough that experience is a most important aspect of a stage manager's future potential.

Martha R. Jacobs
Stage Manager
New York City

[Martha is currently working in an administrative position in live theater in New York City. Her work as a stage manager led to her current position. See Figures 18.8 and 18.9.]

If you accept a job as a stage manager with an Equity company, you must join the union. Thereafter you may never legally work in a non-Equity company without first getting a waiver from Equity.

Actors' Equity Association (AEA)
165 West 46th Street, 15th Floor
New York, NY 10036-2501
(212) 869-8530
fax: (212) 719-9815
www.actorsequity.org

Los Angeles Office
5757 Wilshire Blvd., Suite 1
Los Angeles, CA 90036-3635
(323) 634-1750
fax: (323) 634-1777

San Francisco Office
235 Pine Street, Suite 1200
San Francisco, CA 94104-2733
(415) 391-3838
fax: (415) 391-1108

Chicago Office
203 N. Wabash Avenue,
    Suite 1700
Chicago, IL 60601-2417
(312) 641-0393
fax: (312) 641-6365

Orlando Office
10369 Orangewood Blvd.
Orlando, FL 32821-8239
(407) 345-8600
fax: (407) 345-1522

The Western Region Stage Manager Committee tries to educate stage managers, members, and producers on the roles, duties, and abuses of stage managers. It represents the voice of stage managers within the western region of Actors' Equity Association. The committee would like to remind stage managers that we maintain an interest in and stand in support of their work. In turn, AEA is responsible for serving and assisting stage managers in any grievances, overtime claims, or other problems that might occur with the company that has employed them.

The committee encourages you to contact us if any need arises. Please keep us informed about the progress and problems you encounter. We are interested in what stage managers have to say. We meet on the first Tuesday of the month. Call and get involved.

James T. McDermott
Chairman
Western Region Stage Manager Committee
Actors' Equity Association
(323) 634-1750

Once in a union position, you may quickly find it necessary to deal with members of other unions, depending on the size of your theater staff:

American Federation of Musicians
www.afm.org (national)
Local 47, Hollywood
817 N. Vine
Hollywood, CA 90038-3715
(323) 462-2161
fax: (223) 461-3090
e-mail: local47@afm.org
www.promusic47.org (local)

American Federation of Television
    and Radio Artists (AFTRA)
5757 Wilshire Blvd., 9th Floor
Los Angeles, CA 90036-3689
(323) 634-8100
fax: (323) 634-8194
e-mail: aftra@aftra.com
www.aftra.org

American Guild of Musical Artists
    (AGMA)
1727 Broadway
New York, NY 10019-5284
(212) 265-3687
fax: (212) 262-9088
e-mail: AGMA@AGMANatl.com
www.agmanatl.com

American Guild of Variety Artists
    (AGVA)
184 5th Avenue, 6th Floor
New York, NY 10010-5908
(212) 675-1003
fax: (212) 633-0097
e-mail: agvany@aol.com

American Guild of Variety Artists
    (AGVA)
4741 Laurel Canyon Blvd., Suite 208
North Hollywood, CA 91607-5915
(818) 508-9984
fax: (818) 508-3029
e-mail: agvala@earthlink.net
http://home.earthlink.net/
    ~agvala/agval.html

Association of Theatrical Press
    Agents and Managers (ATPAM)
1560 Broadway, Suite 700
New York, NY 10036-1518
(212) 719-3666
fax: (212) 302-1585
e-mail: atpam@erols.com

International Alliance of Theatrical
    Stage Employees (IATSE)
1515 Broadway, Suite 601
New York, NY 10036-5741
(212) 730-1770
fax: (212) 730-7809
http://iatse.lm.com/

International Alliance of Theatrical
    Stage Employees (IATSE)
Local One (formerly Local 922)
    IATSE
Sound Designers, Lighting Control
    Board Operators, Carpenters,
    Lighting Directors, Spotlight
    Operators
320 West 46th Street
New York, NY 10036-8399
(212) 333-2500
e-mail: snowball@interport.net
www.iatse-local1.org

Screen Actors Guild (SAG)
1515 Broadway, 44th Floor
New York, NY 10036-8996
(212) 944-1030
fax: (212) 944-6774
TTY: (212) 944-6715
e-mail: nypr@sag.org
www.sag.com/newyork/

Screen Actors Guild (SAG)
5757 Wilshire Blvd.
Los Angeles, CA 90036-3600
(323) 954-1600
fax: (323) 594-6603
TTY/TTD (323) 549-6648
www.sag.com

Society of Stage Directors and
    Choreographers
1501 Broadway, Suite 1701
New York, NY 10036-5653
(212) 391-1070
fax: (212) 302-6195
www.ssdc.org

Teamsters Local 399
Studio Transportation Drivers
P.O. Box 6017
North Hollywood, CA 91603-6107
(213) 877-3277
fax: (818) 985-8365
e-mail: callboard@aol.com
    callboard@juno.com
http://members.aol.com/
    tlocal399/399.html

As closely related unions for performers, SAG, AFTRA, and AGVA
have reciprocal agreements as to when and how their members may perform in jurisdictions of the other unions. The producer normally handles
arrangements with the unions and ensures that all members of the cast are
members of Equity, or have been cleared by Equity to work in the production.

Union composition of a staff varies from theater to theater, depending on size and on the arrangements that producers have made with union locals. In a small union house, all of the cast may be Equity and there may be only one non-Equity union member, an IATSE master electrician.

In another larger house, there may be three IATSE members (carpenter, lights, props); two Theatrical Wardrobe Attendants members; five Treasurers and Ticket Sellers members in the box office; two members of ATPAM (publicist and house manager); and five musicians from the AFM (who are paid to play bridge in the wings during a play in which there is no music).

In a huge outdoor theater, Teamster truckers may refuse to leave their trucks and enter the stage area to pick up scenery, insisting that the scenery be loaded out by IATSE stagehands and handed to them on their truck, while IATSE stagehands will refuse to get on a truck, insisting that Teamsters must be present to stack the scenery.

In still another tent theater, four well-paid IATSE crew members may work right alongside six nonunion "apprentices" who are not paid at all; both union and nonunion crew members do the same work, but at the end of the union work call period, the union workers go home while the nonpaid "apprentices" continue to work to the end of the rehearsal period.

The stage manager need never feel that he or she must contest the inequities of union regulations. This is a responsibility of management or the producer. The stage manager should do his or her best to understand the rules that apply to other union members with whom he or she must work: hours, minimum calls, overtime rules, and working restrictions and jurisdictions.

Examples

1. A union property master may be prohibited from moving any lighting equipment, so she looks on while the master electrician, her friend and a member of the same union, toils.
2. A union carpenter may be paid to be on hand for a show in which he has no duties other than pulling the curtain, but his union rules will not allow him to use that paid time to work on the sets of the next show that follows in the same house for the same company.

Start by asking the producer or administrative manager for the information you will need to know about union calls to enable you to plan work calls most efficiently.

If she or he cannot give you sufficient information, request permission to call the business agents of the unions to get this information. Usually the producer or business manager will want to handle this for you.

Discuss work rules with the individual union members concerned. In informal chats find out what union members feel are their obligations to their employer, as well as what they consider the benefits of their union membership.

In the long run, the more you know about the work rules of the other unions, the more money you will be able to save the producer in scheduling calls.

Union rules cannot be summarized here, since they vary from local to local, and since they are also dependent on agreements that each producer makes with each local business agent. It is a mistake to assume that wage scales, hours, and work restrictions are not locally negotiable, regardless of nationally distributed union literature. Stage managers do not negotiate, but producers and business managers do.

Inexperienced stage managers are frequently apprehensive about working with IATSE personnel for the first time. Perhaps this is because the veteran IATSE members are often much older than the new stage managers. There is nothing to fear. Treat members of all other unions with professional courtesy. Give them the same respect for the job they are doing as you expect for yours. Assume that they are trained specialists who know exactly how to carry out their work once you have scheduled it.

It is wrong for a stage manager to harbor contempt or resentment for a member of another union simply because that union prevents his or her exploitation by the producer.

Stage Managers' Association

The Stage Managers' Association (SMA) is not a union, but an association of stage managers who work in the theater, dance, opera, industrial events, and other venues. Members of the SMA include members of AEA, AGMA, AGVA, AFTRA, and other unions, as well as nonunion career-minded stage managers.

Through the SMA website, www.stagemangers.org, stage managers throughout the world can contact one another and exchange information. The SMA posts job openings via e-mail to its on-line membership. Founded in 1982, the SMA has over 400 members. (Stage Managers' Association, P.O. Box 2234, Times Square Station, NY 10108-2020, info@stagemanagers.org.)

Suggested Classroom Exercises

1. Ask students to write to a few manufacturers (pages 255–256) to obtain current catalogs.
2. Have students visit a library to examine *Ulrich's International Periodicals Directory* and select the magazine that they feel would be most useful.

19

Correspondence

As stage manager, you will have little need to write extensive correspondence, but you will want to consider writing a letter to the next stage manager, critiques, letters of recommendation, and thank-you notes.

A Letter to the Next Stage Manager

Turnover of stage managers is very frequent. Sometimes they are there for a season only, and next season a new person is holding the clipboard, starting anew, running into the same problems that you ran into last season. Sometimes stage managers are replaced in the middle of a season, and sometimes a theater has a different stage manager for every single production.

No matter what your length of service, you have found out some things that your replacement can only learn by time-consuming research, trial, and error.

Where did you take the tape recorder to be serviced last time it broke down? When was the last time it was serviced? How frequently should preventive maintenance be done?

Where is the key to the metal bulb protectors for the dressing room lights?

Who services the air conditioning units?

What ceiling outlets are on what lines into the booth?

What mistakes did you make that the next stage manager should avoid?

What working diagrams and templates, applicable to this theater only, can you turn over to your replacement?

There are many little things that only you know. When you leave, the staff cannot be expected to pass this information on to the new stage manager. Some of it may be trivial. Some is important. But all of it would help the new stage manager to adjust to the job more easily.

If you are not going to be around to break in the new stage manager, why not leave a letter to make the adjustment easier? Simply write the same kind of letter that you would like to find if you were coming to the job instead of leaving.

Critiques

The purpose of a written critique is to help you to improve your work on future productions. It is intended to remind you of mistakes you made, problems you solved, and methods you devised. It need not be formal and it need not go anywhere. Don't feel that you have to turn it over to a producer or director because you wrote it. It is for you.

Experience is a great teacher. If the critique reminds you of your experience, it will be a great self-improvement aid. As history students know, mistakes of the past are too soon forgotten and too often repeated.

In your theater career what seems unforgettable to you today will be just a hazy, useless memory tomorrow unless you write it out, review it, and apply it.

As you start into your next production, review your old critiques and try to see how you can contribute more effectively to better theater.

It is the exceptional theater that holds critiquing sessions following productions or seasons. If you should be asked to contribute to such a critique, select one significant item from your written critique to present. Using your most tactful manner, present that one item from the point of view of how best to improve the next production or season. Make sure your suggestions are concrete. Don't offer vague censure or praise. Remember the effective critique should be concerned with locating the "curse" rather than the "culprit." Be hesitant to give adverse criticism on techniques or devices that have produced desired effects.

Letters of Recommendation

You can help capable people with whom you work by writing a letter of recommendation for them (see Figure 19.1). It will help their morale to

```
THE CHECHONOVITZ CIVIC LIGHT OPERA

CHECHONOVITZ, CALIFORNIA


                            August 29

To Whom It May Concern
c/o Mr. George Spelvin
335 Ostrova Drive
Bialistok, California

During the 1997 season I had the pleasure of working with
George Spelvin. He was the company "gopher," a title given
in summer stock to the first person called upon when there
is work to be done.

As a member of the stage crew George set and struck scenery
up and down the aisles of our theater in the round, seven
nights every week. During the day his duties varied. He as-
sisted me as shipping clerk, errand runner, truck driver,
and typist. He helped the property master in collecting and
returning props. On loan to the technical director, he
helped build sets. He painted scenery, properties, and the
stage.

It was always a pleasure to assign George to a job, because
you knew it would be done right — the first time. He always
accepted assignments cheerfully and was alert in seeing if
there was a better way to do a job. Despite his long hours
George was always willing to do a little more, and often
recognized and did work before I could assign it.

George earned the respect of the production staff and cast
members for his dependability and quiet, courteous, unassum-
ing ways.

I would be very pleased to work with George again. I feel
that he is ready for an assignment of greater responsibil-
ity. He would make an excellent assistant stage manager.

                            Sincerely,

                            Lawrence Stern
                            LAWRENCE STERN
                            Production Stage Manager
```

Figure 19.1   Letter of Recommendation from a Manager

know that their work was appreciated, and it may help them to secure better jobs in the future.

Use the theater's letterhead stationery when available.

In your letters of recommendation (1) cite the exact work that the individual performed; (2) give your evaluation of his or her work; (3) state whether you would or would not wish to work with him or her again in the same capacity; (4) evaluate the individual's potential for doing other related work, and for advancement; and (5) be sure to give your title and relationship to the individual.

If the individual was property master this season, do you think she or he might make a good assistant stage manager next season? If the person was assistant stage manager, do you think she or he is ready for stage manager, business manager, or technical director?

If you feel that you have performed well in your position, don't be reluctant to ask for a letter of recommendation from your immediate supervisor.

Copies of letters of recommendation may sometimes be enclosed with résumés when applying for a job.

Thank-You Notes

Don't forget to write thank-you notes, letters of thanks, or letters of appreciation. Let the capable people with whom you worked know that you cared.

Suggested Classroom Exercise

Ask any students who worked in any capacity backstage on the last production to write a critique of their own work, identifying any problems they encountered and explaining what they would do in the future to overcome similar problems.

20

Festivals

There's no such thing as a bad school play.

—Anonymous

Stage managers sometimes find themselves working at festivals and may rise to other staff positions, including manager/producer of a festival. Here's the big picture.

Festivals and *tournaments* are two terms used to describe drama events in which more than one group presents work to an audience or judges, or both. Sometimes *tournament* is used to describe a competitive event and *festival* a noncompetitive event, but generally this distinction is not observed. *Festival* is used here for both.

Purpose of Festivals

Festivals promote the improvement of theater. They give theater people the opportunity to meet, to present their dramatic skills, and to see what their fellow theater workers are doing (and how well). They offer opportunities for exchange of ideas, competition, and social contact. Participants get a chance to "go on the road," to play in an unfamiliar environment. They have an opportunity to evaluate themselves by the reactions of judges and a new audience. Participants may also measure themselves by comparison to the other groups entered.

The festival may be used as a marketplace, bringing together groups and individuals who can hire the groups for appearances at other locations.

A festival should have all of the values of a traditional play. In addition, it should give the festival audience a chance to experience a wide variety of theater in a single day. Audiences become more discerning as a result of attending festivals.

Festivals often result in joyful, stimulating, exciting, and rewarding experiences.

Festival Format

Here are four basic ways to organize a festival. There are a great many variations on these formats.

Plan A

All of the participants prepare a production with a time limit of about 45 minutes. Usually each company chooses its own material, but sometimes the festival rules specify the work to be performed. It may be a scene from a play or musical, a one-act play, or an original script written for the festival, depending on the festival rules. One at a time, each group presents its work to a panel of judges and an audience composed of other festival participants and invited guests. A single auditorium and a single panel of judges are used.

This system is the simplest and works well if the number of entrants is limited. With a dozen entrants, using a schedule that grants 45 minutes to each group, 15 minutes between groups to change sets and to allow the audience to stretch, and 45 minutes to an hour for lunch and dinner, such a festival might start at 9 A.M. and end—by the time the judges have conferred, tabulated their evaluations, and awarded trophies—at midnight. It's a long day for the judges and the festival managers. It is also a long day for any audience members who want to see the entire festival.

In its favor, however, it must be said that this plan is very fair to entrants; they all get to present their work under exactly the same conditions. (But do impatient judges give the last performers the same consideration they give the early ones?)

Plan B

Entrants invite festival judges to see their work at their home theater. From all the entrants, a few are selected to present their works at the finals held in a central location. With just a few plays to be evaluated in the finals, cuttings from each play may be performed during one evening. Or the complete plays may be presented on three successive days, with afternoon and evening performances at a centrally located theater. Or the top three groups may present their complete plays on three successive evenings in competition and the next five groups may present cuttings during the mornings and afternoons, not in competition but as a showcase. The judges in the preliminary rounds need not be the same ones who judge the finals. By performing in their own theaters, some entrants may have initial material advantages (lighting, sets). Judges can compensate for this in their evaluations. In the final rounds, all entrants are on an equal footing.

Award categories may have to be limited or adjusted. For example, if there is usually an award for best lead actress, judges may agree that the finest performer in this category was not invited to the finals. Either they give an individual award on the basis of points during the initial home ground evaluation or they leave out this category and make only group awards. Such a festival might also elect to give no trophies or awards, but rather offer the entrants an evaluation and possibly souvenir pins for participation.

Plan C

The festival is composed of many different 5- to 10-minute events—individual pantomime, group pantomime, individual humorous, individual serious, group humorous, group serious, group special event, and so on. Each group may enter as many events as it chooses. Teams of judges watch the events in rounds and submit ratings. At the end of the first two rounds, after each group in each category has been seen in competition with other entrants by two sets of judges, the ratings are tabulated and the winners proceed to the semifinals.

In the semifinal round another panel of judges rates each entrant, and those with the highest ratings go on to the finals. In this round, entrants are evaluated by still another panel of judges, and winners are selected. The winners then perform for the entire festival audience composed of guests, entrants, and judges.

As complex as this plan is, it can work smoothly and effectively. It can allow some 70 schools in a metropolitan area to take part during a single day with a schedule that may run from 8 A.M. to 5 P.M. Winning entrants have to repeat their scenes five times during the day, but since the scenes are short and there is much time between performances, this is not too much of a hardship. Those eliminated during the early rounds have a chance to watch the work of those still in competition.

Plan D

Plan D must be held at a large facility such as a university or multitheater art complex. From 10 to 25 participating groups perform one-acts, children's theater, or cuttings in a carnival atmosphere. Each entering group presents its selection two to five times during a period of one to three days. There may be 10 to 15 different "theaters" operating simultaneously, with starting times overlapping. Audience groups may be scheduled to see specific performances, or they may arrive at the festival at any time during the day, examine the schedule, and then go to see the entrant that is performing next or wait and see another group that is scheduled to perform 15 minutes later. In this type of festival the entire audience is not expected to see every entering group, but it is hoped that there will be something for everyone. Entering groups do not usually compete for trophies, but judges may submit written evaluations or critique orally.

Planning

Regardless of the format you choose, organization and long-range planning are absolutely essential to success. Festival planning should start with a meeting of the festival staff, at least six months to a year before the festival. It is important to allow enough time to organize the festival and to do all the supporting work.

The number of participants and the size of the audience should be carefully estimated at the initial meeting. The number of invitations, programs, judges, and so on, will depend on this estimate, and very little advance work can be done without it. The date(s) of the festival, the host campus or theater, and the overall festival theme, if any, should also be determined at that meeting, because all publicity from then on should emphasize the date(s), place, and theme.

Here are some of the individuals and committees usually needed to make a festival run smoothly:

1. Producer (Executive Director, Chairperson)
2. Rules
3. Registration
4. Judges/Evaluators
5. Tabulations/Evaluations
6. Programs
7. Publicity
8. Guests/Hospitality
9. Facilities (Technical Director, Room Chairperson)
10. Stage Crew (Stage Manager)
11. Associate Producer or Reviewers
12. Food/Refreshments
13. Business Manager/Trophies

Some of the committees may be combined (such as rules and registration, business manager and trophies, and judges and evaluation). But it is desirable to break up duties as much as possible so that individual chairpersons can do a small job very well rather than accepting a lot of responsibility and carrying it out marginally.

It is also usually preferable to have one individual responsible for the work of each committee rather than appointing cochairs. Each chairperson may recruit a deputy chairperson (next year's chair) and should recruit as many committee members as are needed to carry out the work of the committee.

Following are brief descriptions of the work of individuals and committees, with some discussion of the problems that must be faced. Since the specific work of individuals and committees varies with the type of festival, letters A through D are used following each entry to denote the types of plan to which it applies.

Festival Producer (A, B, C, D)

The top executive officer, regardless of title, coordinates all committees, troubleshooting any problem that the committees cannot resolve. He or she presides over festival planning and preparing of critiques, and serves as figurehead for the festival.

The producer's most difficult problem is delegating authority to individuals and committee chairpersons. An effective producer motivates capable individuals to accept responsibility.

The producer does not get bogged down in the actual work of the committees. If a committee chairperson becomes ill during a critical period before the festival, the producer finds a new chairperson; the producer does not take over the sick person's work.

A producer's effectiveness is not measured by how much he or she does, but by how much he or she gets done by others. (Before you accept a job as a festival producer, embroider that last sentence on a sampler.)

The initial planning meeting is very important for the producer. He or she should review the production calendar or schedule with all the chairpersons and ask them to determine deadlines for the completion of their work.

Three important principles should be applied in setting up the production calendar:

1. Expect and plan for delays! Play the "What if . . . ?" game. Example: What if it takes the registration chairperson two more days than planned to get in all the names of the entrants? How will this delay affect the work of the program chairperson? After answering such questions, space deadlines so that there is room between interdependent deadlines. You now plan a three-day period between the registration deadline and the deadline for the program chairperson to get the names to the printer.

2. Set up minor checkpoints with each chairperson. Instead of establishing one deadline for each chairperson's completed work, set up deadlines or checkpoints for small parts of that work. Example: Instead of establishing a single deadline for the program chairperson, establish deadlines for artwork completed, copy edited material to the printer, and so on.

3. Plan deadlines as far in advance of the festival as is comfortable. Example: At the initial planning meeting, decide on the type of trophies. What deadline should be established for obtaining the trophies? Two weeks before the festival? Three? Four? When possible, schedule deadlines so that they do not coincide with other deadlines. This will allow you to deal with one item at a time.

Applying these three principles allows the producer the comfort of checking on minor problems throughout the organization stage rather than facing total panic the day before the festival.

Committee chairpersons should be encouraged to submit an information copy of all work to the producer as it is completed. The producer should also call and meet with chairpersons periodically to ensure that they have not run into snags or delays.

The producer also works with the chairpersons, especially the publicity chairperson, when a figurehead is needed. If a newspaper runs a picture headed, for example, "Mayor Presents Festival Proclamation," the smiling, relaxed individual accepting the proclamation is likely to be the producer.

After the festival the producer should hold a critiquing session with all committee chairpersons. Each chairperson should discuss the major problems he or she encountered. Emphasis must be placed on what the chairperson had not been adequately prepared to do. The chairpersons should then write brief notes to their hypothetical successors (even if they plan to be around next year). They can attach samples of their work, such as the illustrations in this chapter. With the materials gathered into a festival procedures file or book, the next year's chairperson can start planning with the benefit of past years' experience.

The person who is appointed festival producer should be someone who has had experience as chairperson of one or more committees during prior festivals. It should be clear to all committee chairpersons that their work will be considered when staff appointments are made for future festivals.

The work of a festival producer is unquestionably time consuming. Principals and department chairpersons must recognize this fact. If possible, they should reduce the teaching hours or other responsibilities of producers to allow them adequate time to devote to their festivals. In some cases, student teachers, teaching assistants, or students can be recruited to assist producers. Above all, however, producers must delegate authority and not overcommit their own time.

Rules (A, B, C, D)

The rules chairperson is responsible for writing, updating, and distributing the rules of the festival. At some Plan C festivals, the rules committee holds sessions during the entire festival to make judgments on reported infractions. Some rules that have worked for various festivals in southern California are given in Appendix E at the end of this book.

Rules should be reviewed prior to the initial planning meeting for the festival. Any proposed revisions should be brought to the attention of the entire committee—and sometimes to the attention of the entire membership of the sponsoring organization—before they are made.

Complete rules should be mailed out with the invitations to participate. You might want to send out two copies with instructions that the second copy be signed and returned with the registration forms. This might promote study of the rules and compliance. It is also helpful to underline or use asterisks to call attention to rules that have been changed since the last festival.

One possible system for handling infractions at a Plan C festival is as follows: Anyone (participant, judge, or observer) may report an infraction to a room chairperson. The room chairperson then fills out an infraction form (see Figure 20.1) and sends it to the rules committee. The event is allowed to continue, but after the event, the rules committee summons the parties involved and decides whether a participant has indeed violated a rule and whether the participant is disqualified.

```
         Report of Suspected Rule
                Infraction

School Code Number:_____

Room Number:_____

Category:_____

Reported by:_____

Date/Time:_____

Suspected Infraction:_____

_____

_____
-------------------------------------
(for rules committee use:)

Judges:_____

Findings:_____

Action Taken:_____

_____
```

Figure 20.1   Rule Infraction Report Form

In Plan C tournaments, possible violations can also be examined by dispatching judges to observe in subsequent rounds.

Registration (A, B, C, D)

The registration chairperson is responsible for soliciting entrants. He or she mails to potential entrants flyers announcing the festival along with registration forms (Figure 20.2). When mail response is not adequate, the chairperson follows up with phone calls. He or she is also responsible for collecting entry fees, photographs, and other entry requirements.

In some cases the chairperson is responsible for assigning entries a code. In competitive festivals some entrants feel that judges will be influenced by the name of the school rather than the performance of the actors, particularly in cases where that school has won the past competition or several past competitions. Codes (like X, Y, Z, 25MM, 40ZZ) replace school names in programs and the judges' ballots, thus lessening the possibilities of prejudice.

In Plan C festivals, to handle registration of several different events, registration forms for each event (individual humorous, individual pantomime, group pantomime, etc.) should be color-coded.

The registration chairperson schedules the entrants and in some cases mails back to them confirmation of their entry along with their specific performance schedule (see Figure 20.3) and a festival information packet.

Judges (A, B, C, D)

The judges (evaluators) chairperson is responsible for obtaining the judges, or evaluators, needed for the festival. The number of judges will depend on the type of festival and the number of entrants.

The chairperson should be aware of a common tendency of entrants to accept decisions more readily when there are more judges for each round. For instance, entrants would prefer to be rated by five judges rather than three. But if some 50 sections are to be judged simultaneously (Plan C), an increase in the number of judges required can involve recruiting 100 extra judges!

Qualifications for judges should be set up within the festival rules; for example, a judge for a high school festival should be out of high school for at least four years.

The judges chairperson should look for theater-knowledgeable people. Schools and theaters can each recommend several judges. High school drama teachers may judge junior high festivals, and college instructors may judge high school festivals.

The chairperson should also try to bring in VIPs as festival judges—the artistic director of a local resident theater, the manager of a television station, actors and actresses from the community, newspaper critics and editors, and so on. Sometimes VIP judges may also serve as presenters of

---

SCETA HIGH SCHOOL THEATRE FESTIVAL
REGISTRATION FORM

(PLEASE PRINT OR TYPE)

1. _____
   Name of person to whom all correspondence should be addressed

2. _____
   Street   City   Zip

3. _____
   Telephone (including area code)

4. _____
   Name of entering school

5. _____
   Street   City   Zip

6. _____
   Title of Play

   _____
   Playwright   Adaptor or translator

7. _____

   _____
   Dates and times of local performance

8. _____
   Name and address of theatre if different from participating school

9. _____
   Name of director   School phone (including area code)

10. Enclose five copies of maps to your school indicating freeway exits and location of your theatre on campus.*

11. Form letter will be sent at a later date to be signed by the appropriate administrative officer giving your school permission to participate and releasing the Festival and C.S.U.N.** from liability.

12. Please have black and white 8 x 10 glossy photographs available for newspaper publication and photographs for the "all schools" display at Northridge.

13. List below the names and addresses of local newspapers, TV, radio stations, and drama editors.

14. The participating school agrees that all interpretations of regulations and decisions of the Festival committee are final, including the selections of participating schools, and that no recourse shall be initiated against the Festival committee, SCETA, or the sponsors of the Festival.

    _____
    Signed

    _____
    Title   Date

Please send registration form, maps, and entry fee of $35.00 to:

           H.K. Baird   (Make check payable to SCETA,
           144 So. 1st Avenue   If not a member, you must
           Covina, Calif. 91723   join SCETA.)

*One copy is sent to each judge.
**C.S.U.N.: California State University, Northridge

Figure 20.2   Festival Registration Form

Used by permission of the Southern California Educational Theatre Association.

```
John Actor

1437 Broad Street

Santa Monica, California   90404


Friday, April 23


TIME                    EVENT                   PLACE
_____

10:00 A.M.              A & J Storytellers      Outdoor Theatre #5
                        Story Theatre

11:00 A.M.              A & J Storytellers      Reader's Theatre
                        Story Theatre

12:30 P.M.              A & J Storytellers      Outdoor Theatre #3
                        Story Theatre


Saturday, April 24

1:00 P.M.               A & J Storytellers      Reader's Theatre

3:30 P.M.               A & J Storytellers      Reader's Theatre


Sunday, April 25

3:30 P.M.               A & J Storytellers      Reader's Theatre



On Saturday, April 24, and Sunday, April 25, I intended that the
storytellers might stroll around and gather their own small groups to
tell stories to.
```

Figure 20.3   Registration Confirmation and Assignment Used in a Plan D Festival
Used by permission of the Southern California Educational Theatre Association.

awards at the conclusion of the festival. If so, they should be advised in advance, not on the day of the festival. A postcard invitation with a mail-back reply card attached (see Figure 20.4) is a handy way to recruit new judges and invite former ones.

The chairperson should keep a file of willing and capable judges, listing their names, addresses, and telephone numbers on 3" × 5" or 5" × 8" cards. Such a file can shorten recruiting time for each successive festival. A code

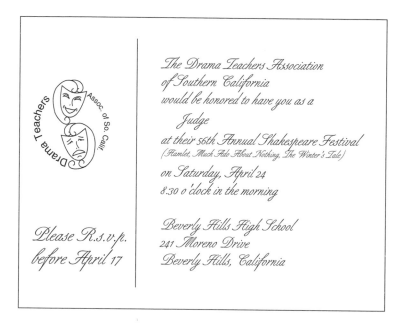

The Drama Teachers Association
of Southern California
would be honored to have you as a
Judge
at their 56th Annual Shakespeare Festival
(Hamlet, Much Ado About Nothing, The Winter's Tale)
on Saturday, April 24
8.30 o'clock in the morning

Beverly Hills High School
241 Moreno Drive
Beverly Hills, California

Please R.s.v.p.
before April 17

☐ *I will be able to attend*

☒ *I will not be able to attend*

☐ *but wish to remain on list*

Are there any events you prefer not to judge?

_____

_____
Name   *(Please Print)*

_____
Address

Figure 20.4   Postcard Invitation to Prospective Judges. The card was perforated so that the two sections could be easily separated. It was folded and stapled for mailing. The reverse side of the top part is addressed to the judge; the reverse side of the bottom part is addressed to the judges chairperson.

Courtesy of DTASC.

is useful for making concise notes on the file cards. For example, as the returns come in, the chairperson should indicate whether or not each person is coming, along with the date the reply was received. The letter "R" would indicate that the judge sent regrets. After a few regrets from the same individual, that chairperson would know not to invite him or her again.

If any judges accepted the invitation and then did not participate, the chairperson would mark their file cards "NS" for "no show" and might not invite them the next year. Some judges chairpersons find it necessary to invite more judges than are needed to make up for the few no-shows. If there is a surplus of judges, some may be asked to observe the first rounds and then be held for use in later rounds, when other judges may be dismissed.

Those judges who have proven their dependability at prior festivals should be given a coded mark on their file cards (e.g., "X") so that the judges chairperson will schedule them for all the rounds. Those so coded should be programmed first, for all rounds. Unproven judges should be assigned only to preliminary rounds (when more judges are needed).

When you mail out double postcards to prospective judges to request their participation, you will find that roughly 3 percent will return postcard tearoffs *without their names* (see Figure 20.4)! Some of them will show up at the festival even though you didn't send them final instructions in the mail. We call them "mystery" judges.

There are two ways to prevent this minor annoyance. The hard way: Print two sets of address labels and place one set on the return tearoffs. This requires a lot of work. The equally hard but less expensive way: Number your list of judges and write each judge's number on his or her return tearoff; then look up the names and addresses of the mystery judges on your list when you get their blank responses.

If a judge is assigned to several rounds in a Plan C festival, it is desirable that the rounds be in a variety of categories, to make participation more interesting. Instead of judging four rounds of individual pantomime, for example, the judge should be given one round of group serious, one round of individual comedy, one round of individual pantomime, and one round of group special event.

About 10 days prior to the festival a reminder note should be sent to all judges who have accepted the invitation, asking them to phone in last-minute cancellations (see Figure 20.5). It is a good idea to enclose a rough map showing how to get to the festival, with a note on where to park.

Upon arrival at the festival, each judge should be greeted by the judges chairperson and presented with the festival rules pertaining to judging (see Figure 20.6), an envelope containing ballots and evaluation forms, a name tag, and an identification ribbon. The judges chairperson should then address the judges as a group, thank them for their participation, and review the procedures with them.

Some method should be set up for getting feedback from judges. Either they should be provided with a festival evaluation form to encourage their

THE DRAMA TEACHERS ASSOCIATION OF SOUTHERN CALIFORNIA

Thank you for accepting our invitation to judge at the 56th annual Shakespeare Festival, to be held on Saturday, April 24.

Enclosed please find a map to Beverly Hills High School, located at 241 Moreno Drive, Beverly Hills, California.

Please plan to arrive by 8:30 A.M. and to report to the library.

If for any reason your plans change and you cannot attend, please call me at Burbank High School, 555-3138, and leave a message, or in the evening at my home number 555-6904 (Area code 213).

Again, thank you for taking the time to make our festival a worthwhile experience for our students.

Deane Wolfson

Deane Wolfson
Third Vice-President
DTASC

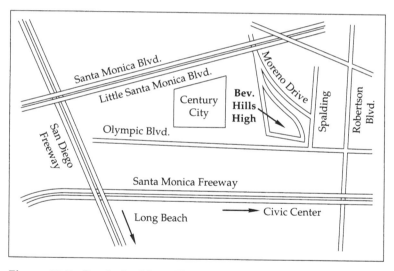

Figure 20.5 Reminder Note. This is sent to judges about 10 days prior to the festival. A map and parking instructions can be helpful.

Courtesy of DTASC.

suggestions, or they should be debriefed orally by the judges chairperson. Example: At one Plan C festival, judges felt that it was too difficult to render evaluations in the improvisation category. They did not feel comfortable in applying the rules. As a result, the category was dropped in subsequent festivals. Perhaps the rules should have been changed or clarified.

In some cases there will be honoraria for the judges, ranging from travel and hotel expenses to a free lunch pass. The judges chairperson should take responsibility for distributing such honoraria.

```
               SHAKESPEARE FESTIVAL — INSTRUCTIONS TO JUDGES

  1. Room chairpersons will list the code numbers of contestants on the blackboard in
     the order in which they are to perform. PLEASE COPY THESE CODE NUMBERS, IN
     ORDER, ON YOUR BALLOT. Note the character name, if you wish.

  2. Room chairpersons will time each performance and will stop the performers at the
     expiration of the allotted time. Contestants must stop when time has expired
     whether they have finished or not. Please evaluate each performance on the basis
     of its quality, even if performance has been stopped. DO NOT DISQUALIFY ANY
     CONTESTANTS. (It is assumed that an unfinished performance may have an effect
     upon its quality and upon your rating.)

  3. PLEASE DO NOT CONFER with other judges or others in the room before marking and
     sealing your ballot. We want your private judgment.

  4. Please do not announce your ratings to ANYONE. Winners will be announced in the
     assembly at the close of each round.

  5. Please report to the chairperson of judges any attempt by students, teachers, or
     parents to influence or dispute your judgment.

  6. At the close of each round, give your SEALED AND SIGNED ballot to the room
     chairperson, who will deliver it to the Tabulations Room.

  7. Please stay available in the judges' room in case of questions.


FESTIVAL RULES
    * All selections are to be memorized.
    * Students may portray more than one character and may play characters of the
      opposite sex.
    * No props are to be used.
    * Classroom furniture, such as tables and chairs, may be used with no limitations.
    * Clothing worn may be used (i.e., hands in pockets) but may not be removed or put
      on during the scene.
    * A memorized introduction is recommended but not required.
    * Introductions may be either dramatized or narrated.
    * Directors, parents, and students may not discuss performances with judges or
      attempt to influence decisions.
    * Protests or questions must be handled by the Rules Committee. This committee can
      be contacted by room chairperson.

RULES FOR SPECIAL SCENE — WINTER'S TALE
    * This scene must be done exactly as cut. No deletions or changes of any kind will
      be allowed.
    * No introduction at all may be given, not even the title of the play.
    * This scene will not be timed.
    * All other general festival rules apply to the special scene.

VIOLATIONS OF RULES
      Please report any suspected violation of rules to the Rules Committee as soon as
      possible. DO NOT DISQUALIFY CONTESTANTS! Only the Rules Committee may disqualify
      an entry.

                  PLEASE SIGN YOUR COMPLETED BALLOT!
```

Figure 20.6 Rules for Judges. These should be an abbreviated form of the complete festival rules. They should be reviewed orally before the festival.

Courtesy of DTASC.

Tabulations/Evaluations (A, B, C, D)

The tabulation chairperson is responsible for tallying the ballots of the judges during a competitive festival. The chairperson should design the judges' ballots (see Figure 20.7) and prepare tally forms (see Figure 20.8) in advance so that ballots can be quickly processed at the end of each round.

BALLOT

Drama Teachers Association of Southern California

Event: __VI__   Section: __—__   Room Number: __212__

Round (Circle one):   I   II   Semi-final   Final

Order	Code Number	Notes	Placement
1	HH	C	6
2	C	A	2
3	VV	A⁺	1
4	BB	B⁻	5
5	T	B⁺	3
6	A	B	4
7	P	EXCESSIVE SHOUTING	
8	LL	DROPPED LINES	
9			
10			
11			
12			

Winners' code numbers: only six places are to be listed,
other performances need to be rated.

First place: __VV__

Second place: __C__

Third place: __T__   Please do not list ties
                                     for any places! Ties
Fourth place: __A__   must and will be broken
                                     by tabulation!
Fifth place: __BB__

Sixth place: __HH__

Judged by: ___CAROL KATO___ *Carol Kato*
           (Please print your name.)

Please give this ballot, in a sealed envelope, to the room chairman who
will deliver it to tabulations. Thank you!

Figure 20.7   Judges' Ballot for a Plan C Festival
Courtesy of DTASC.

Code	Judges 1	2	3	4	5	6	7	Total	Place	Sweep
Tally Event: vi Section: — Room Number: 212 Round: F										
HH	6	7	7	3	7	6	6	42		
C	2	3	7	5	6	7	3	33		
UU	1	1	5	6	4	4	1	22	2	4
BB	5	4	6	4	7	7	7	40		
T	3	2	4	1	1	2	4	17	1	6
A	4	7	1	2	2	5	5	26	3	2
P	7	6	2	7	5	3	7	37		
LL	7	5	3	7	3	1	2	28		

Figure 20.8 Tally Form for a Plan C Festival. The placements awarded to an entry by each judge are totaled, and the entry with the least number of points is awarded first place in the place column. If a sweepstakes trophy is to be awarded, winning entries are given sweepstakes points. First place in a group event (one in which two or more actors participate) wins six sweepstakes points; second place, four points; and third place, two points. In an individual event (one in which a single actor participates) first place gets three points toward sweepstakes, second place gets two points, and third place gets one point. In Event VI, Group T took first place, Group UU took second place, and Group A took third place. Since this was a group event, Group T earned six points toward the overall festival sweepstakes.

Courtesy of DTASC.

Last-minute, roughly drawn tally sheets can lead to confusion in adding the judges' votes.

The chairperson recruits a tabulation committee to work during the festival.

The tabulation chairperson may also distribute a summary of votes (see Figure 20.9) to interested teachers immediately following the festival so that they can see how their students fared in various rounds. Sometimes it is desirable that teachers show these results to their students so that they can see just how subjective the judging was. (Example: An entry that does not even take third place in the final rounds of a Plan C festival may have had several first-place votes from judges in earlier rounds.)

Finals

Event II

UU	20	7757776		C 20 777 2775
BB	20	7475674		
R	25	5777777		
X	20	1113227	②	
CC	20	3521111	①	
P	20	4267352	③	
K	20	7336747		
LL	20	6644537	④	
P	25	7777777		
C	25	2777463		

Event IV

LL	40	4777376	
E	40	3121433	①
X	45	2734224	③
W	40	1242542	②
LL	45	7567717	
Z	40	7677777	
CC	45	7415171	④
OO	40	7776777	
C	40	5353655	
WW	40	6777767	

Event VI

HH	6773766	
C	2375673	
UU	1156441	②
BB	5464777	
T	3241124	①
A	4712255	③
P	7627537	
LL	7537312	④

Event III

C	30	4277727		P	302672475 ②
L	30	3376754		P	357777177
YY	30	7771277		JJ	301417577 ①
RR	35	7124776 ④		DD	307725667
ZZ	30	6553771 ③			
C	35	7777313			
GG	35	7747732			
LL		305767747			

Event V

LL	142111	①
CC	6566544	
Y	5674256	
P	2374465	③
RR	773772	
M	4242677	④
B	77577	
WW	3113332	②

Event VII

XX	2115345	②
LL	4242231	①
L	7437456	
CC	7564667	
E	3376777	
Y	5623122	②
G	1751513	④
A	6777774	

Figure 20.9 Duplicated Summary of Votes. This may be distributed to teachers after the final rounds of a Plan C festival to allow the teachers to point out to their students just how subjective the judging was. Note, for instance, that in Event VII Entry LL was judged best by only one judge, but came in first; Entry XX was judged best by two judges, but came in second; and Entry G was judged best by three judges, but came in fourth! Because there was a tie for second place, no third place was awarded.

Courtesy of DTASC.

It is desirable that the tabulations room be near the stage or room where the winners of rounds are to be announced. This can eliminate some footwork.

In noncompetitive festivals (Plan D) an evaluations chairperson may be appointed to design evaluation forms (see Figure 20.10), supervise the collection of the forms from judges or evaluators, and distribute the forms to the participants. At children's festivals, children may be asked to serve as evaluators, in which case evaluation forms should be specially prepared for them (see Figure 20.11). If oral critiques are held, the evaluations chairperson is responsible for scheduling and moderating the sessions. Getting critiques to participating individuals and groups may necessitate forms distributed to judges on which they can write the code number of the

(text continues on p. 301)

```
                   FOURTH ANNUAL CHILDREN'S THEATRE FESTIVAL
                     California State University, Los Angeles

                        Reviewer's Evaluation and Critique


Reviewer _____ Production _____

Date and time reviewer saw production _____

Style of Production _____
(formal, audience participation, musical, improvisational, educational, other)

Please rate and/or comment on the following aspects of the production.
Suggested ratings are: excellent, very good, good, adequate, needs improvement.

   1.  ENTIRE PRODUCTION
       a. Overall rating of relative success of production   _____
       b. Audience response                                  _____
       c. Consistency of style                               _____

Comments:
       _____

       _____

       _____

       _____

       _____

       _____



   2.  DIRECTING
       a. Appropriateness of production concept              _____
       b. Development and execution of production concept    _____
       c. Development of ensemble                            _____
       d. Casting and role development                       _____
       e. Blocking and design of space
       f. Respect for and ability to control and entertain
          an audience of children                            _____

Comments:
       _____

       _____

       _____

       _____

       _____

       _____
```

Figure 20.10   Evaluation Form for a Plan D Festival

Used by permission of the Southern California Educational Theatre Association.

3. <u>ACTING</u>
   a. Development of characters
   b. Clarity of speech   _____
   c. Control of movement   _____
   d. Ability to relate to other actors and the audience _____
   e. Illusion of the first time
   f. Flexibility   _____

Comments:

_____

_____

_____

_____

_____

_____

4. <u>DESIGN ELEMENTS</u>
   a. Overall reaction   _____

Sets _____   Costumes _____

Lights _____   Makeup _____

Sound _____   Props _____

Comments:

_____

_____

_____

_____

_____

_____

5. <u>SCRIPT</u>
   a. What age child is the script appropriate for?
   b. Consistency of style of script   _____
   c. Integrity and validity for an audience of children _____

Comments (particularly appropriate if script is original):

_____

_____

_____

_____

_____

_____

Figure 20.10 *(Continued)*

SOUTHERN CALIFORNIA
CHILDREN'S THEATRE FESTIVAL
California State University, Los Angeles

JUNIOR REVIEWER'S PLAY EVALUATION FORM

Reviewer _____ Production _____

Date and time reviewer saw production _____

1. The first questions are about how you like the play. (Circle your response.)

   Did you like the play?   Yes   No   Parts of it
   Was the play interesting?   Yes   No   Parts of it
   Was the play fun to see?   Yes   No   Parts of it
   Could you follow the story?   Yes   No   Pretty well
   Would you like to see this play again?   Yes   No

2. Circle the comments below that describe the way you felt about the play.

   Great!!   Pretty good   Too noisy   Too fast

   Exciting   Dull   Too violent   Too long

   OK   Scary   Too slow   Too boring

   Hard to understand   Easy to understand   Part good, part bad   Too scary

3. Give short answers to the following questions about the play.

   What did you like best about the play?

   What did you like least about the play?

   What did you learn from this play?

Figure 20.11   Evaluation Form for Use by Children at a Children's Festival
Used by permission of the Southern California Educational Theatre Association.

4. What age kids do you think this play is best for?

   (Circle one age group)   3 - 6   6 - 9   10 - 14

   Would this play be fun for grownups, too?   Yes   No   I don't know

5. Please answer the following questions about the actors and the acting.
   (Circle your response)

   Did the actors have fun?   Yes   No   I don't know

   Were the actors nervous?   Yes   No   I don't know

   Did the actors have lots of energy?   Yes   No   Some of them

   Were the characters believable?   Yes   No   Some of them

   Could you hear the actors well enough?   Yes   No   Some of them

   Could you understand what they were saying? Yes   No   Sometimes

   Which character did you like best? _____
   Why?

   Which character did you like least? _____
   Why?

Figure 20.11   *(Continued)*

6. If this was the kind of play where the actors ask the audience to answer questions or do things on the stage, please answer the following questions. If it wasn't, skip #6 and go on to #7.

Did the actors talk <u>to</u> the audience?	Yes	No	Sometimes
Did the actors listen to the answers the audience gave?	Yes	No	Sometimes
Do you think it was a good idea for the actors to ask the audience's help with this particular play?	Yes	No	I don't know

7. Please answer the following questions about the scenery and costumes. (Circle your response.)

Was the scenery practical for the play?	Yes	No	I don't know
Did you enjoy looking at the scenery?	Yes	No	
Was the scenery easy for the actors to work with?	Yes	No	I don't know
Did the scenery take away from the play?	Yes	No	I don't know
Did you enjoy looking at the costumes?	Yes	No	
Were the costumes easy for the actors to work in?	Yes	No	I don't know
Do you think the scenery and the costumes went well together?	Yes	No	I don't know

8. Is there anything else you would like to say about this play?

Figure 20.11   *(Continued)*

participant and their comments (see Figures 20.12, 20.13, and 20.14). The forms are collected at the end of each round by room chairpersons and later distributed to the drama teachers. Drama teachers are encouraged to pass

(text continues on p. 305)

Room No. _____   FULLERTON COLLEGE HIGH SCHOOL THEATRE FESTIVAL
Round No. _____   PERFORMANCE-CONTEMPORARY

CONTESTANT'S NUMBER _____   SELECTION _____

JUDGE'S NAME _____   DATE _____
                    (print)

SELECTION	+/-	COMMENTS
A. Was the selection suited to the category? B. Did it match the performer's abilities?		
COMPREHENSION OF THE SELECTION A. Did the actor understand the purpose and point of view of the author?		
CHARACTERIZATION A. Is the character believable and convincing? B. Is the character portrayal energetic and focussed?		
TECHNIQUE A. Were the actor's face and body responsive to the mood of the selection? B. Was the actor's voice appropriate and consistent to the character? C. Were the tempo and pace appropriate to the material?		

TIME LIMIT: Selections exceeding the 3-minute time limit shall be disqualified from the round.

ADDITIONAL COMMENTS: Please use back of ballot.

RATING: Superior (I), Excellent (II), Good (III), Average (IV).

JUDGE'S SIGNATURE _____

NORTH ORANGE COUNTY COMMUNITY COLLEGE DISTRICT

Figure 20.12   A Response Sheet (Critique Form) Supplied to Festival Judges with Springboard Questions Specifically Designed for the Performance-Contemporary Category. Compare to Figures 20.13 and 20.14. The forms have two purposes: (1) to assist a judge in organizing his or her own thoughts about the relative merits of 6 to 12 entrants in a round and (2) to help the judge write some feedback in the comments section to student actors.

Courtesy Theatre Arts Department, Fullerton College, Fullerton, California.

Room No. _____   FULLERTON COLLEGE HIGH SCHOOL THEATRE FESTIVAL
Round No. _____   ONE-ACT PLAY

CONTESTANT'S NUMBER _____   SELECTION _____

JUDGE'S NAME _____   DATE _____
                            (print)

	+/−	COMMENTS
SELECTION OF MATERIAL A. Was the play of literary merit? B. Was the play of acceptable taste? C. Is the script suitable to the actors' abilities?		
DIRECTING A. Is the play well cast? B. Is arrangement of stage properties suitable for effective blocking, movement, and picturization? C. Does the performance have appropriate mood? D. Does the performance move? build? reach a climax? E. Are the stylistic conventions consistent?		
ACTING A. Do the actors create and maintain believable characters? B. Are the characters' relationships clearly defined? C. Are the actors audible and articulate? D. Do the actors reflect motivated movement, action, and reaction?		
TOTAL EFFECT A. Was there purpose and unity to the production? B. Was the theme of the play projected to the audience? C. Was this a satisfying theatrical experience?		

TIME LIMIT: Selections exceeding the 3-minute time limit shall be disqualified from the round.

ADDITIONAL COMMENTS: Please use back of ballot.

RATING: Superior (I), Excellent (II), Good (III), Average (IV).

JUDGE'S SIGNATURE _____

NORTH ORANGE COUNTY COMMUNITY COLLEGE DISTRICT

Figure 20.13 A Response Sheet (Critique Form) Supplied to Festival Judges with Springboard Questions Specifically Designed for the One-Act Play Category. Compare to Figures 20.12 and 20.14.

Courtesy Theatre Arts Department, Fullerton College, Fullerton, California.

Room No. _____   FULLERTON COLLEGE HIGH SCHOOL THEATRE FESTIVAL
Round No. _____   MUSICAL THEATRE

CONTESTANT'S NUMBER _____   SELECTION _____

JUDGE'S NAME _____   DATE _____
                        (print)

SELECTION OF MATERIAL	+/–	COMMENTS
A. Was the selection suited to the category? B. Did it challenge the performers' abilities? C. Was the selection well edited, balanced between performers? D. Does it have continuity? Does it build to a climax?		
COMPREHENSION OF THE SELECTION A. Did the actors understand the purpose and point of view of the author? B. Are the relationships between actors clearly defined? C. Was the relationship between the actors and audience clearly defined?		
CHARACTERIZATION A. Are the actors believable? B. Is the cutting suitably cast?		
TECHNIQUE A. Is the blocking well motivated? B. Was the choreography motivated or original? C. Are the actors audible and articulate? D. Do the actors have distinct characters projected both physically and vocally? E. Did the actors find an appropriate concept of the piece?		

TIME LIMIT: Selections exceeding the 3-minute time limit shall be disqualified from the round.

ADDITIONAL COMMENTS: Please use back of ballot.

RATING: Superior (I), Excellent (II), Good (III), Average (IV).

JUDGE'S SIGNATURE _____

NORTH ORANGE COUNTY COMMUNITY COLLEGE DISTRICT

Figure 20.14 A Response Sheet (Critique Form) Supplied to Festival Judges with Springboard Questions Specifically Designed for the Musical Theater Category. Compare to Figures 20.12 and 20.13.

Courtesy Theatre Arts Department, Fullerton College, Fullerton, California.

on significant comments to their students (and screen out any comments that might be detrimental to their growth as actors).

The "response" forms (avoiding the use of the word *critique*) used by Fullerton College list questions in various categories to trigger judges' ideas about how high school actors are dealing with the challenge of presenting dramatic materials in front of a panel of judges and audiences of their peers. These questions are merely springboards. Judges are encouraged to be "positive" in their comments.

Giving supportive criticism to young actors is an art in itself. How can you motivate improvement without citing weaknesses and dampening creative spirit? Fullerton College recommends that judges consider writing questions instead of statements on their response forms. (See Figure 20.15 for Fullerton's suggested list of questions.) Instead of writing on a response form, "Your voice was all wrong for that part and as irritating to me as nails scraping on a blackboard; think of working backstage," it is suggested that the judge write "How did you prepare vocally for the performance?" The thinking behind this shift to questions is (1) young actors might be offended and discouraged by blunt, nonsupportive criticism and (2) although young actors might not be able to understand the relevance of the question to their performance, they might discuss it with their drama coach and the resulting dialogue might lead to exercises to help the students modulate their voices.

Programs (A, B, C, D)

It usually takes at least two months to write, rewrite, proof, and publish a festival program. The following items should be included:

1. Statement of the festival's philosophy
2. History of the festival or the host institution
3. Statement of the festival's theme
4. Schedule (see Figure 20.16, Plan C, and Figure 20.17, Plan D)
5. Map of grounds and room maps of the larger buildings
6. List of officers of the producing association and festival committee chairpersons
7. List of participating schools, theaters, and so on
8. Program of events with room assignments for Plan C (see Figure 20.18)
9. Background information on plays and playwrights whose works are to be presented
10. Background information on groups participating, with synopses of the works they will present (see Figure 20.19, Plan D)
11. Page with blanks on which to record names of festival winners (see Figure 20.20)

NORTH ORANGE COUNTY COMMUNITY COLLEGE DISTRICT

FULLERTON COLLEGE

THEATRE ARTS DEPARTMENT

RESPONSE SHEETS:

1. THESE ARE THE MOST IMPORTANT PART OF THE FESTIVAL FOR THE STUDENTS AND TEACHERS, WHY THEY RETURN EACH YEAR!!!
2. KEEP THE REMARKS POSITIVE!!!
3. FEEL FREE TO COMMENT TO AN INSTRUCTOR ON CRITIQUES. (NONE OF WHOM GET ANY REIMBURSEMENT FOR ALL THEIR EXTRA TIME.) A POSITIVE (EARNED) COMPLIMENT TO AN INSTRUCTOR ON THE CRITIQUE CAN READILY BE PASSED ON TO THEIR ADMINISTRATORS.

4. CONSIDER QUESTIONS RATHER THAN STATEMENTS:

   —WHO WERE YOU TALKING TO? WHY? WHAT WAS YOUR RELATIONSHIP?

   —WHAT ARE YOU FIGHTING FOR? WHAT ARE THE RISKS-OBSTACLES?

   —WHAT DREW YOU TO THIS CHARACTER? HOW IS HE/SHE LIKE YOU?

   —WHAT HAPPENED BEFORE? WHAT HAPPENS AFTER THE SCENE?

   —HOW LONG HAVE YOU BEEN REHEARSING? WHAT DID YOU LEARN?

   —HOW ABOUT AN ACTIVITY — TYING SHOES, FIXING BUTTON, CLEANING PURSE, WORKING OUT, EATING, DRINKING, TUNING GUITAR, ETC.

   —HOW DID YOU PREPARE PHYSICALLY/VOCALLY FOR THE PERFORMANCE?

(714) 992-7425   321 East Chapman Avenue, Fullerton, California 92632-2095 (714) 992-7000 • FAX (714) 447-4097

Figure 20.15   Handout to Festival Judges That Gives Some Guidance on How to Fill Out Response Sheets and Suggests Questions as a Form of Feedback. Judges are briefed before the first round on how to write positive, constructive comments and on how questions rather than statements can be effective.

Courtesy Theatre Arts Department, Fullerton College, Fullerton, California.

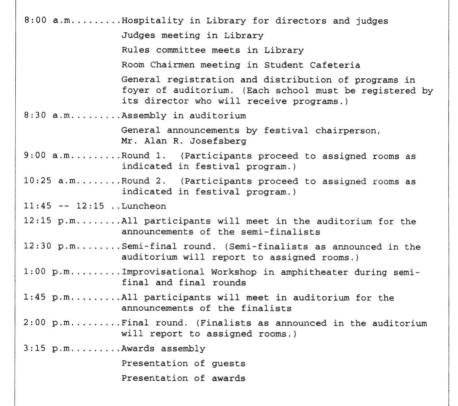

FAIRFAX HIGH SCHOOL
7850 Melrose Avenue
Los Angeles
<u>November 15</u>

SCHEDULE FOR THE DAY

8:00 a.m.........Hospitality in Library for directors and judges

Judges meeting in Library

Rules committee meets in Library

Room Chairmen meeting in Student Cafeteria

General registration and distribution of programs in foyer of auditorium. (Each school must be registered by its director who will receive programs.)

8:30 a.m.........Assembly in auditorium

General announcements by festival chairperson, Mr. Alan R. Josefsberg

9:00 a.m.........Round 1. (Participants proceed to assigned rooms as indicated in festival program.)

10:25 a.m........Round 2. (Participants proceed to assigned rooms as indicated in festival program.)

11:45 -- 12:15 ..Luncheon

12:15 p.m........All participants will meet in the auditorium for the announcements of the semi-finalists

12:30 p.m........Semi-final round. (Semi-finalists as announced in the auditorium will report to assigned rooms.)

1:00 p.m.........Improvisational Workshop in amphitheater during semi-final and final rounds

1:45 p.m.........All participants will meet in auditorium for the announcements of the finalists

2:00 p.m.........Final round. (Finalists as announced in the auditorium will report to assigned rooms.)

3:15 p.m.........Awards assembly

Presentation of guests

Presentation of awards

Figure 20.16   A Festival Schedule. Four rounds are scheduled during one day. Courtesy of DTASC.

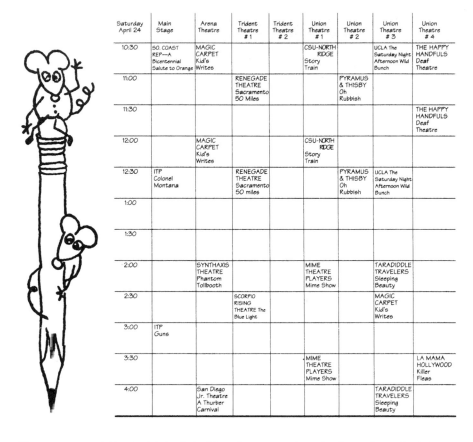

Saturday April 24	Main Stage	Arena Theatre	Trident Theatre #1	Trident Theatre #2	Union Theatre #1	Union Theatre #2	Union Theatre #3	Union Theatre #4
10:30	SO. COAST REP—A Bicentennial Salute to Orange	MAGIC CARPET Kid's Writes			CSU-NORTHRIDGE Story Train		UCLA The Saturday Night Afternoon Wild Bunch	THE HAPPY HANDFULS Deaf Theatre
11:00			RENEGADE THEATRE Sacramento 50 Miles			PYRAMUS & THISBY Oh Rubbish		
11:30								THE HAPPY HANDFULS Deaf Theatre
12:00		MAGIC CARPET Kid's Writes			CSU-NORTHRIDGE Story Train			
12:30	ITP Colonel Montana		RENEGADE THEATRE Sacramento 50 miles			PYRAMUS & THISBY Oh Rubbish	UCLA The Saturday Night Afternoon Wild Bunch	
1:00								
1:30								
2:00		SYNTHAXIS THEATRE Phantom Tollbooth			MIME THEATRE PLAYERS Mime Show		TARADIDDLE TRAVELERS Sleeping Beauty	
2:30			SCORPIO RISING THEATRE The Blue Light				MAGIC CARPET Kid's Writes	
3:00	ITP Guns							
3:30					MIME THEATRE PLAYERS Mime Show			LA MAMA HOLLYWOOD Killer Fleas
4:00		San Diego Jr. Theatre A Thurber Carnival					TARADIDDLE TRAVELERS Sleeping Beauty	

Figure 20.17 A Festival Schedule. This shows one day of a three-day schedule.

12. Decoration (an artistic cover design can make the program a valuable souvenir; designing a children's theater festival program as a coloring book is a clever idea)
13. A tear-out feedback form, addressed to the festival producer, that will encourage constructive criticism (see Figure 20.21)
14. Acknowledgments

Most of the items listed are self-explanatory, but a few need further comment.

The artwork for the program cover might take more time than the other items. The program chairperson should recruit an artist well in advance of other production work on the program.

The program chairperson should tell other chairpersons (registration, room chairperson) the deadline for submitting information for the program. Late entries are a major problem for the program chairperson; therefore, a definite deadline should be determined at the first planning meeting.

EVENT 2 -- GROUP PANTOMIME

Semi-finals in Rooms 110, 112, 114

Finals in Room 112

Section 6	Round 1	Round 2		Section 9	Round 1	Round 2
AAA 20 ·	· 110 ·	· 110		EEEE 20 ·	· 113 ·	· 113
MMM 20 ·	· 110 ·	· 111		EEE 20 ·	· 113 ·	· 115
SS 20 ·	· 110 ·	· 112		ZZZ 20 ·	· 113 ·	· 110
S 20 ·	· 110 ·	· 112		PPP 20 ·	· 113 ·	· 113
B 20 ·	· 110 ·	· 114		LL 20 ·	· 113 ·	· 115
R 20 ·	· 110 ·	· 115		NNN 20 ·	· 113 ·	· 114
CC 20 ·	· 110 ·	· 110		UU 20 ·	· 113 ·	· 115
TT 20 ·	· 110 ·	· 111		E 20 ·	· 113 ·	· 111
Z 20 ·	· 110 ·	· 113		UUU 20 ·	· 113 ·	· 110

Section 7	Round 1	Round 2		Section 10	Round 1	Round 2
N 20 ·	· 111 ·	· 113		AAAA 20 ·	· 114 ·	· 110
LLL 20 ·	· 111 ·	· 114		L 20 ·	· 114 ·	· 115
FFFF 20 ·	· 111 ·	· 115		HH 20 ·	· 114 ·	· 112
BB 20 ·	· 111 ·	· 114		J 20 ·	· 114 ·	· 115
JJ 20 ·	· 111 ·	· 113		AA 20 ·	· 114 ·	· 114
K 20 ·	· 111 ·	· 112		BBB 20 ·	· 114 ·	· 111
SSS 20 ·	· 111 ·	· 115		OO 20 ·	· 114 ·	· 111
A 20 ·	· 111 ·	· 111		X 20 ·	· 114 ·	· 110
Y 20 ·	· 111 ·	· 110		OOO 20 ·	· 114 ·	· 113

Section 8	Round 1	Round 2		Section 11	Round 1	Round 2
H 20 ·	· 112 ·	· 111		ZZ 20 ·	· 115 ·	· 112
C 20 ·	· 112 ·	· 112		GG 20 ·	· 115 ·	· 114
YYY 20 ·	· 112 ·	· 114		CCC 20 ·	· 115 ·	· 114
RRR 20 ·	· 112 ·	· 113		CCCC 20 ·	· 115 ·	· 113
TTT 20 ·	· 112 ·	· 110		DD 20 ·	· 115 ·	· 114
NN 20 ·	· 112 ·	· 112		P 20 ·	· 115 ·	· 113
XX 20 ·	· 112 ·	· 111		U 20 ·	· 115 ·	· 112
JJJ 20 ·	· 112 ·	· 112		DDDD 20 ·	· 115 ·	· 111
F 20 ·	· 112 ·	· 110		FFF 20 ·	· 115 ·	· 115

Figure 20.18 Room Assignments for First Two Rounds of Plan C Festival. These rounds are scheduled in advance, letting entrants know in which rooms they will perform. Room assignments for later rounds are announced as judges eliminate entrants from competition.

Courtesy of DTASC.

THE TWELFTH NIGHT REPERTORY CO.

12732 Moorpark Street Studio City, Calif. 91604 (213) 760-2112

GREEK MYTHOLOGY

On October 18, 1974 we first presented GREEK MYTHOLOGY to Vintage Street School, in Sepulveda. The performance was for the Los Angeles City Schools Principal's Cultural committee. This committee rated GREEK MYTHOLOGY as "Excellent," and we began a massive tour of the Los Angeles City Schools.

This tour resulted in establishing Twelfth Night as a major source of educational theatre in Los Angeles. We played GREEK MYTHOLOGY to over 75,000 youngsters during the 1974-1975 school year. It remains one of our most requested presentations. In December of 1974, members of the Office of Multicultural Education for the L.A. City Schools came and saw GREEK MYTHOLOGY. They were very enthusiastic about the potential of using this same theatrical format as a means of multicultural education, and they proceeded to help us secure a $30,000.00 grant from HEW for that purpose.

In short, GREEK MYTHOLOGY was the start of something very good for Twelfth Night.

THE CAST

STEVE MUNSIE (Pantomimist) is a founding member of Twelfth Night, and was the first to perform in GREEK MYTHOLOGY. Although his role has been successfully repeated by Don Lewis and Michael Ross Oddo, much of GREEK MYTHOLOGY has always been Steve's inspiration. Steve has taught at ISOMATA (Idyllwyld School of Music and the Arts), an extension of USC.

SCOTT CATAMAS (narrator) first founded Twelfth Night in June of 1973. Scott has played many leads, directed, and produced numerous productions. He was the original narrator for GREEK MYTHOLOGY in 1974. Scott is the President of Twelfth Night.

AARON HASSMAN (musician) MA in educational psychology, BA in Theatre Arts, BA in Music. Aaron first joined Twelfth Night in January 1975. He is currently performing every day for us with his MUSICIAN'S SEMINAR program. Aaron also teaches Creative Dramatics and Creative Guitar to Los Angeles City School teachers (through the In-Service Workshop program).

GREEK MYTHOLOGY was written and produced by Scott Catamas.

The Twelfth Night Repertory Company is an independent, Non-Profit Organization.

Figure 20.19 Description of a Group Participating in a Plan D Festival. This information may be printed in the program or on a flyer distributed to the audience.

Courtesy of the Twelfth Night Repertory Co.

AWARD WINNERS

Event 1 — Individual Pantomime

_____
Third
_____
Second
_____
First

Event 2 — Group Pantomime

_____
Third
_____
Second
_____
First

Event 3 — Individual Humorous

_____
Third
_____
Second
_____
First

Event 4 — Individual Serious

_____
Third
_____
Second
_____
First

Event 5 — Group Special Event

_____
Third
_____
Second
_____
First

Event 6 — Group Humorous

_____
Third
_____
Second
_____
First

Event 7 — Group Serious

_____
Third
_____
Second
_____
First

Event 8 — Group Improvisation

_____
Third
_____
Second
_____
First

Sweepstakes Trophy

_____
Third
_____
Second
_____
First

Figure 20.20　A Page for Listing Award Winners in the Program
Courtesy of DTASC.

Illegible names and partial names on registration forms also create problems for the program chairperson. He or she should remind the registration chairperson to ensure that the forms ask entrants to print clearly and to submit complete names.

After cost, proximity is the most important factor in selection of the printer because the program chairperson will have to visit the printer often. An ideal arrangement is for the program chairperson to work with the school printshop.

To determine the number of programs to be printed, the chairperson should add the estimated number of entrants, judges, festival workers,

FESTIVAL EVALUATION FORM

What did you like best about the festival?

_____
_____
_____
_____
_____
_____
_____
_____

What could we do to make it better or different?

_____
_____
_____
_____
_____
_____
_____

Were you well provided for in terms of facilities and courtesy?

_____
_____
_____
_____
_____
_____
_____
_____

_____ I am willing to work on a committee for next year's festival.

_____ I would like to serve as a reviewer for next year's festival.

_____ I would like to be invited to bring a production next year.

What day or days did you attend the festival? _____
In what position did you attend the festival? (Circle one) Producer, Director,
Reviewer, Performer, Audience member, Other _____

Name _____   Position _____
Address _____   City _____ Zip _____
Home Phone _____   Office Phone _____

Figure 20.21   Festival Evaluation Form
Used by permission of the Southern California Educational Theatre Association.

expected audience, and guests, and then add a large number of extras. It is better to order too many than not to have enough.

Publicity (A, D)

The publicity for a festival requires all the effort that would be expended on a single production and then some. The publicity chairperson should devise a schedule of publicity releases starting five weeks before the festival and building to a peak the weekend before the festival. (Some large annual festivals start their publicity work 9 to 12 months ahead of the festival date.) The chairperson should attempt to obtain coverage from all media in the area of the festival and all media in the areas of prospective audiences. Releases to junior high, high school, college, and teacher organization newspapers will be especially useful (see Figure 20.22).

The publicity chairperson might issue releases on the following subjects (separately or in combinations):

1. Dates, places, chairperson, and intended audience for the festival
2. History of the festival
3. Judges named for festival
4. Participants listed for festival
5. VIPs planning to attend festival
6. Trophies, scholarships, and future competitions announced for festival winners
7. Winners selected and trophies presented

Sometimes it is better to divide the work of the publicity committee between two or more people. For example, the publicity chairperson can handle all public relations (face-to-face and telephone contacts) and the deputy or assistant chairperson can handle all written releases to the media.

All public relations contacts should be logged and copies of all media releases should be filed so that successive publicity chairpersons can build on the work of their predecessors.

Guests/Hospitality (C, D)

The guests, or hospitality, chairperson is responsible for guides. Ways to obtain guide services include the following:

1. The host campus is asked to provide guides from one of its service organizations (Honor Society, ROTC, etc.).
2. Each entering school is required to bring one student to serve as a guide.
3. Students in the drama department earn classroom points by serving as guides (usually on college campuses).

Children's theatre festival '76

The spring of 1973 marked the beginning of a rather special theatrical enterprise: Immaculate Heart College of Los Angeles hosted the initial outing of the Children's Theatre Festival.

Appreciative of the concept which launches the American College Theatre Festival, members of the Southern California Educational Theatre Association hoped to bring together a diverse group of performers specializing in entertainment for children. It was of equal importance to provide good examples of Children's Theatre fare being produced throughout Southern California, and to present such programs at a reasonable cost to Southland families. An opportunity for children's theatre artists to meet and see one another's work (and a chance to broaden the audience for such artists) was also of special interest to festival planners.

The gathering at Immaculate Heart joined a dozen producing companies and an enthusiastic audience nearing a thousand people. The 1974 Festival held at Cal Poly, Pomona doubled the 1973 attendance and last year's festival, produced at California State University, Northridge, drew an audience of over 8,000. Since the beginning of the festival, many innovations such as strolling players on the grounds, a playwriting contest, and premiere performances of a number of original plays have been introduced to the weekend's activities.

Children's Theatre Festival '76 will be presented on Friday, April 23rd; Saturday, April 24th; and Sunday, April 25th at California State University, L. A. Over forty companies of performers will provide entertainment on Friday from 9:00 a.m. to 2:00 p.m. and on Saturday and Sunday from 10:30 a.m. to 5:00 p.m. Admissions will be $2.00 for adults, $1.00 for children. Families are again encouraged to picnic in a lovely campus setting — refreshments will be available at convenient locations — while enjoying the most diversified theatrical afternoon available at the price.

New representation in this year's festival of educational, professional, and community theatre groups will include a presentation of **Colonel Montana** by the Improvisational Theatre Project from the Mark Taper Forum; San Francisco's Magic Carpet presenting the critically acclaimed production of *Kid's Writes, Multicultural Mythology* produced by The Twelfth Night Repertory Co.; the L.A. Mime Company; a zany production of *Castle Hassel At Rainbow's End* presented by the Trobadoor Puppets; and an exciting production of *Winnie-the-Pooh* produced by the University of Nevada.

Muscial theatre, always a part of the festival, is represented this year by productions such as *H20 Where Are You?* produced by the Space Place Players in conjunction with the California Museum of Science and Industry and *Sacramento Fifty Miles* from Bakersfield College.

Among returning favorites are Betsy Brown in *Carnival of the Animals*, a salute to Orange County from the talented South Coast Repertory, John and Pam Wood as *J. P. Nightingale*, and *Macaroni Feathers* by McKerrow and McClelland produced by San Diego State University.

An exciting line-up, and only a part of all the entertainment to be staged in the theatres and on the lawns of the Cal. State L. A. campus.

Executive producer Pam Woody of the Cal. State L. A. faculty is busy collecting a distinguished group of theatre experts to act as production reviewers; for, though the festival remains a noncompetitive event, a basic part of its philosophy is the improvement of quality and communication in children's theatre. However, the most expert of opinions may be provided by a panel of junior reviewers also being assembled. This year we will again ask young people of the general age of the festival audience to express their thoughts and preferences to the performance companies and to the festival committee.

Plays, improvisational adventures, creative dramatics, clowns, strolling singers and dancers; a lively two-day presentation of theatre arts for children. Sponsored by the Southern California Educational Theatre Association, the 1976 Children's Theatre Festival presents its fourth annual gathering — a reflection of the unprecedented growth in theatre for children in California.

Further inquiries may be directed to Pam Woody at (213) 224-3342 or 224-3350, or to:

The Childen's Theatre Festival
c/o California State University, L.A.
5151 State University Drive
Los Angeles, California 90032

Figure 20.22   A Festival Publicity Release Placed in a Teachers' Newspaper
Used with the permission of United Teachers–Los Angeles.

The guest chairperson briefs the guides before the festival, explaining the layout of the host campus and taking the guides on a quick tour of important locations. Each guide receives a map to keep, some handout maps, and an identifying ribbon.

The guest chairperson might establish an information (and lost-and-found) booth, at the main entrance or in the central corridor, to which guides can direct people whose problems they can't resolve.

The guest chairperson should have emergency information at hand—such as phone numbers for police, fire, and ambulance.

The guest chairperson is also responsible for personally greeting and hosting VIPs.

For a Plan D festival the hospitality chairperson might also want to plan social events for participants (such as a welcoming cocktail party). If many of the festival participants are from out of town, the hospitality chairperson might provide a memo to each on accommodations, entertainment, and points of interest in the vicinity of the festival.

Facilities (Technical Director) (A, B, C, D)

Generally, the responsibility of the facilities chairperson (or technical director) is to ensure that the participants can perform comfortably in the space assigned to them.

For a Plan D festival the facilities chairperson drafts stage plans or floor plans for every production area of the festival. He or she consults with the technical director of each entry to ensure that the stage or room scheduled for use by that entry can accommodate its scenery and lighting requirements.

It is best to set up separate appointments with each technical director to inspect the site before the festival and review the production requirements. Arrangements can be made for any necessary adjustments to the allotted facilities. Sometimes this will simply mean finding an extension cord. But in other cases more serious steps must be taken. For example, background flats that won't fit through the door to the stage area may require rescheduling of two presentation areas.

If entrants will have to travel a great distance to participate and technical directors cannot inspect sites in advance, the facilities chairperson must make special efforts to ensure that complete floor plans are reviewed through the mail. Incoming groups should be advised of the height of the playing area, the diagonal length of the largest door (for entering scenery), the number and capacity of electric outlets and their distance from the playing area, and any other limiting factors.

Another especially important function of the facilities chairperson is checking with the host campus early in the planning stage to ensure that there is adequate seating capacity for the expected participants and audience. For a Plan C festival, for example, there must be enough large rooms to accommodate the group events.

The facilities chairperson is also responsible for negotiating with the supervisor of the host campus for any special requirement—space, telephones, custodian time, and so on. Therefore, it is convenient for the chairperson to be on the staff of the host school.

The chairperson, the festival producer, and the supervisor of the host campus should also discuss facility problems that arose during past festivals to determine how to prevent similar problems during the current festival.

Examples

1. A home football game and a high school Shakespeare festival were scheduled at the same time. No conflict was expected, but the blare of the public address system from the field drifted through the open windows on that hot day and interrupted every Shakespearian scene. Can the host campus be persuaded not to schedule any event other than the festival? If an athletic event must be scheduled, can the volume of the public address system be limited?

2. On the weekend of a three-day children's theater festival, the host state college also scheduled national debate finals, a national piano competition, and a gymnastics event. The resulting parking situation was impossible. Many people who might have attended one of those events were discouraged when they could not find parking within three city blocks of the campus. Can the facilities chairperson convince the campus supervisor to limit the number of events scheduled? Can a separate parking area be set up for the festival with large signs at the theater directing drivers to the lot with a shuttle bus to run drivers from the lot to the festival?

The chairperson should ensure that notes are written to the faculty and staff of the host campus, letting them know that guests will be on their campus and in their rooms.

Room Chairperson (C)

The festival room chairperson sees that the host custodian unlocks the schoolrooms on time. This chairperson also organizes student room chairpersons to serve in each room to monitor and time events.

Usually each entering school is required to bring along with its participants two or more students to serve as room chairpersons. They ensure that the judges and participants are present, time events, and supervise the running of the festival within each room.

The festival room chairperson should brief the student room chairpersons just before the festival by orally reviewing a written handout (see Figure 20.23). He or she is also responsible for distributing stopwatches, instructing students in their use, and recovering them. The festival room chairperson should number the stopwatches and have the room chairpersons sign for them.

```
                    INFORMATION FOR ROOM CHAIRPERSONS


      8:00  —  8:30    Registration
      8:30  —  8:45    Assembly
      9:00  — 10:20    Round 1 — Prelim
     10:25  — 11:45    Round 2 — Prelim        Important Rooms
     11:45  — 12:15    Lunch
     12:15  — 12:30    Assembly — Semi-finalists
                       Announced               Room Chairpersons — Room 52
                       Semi-final Round         Judges            — Library
     12:30  —  1:40    Semi-final Round         Tabulations       — Faculty Lounge
      1:40  —  1:55    Assembly — Finalists     Rules             — Cafeteria
                       Announced
      1:55  —  4:00    Final Round
      4:00  —  4:30    Awards Assembly
```

1. Report to Room 52 on Saturday at 8:00 to get instructions and materials which will include program.
2. Go to your assigned room.
3. List code numbers for the entrants on the board.
4. Check to see that all entrants are there by calling numbers.
5. Be certain to start each round at the time indicated, if possible. If late entrants arrive they may perform when others are finished. Cross out code numbers of entrants who do not participate.
6. Check to be certain that the indicated number of judges is present. If not, send a runner to the library. (Preliminary round --- 3 judges; semi-finals --- 5 judges; finals --- 7 judges.)
7. Explain that if anyone feels there has been a rules violation he or she should speak to the room chairperson as soon as the scene in question has finished. Send a runner with a rules infraction slip to the cafeteria. A member of the rules committee will review the situation and determine whether it has been disqualified. Important: no judge or room chairperson can disqualify a scene for any reason.
8. There is to be no talking during scenes and no applause or comments which could influence the judges. You may ask anyone who misbehaves to leave the room.
9. Time each scene from the moment the players begin. (Individual pantomime, group pantomime, individual humorous, and individual serious --- 5 minutes; group special event, group humorous, and group serious --- 9 minutes; improvisation --- 5 minutes.)
10. If a scene runs over, you must say "time," and stop the scene. The entrant is to be judged on what was performed, not penalized for running over time.
11. At the end of the round, try to hold people in the room until the end of the time period to avoid noise in the halls.
12. When judges have finished voting, take their ballots immediately to the tabulations room.
13. Thank judges and participants and proceed to your next assignment.
14. At the end of the final round, or before if you do not have an assignment, return your stopwatch to Room 52.

                       Thank you!

Figure 20.23 Room Chairperson's Briefing Form
Courtesy of DTASC.

Stage Crew (Stage Manager) (A, B, C, D)

The stage crew chairperson, or festival stage manager, is responsible for the stage and backstage areas before, during, and after the festival. He or she ensures that the stage, lighting equipment, and scene-changing facilities are ready. The chairperson also meets with the technical directors and stage managers of each entry to ensure efficient use of the stage.

In a Plan C festival the stage is used primarily for the presentation of trophies and sometimes for the performance of winning entries. Another important use of the stage in a Plan C festival is the announcement of winners of the preliminary rounds. The use of an overhead projector is highly recommended. So much screaming and yelling follows the announcement of each preliminary winner that the reading of the entire list will be delayed without the use of a projector. With a projector, winners and their room assignments for the next round can all be projected at once. The projector operator is warned to wear ear plugs!

Associate Producer and Reviewers (D)

In festivals where groups are invited to perform, the festival producer might insist that the group's work be seen and evaluated prior to a formal invitation. In this case, an associate producer may recruit committee members (reviewers) to preview, individually or as a committee, the work of prospective entrants.

Food/Refreshments (A, B, C, D)

The food/refreshments chairperson is responsible for food services at the festival. In some cases, service will be limited to providing coffee and doughnuts for the judges and festival staff. In other cases, the host campus cafeteria will be set in operation to provide lunch for all participants in the festival. In still other cases, the chairperson might supervise a string of concessions from one day to a week.

At one large, three-day children's festival the food chairperson decided to sell a box lunch of sandwiches, potato chips, and fresh fruit to the audience and provide the same, free, to participants, workers, and judges. The price was kept low. The overall cost of the food program was not entirely covered by sales, but most felt that the program, though simple, was adequate and desirable.

In all cases the chairperson is advised to confer with the supervisor of the host campus cafeteria and to check on local government regulations concerning food services.

Business Manager/Trophies (A, B, C, D)

It is desirable that the treasurer of the organization sponsoring the festival serve as the business manager of the festival. The business manager is responsible for all income and expenditures. He or she approves payment of all expenses, makes out the checks, and receives income from the registration chairperson and the food/refreshment chairperson (assuming a profit from concessions).

The business manager submits a written report on the festival's finances (see Figure 20.24) at the critique following the festival.

The business manager may be given the additional responsibility of obtaining trophies, or that duty may be assigned to a separate chairperson.

```
                              DTASC
                        Financial Statement
                        September 20, 20XX


Balance--February 1, 20XX                                    $3129.53
      (Last Financial Statement)

Receipts
      Entry Fees--Shakespeare Festival

            Sr. High        $1819.00
                             1024.50
                                                              2843.50
                        TOTAL BALANCE & RECEIPTS TO DATE     $5973.03


Expenses
      General
         Coffee & Food Services
                  (Planning Meetings)         77.45
         Art Work & Printing                 221.64
         Programs                            849.54
         Queen's Costume Rental (Jr. & Sr.)  100.00
         Trophies & Ribbons                  923.53
         High School Theatre Festival (SCETA) 1000.00
         Rental, CTA Auditorium               37.50
         Postage, Supplies, Phone            146.60
                                                             $3356.26


      Shakespeare Festivals—Facilities, etc.
         Sr. High
               Judges Inv. & Postage    65.00
               Postage, Fest. Question.  8.20
               Luncheon & Food Services196.18
                                                269.38

         Jr. High
               Lunches & Food Services 173.36
               Custodial                105.28
               Photography               52.84
               Supplies                  11.00
                                                342.48
                                                              611.86
                        TOTAL EXPENSES TO DATE              $3968.12

Balance in Bank, September 20, 20XX
      Savings    $2000.00
      Checking       4.91
                                                            $2004.91
(TWO SCHOLARSHIPS AWARDED, BUT NOT PAID AS YET.)
```

Figure 20.24 Festival Financial Statement
Courtesy of DTASC.

Consideration should be given to awarding special trophies to individuals who have worked especially hard in mounting the festival over a period of years and to the individual or institution that hosts the festival.

To Compete or Not to Compete

Many teachers with whom I've spoken resent competitive festivals. They state that they don't want to put their students in pressured situations. Some feel that competition is alien to art. Some say they don't want to attend festivals where year after year the same few schools win trophies both in events and in the festival sweepstakes (most points earned by a school in all events). Some feel that returning from festivals year after year without trophies reflects poorly on their teaching, and others say that they simply don't have the student talent to make their schools competitive. It feels good to win and it feels bad to lose, and at every competitive festival there are many more losers than winners.

On the other hand, those who favor competitive festivals say that they merely reflect society. Students live in a world of Olympic Gold Medals, Emmys, Tonys, Obies, and Oscars. Outstanding talent should be rewarded. Students must learn to win and to lose, to live with success and failure, to rise above setbacks, and, most important of all, to rise above accolades. The first time students go to an open reading at a community theater, they will be competing. Why shouldn't we prepare them?

Some teachers find that their students, particularly the shy and the overconfident, benefit enormously from the experience of competitive work.

"I love to take my students to festivals," one drama teacher told me. "They get off their high horse when they see so much talent at other schools. They go with such exaggerated ideas of their own importance and they return with such wondrous humility."

Festivals can also be run on a noncompetitive basis. Instead of trophies, all entrants get medals for participation. Instead of points, judges render evaluations that are forwarded to the students' teachers. Following the festival, each teacher reviews the evaluations and decides which items would be useful for the students. This takes massive amounts of paper shuffling and sorting. Participants still gain the major rewards of a festival—playing in a different environment to a different audience, sharing experiences, and measuring their own work against the work of others. But there are no winners or losers.

Drama teachers should make their feelings known on the matter of competing to festival planning committees. Festival planners must be responsive to the majority of their constituents. If teachers simply return their registration forms with a statement that they are not entering this year, the festival is likely to continue as it always has. But if they state their reason for declining, they may get some response.

Teachers who are going to compete should prepare their students for it. Tell them how you feel about competing. Ask how they feel about it. Discuss what behavior they expect of themselves during and following the festival. Ask what they expect to gain by competing, and follow up afterward by asking if they got out of it what they expected.

One teacher has his entrants present their work to an audience of parents the night before the festival. Another drama teacher has his entrants tour selected classrooms to present their work during the week before the festival. Both systems give the students extra experience and get them "up" for the festival.

Websites

Visiting websites can give you a quick glimpse into what festivals are like. Some even include photographs of recent activities. The Ohlone College High School Theatre Festival (www.ohlone.cc.ca.us/instr/ theater/tdd high.htm) gives the dates of their next festival and information on how to participate. The Fullerton College High School Theatre Festival (http:// theatre.fullcoll.edu/festival.htm), with a 20-year track record, posts the names of the winning high schools in each category and the names of the pieces that each presented.

Conclusion

Festivals do not just happen. The major factors contributing to their overall success are painstaking planning and careful problem solving. With these and a few years of experience, your festival should run smoothly and effectively.

Suggested Classroom Exercise

Assign students to work on the staff of a high school festival, and then to report to the class on what they did and what they observed. If this is not possible, ask students to evaluate which plan they would use (see "Festival Format") to institute a festival at your school.

21

Getting a Job

*I honestly think it is better to be a failure at something you love
than to be a success at something you hate.*

—George Burns

It takes twenty years to make an overnight success.

—Eddie Cantor

There is no security on this earth. There is only opportunity.

—General Douglas MacArthur

Your First Job as Stage Manager

There is no minimum number of college credits that qualifies an individual
to become a professional stage manager. Outside of educational theater situations, no producer (or anyone else who hires stage managers) will ask to
see your college diploma, your high school diploma, or any other kind of
certificate. Producers might ask to see your résumé and will probably ask
you about your past experience.

The two factors that count most heavily are your feeling of competence
and your ability to sell yourself. If you have read this book this far, understand it, and feel that you can apply everything in it, you are ready to stage-
manage. Now, can you convince someone else that you are ready?

In seeking your first job, my recommendation is that you apply immediately as stage manager at the theater closest to your home. If you are not
accepted, ask if you may work as assistant stage manager, property person,
assistant property person, or on the crew. Once working in any subordinate position, demonstrate your competence and tell the producer that you
want to work your way up.

The frequent pattern is that if hired as props, no matter how competent
you prove yourself, you will always be seen by that producer as props. So,
with the experience you have, start applying to other theaters for positions

of greater responsibility. Later, when you have worked at another theater as stage manager, the producer for whom you propped will welcome you back as stage manager.

The best time to get a paid stage management position is when you already have a job in community, educational, or showcase theater. This might mean taking a bread-and-butter daytime job while you work in community theater at night until you can get the experience and credits you need.

If you are considering going to college with a career in theater in mind, I suggest that you visit possible campuses and talk to the students who are in the theater program. It is too easy to be misled by advertisements and catalogs. Ask the students for the answers to the following questions:

1. How many main stage and little theater productions are put on every year? Some colleges provide the opportunity to make theater happen. Others have very limited production opportunities even though they may have fine academic programs. Your concern is whether or not you will have a chance to work. In some schools where there are many productions every year, there may also be very large numbers of students. Will you be a small fish in a large pond? Perhaps it would be better to go to a smaller school where everyone works without waiting to be in the junior class. Ask the students about this; they know.

2. Does any one faculty member teach with passion? Well, if not passion, a point of view? Well, lacking a point of view, how about a sense of joy? You can't write to a prospective teacher and ask, "Will you light my fire?" But you can ask the students if they have found any faculty members they can endorse as enthusiastic. Again, the students generally know.

By the time you have discussed these two questions with prospective fellow students, you will have a good idea if you will fit into their theater community just from the vibes you get.

There are many different atmospheres in which to study theater. Check around at junior colleges, private and state-supported colleges and universities, and independent theater programs before making up your mind. Don't feel trapped if you don't find what you want the first semester; you can usually transfer credits to other institutions.

Résumés

A résumé is a letter of introduction that you write on behalf of yourself to a prospective employer.

Put yourself in her or his shoes. What does she or he want to know about you? Your past experience is most important. What have you done? Put your most recent credit at the top of the page. Whom did you work with? At what theaters? The faster the prospective employer can find the information she or he wants, the better (see Figures 21.1 and 21.2).

It's a good idea to list the names of a few prominent cast members along with your credits. It is name dropping in its most obvious and honest application.

Your address and phone number(s) are essential on your résumé. Note that race, religion, national origin, and age are not included.

Send your résumé out regularly to every theater in town, and if you're willing to travel, to selected theaters out of town. Every three months is not too often. It is absolutely impossible for you to know exactly when a theater will be in need of new personnel.

A résumé is usually worthless unless it is followed up with personal contact. Start with a phone call. Ask if your résumé arrived. Then ask if there are any openings now or if any are expected. Ask if you might drop by for a chat to get acquainted and to be kept in mind for some future opening. At the very least, get the name of the person who actually hires the stage manager at that theater.

In your contact file keep a record of the theaters to which you've sent your résumé, and the names of the people to whom you've spoken in your follow-up phone conversations. Note their comments carefully. Who is the stage manager now? Could you work without salary on the crew until a paying slot opens up? During pre-opening rush, could you work with the crew just to get acquainted with their staff?

Hiring is usually done face to face, and personality may be a much more significant factor than experience. For the novice it is important to realize that although you may be the best stage manager in the world, there are directors, production managers, and producers who will not care to work with you because they feel that your personality will not mesh with theirs in what they consider to be the best interest of production. Over the years they have become able to make this evaluation instantaneously. It is something that does not lend itself to open expression in the interview process. If you are rejected and feel there is no reason other than the interviewer's feeling against you, trust his or her judgment and try someplace else.

When your level of experience warrants it, you may wish to submit your résumé to the Theatre Communications Group (TCG), 355 Lexington Avenue, New York, NY 11107-0217, phone: (212) 697-5230, fax: (212) 983-4847, www.tcg.org, e-mail: custserv@tcg.org. TCG assists in the nationwide exchange of information among regional, not-for-profit theaters. The organization publishes *ArtSearch*, a bi-monthly employment bulletin for the performing arts. Positions for stage managers are listed in the production section. TCG also publishes *American Theatre Magazine*.

When you have several credits and are ready for the New York stage, you may wish to have a capsule résumé published in the *Players' Guide*, an annual pictorial directory for stage, screen, radio, and television. The section devoted exclusively to stage managers might bring your name to the

JILL JOHNSON

NATIONAL TOURS

1st/2nd SM

Les Miserables dir	R.J. Alexander
City of Angels	Michael Blakemore
The Unsinkable Molly	John Bowab
Brown	
Bye Bye Birdie (reh 1 stop)	Gene Saks

SHUBERT THEATRE (L.A.)

ASM

Cats	Trevor Nunn
Les Miserables	R.J. Alexander
City of Angels	Michael Blakemore

LONG BEACH C.L.O.

Resident PSM

Chess	David Bell
Funny Girl	Alan Johnson
1776	Gordon Hunt

CALIFORNIA MUSIC THEATRE

SM

Kismet	Gary Davis
Strike Up the Band	Gary Davis

LOS ANGELES THEATRE CENTER

PSM 15 shows inc:

Joe Turner's Come and Gone	Claude Purdy
Sarcophagus	Bill Bushnell
Barabbas	Stein Winge
Diary of a Hunger Strike	Peter Sheridan
The Promise	José Luis Valenzuela
Antony and Cleopatra	Tony Richardson
I Don't Have to Show You	Luis Valdez
No Stinking Badges	

MARK TAPER FORUM

SM 10 shows inc:

Quilters	Barbara Damashek
Hunting Cockroaches	Arthur Penn
Moby Dick: Rehearsed	Edward Payson Call
Cat on a Hot Tin Roof	José Quintero
Wild Oats	Tom Moore
Passion Play	Gwen Arner
Frankie & Johnny in the	Paul Benedict
Clair de Lune	

REFERENCES

Don Hill	Scott Faris	Maureen Gibson
Assoc. Producer,	PSM	PSM
LBCLO		

Figure 21.1 Jill Johnson's Résumé. What a pleasure it is to present Jill Johnson's résumé as an example. Jill first wrote to *Stage Management* when she was a student at Occidental College. Now look at her credits! She is currently Production Stage Manager at the Pasadena Playhouse.

Courtesy Jill Johnson.

CREDITS

PLAY	THEATRE	DIRECTOR (PRODUCER)
* MIDDLE OF THE NIGHT (Jonas Rimson, Arlene Schwimmer)	JCA Center Playhouse	(Bill Miller)
* THE TUNNEL OF LOVE (Ron Doyle, Linda Priest)	Theatre Rapport	(Bob Cole)
• THE ANTHEM SPRINTERS (Patrick Burke, Gary Walberg)	Actors Studio West	Charles Rome Smith
* A MY NAME IS ALICE (Dina Babbitt, Wadsworth Taylor)	JCA Center Playhouse	(Bill Miller)
† THE GLASS MENAGERIE (Piper Laurie, Ann Sothern)	Huntington Hartford	George Keathley
– THE FANTASTICKS (Janice Hague, Michael McGiveney)	Immaculate Heart	Patricia Madsen
– THE VOYAGE (Ron Stevens, Wadsworth Taylor)	" " "	R. Montgomery
* CRAWLING ARNOLD (Hal Adelson, Shirley-May Pilnick)	JCA Center Playhouse	(Bill Miller)
• AFFAIRS OF STATE (Joan Caulfield, John Himes)	Orange County Theatre	Reid Lowden
• FUNNY THING HAPPENED ON THE WAY TO FORUM (Sterling Holloway, Gil Lamb)	Fresno Music Circus	Jonathan Lucas
† FUNNY THING HAPPENED ON THE WAY TO FORUM (Danny Dee, Sherri Spilane)	Sacramento Music Circus	" "
• SHOW BOAT (Alan Gilbert, Marvin Miller)	" " "	Milton Lyon
• GUYS AND DOLLS (Ed Ames, Joyce Jameson)	" " "	Jonathan Lucas
• TAKE ME ALONG (John Conte, Danny Lockin)	" " "	" "
† 110 IN THE SHADE (John Davidson, Gaylea Byrne)	" " "	" "
† MUSIC MAN (Kathleen Freeman, Norwood Smith)	" " "	" "
† PAJAMA GAME (Wally Griffin, Patti Karr)	" " "	" "
† BYE BYE BIRDIE (Peter Marshall, Jess Pearson)	" " "	" "
† CAMELOT (Kenneth Nelson, Lyle Talbot)	" " "	" "
• NOBODY LOVES AN ALBATROSS (Frank Aletter, Kathleen Freeman)	Las Palmas	Alan DeWitt
• ONE FLEW OVER THE CUCKOO'S NEST (Warren Oates, William Smith)	Player's Ring	John Erman
• ENTER LAUGHING (Lillian Adams. Arthur Peterson)	" " "	Harvey Korman
• THE TORCH BEARERS (Jeanne Arnold, Len Lesser)	Equity Library Theatre	" "
• THE EMPEROR (Henry Darrow, Bart Heyman)	Cahuenga Playhouse	Bill Wintersol

* director
– technical director
• stage manager
† assistant stage manager

résumé
Lawrence Stern
Main P.O. Box 1901
Los Angeles, California 90053
(213) 555-2424

Figure 21.2   Short-Form Résumé Showing Varieties of Theatrical Management Experience

attention of a Broadway producer. The *Guide* is published by Players' Guide, 123 West 44th Street, #2J; New York, NY 10036-4031, phone (212) 302-9474, fax: (212) 302-3495, www.players-guide.com; e-mail: info@players-guide.com. Worldwide employment agencies specializing in live theater use the Internet to publish résumés of job seekers. For example, try www.BackstageEmployment.com (Backstage Employment & Referral, Inc., 4137 Hinsdale Road, South Euclid, OH 44121-2703).

The trade papers rarely contain advertisements for stage managers. It is definitely a producers' market, with supply exceeding demand in situations where the stage manager is paid. If the job is dreadfully underpaid, it is almost impossible to get competent people to serve as stage manager. This means that the novice can easily gain the valuable experience needed if she or he wants to work up to the level of the professional stage manager.

Do not underestimate yourself. Send your résumés to theaters that you feel require greater experience than you possess. You may make a valuable contact that will pay off later. Or you may be hired for a slot far above what you're seeking by a producer who recognizes your potential.

When you are "at liberty," you will have plenty of time to send out résumés and to update your contact file so that you can get off your next round with far less effort. From your file you will be able to pull the addresses of the theaters, and you can send them out marked to the attention of the specific individual who does the hiring.

It is a Hollywood aphorism that "the best time to get a job is when you have one." Even if you are happily employed in what seems like a long-range situation, get out your résumé regularly and keep up your contacts.

Some people with experience in stage management are able to find work in the related fields of television, movies, and advertising. Jobs in these fields are just as scarce or scarcer than in live theater. If you search for a job in television, movies, or advertising, you may be competing with people who have studied those specific fields at the college level. Sometimes executives in those fields recognize the organizational and people skills that are honed in stage management.

Figure 21.3 is the résumé of a person whose career path has shifted from live theater into television production. Leslie Ann Kent studied theater at the college level and then worked as a stage manager. She got several live theater productions under her belt before working in film and television. (The production assistant title in television seems equivalent to gopher in live theater.)

Personal Mailing List

In addition to mailing out résumés to prospective employers, you may wish to keep up your contacts with people in the business by regularly

<table>
<tr><td colspan="3" align="center">**Leslie Ann Kent**</td></tr>
<tr><td>**Production Management**</td><td></td><td></td></tr>
<tr><td>"Maybe This Time"
(a Stabilizers video)</td><td>Avocado Films</td><td>Patrick Welborn</td></tr>
<tr><td>*Chip's Hardware*</td><td>Artist in Torment Productions</td><td>Michael Jung</td></tr>
<tr><td>*Everything I'm Not*</td><td>Artist in Torment Productions</td><td>Jonathan J. Casson</td></tr>
<tr><td>1989 Solo Showcase</td><td>University of the Arts</td><td>Walter Dallas</td></tr>
<tr><td>**Stage Management**</td><td></td><td></td></tr>
<tr><td>*New World Order*</td><td>California Institute of the Arts</td><td>Kelly M. Johnston</td></tr>
<tr><td>Caught in the Act
(an Improvisational Comedy Troupe)</td><td>California Institute of the Arts</td><td>Anne West</td></tr>
<tr><td>An Evening of Cabaret</td><td>Colorado Shakespeare Festival</td><td>Richard Devin</td></tr>
<tr><td>*The Rivals* (ASM)</td><td>Colorado Shakespeare Festival</td><td>Joel Fink</td></tr>
<tr><td>L.A. Showcase '92</td><td>Odyssey Theater</td><td>Roxanne Captor</td></tr>
<tr><td>Mardi Gras with
Queen Ida's Zydeco Band</td><td>California Institute of the Arts</td><td>Christopher Gratton</td></tr>
<tr><td>*Tempest* (ASM)</td><td>Modular Theater</td><td>Craig Belknap</td></tr>
<tr><td>*Drums in the Night*</td><td>California Institute of the Arts</td><td>William Kasper</td></tr>
<tr><td>*The Importance of
Being Earnest* (ASM)</td><td>Colorado Shakespeare Festival</td><td>Joel Fink</td></tr>
<tr><td>L.A. Showcase '91</td><td>Odyssey Theater</td><td>Peter Frisch</td></tr>
<tr><td>*Bonjour la Bonjour*</td><td>The Off Ramp Theater</td><td>Judy Goff</td></tr>
<tr><td>**Additional Experience**</td><td></td><td></td></tr>
<tr><td>*Dr. Quinn, Medicine Woman*
(production assistant)</td><td>CBS Entertainment Productions</td><td>John Liberti</td></tr>
<tr><td colspan="2">Bachelor of Fine Arts - Theater Management</td><td>California Institute of the Arts - May 1993</td></tr>
<tr><td colspan="3">References available on request</td></tr>
</table>

Figure 21.3 Résumé Showing Transition from Live Theater to Television Production. Leslie Ann Kent read *Stage Management* while in college. She worked as a stage manager in several live theater productions before looking for work in television production.

Courtesy Leslie Ann Kent, Production Assistant, CBS Entertainment Productions.

sending them notes on your progress, invitations to shows you're doing, and programs of shows you've done (not to mention holiday greetings).

It takes very little effort and does not cost much in postage and stationery to let your theater acquaintances know what you're doing—and it can pay off in many pleasant ways.

Three months after your present show closes, 10 members of your cast, staff, and crew may be working in 10 different theater situations. Each represents a possible introduction for you to another set of directors and producers. But three months after you close you may run into an actor with whom you worked nightly, and he or she may not remember your name.

The theater scene is both fluid and forgetful. To exploit the former quality, you have to overcome the latter.

The best thing about being a production assistant is that you have nowhere to go but up. You get to watch all of the departments function simultaneously. There are about 110 people on a set at any given time working in many different departments. Over the last year, there is not a single one that I have not helped out in some capacity—some many times. Being a production assistant gives you the opportunity to get closer to the people who can teach you what you want to learn.

Production assistant is a common first job for industry insiders. Most of them have been a production assistant at one time and understand that a person in that position aspires to move up. If you show enough intelligence, diplomacy, and skill, people will notice and, hopefully, remember you.

> Leslie Ann Kent
> Production Assistant
> *Dr. Quinn, Medicine Woman*
> CBS Entertainment Productions

Your personal mailing list might consist of all of your cast lists with crew and staff members added.

I worked for many years outside of New York as a non-union stage manager. When I came to New York, I stage-managed showcases for about two years, getting paid next to nothing—working with Equity and non-Equity actors. One of the actors I worked with recommended me to a producer, and I got an interview. I know that the actor's recommendation helped, but I had to put myself on the line—let the producer know that I had the experience and the background that would make me an asset to his company. I got the job and the Equity contract. Once that job was over, I was back looking for paying work and stage-managing Equity showcases—to keep growing as a stage manager until I landed my next Equity job—and so it continued for the seven years I actively stage-managed as an Equity stage manager.

> Martha R. Jacobs
> Stage Manager
> New York City

[Martha's work as a stage manager led to her current administrative work in live theater.]

Long-Range Goals

Where are you going, Stage Manager? Do you want to stage-manage for the rest of your life? Do you want to find some big, cushy theater with stable management and move in to stay—to age 65 or senility, whichever comes first?

There seem to be too few career stage managers in the business. There are many aspiring actors, aspiring directors, aspiring producers, and aspiring writers who call themselves stage managers. There are many stage managers who are on their way out of the theater—on their way to law school, teaching English, programming a computer, or selling shoes. Stage management seems frequently to be a phase rather than a career.

If you make a career of it, you can hope for a salary of $600 to $1,000 per week in regional theaters, depending on contract. Smaller-sized theater salaries begin at $170 per week. If you get to Broadway, your salary might go as high as $1,939 per week as production stage manager for a musical. (These figures reflect the Equity contracts as of 1999. For more current information, call your local Equity office.) (If you want to know what it's like to be a highly paid Broadway SM, please read "The Stage Manager: Off-Broadway or On, the Buck Stops Here." This February 1987 article in *Smithsonian* details SM Alan Hall's work on the Broadway musical *Smile*. If your sights are on Broadway, read it!)

But that's the optimistic viewpoint. You must expect feast and famine, periods of high pay and periods of unemployment.

Unlike many careers, stage management does not offer regular promotions, hours, vacations, and retirement. A few benefits are provided by union membership, but it is up to the individual to plan her or his own career progress. Promotions are yours for the getting, the hustling, and the self-promoting. If you plan to be a career stage manager, you must evaluate your own aggressiveness as a very significant factor in your potential career. If you are not aggressive, you will drift from one union minimum situation to the next.

A big-name visiting director at our school said that no one important he had ever met started out as a stage manager. I'm pushing to be the first.

Jill Johnson
Theater arts student
Occidental College, CA

[Former stage managers don't wear miniature gold clipboards around their necks. So sometimes it's hard to tell. Your visiting director had obviously not met Humphrey *(Casablanca)* Bogart, Dale *(Man of La Mancha)* Wasserman, or Gordon *(Mark Taper Forum)* Davidson. Hal *(Pajama Game, Fiddler on the Roof)* Prince started his Broadway career as third assistant stage manager. I'm sure that these four (actor, writer, director, producer) do not exhaust the list. (William Shakespeare was a stage manager before he wrote his first play. Is that why his plays contain no stage directions?) Stage management is not a mandatory prerequisite for any other job in theater. But it is a potentially valuable way to enter the very competitive world of the theater and meet others who can help you along the way.]

If stage management is just a phase for you, here is my best advice: Get out just as soon as you can and do your thing. Stage management demands too much of your organizational ability, energy, time, and emotional juices for you to think of it as a bread-and-butter job to support your real interest in life. When you have stage-managed three or four shows in two or more theaters, you will have a fair understanding of the job, and certainly adequate background for any related theater work. It won't take you more than six months of steady work to know if you want to make it a career. Then if you want to be an actor, director, producer, writer, or shoe salesperson, get out and act, direct, produce, write, or sell shoes.

I've come a long way since my last letter. I am an Equity stage manager, and have worked the past three years at the Mark Taper Forum (for, ironically, Gordon, who was indeed a stage manager and who consequently demands a great deal of his stage manager teams). My best advice is to start wherever you can, experience any and all aspects of theater, and make it known to those around you what your ultimate goals are. I began as an intern in the Taper casting office and told *everyone* that I wanted to stage-manage. That information reached someone who needed a production intern, a position which let me prove myself as well as learn the ways of professional theater. I was offered a year-long position as resident production assistant, which enabled me to work with various directors, designers, and stage managers. Then they needed a stage manager for *Moby Dick: Rehearsed,* and here I am, one year later, resident Production Stage Manager in a brand new four-theatre complex.

Jill Johnson
Production Stage Manager
Los Angeles Theatre Center
Los Angeles, CA

But if you want to be a stage manager, give it all you've got. Be a *great* stage manager!

Suggested Classroom Exercise

Ask each student to write his or her résumé. Have students exchange and critique résumés.

Appendix A

Production Checklist from a Stage Manager's Point of View

A Chronological Approach and Priorities

Don't be deterred by the size of the job! Begin with the possible. Begin with one step.
—G. I. Gurdjieff and P. D. Ouspenski (Russian philosophers)

Those two priceless abilities: first, the ability to think. Second, the ability to do things in the order of their importance.
—Henry L. Doherty

YOU DO NOT HAVE TO DO ALL OF THE ITEMS IN THIS CHECKLIST! You need to know if the task needs to be done and who in your theater will do it. If you determine that the stage manager needs to do it, you may still be able to assign the task to a coworker or subordinate.

In the first hardcover edition of *Stage Management*, the following chart appeared as end papers. In the subsequent five softcover editions, it appeared prior to the first chapter. In both cases, this chart's placement reflected my hope that it would help the novice stage manager get a basic understanding of his or her job and allow the reader to access critical information directly, without reading the book from cover to cover.

Generally, reader reaction to this chart has been favorable. Some producers told me that they amended it for their own production checklist. The negative reaction was that it intimidated students and amateurs ("I can't possibly accept a job where I have to do all that!").

My hope is that now that you have found it, you will use it to help you determine what you have to do to get the show on the road.

Hopefully, you understand that YOU DO NOT HAVE TO DO ALL OF THE FOLLOWING, and you're ready to turn the page.

A CHRONOLOGICAL APPROACH AND PRIORITIES

TASK	PAGE	PRIORITY	COORDINATE WITH
BEFORE REHEARSALS BEGIN			
Get things to run smoothly on stage and backstage	1	A	
Gather equipment	57–60	B,E,F	
Be aware of police, fire, and municipal regulations	264–268	A	Producer, Tech Dir
Get to know the theater	51–69	B	
Inspect safety conditions	127–138	A	
Make a diagram of the stage	60–62	C	Tech Dir
Check out the electric boxes	62	C	Tech Dir
Make a diagram of lighting instruments	62–66	C	Tech Dir, Light Design
Keep a do list	138–139	B	
Make a prompt script	19–25	A,B,D	Director
Identify the problems of the script	25	A	Director
Hold preproduction staff meetings	34–40, 55	C	Producer, Director
Write out plots	26–29	B,C,G	Dir, Technicians
Make master calendar	36–39	B,C	Everyone
Distribute rehearsal schedules	40–45	B,C	Producer, Director
Arrange the callboard	47–50	C	Producer
Post emergency numbers	49	A	
Distribute/explain company rules	45–46	C,G	Producer, Director
Keep a budget and record your expenses	92–99	A	Producer
Obtain audition forms	71–85	B,C	Producer, Director
Prepare staff, crew, cast lists	85–88	C	Prod, Dir, Staff, Crew
Make gel patterns	170–171	D	Tech Dir, Light Design
Make supply directory	254–257	E	
DURING READINGS AND REHEARSALS			
Prepare audition rooms	70	B,C,D	Producer, Director
Post notes for readings	73–76	B,C,D,F,G	Prod, Dir, Publicist
Accept résumés	76	E	Director
Control scripts	79	B	Director
Make preset diagrams	103–104	A	Dir, Tech Dir, Sc Des
Prepare for rehearsals	104–105	B,D	Director
Brief cast, crew on safety	127–138, 194–195	A	Producer, Director
Post running order	121–124	B,D	Director
Supervise department heads	150–152	C	Prod, Dept Heads
Control required forms	82–85	C	Producer, Director
Conduct deputy election	89–91	B	Union, Cast
Keep cast on time	144–149	A,B	Director, Cast
Distribute itineraries	224–225	C	Producer, Cast
Distribute touring agreement	244–247	C	Cast
Post duty roster	229–231	C	Everyone
Make checklists	209–212	B	
Supervise props	152–162	A	Prop Mast, Prod, Dir
Distribute scene-shift diagrams	198–201	B,C,D	Scene Designer
Contribute to advance letters	249–250	C	Producer
Maintain order	118–119	B,E	Director
Call rehearsal cues	105–106	A	Director
Take blocking notation	110–117	B,C,D	Director
Make French scene diagrams	118	E	

KEY:
A. I've got to do this first. The quality of the production will be adversely affected if I don't.
B. I've got to do this because if I don't, time and energy of staff and cast will be wasted.
C. Someone else may do this well, but I've got to make sure it gets done.
D. I can assign this task to a subordinate if I make sure it gets done.
E. I'll do it if I have time, and it would help, but we'll survive without it.
F. A luxury; leave it for last.
G. This might be helpful for another show in a different theater, but will be useless here.

A CHRONOLOGICAL APPROACH AND PRIORITIES

TASK	PAGE	PRIORITY	COORDINATE WITH
Spike set pieces	106–107	A,C	Tech Dir
Prompt	107–110	C	Director, Cast
Give rehearsal, publicity, costume calls	119	A	Everyone
Warn cast	110	E	Director, Cast
Keep rehearsal log	126	E	
Submit rehearsal reports	126–127	B,G	Producer
Time rehearsals	124–126	B,D	Dir, House Manager
Post photo calls	120	E	Publicist, Dir, Costumes, Cast
Check lighting cue sheet	167–169	C	Lights
Work on take-in, brief crew	194	C,B,D	Scene Designer, Dir Tech Dir, Crew
Make shift plot chart	198–201	C,D	Tech Dir
Supervise arrangement of scene dock	195–197	C,D	Tech Dir
Supervise technical rehearsal	205–208	A	Director, Tech Dir
Choreograph scene changes	189	B,D	Tech Dir
Prepare area lighting diagram	172	C	Light Designer
Prepare re-gelling plans	169–171	C	Light Designer
Post sign-in sheets	145–147	B,C	
Place curtain call light cues on lighting sheet	216–219	B	Director, Light Techs

DURING PRODUCTION

TASK	PAGE	PRIORITY	COORDINATE WITH
Conduct lighting check	164–167	A	Light Designer, Techs
Post scene-shift diagrams	198–201	B,C,D	Tech Dir
Give calls (prior to curtain)	148–149	A	Cast
Caution audience	201	C	Producer
Call late actors	146–147	A	Cast
Coordinate with house manager	221–222	A	House Manager
Give cues	212–216	A	Technicians
Check immediate effect of each cue	215	A	
Supervise shifts	189–194	C,D	Tech Dir
Inspect shifts	197–198	B,C,D	Tech Dir
Time performances	124–126	B	Director
Walk the curtain	219	D	Tech Dir
Time curtain calls	216–219	A	Director
Maintain sets	202–204	B,C,D	Tech Dir
Be aware of cast morale	236–237	A	Cast
Keep the show in hand	234–236	A,C	Director, Cast
Post V.I.P list	232–233	F	Producer
Rehearse understudies, block replacements	237–238	C	Producer, Director

POSTPRODUCTION

TASK	PAGE	PRIORITY	COORDINATE WITH
Distribute strike plan	240–242	B,C,G	Tech Dir
Post changeover schedule	242–243	C,G	Producer, Tech Dir
Supervise moves	244–249	A,B,C	Producer
Write letter to next stage manager	276–277	F	
Write critique	277	D	
Write letters of recommendation, thank-you notes	277–279	F	

IN GENERAL

TASK	PAGE	PRIORITY	COORDINATE WITH
Make contact file	257–258	E	
Make a theater information packet	66–69	C,F,G	Producer, Tech Dir
Get acquainted with unions	271–275	C,E	
Send out résumés	323–327	A	
Read theater news	251–253	E	
Keep in contact with theater acquaintances	327–329	F	
Start a theater library	257–260	F	

Suggested Classroom Exercise

Collectively review this list to select items that are appropriate to the work of stage managers at your theater. Have the class write an abbreviated list that could be used as a stage manager's guide at your theater.

Appendix B

Forms

Try to be a problem solver, not just a problem.
—Elbin Cleveland

There are many forms and checklists used by a stage manager in the course of his or her work. Not all of the forms are necessary for every production. All of the following have been explained in this book. For quick reference, they are listed here in alphabetical order with page number.

Suggested Classroom Exercise

Select and list those forms that are used at your theater. Have students make a book of master forms that will be used in your future productions.

Appendix C

A Few Theater Stories

A sense of humor is part of the art of leadership, of getting along with people, of getting things done.

—Dwight D. Eisenhower

Knowing jokes is not a substitute for having a sense of humor. There are occasions, however, when a good theater anecdote can be helpful.

1. The wedding of the daughter of a very famous Hollywood character actor brought out many producers, directors, and agents. As the proud father escorted the bride down the aisle, this whisper was overheard: "Will you look who they got to play the father!"

2. The old circus worker came home drenched from a storm. For years and years his job had been to follow the elephants in the parades and clean up after them.

His wife pleaded with him. "Why do you do it? You're past retirement age. It's bad for your health—out in all kinds of weather. Please, I beg you, retire."

"What," he answered, "and give up show biz!"

3. The novice actor was elated by a call from his agent. It was just a one-line walk-on in a historical play, but it was work. The actor who was to do the part had been taken ill. They opened that night. The agent explained that he would get his costume and full particulars at the theater.

"By the way," said the agent, "your line is, 'Hark, I hear a cannon.'"

On the way to the theater the novice rehearsed his line: "**Hark,** I hear a cannon." "Hark, **I** hear a cannon." "Hark, I hear a **cannon.**" He was absolutely determined to deliver his one line well.

He got into his costume and the stage manager briefed him. His cue would be the firing of the cannon.

He went on stage. He waited. His moment was coming. He became more and more excited. Finally the cannon exploded.

And the novice delivered his line as follows: "What the hell was that?!!"

4. Cecil B. De Mille was about to shoot his greatest, most costly epic scene. He had stationed his three best cameramen strategically. In the scene a herd of elephants stampeded through a primitive village, an earthquake swallowed up half the village, a tidal wave covered everything else, and, as the waters receded, a volcano erupted spewing hot lava and burning the remaining huts. Then the Yugoslavian army on horseback, dressed as the hordes of Ghengis Khan, swept through the remains, raping and pillaging, only to be in turn swept off by a tornado.

Eighty-seven assistant directors and the headquarters staff of the Yugoslavian army held the thousands of extras in place. Three hundred and seventeen special effects men readied the wind machines, dynamite, and chicken feathers.

Then C.B. gave the command, "Lights, cameras, action."

And it all happened beautifully—the elephants, earthquake, tidal wave, lava, burning, the Yugoslavian army, raping, pillaging, and the tornado. And when the last chicken feather had settled to the ground, Cecil B. De Mille knew that he had produced the most incredible sequence ever captured on film.

"Did you get that, Dick?" he asked his ace cameraman. "Gosh, C.B., I forgot to take the lens cover off the camera."

"Never mind," said C.B. "Did you get that, Roger?" he asked his second cameraman.

"Oh, boy, C.B. I forgot to load the film."

"Never mind," De Mille said and shouted up to the third cameraman on the dolly, "Did you get that, Arthur?"

Arthur shouted back, "I'm ready when you are, C.B."

5. The Boy Scout saw a nun trying to cross a busy intersection near Broadway. He offered to help her.

"Oh, thank you, young man, but I can make it."

"Please, sister, let me help," said the scout. "We're supposed to do good deeds."

When they had crossed, he said, "May I ask what order you're with so I can tell my scoutmaster?"

"Oh, for Pete's sake," she said, "I'm with *The Sound of Music.*"

6. The last act of a college's production of *Hedda Gabler* was building to its melodramatic conclusion in which Hedda takes the pistols, which the playwright had so conspicuously planted, and exits into the library to shoot herself. After a shot is heard, Tesman crosses to the library door, peers offstage, and announces to the audience, "Shot herself. Shot herself in the temple. Fancy that."

The student actor playing Tesman waited for the shot. Finally he heard— click, click. He crossed to the library door, peered offstage, and said, "Oh my God, she stabbed herself to death."

7. We were rehearsing a play called *Golden Boy.* Charlie Lynch was playing the part of Tom, a prize fighter, and Dorothy Kilheffer was playing the part of Lorna. These two are in love. In the process of finding out that they are in love they have a violent quarrel. During this quarrel he says to her, "I wouldn't look at you twice if they hung you naked from a Christmas tree."

At this moment I heard a quite audible gasp from John Schaeffer (President of the College). I thought to myself, "Uh-uh, we may be going to get the blue pencil." But we went on without interruption.

At the end of the scene Dr. Schaeffer called Dotty to him and said something to her in a rather agitated whisper.

After rehearsal I asked Dotty what happened. He had said to her, "Dotty, that's a terrible thing for a man to say to a woman. That's the worst thing he can possibly say. Don't worry, Dotty, if they hung you naked from a Christmas tree, I'd look at you twice." (Darrell D. Larsen, retiring after 35 years as director of theater for Franklin and Marshall College, *Alumnus Magazine*, July 1962).

8. Sammy Ginsburg had been in show biz for 80 years as a stunt man in a circus. His specialty was diving 100 feet into a barrel of water. As he began his act, he addressed the crowd.

"Ladies and gentlemen, good evening. Tonight for the 47,453rd consecutive time you will see me climb up on this 100-foot ladder and dive into this barrel of water."

A hush fell over the audience. The drums started to roll.

"Of course," Sammy continued, "it's not like in the old days. I've been doing this same stunt for 65 years, and I'm a little slower now—my arthritis."

He reached for the ladder and moaned. "Also a little bursitis. I have it in my right arm. But I have to go on with the show because I'm the sole support of a family of 14."

He slowly pulled himself up on the second rung and groaned low again.

The crowd became apprehensive at the sight of this old man groaning up the ladder. "Don't jump," shouted a member of the audience. Soon several others joined in and it became a chant, "Don't jump, Sammy, don't jump." Finally the whole audience was standing up, chanting, shouting, imploring Sammy not to go through with it.

"Okay, okay already," said Sammy, stopping his climb and addressing the audience. "The next performance is at 10:30."

9. Edward G. Robinson once said that you could always tell if he was a good guy or a bad guy in a movie by the angle of the brim of his hat. If it was up, he was usually a detective, and if it was down, he was the heavy. While filming a flick in which he was a terrible villain, his hat brim suddenly popped up.

"What did you do?" asked a friend.

"What could I do?" replied Robinson. "Why, I arrested myself, of course."

10. When Cecil B. De Mille arrived at the Pearly Gates, St. Peter asked him to produce a film.

C.B. said no.

"But you can use all the greatest talent we have here," St. Peter persisted. "Directors: Stanislavsky, Eisenstein, Griffith..."

"No," said C.B.

"Actors: Barrymore, Gable, Cooper, Bogart..."

"No," said C.B.

"Composers: Beethoven, Tschaikovsky, Mozart, Gershwin, Hammerstein..."

"Well," said C.B.

"Writers: Shakespeare, Shaw, O'Neil, anyone you want."

"Okay," said C.B., "with talent like that, how can I refuse. I can start this afternoon."

"Great," said St. Peter, "but first I'd like you to read this girl I know. She sings."

11. Dustin Hoffman was scheduled to shoot a scene from the movie *The Marathon Man*. He arrived on set looking totally bedraggled. Sir Laurence Olivier asked what had happened. Hoffman explained that in order to prepare for his scene as a runner, he had stayed up all night running. "My dear young man," asked Olivier, "have you thought of acting?"

12. A lovely Hollywood lady was complaining to her friend that she couldn't sing. The friend sympathized. "And I can't dance." The friend sympathized. "And worst of all, I can't act."

"Why don't you give up show business?" her friend asked.

"I can't quit. I'm a star."

13. The rabbi was running late when he arrived at the funeral. Flustered, he tried in vain to find the notes that would help him to personalize his eulogy. "He was so loved by his brothers. Although they all live far from here, they have gathered with us to pay their last respects. His brother . . ."

"Arthur," someone whispered.

". . . his brother Arthur," continued the rabbi, "is from . . ."

"a doctor in Cleveland," the same person whispered.

"Cleveland," continued the rabbi, "where he's a doctor. And his brother . . ."

"Leonard," came the whisper.

"His brother Leonard is . . ."

"an accountant in Kansas City," whispered.

". . . here from Kansas City where he's an accountant. And his brother . . ."

"Sam," whispered.

"and his brother Sam, who . . ."

"An agent in Hollywood," whispered.

"Sam enchanted evening, you will meet a stranger . . ."

14. Phillip runs into his old friend Elliot, an actor on Broadway.

"How are you, Elliot?"

"Terrific. Couldn't be better. I've been running over at the Helen Hayes Theatre for the last three months and it looks like we'll run forever. Before that I shot a spaghetti Western in Yugoslavia. My TV series is in reruns nationally. I've been selected as spokesperson for Campbell Soups and my last three commercials are all still running. And Neil Simon wants me to do the lead in his next play. But enough about me. How about you? How did *you* like my last movie?"

15. The late Ruth Gordon was performing in a play. The phone on the set rang and she knew it was her cue, but she went up on her lines. She picked up the phone, turned to the actress standing next to her, and said, "It's for you."

16. A director dies and goes to heaven. On his very first day there he is delighted by St. Peter's tour of the Heavenly Civic Theatre. The actors in rehearsal are first rate. The facilities are without equal—state of the art lighting,

sound, and stage equipment. "This is terrific!" exclaims the director, "I can't imagine what hell must be like."

With a snap of his finger St. Peter transfers the director to the Satanic Civic Theatre. The director is equally impressed—from the chandeliers in the lobby to the ornate barber chairs in the makeup room, the facilities are equal. "I can't see any difference," protests the director.

"No," says St. Peter knowingly, "but in Heaven the critics aren't allowed at opening night."

17. A producer and a writer are on their way to Palm Springs for a weekend of work on a script when their car breaks down in the desert. They walk and then crawl across the burning sands. Finally, almost totally dehydrated, they come upon a tiny stream of cool water. The writer scoops up some water in his hands and is about to bring it to his lips when the producer throws some desert sand into the water in the writer's hands. "Why did you do that?" shouts the writer.

The producer answers, "Just trying to help you fix it up a little."

18. An actor returns home to find his home burned to the ground. He asks his neighbor what happened. The neighbor says, "Sorry to tell you, but your agent came to your home, beat up your wife and kids, locked them in the basement, stole your TV and VCR, and torched your house."

"What," stammers the actor incredulously, "my agent came to my home?!!!"

19. Two guys are sitting in a bar. One asks, "What's your IQ?"

"One eighty-five," replies the second.

"How do you feel current sub-particle quantum research will impact on Einstein's theory?" They chat for a while.

In another part of the bar two others are talking. "What's your IQ?" asks the first.

"It's 120," answers the second.

"Did you catch the Dodgers game last night?"

They chat. In a dimly lit corner two others are talking. "What's your IQ?" asks the first.

"About 39," replies the second.

"Have you read any good scripts lately?"

20. Experiencing stagefright while waiting in the wings, Renee Taylor noticed that Helen Hayes was crossing herself.

"Will that help me? I'm Jewish."

Ms. Hayes answered, "Only if you can act."

21. Julie Andrews tells a Moss Hart story. They were rehearsing for *My Fair Lady* in London. The rehearsals were going badly. Hart complained to his wife, Kitty Carlisle, that if these were the old days, he would have taken Julie to the honeymoon suite of the Savoy for some private rehearsal time. He was sure that would have improved the production. Kitty said fine, go right ahead.

Julie concluded the story by saying that "the honeymoon suite of the Savoy is just marvelous" (after a pause), "I've been told."

22. Long ago on Broadway it was the stage manager's responsibility to deliver dismissal notices to actors who had rehearsed but would not be used

in the run of the show. If the actor was not personally notified by the end of dress rehearsal, the producer would have to pay him for the run of the show.

One worried actor took to sneaking out of the theater during the last week of rehearsals in the hopes of avoiding the stage manager. But alas, after dress rehearsal, and after hiding in a closet for hours, and just as he was exiting the theater from a fire escape, he heard the stage manager calling him. He accepted the small envelope, read the contents, and smiled. "What a relief. My mother died."

23. He stepped from the stage to scant applause. As he removed his buskins, his mother approached.
"What was that, son?"
"Acting."
"That's acting?"
"Yeah, Mom. I'm an actor."
"What's an actor?"
"Someone who does what I just did."
"You get paid for that?"
"A hundred drachmas."
"One hundred drachmas for that little nothing?! I'm impressed. Tell me, Thespis, my big shot, do you need an agent?"

24. "An associate producer is the only guy in Hollywood who will associate with the producer." (Fred Allen)

25. From correspondence between George Bernard Shaw and Winston Churchill:
Dear Winnie, here are two tickets to my new play. Bring a friend, if you have one. GBS
Dear GBS, sorry, but I can't make it to the opening night of your new play. However, I would appreciate tickets to the second night performance—if you have one. WSC

26. "I didn't like the play, but then I saw it under adverse conditions—the curtain was up." (Groucho Marks)

27. A man arrives at the theater to find another man lying across his seats.
"Sir, you're in my seats."
The man groans faintly, "Ohhhh!"
"I say, you're in my seats."
The man groans again a little louder, "Ohhhhhh."
"Sir, where are your seats?"
The man groans, "In the balcony."

28. Two stage managers, nearing the ends of their careers, were discussing the likelihood of there being some form of theatrical endeavor in the hereafter. They first consulted a friendly medium. Later the following exchange took place between the two stage managers:
SM1: "I have some good news and some bad news. The good news is that there is a wonderful theater in heaven—well equipped, spacious, plenty of wing space. In fact, there's a show opening tomorrow night."
SM2: "That's wonderful! So what's the bad news?"
SM1: "You're calling the show."

29. An old stage manager arrived at the Pearly Gates. As a reward for years of patience, discretion, and endeavor, St. Peter granted him a single wish. "I've never seen a perfect blackout—can that be arranged?"

St. Peter snapped his fingers, and the darkness descended. There was not a hint of spill from worklights or prompt corner. There was total silence, not a whisper, not a footstep, not a pin drop—just complete silence and total darkness. It lasted 18 seconds.

When the lights came up again, St. Peter was gone and the Pearly Gates had been struck.

These last two stories were sent in by Garry McQuinn, Head of Technical Production at the National Institute of Dramatic Art in Australia. I love old theater stories. If you have any that you would like to share, please see the Reader's Comments Form, page 383, for my address. Thanks!

For additional theater stories and backstage humor, visit www.geocities.com/Broadway/Stage/2203/theatrejokes.html.

Suggested Classroom Exercise

Have students apply a black marker to their personal copies to eliminate any of the entries above that they feel are sexist, racist, too vulgar, in bad taste, or not funny. Discuss the difference between knowing jokes/anecdotes and having a sense of humor.

Appendix D

Websites of Interest
to Stage Managers

*When everything is said and done, a lot more will
be said than done.*

—Anonymous

Here are a few websites referenced in the text with selected others. This is in no
way a comprehensive list. The following are only a mouse click away at
www.ablongman/stern/

Lists of Lists/Links

www.theatre-central.com
www.theatre-link.com

A.S.K. Theater Projects
www.askplay.org/links.html

Ken McCoy, Ph.D. Stetson University
www.stetson.edu/departments/csata/thr_guid.html

University of Virginia
www.people.virginia.edu/~rlk3p/desource/links/LinkList.html

Audio Terms

Rane Corporation
www.rane.com

Books, Publishers, and Book Stores

Allyn & Bacon, Inc.
www.ablongman.com

Cornell University Press
www.cornellpress.com

The Drama Bookshop
www.playbill.com/cgi-bin/plb/dramabooks?cmd=search

Drama Publishers
www.quitespecificmedia.com

The Internet Theatre Bookshop
www.stageplays.com

Colleges/Universities

Case-Western Reserve University
www.cwru.edu/artsci/thtr/website/theahome.htm

Fullerton College
http://theatre.fullcoll.edu/

Ohlone College
www.ohlone.cc.ca.us/instr/theater/

SUNY–Stony Brook
www.sunysb.edu/theatrearts/

Yale University
www.yale.edu/drama

Consultants

Theatre Projects Consultants
www.tpcworld.com

Costumes

Eastern Costume Company
www.easterncostume.com

Patternmaker
www.patternmaker.com

Directories of Theatrical Resources

Contacts (British)
www.spotlightcd.com/spotpubs/pub7.html

ESTA
www.esta.org

Princeton University Theatrical Supplies
http://webware.princeton.edu/theater/VENDORS.HTM

University of Virginia
www.people.virginia.edu/~rlk3p/desource/links/LinkList.html

World's Greatest Lighting Manufacturers
www.lighting-inc.com/manufacture1.html

Employment

Backstage Employment & Referral, Inc.
www.BackstageEmployment.com

Players' Guide
www.players-guide.com

High School Festivals

Fullerton College
http://theatre.fullcoll.edu/festival.htm

Ohlone College
www.ohlone.cc.ca.us/instr/theater/tddhigh.htm

Humor

Carissa Dollar's Theatre Jokes
www.geocities.com/Broadway/Stage/2203/theatrejokes.html

Lighting

A. C. Lighting
www.aclighting.com

Altman Stage Lighting Company, Inc.
www.altmanltg.com

Bulbtronics
www.bulbtronics.com

Colortran-Leviton Controls Division
www.colortran.com or www.nsicorp.com

Diversitronics, Inc.
www.diversitronics.com

Electrol Engineering, Inc.
www.electrol.net

Electronic Theatre Controls, Inc.
www.etcconnect.com

High End Systems, Inc.
www.highend.com

Martin Professional, Inc.
www.martin.dk

The Phoebus Co., Inc.
www.phoebus.com

Rosco Laboratories, Inc.
www.rosco.com

Strand Lighting
www.strandlight.com

Strong Entertainment Lighting
www.strongint.com

Tomcat USA, Inc.
www.tomcatglobal.com

Vari-Lite, Inc.
www.vari-lite.com

Vincent Lighting Systems
www.virtualightstore.com

World's Greatest Lighting Manufacturers (Lighting Internet Service)
www.lighting-inc.com/manufacture1.html

Lighting Instrument Template
www.fieldtemplate.com

Magazines/Newspapers/Information

American Theatre Magazine
www.tcg.org

Back Stage
www.backstage.com

Back Stage West
www.backstagewest.com

Contacts
www.spotlightcd.com/spotpubs/pub7.html

Dramatics
www.etassoc.org

Entertainment Design Magazine
www.entertainmentdesignmag.com

Hollywood Reporter
www.hollywoodreporter.com

Lighting Dimensions
www.etecnyc.net

Plays
www.channel1.com/plays

TDR (The Drama Review)
http://mitpress.mit.edu

The Technical Brief
www.yale.edu/drama/publications

Theater
www.yale.edu/drama/publications

Variety
www.variety.com

Opera Scores

T.I.S., Inc. (bookstore)
www.tisbook.com

Organizations

A.S.K. Theater Projects
www.askplay.com

Educational Theatre Association
www.etassoc.com

Stage Managers' Association (SMA)
www.stagemanagers.org

USITT United States Institute for Theatre Technology
www.usitt.org

Publishers, Plays, and Musicals

Baker's Plays
www.bakersplays.com

Dramatic Publishing Company
www.dramaticpublishing.com

Dramatists Play Service, Inc.
www.dramatists.com/dramatists

Eldridge Publishing Company
www.histage.com

The Heuer Publishing Company
www.hitplays.com

Institute for Readers Theatre
www.readers-theatre.com

Show Control

On Line Exchange of Sound Control Information
www.show-control.com/sclist.html

Prophet Systems Innovations
www.prophetsys.com

SM Equipment

Tools for Stagecraft
www.toolsforstagecraft.com

Zee Medical, Inc.
www.lifeessentialsbyzee.com

Sound

Audio Manufacturers, list of
www.tiac.net/users/auldwrks/theater/proaud1.htm

Clair Brothers Audio
www.clair-audio.com

Clear-Com Intercom Systems
www.clearcom.com

Crown International, Inc.
www.crownaudio.com

Eastern Acoustic Works
http://www.eaw.com

JBL Professional
www.jblpro.com

Level Control Systems
www.LCSaudio.com

Mackie Designs, Inc. (mixer manual can be downloaded free)
www.mackie.com

Online Exchange for Sound Information
www.brooklyn.com/theatre-sound/

QSC Audio Products, Inc.
www.qscaudio.com

Rane Corporation
www.rane.com

Sound Designers

Garth Hemphill
www.glhdesign.com

Sound Effects

Gefen Systems
www.sfxsearch.com

Hollywood Edge
www.hollywoodedge.com

Sound Dogs
www.sounddogs.com

The SoundFX Gallery
www.sfx-gallery.co.uk

Sound Ideas
www.sound-ideas.com

Special Effects

MDG Fog Generators, Ltd.
www.MDGFOG.com

Technical Information for Visiting Companies

Theatre Royal
www.theatreroyal.demon.co.uk.

Theaters

ACT San Francisco
www.act-sfbay.org

American Musical Theater of San Jose
www.amtsj.org

Theatrical Supplies

Dudley Theatrical
www.dudleytheatrical.com

ESTA (Entertainment Service and Technology Association)
(lists/links of suppliers)
www.esta.org

International Theatrical Truss Corp.
www.ITTCORPORATION.com

Jeamar Winches
www.jeamar.com

Musson Theatrical TV Film
www.musson.com

Paco Corp.
www.pacocorp.com

Princeton University Theatrical Supplies (lists/links of suppliers)
http://webware.princeton.edu/theater/VENDORS.HTM

Stagecraft Supplies/Information
www.theprices.net/lists/stagecraft/archive.html

Unions

Actors Equity Association (AEA)
www.actorsequity.org

AFM Local 47
www.promusic47.org

American Federation of Musicians
www.afm.org

American Federation of Television and Radio Artists (AFTRA)
www.aftra.org

American Guild of Musical Artists (AGMA)
www.agmanatl.com

American Guild of Variety Artists (AGVA)
http://home.earthlink.net/~agvala/agva1.html

International Alliance of Theatrical Stage Employees (IATSE)
http://iatse.lm.com/

Local One (formerly Local 922) IATSE
www.iatse-local1.org

Screen Actors Guild (SAG)
www.sag.com/newyork/
www.sag.com

Society of Stage Directors and Choreographers
www.ssdc.org

Teamsters Local 399
http://members.aol.com/tlocal399/399.html

If you should find a website, not listed above, that is particularly useful to stage managers, please advise. See the Reader's Comments Form, page 383.

Suggested Classroom Exercise

Ask each student to visit a few sites on the preceding list, then report to the class on usefulness of each site to stage managers.

Appendix E

Rules for High School Festivals

We must laugh and we must sing. We are blest by everything.
—William Butler Yeats

Four examples are given here of rules that have worked for various festivals in southern California: the Adult Drama Association of Los Angeles (Plan A festival); the Southern California Educational Theatre Association (Plan B festival); the Drama Teachers Association of Southern California (Plan C festival); and the Southern California Educational Association (Plan D festival).

ADULT DRAMA FESTIVAL

WHERE: Bing Theatre
          Los Angeles County Museum of Art
          5905 Wilshire Boulevard
          Los Angeles, California
WHEN: Saturday, March 19, 1977
          10:00 am to 11:00 pm
          NOTE: If more than fifteen (15) groups apply, we shall extend the Festival to Friday, March 18, 1977, 7:00 pm to 10:00 pm
WHO: All community theatre groups are eligible to participate.
WHAT: Community theatre getting together to present their best.
WHY: To promote and promulgate proper community theatre.

RULES AND REGULATIONS

PARTICIPATION
1. Theatre groups must be members of the Adult Drama Association in order to compete in the Festival.
2. Participation is limited to theatre groups in Los Angeles County.
3. Audience: admission is free, but no one will be allowed entry while a production is underway.

PRODUCTION MATERIAL
1. Scripts can be one-act plays, one act from a larger play, or adaptations. Rights and royalties for copyrighted materials are the responsibilities of the individual theatre groups.
2. Maximum time limit for a production is 30 minutes, curtain-to-curtain. A total of 15 minutes is allowed for set-up and strike; the 15 minutes can be divided between set-up and strike at the discretion of the theatre group. The 30 and 15 minute time limit are separate units.
   PENALTIES for time overruns are as follows:
      A production is "downed" one level (e.g., from first place to second place) for a one minute overrun, two levels for two minutes overrun, etc. and disqualified for anything over five minutes.
      Penalties apply to production and direction categories, but not acting categories.
3. In fairness to all participants, it is recommended that participating groups try to stay relatively close to a 30-minute production time. We can thus stay "on schedule" for the total time of the Festival.
4. Material should be selected on its potential for demonstrating acting and directing capabilities of the participants, for these are the sole criteria upon which the productions will be judged.

   Friday evening, March 18, has been reserved so that groups may make a visual inspection of the Bing Theatre. It is hoped that the technical crew will be at their stations to demonstrate the capabilities of the theatre, e.g., how a sound system might be patched in, a curtain pulled, or a light dimmed. No rehearsals will be allowed at this time. Each participating group will be sent a floorplan of the Bing Theatre stage when their entry is received, so that they may rehearse accordingly. However, Friday, March 18, may be used as part of the competing Festival if more than 15 groups participate. If so, another evening will be designated for inspecting the theatre.
5. Simple risers, chairs, tables, couch, and cubes will be provided. Should a group wish to rely on specific furniture units that hold a play together, the transport and storage of these materials must be their responsibility.
6. The theatre is beautifully equipped to brightly light the stage (or moodily dim it). Special lighting plots cannot be accommodated.

ENTRY PROCESS
1. Send in the NOTIFICATION OF ENTRY as soon as possible to get the time slot of your choice. The nonrefundable entry fee of $10.00 must accompany this Notification. Details such as cast members are not required when you send in this Notification.
2. When your Notification of Entry is received, you will be mailed an entry packet which includes (1) The Bing Theatre floor plan, (2) A form to fill in with program information, i.e., name of play, cast members, director, publisher, and selection of scene, (3) A complete list of flats, risers, furniture that you will need. The form must be returned by February 15, 1977, to get your information in the program.
3. THE DEADLINE FOR RECEIPT OF THE NOTIFICATION OF ENTRY IS FEBRUARY 1, 1977. It is important that your prompt attention be paid to this deadline, because Los Angeles County insists that you adhere to these rules.
4. The Notification of Entry must be accompanied by an application form for membership in the Adult Drama Association if you are not already a member group. The membership fee is $10.00 per year. Enclose the check with application.

MISCELLANEOUS
1. Three to five judges from the field of professional theatre will critique performances; these will be written and presented to participating groups at an A.D.A. meeting.
2. Awards of Best Production, Second Place and Third Place, Honorable Mention, Best Director, Best Actor, Best Actress, Best Supporting Actress, and Best Supporting Actor will be made at the conclusion of the festival.
3. The first fifteen (15) entrants will perform on Saturday, March 19, 1977. Should more than 15 groups enter, latecomers will perform on Friday, March 18, 1977, and awards will be made after the Saturday performance.
4. As many of you know, the best way of getting to know other members of the A.D.A. is by working with them. How about volunteers for house management, backstage coordination, etc.? We need you.

Figure E.1   Rules for a Plan A Festival—Adult Drama Association

Courtesy of Los Angeles County Department of Parks and Recreation.

```
                RULES FOR HIGH SCHOOL THEATRE FESTIVAL 1975


  I. Eligibility:
     1. Any secondary school in Southern California is eligible to enter.
        (See Section VI)
     2. Members of the company must be duly enrolled in the entered high school.
        (Exceptions: A production requiring children's roles incapable of being
        played by high school actors, i.e., the boys of Medea and Jason in Medea,
        may be included.)
     3. Only one play may be submitted by each high school.
     4. Productions must be directed by an accredited faculty member within the
        entered school.
     5. Each production must adhere to the rules and regulations as herein stated or
        be disqualified. Evaluators may report possible violations which the
        Committee will investigate and determine whether disqualification is
        necessary. Entry fees will not be refunded.

 II. Type of Play:
        Any type of full length play of educational value that is generally intended
        for adult audiences, i.e. not child audiences, is acceptable.
        Musicals and original material are not acceptable.
        Music may be included if it is incidental to the production, leaving a
        production that is clearly recognizable as a drama rather than a musical
        comedy or musical play.

III. The Company:
        The company must be limited to thirty students including cast and crew.
        The company screened by the evaluators must be that which is used at
        C.S.U.N.

 IV. Production Requirements:
        To avoid difficulties in executions at C.S.U.N., plays must be produced for
        or adaptable to the proscenium stage. Weight and size of scenery should
        correspond to the limitations specified by the American College Theatre
        Festival. Simplicity in setting and technical effects is recommended. (1,000
        cubic feet)

  V. Evaluations:
        The Festival Committee will provide qualified evaluators to screen the
        production during the play's scheduled run at its campus site.

 VI. Costs:
     1. Entry fee is $35.00 and membership in SCETA.
        Each school provides its own production costs.
     2. The Festival Committee will provide, through entry fees, ticket sales, the
        following to the shows selected for reproduction:
        a. Costs for the play's reproduction, i.e. additional royalty, additional
           rental of costumes and props (not to exceed Festival revenue).
        b. Transportation costs for the companies and their theatrical baggage.

VII. The Festival Committee reserves the right to refine, expand, or adjust the
     rules of the Festival if circumstances demand such action.

VIII. Directors must participate in Festival Activities.

 IX. Deadlines:
     1. The deadline for Festival entries is October 20th.
     2. Productions must be presented by December 13th. No evaluations will be made
        after that date.

  X. Each Director & School is responsible for 10 tickets to each of the three
     performances at C.S.U.N.
```

Figure E.2   Rules for a High School Festival (Plan B). C.S.U.N. stands for California State University, Northridge. SCETA is the Southern California Educational Theatre Association.

Used by permission of the Southern California Educational Theatre Association.

```
                      FALL DRAMA FESTIVAL--1975


        EVENTS                  TIME LIMITS         POSSIBLE ENTRIES

   I    Individual Pantomime    5 min.                     1
  II    Group Pantomime         5 min.              2 to 8
 III    Individual Humorous     5 min.                     1
  IV    Individual Serious      5 min.                     1
   V    Group Special Event     9 min.              2 to 8
  VI    Group Humorous          9 min.              2 to 8
 VII    Group Serious           9 min.              2 to 8
```

SCHEDULE

```
     8:00—8:30          Registration
     8:30—8:45          Assembly
     9:00—10:20         Round I
    10:25—11:45         Round II
    11:45—12:15         Luncheon
    12:15               Assembly: Semi-finalists announced
    12:30—1:40          Semi-final Round
     1:45               Assembly: Finals announced
     2:00—3:15          Final Round
     3:15—4:15          Awards Assembly
```

ENTRY FEE

Entry fees are $2.50 per participant up to $50.00 maximum fee per school. This entry fee includes programs for each participant up to 20. To order more programs, $.25 per additional program must be sent. (A limited number of programs may be sold at the festival for $.25 each.) DTASC MEMBERSHIP DUES ($6.00) must also be sent with entries unless paid earlier this school year.

ENTRY DEADLINE

SENIOR HIGH: Entries and fees must be postmarked or delivered not later than MIDNIGHT, WEDNESDAY—OCTOBER 15.

JUNIOR HIGH: Entries and fees must be postmarked or delivered not later than MIDNIGHT, WEDNESDAY—OCTOBER 8.

LATE ENTRIES WILL NOT BE ACCEPTED. ANY HARASSMENT REGARDING THE ENTRY DEADLINE SHALL BE REFERRED TO RULES COMMITTEE WHICH CAN DISQUALIFY ENTRIES FOR THE NEXT FESTIVAL.

TIME LIMITS

TIME LIMITS WILL BE STRICTLY OBSERVED. PARTICIPANTS WILL BE STOPPED WHEN TIME HAS EXPIRED, BUT WILL NOT BE DISQUALIFIED.

GENERAL STANDARDS FOR JUDGING OF ACTING EVENTS

1. Manner of approach to the audience.
2. Use of appropriate speech and acting techniques.
3. Characterization.
4. Theatrical effectiveness and general excellence of performance.

SPECIFIC RULES

1. A memorized introduction is recommended though not required. If it is given it must be included in the time limit.

2. Where an introduction is used, the student making the introduction is considered a participant. In individual events, the participant must make his own introduction if he chooses to have one.

3. Selection is to be memorized.

4. No participant may perform in more than one event. However, a participant may portray more than one character and may enact a character of the opposite sex.

5. Sound effects are permissible but only through the use of a participant's hand, feet, or mouth. No manufactured devices may be employed.

(continued)

Figure E.3   Rules for a High School Festival (Plan C)

Used by permission of the Drama Teachers Association of Southern California.

6. No director, parent, or student may attempt to influence the decision of any judge or discuss in the hearing of a judge the merits of any participant.

7. No director or parent may act as a judge in a section in which he has a participant.

8. The opinion of the judges as to the excellence of the performance and the judges' decision as to the ranking of the contestants should not be challenged. Any protest regarding rules violations should be made to the Rules Committee.

9. Only published or professionally produced material is to be performed in any event, except pantomime.

10. No Shakespearean material may be used. Verse drama is acceptable.

11. The terms "serious" and "humorous" refer to the mood of the selection performed, not necessarily to the form of the work from which the cut is taken. (That is--a humorous scene or monologue might be cut from a tragedy, for example.)

12. No properties may be used except available classroom furniture, such as a table and chairs. They may be used in any manner, except in pantomime.

13. Participants shall wear acceptable school clothing, including shoes, but no costumes may be worn. It is permissible to color coordinate and to dress in the mood of the scene. Special footwear (i.e., tennis shoes, ballet slippers, etc.) is acceptable for all events.

14. Clothing may be used (example: hands in pockets) but not removed or put on.

15. Each participating director must serve either as a judge or on a committee. The Rules Committee is given the authority in extreme circumstances to disqualify all entries of an entire school for unsportsmanlike conduct and/or discourteous behavior by the director, students, or parents.

16. Students are not to be notified of placement in any rounds. Semi-finalists and finalists will be announced at the scheduled assemblies.

17. A school with only boys or only girls enrolled in its student body may join with one other school which has only the opposite sex enrolled to enter as a "team" in competition. Rules and fees will apply to such a team as to a single school.

18. Specific events, such as pantomime and the Special Event, have specific rules which are given herein following the standard rules.

19. All entries must be directed and/or supervised by members of DTASC.

20. In a four-year school, 9th grade is considered part of the junior division, while 10th, 11th, and 12th grades are part of the senior division.

RULES FOR PANTOMIME

1. Pantomime is defined as a dramatic (either humorous or serious) performance by actors using only dumb show.

2. No music is to be used in pantomime.

3. The pantomime is to be prepared and to have an introduction consisting of a title which is not more than ten words.

4. The pantomime is not to exceed five minutes.

5. Words may be mouthed in pantomime, as long as there is no vocal utterance.

6. Chairs are allowed in pantomime. No other furniture or property is to be used. No chairs may be moved during the pantomime.

7. Each performer may pantomime any number of characters and may pantomime characters of the opposite sex.

SPECIAL EVENT RULES

1. To honor the Bicentennial, DTASC chose Carl Sandburg's poem, The People, Yes. A composite or straight cutting may be taken from any part or parts of the poem.

2. Participants may number 2 to 8 and the time limit imposed is nine minutes.

3. Humming or chanting of any music may be used as background, but no lyrics may be used from any other sources.

Figure E.3   *(Continued)*

DRAMA TEACHERS ASSOCIATION OF SOUTHERN CALIFORNIA

IMPROVISATION

RULES -- STANDARDS -- PROCEDURES -- EXAMPLES

1. Four participants must be entered, no more, no less. May be four boys, or four girls, or three and one or two and two. The sex does not matter, nor does the combination.
2. Spectators will be allowed to watch all rounds of improvisations, including semifinal and final. They must, however, remain in the room until the round is over.
3. In rounds one and two, and in the semifinal round, the participants will be in the room and may watch because in the first three rounds the situations will be different. In other words, the same situations will not be given to each group in a room in Rounds one, two, and semifinal.
4. Situations will be in a sealed envelope for each room. Participants will select their own envelope.
5. Improvisation introductions will consist of a title of not more than ten words.
6. In the final round, the participants will not be allowed to watch. They will be placed in another room, well out of hearing distance, and will perform one group at a time. After performing, the group may watch the others perform. The order of the final performance will be determined by drawing numbers.
7. Up to two minutes of preparation time will be allowed within the five-minute time limit. Less time in preparation may be taken and the entire five minutes does not have to be used up in Rounds one, two, and semifinal.
8. A visual warning will be given to all performers at the end of three minutes and at the end of four minutes.
9. At five minutes, if the improvisation is not completed, the group will be told to stop.
10. In the final round, the improvisation must be (including the preparation time) over three minutes.
11. In the final round the situation, as in the first three rounds, will be in a sealed envelope. However, in the final round there will be two sealed envelopes for each group. The four finalists in each group must choose a member who will not be involved in the situation until the final two minutes. This member will have the second sealed envelope, which may be opened once the other three begin. The fourth member who has the second envelope will act as the <u>deus ex machine</u>, the surprise element. He or she will enter the situation during the final two minutes (at the time the three-minute mark is reached).

Figure E.3   *(Continued)*

CHILDREN'S THEATRE FESTIVAL

PHILOSOPHY, RULES AND EXPLANATIONS

(ABBREVIATED FORM)

I. Statement of Philosophy

Recognizing a continuing need to raise the standard of theatre for the child audience, the Southern California Educational Theatre Association has established the following goals for their annual Children's Theatre Festival:

A. To encourage educational, commercial, community and recreational theatre for the child audience, to enrich the lives of children, and to contribute to the development of discerning audience members of the future.

B. To bring selected professionals in contact with one another and their productions in order to promote sharing of talents, techniques, and goals.

C. To provide a showcase for productions and focus the attention of the media and the public on the productions created by professionals from the educational, commercial, community, and recreational theatres.

D. To strive to obtain sufficient profits and subsidies in order to underwrite the expenses of all festival participants, thus eliminating artist exploitation.

E. To provide a weekend of family entertainment at a reasonable cost to the public.

Since the festival strives to create an atmosphere of mutual support, no awards or ratings will be given to the participants. A board of reviewers will evaluate each performance in order to encourage each member of each production company to improve his theatrical skills. Critics from the commercial media will be invited to review each production.

II. Eligibility

A. Any Children's Theatre Producer in Southern California who is invited by the Festival Committee and whose producer or director is a member of SCETA.

B. Members of the acting company must be of college age or older. Exception: an occasional child's role, i.e., Tiny Tim in "A Christmas Carol."

Figure E.4   Children's Festival Rules (Plan D)

Used by permission of the Drama Teachers Association of Southern California.

2

III. Size of Company

The company must be limited to a maximum of 20 persons.

IV. Type of Play

Any type of full length production, scripted or improvisational, including scripted puppet theatre.

V. Production Facilities

The Executive Producer of the 1976 Festival will supply technical details to invited companies.

VI. The Executive Festival Producer will forward application forms to producers selected by the Festival Advisory Committee. All companies will be reviewed. The Festival Advisory Committee reserves the right to refuse participation to companies whose shows do not meet the expected criteria.

January 18.......Deadline for receiving application forms, plot synopsis, background information on Company, 8 x 10 action shots of group (rehearsal pictures or shots from previous productions) and $35.00 deposit. $25.00 is refunded if Festival commitments and deadlines are met.

March 15........Deadline for sample program (printed by individual producer) 8 x 10 glossy black and white photographs from production, for newspaper publication and media. 35mm color slide for TV. Glossy pictures are not acceptable for television.

VII. Expenses

A. The Festival Committee will provide theatre facilities for the individual and collective companies participating in the 1976 Festival.

B. The host campus will provide minimum technical assistance without cost to the producer.

C. Participating producers will pay their own production costs and author's royalties and provide transportation for their company and their theatrical baggage, including scenery.

D. When Festival revenues permit, companies may be assisted in defraying expenses.

Figure E.4   *(Continued)*

3

    E. Each participating producer will provide a sufficient number of programs for each performance -- delivered to the house staff upon arrival.

    F. Companies seeking financial assistance must submit detailed estimates 30 days in advance of the festival dates.

    G. The $35.00 entry fee will be considered a deposit guaranteeing appearance at the festival. If the company exhibits its production and meets scheduled deadlines for sample programs, pictures, etc., $25.00 will be refunded. If the $5.00 process fee was included with indication of interest form, the entry fee is $30.00.

VIII. Liability

The Festival liability waiver must be signed by the chief administrative officer of the production organization or his designee. If the policy of the individual company requires release or field trip permission forms for its members, all arrangements relating to those forms are the sole responsibility of the producer.

  IX. Board of Reviewers

    A. The appointed Director of the Reviewing Board will select a panel of reviewers from the educational and professional theatre community to review each show presented. Although no prizes or awards will be given, a written critique will be presented to each producer by a minimum of three reviewers. Specific procedures and evaluation forms will be provided by the Director of the Board of Reviewers.

    B. Each producer is expected to serve as a reviewer for at least one production other than his own.

   X. Registration

    A. The producer must submit the final registration form along with the thirty-five dollar ($35.00) check by January 18, 1976.

    B. Make checks payable to: Children's Theatre Festival.

        Mail to: Children's Theatre, Executive Producer
                 Dr. Pam Woody
                 Department of Speech, Communication, and Drama
                 California State University, Los Angeles
                 5151 State University Drive
                 Los Angeles, California 90032

Figure E.4 *(Continued)*

CRITERIA FOR PLAYS FOR CHILDREN
PARTICIPATING IN THE SOUTHERN CALIFORNIA
CHILDREN'S THEATRE FESTIVAL

All children's theatre productions entered in the Southern California Children's Theatre Festival will be previewed by members of the Festival Advisory Committee or an approved evaluator. Shows may not be changed between preview performance and the Festival, except for changes approved by the Festival Advisory Committee. The Festival reserves the right to refuse participation to companies whose shows do not fulfill the criteria stated below.

A.   Shows should be designed to appeal to children rather than adults and should be intended for a stated age range.

B.   Shows should demonstrate an integrity of style, whether it be audience participation, formal theatre, improvisational theatre, or story theatre.

C.   If a show is audience participation oriented there must be built-in audience controls and the actors must work with and listen to the children.

D.   The direction should demonstrate an understanding of pace, reasonably creative movement, the necessity for variety, appropriate casting, and respect for children.

E.   The acting should be consistent and the actors should appear to enjoy performing for and working with children. The illusion of the first time is vital, particularly with shows that tour and do many performances.

F.   The literature should not show characters rewarded for evil or include unnecessary violence. The play should treat all characters fairly and not poke fun at any race, religion, nationality, sex, color, or way of speaking with the exception of regional accents.

G.   The costumes, sets, and makeup should be executed with some style and unity and should be appropriate for the production. They must be in good condition.

H.   The length of the show should be appropriate to the style of the show.

Audience participation plays for K-3   30 - 50 minutes
Formal play for 2-6 grade   60 - 75 minutes

I.   No intermissions are allowed.

Figure E.4   *(Continued)*

NOTE: The Festival Advisory Committee reserves the right to refine, expand, or adjust the rules of the festival, if circumstances demand such action.

The participating producers agree that all interpretations of regulations and decisions of the Festival Committee are final, including the selection of participating companies, and that no recourse will be initiated against the Executive Festival Producer, the Festival Advisory or Working Committees or SCETA.

I have read these rules and criteria and agree to abide by them and return one copy with my entrance fee to the Executive Producer, by the stated deadline:

Signed _____

Date   _____

Figure E.4   *(Continued)*

Suggested Classroom Exercise

Distribute rules for your school's high school drama festival. Ask students to review rules and suggest revision of any that are not clear.

Glossary

The terms compiled in this glossary are the special vocabulary of the stage manager.

Abstract Set   Nonrepresentational set that suggests rather than simulates appropriate surroundings.

Accent   Emphasis placed on an action or phase of a play by lighting or staging technique.

Achromatic Lens   A lens that transmits light without separating it into its spectral colors. Lenses should be achromatic.

Acoustics   The qualities of sound transmission within a theater.

Act Curtain   *See* Curtain.

Acting Area   That part of the stage used by actors during the performance; may be extended to aisles or elsewhere if the action of the play takes place there.

Adaptor   Short length of cable with a different type of plug on each end (i.e., twistlock to pin, or pin to stage plug); also, a plug inserted into a socket so that it will accept a different type of lamp base.

Ad-lib   (1) Anything said by actors on stage other than the lines of the script; (2) to extemporize in a performance or interpolate impromptu remarks possibly because of a lapse of memory, as a reaction to an unplanned incident, or to cover a late entrance.

AEA   Actors Equity Association. Union for stage actors and stage managers.

AFTRA   American Federation of Television and Radio Artists. Radio and TV entertainers' union.

AGVA   American Guild of Variety Artists. Nightclub entertainers' union.

Amateur   Anyone whose work in or for the theater is without financial reward.

Amber   A popular yellowish-orange color.

Ampere   Unit of electric current; one ampere is the amount of current sent by one volt through a resistance of one ohm.

Amphitheater   An oval or circular building with rising tiers of seats about an open space.

Analog   Signal sent from control to dimmer by way of intensity of electrical current (compare to digital).

Analog Input Channels   Allows input from manual console to computer/memory console that has no manual slider control of channels.

Analog Input Switches   User-programmable switches that can cause a variety of actions to occur at the touch of a switch (also called "macros").

Anchor   To fasten to the floor.

Angel   One who invests money in a production.

Antagonist   Adversary of the hero or protagonist.

Anticipate   React to a cue that has not yet occurred (e.g., actor falls before shot is fired; actor turns to door before knock, etc.).

Anti-pros   Lighting instruments hung in front of the proscenium; front-of-house positions.

Antique   To make props or set pieces appear old.

Appliqué   Ornamentation cut from one material and applied to another.

Apprentice   Individual who works in the theater for the learning experience, usually not paid.

Apron   The part of the stage in front of the proscenium.

Arbor   Metal frame supporting counterweights in system for flying scenery.

Arc Spotlight   Spotlight in which the source of light is an arc of electric current jumping a small gap between two carbon sticks; the carbon sticks are either hand-adjusted or driven electrically to remain a constant distance apart; an iris shutter is used to control the size of the beam or to shut it off completely.

Arena Theater   A theater having the acting area in the center of the auditorium with the audience seated on all sides.

Arm   A batten supporting a curtain; usually a short batten used for wings.

Asbestos Curtain   Fireproof curtain located immediately in front of the front curtain. In some areas it is required by law that this curtain be raised and lowered in sight of the audience during a performance. Also called fire curtain and fireproof curtain.

Aside   Dramatic device in which the character speaks directly to the audience while other characters on stage supposedly do not hear him or her.

At Liberty   Euphemism for unemployed.

ATPAM   Association of Theatrical Press Agents and Managers. Union for theater publicists and house managers.

Audition   Tryout performance before producers, directors, casting directors, or others for the purpose of obtaining a part in a production; may be acting, singing, or dancing.

Auditorium Lights   *See* House Lights.

Auto Sketch   One of several CADD programs (Trademark by Autodesk).

Baby Spot   Small spotlight, usually 100, 250, or 400 watts; lens is ordinarily 5", 4½", or smaller in diameter.

Backdrop   A large area of painted canvas fastened to a batten and used for a background that hangs straight (e.g., sky drop, woodland drop, lake drop, etc.); contrast to Cyclorama, which is not painted but lighted.

Backing Light   Illumination behind a set used to give a lighting effect on a backdrop.

Backing Unit   Any piece or pieces of scenery placed behind an opening (door, window, etc.) to limit the view from the audience of the offstage areas.

Backlight   To focus lighting instruments on the backs (shoulders) of actors to produce emphasis or separation from background.

Backstage   (1) The entire area behind the curtain line: stage, dressing rooms, green room, etc. (2) any part of the stage outside of the acting area during a performance.

Baffle   Metal or wood screen used to prevent light spill.

Balcony Front Spotlights   Spotlights that are mounted on the front of the balcony or related locations to light the acting area.

Barn door   A metal shutter with doors to control light spill.

Batten   (1) A length of rigid material, usually wood, fastened to the top and bottom of a drop or leg; (2) the 1" × 3" lumber used to construct scenery; (3) the wood or pipe on a set of lines to which scenery or lights are fastened.

Beam, Ceiling   Beam in ceiling of an auditorium in which spotlights are concealed.

Beam Front Spots   Spotlights mounted high in the beams (or prepared slots) of the auditorium ceiling for the purpose of lighting the acting area from above.

Belaying Pin   A hardwood pin or pipe used in pin rails to tie ropes from gridiron.

BEP   Break-even point.

Bit Part   Small role in a production, rarely with more than two or three lines. *See* Walk-On.

Black Light   Light that causes certain colors and materials to glow in the dark.

Blackout   Closing of a scene, act, or the play itself, usually on a particularly effective line, by a sudden extinguishing of the lights. Used frequently in musical revues.

Blacks   Black draperies or curtains.

Bleed   When a prior color is seen through a subsequent coat, it is said to bleed.

Block   A pulley or pulleys in a frame, part of counterweight flying system.

Blocking   Movement of actors in the acting area.

Blocking Notation   Written description of actors' movement.

Boards   The stage. "To walk the boards" means to appear on stage.

Bobbinet   Transparent curtain of silken texture. *See* Scrim.

Book   Play manuscript. In musical productions, the libretto without the music.

Boomerang   Color wheel. A box attached to a lighting instrument to hold color frames. Makes color changes convenient. *See* Color Box.

Border   *Scenery:* An abbreviated drop at the top of the set, which masks the flies from the audience. May represent sky, foliage, etc. *Lighting:* Row of overhead lights on stage. First row behind the proscenium arch is called the concert border, X-Ray border, or first border. Others are numbered from down- to up-stage: second border, third border, etc.

Border Lights   Strips of lights mounted in a metal trough divided into compartments with individual color frame holders. Instruments are normally wired into three or four different circuits and are used for general lighting in the stage area.

Bottle   Slang for lamp that is used in a stage lighting instrument.

Box Set   Traditional set of three walls.

Brace Cleat   A small metal plate attached to the frame of a flat. A stage brace is hooked into it to brace a flat.

Brace, Stage   An adjustable device made of two lengths of 1" × 1" wood held between clamps, used to support scenery from behind. A forked iron hook fastened to one end of the brace is twist-hooked into a brace cleat attached to the unit requiring support, and an iron foot at the other end of the brace is secured to the floor by means of a stage screw.

Break Character   To say or do anything, as an actor, during a rehearsal or performance, that is not consistent with what the character portrayed would say or do.

"Break a Leg"   Traditional wish of good luck exchanged between theatrical people prior to opening night curtain instead of "good luck."

Breakaway   Scenery or props that disappear, break, or change form in full view of the audience.

Bridge   A long, narrow platform hung from the grid immediately adjacent to a light pipe or attached to it, for the purpose of allowing a technician access to lighting instruments.

Bridge Lights   Those lights that are mounted on the bridge.

Bridge, Paint   A long narrow platform hung from the grid at the back wall, upstage from which a scenic artist may paint scenery or drops attached to a frame on the wall.

Bring Up   To increase the intensity of the lights. *See* Dim In.

Build   Accumulation and gradual acceleration of tempo, emotional intensity, and action by dramatist, actors, or director at any point in a play, but particularly in the approach to the climax.

Bump It   To hit the floor forcefully with flown scenery in order to trim scenery.

Bump Up   To bring lights up as fast as possible.

(To) Burn   To transfer sound data onto a hard drive.

Burn In   The first red glow emitted by the filament of a lighting instrument before full intensity light is emitted.

Bury the Show   To strike sets, costumes, and props after the final performance.

Cable   Flexible wire for conducting current from dimmers to lighting units or effects equipment.

CADD   Computer-aided design and drafting, now used by theater designers.

Cage   Wire enclosure used to separate lighting equipment or sound equipment from the stage.

Call   (1) Notice to actors backstage announcing the amount of time before the curtain, normally half-hour call, fifteen-minute call, and five-minute call; (2) notice of rehearsal or performance placed on the callboard and reiterated by the stage manager.

Call Boy Individual who gives calls to the actors. It is advised that the stage manager do this herself or himself.

Callboard Bulletin board for actors.

Candlepower Illuminating capacity of an instrument.

Carpenter Stagehand responsible for handling scenery, building and repairing the set.

Cast (1) Players in a play; (2) to select actors to play roles.

Caster A small wheel used to make scenery movable.

CD Compact disk, now used for sound effects.

Ceiling A large horizontal canvas-covered frame hung on two or more sets of lines, used to close in the top of an interior set. *Book ceiling:* built in two pieces that fold together at the middle (book-like) parallel to the footlights, to permit flying. *Roll ceiling:* canvas is attached to front and back battens and rolled around them for storing and transportation.

Ceiling Plate A plate for bolting together and hanging a ceiling piece.

Center Stage The area in the center of the acting area.

Central Staging Placing the audience area on all four sides of the acting area.

Chalk Line A long length of string rubbed with chalk that is snapped to transfer a straight chalk line to floor or flat.

Characterization Delineation by dramatist of a role in a play or portrayal by an actor of a role on stage.

Cheesecloth An open-weave cotton cloth sometimes used as scrim.

Chew the Scenery To rant and rave on stage.

Cinemoid A colored plastic sheet used for producing color in light.

Clamp Most lighting instruments come with a C-type clamp to fasten them to a pipe. There is a similar cable clamp used to hold heavy quantities of cable to a light batten, but this is most frequently done with tape.

Claque Paid members of an audience hired to applaud.

Clavilux An instrument invented by Thomas Wilfred for throwing upon a screen varying patterns of light and color that permit combinations analogous to the successive phrases and themes of music.

Clear, Please (1) Order to strike props or get out of the way; (2) warning that the curtain is going up.

Cleat Metal hardware used for securing flat.

Clew A metal plate that holds several lines so that they can be handled by a single line.

Climax That part of the central action, usually near the close, in which tensions are greatest and in which the theme is finally and fully revealed.

Clincheplate A metal plate used to back clout nails.

Clip Cues To speak one's lines before the preceding actor has had time to finish the cue phrase. This usually destroys the meaning or effectiveness of the final words.

Clipboard A board with a metal clamp on the top for holding plots, cue sheets, etc.

Clout Nails A type of nail used in scenery construction, which bends to hold materials together when it strikes the clinchplate.

Color Box A metal container of six color frames that can be attached to the front of a spotlight for color changes. Some of these are controlled remotely from a switchboard or from the spotlight. *See* Boomerang.

Color Frame A metal, wood, or cardboard holder for the color medium in the front of a lighting instrument. More frequently called a gel frame.

Color Medium A transparent material, such as glass, gelatine, or cinemoid, that is placed in front of lighting instrument to produce color.

Color Wheel   A device to make color changes. A large, cumbersome wheel mounted on the front of a spotlight, that has four to six openings for different colored gelatines. It may be manually operated by the spotlight operator or it may be motor driven.

Come Down   To move toward the downstage area, or toward the audience. *See* Downstage.

Comedy   (1) Style of drama characterized by the humorous and amiable; (2) a play in which the protagonist fights a winning battle.

Composite   (1) Several pictures showing an actor in various costumes and poses; (2) part of an actor's résumé.

Concert Border   Lights mounted on the first pipe upstage of the proscenium.

Connector   A device for connecting two cables together or a cable to a switchboard or unit. Each connector consists of two parts, a female or receiving part and a male that has studs or prongs that fit into the female. Multiple connectors are female connectors to which more than one male connector can be fastened. A number of units can be attached to one cable easily by use of branchoffs or multiple connectors.

Contour Curtain   A curtain that is gathered up in scallops.

Conversation Piece   A comedy in which there is much talk and little action.

Corner Iron   Right-angle iron strap or L-shaped plate used for support or reinforcement.

Corner Plate   A triangle of 3/16" or 1/4" plywood used to reinforce corners of flats in scenery construction.

Counterweight System   Mechanical use of weights to help balance heavy scenery, curtains, etc.

Cover   Understudy (British and opera)

Crash Box   A box filled with broken glass or small metal parts used for sound effects.

Crisis   Turning point in a play.

Crosspiece   Horizontal batten in a flat.

CRT   Cathode ray tube, the TV-like screen that is appearing in more and more control booths as the window into the computer control board.

Cue   A signal in dialogue, action, or music for an actor's action or speech or a technician's duty backstage.

Cue Sheet   A list of the exact cues for the execution of specific duties by the crew.

Curtain   A hanging drapery that conceals the stage or scene from the audience. It may rise, part, fold, drape, or sink. Also called front curtain, main curtain, act curtain, house curtain, flag, and rag.

Curtain Line   (1) An imaginary line across the stage that marks the position of the front curtain when it is closed; (2) the last line of a scene or act that is the cue for the curtain to close.

Cut   (1) To remove a line or lines from a script; (2) order to stop rehearsal.

Cut Drop   A drop that has pieces cut out or is edged to represent leaves, foliage, or other decoration.

Cut Line   A trip line that is cut to release the asbestos curtain in case of fire.

Cutout   *See* Ground Row.

Cutting List   A list of the pieces of wood with their dimensions needed for scenery and set pieces.

Cyclorama (Cyc)   A huge, seamless backing sheet of material, usually white, that can be lit to indicate sky. Sometimes it is hung in a semicircle with the sides coming well downstage to enclose the acting area.

Cyclorama Lights   High-powered individual reflector-type border lights mounted on a castered frame (or hung from a light batten) to light the cyclorama.

Dark Night(s)   Period when theater is not open to the public.

Dead Spot   Area in acting area that is insufficiently lit.

Diffused Light   Nearly shadowless light.

Digital   Signal sent from control to dimmer via ones and zeros (compare to analog).

Dim   To decrease the intensity of the light on the stage by means of rheostats or dimmers. Also called takedown.

Dim In   To increase the intensity of the light. Also called dim up or bring up.

Dimmer   An electrical device used in a switchboard to regulate current. Types: resistance, slide, plate, transformer, vacuum, remote control, silicon rectifier.

Dip in Intensity   Unplanned lowering in intensity of stage lighting.

Direct Beam   Lenseless projection equipment used to cast shadow or project translucency on a screen, cyclorama, or flat.

Discovered at Rise   On stage when the curtain goes up.

Distemper   Paint made by mixing dry pigment with size. Scene paint.

DMX512   Standard protocol for communication between consoles and dimmers.

Dolly   A low truck with casters used for moving scenery, set pieces, or theatrical equipment.

Dome   A permanent plaster cyclorama.

Dope   Glue used for attaching canvas flats.

Douser   Cutoff device in arc light or follow spot.

Downstage   Toward the footlights (or if no footlights, toward the pit, apron, or audience).

Draw Curtain   A type of curtain suspended from an overhead track that opens from center to each side. Also called a traveler curtain.

Dress Parade   On stage, under the lights (preferably before appropriate flats) check of costumes to be worn by each character.

Dress Rehearsal   Final rehearsal before opening.

Dressing a Set   Adding minor decorations to the set, usually the ornamental touches as opposed to functional props that must be on the set for use of actors.

Drop   *See* Backdrop.

Drop Curtain   A curtain that rolls up from the bottom.

Duck   Strong cotton material.

Dutchman   A strip of material, usually muslin, about three inches wide, which is used to cover cracks where flats meet. Masking tape is sometimes called instant Dutchman.

Duvetyn   Velvety cotton fabric.

Effect   The impression given to an audience of a particular thing by a technical achievement: a rainbow produced by lights, wind produced by a windmachine, etc.

Electrician   The operator of the control board and lighting instruments. Not necessarily an electrician in the nontheater meaning of the word. Also called boardman, lighting technician, or tech.

Elevations   (1) Working drawings of the flats of a setting; (2) risers, platforms, etc., that give variety to the stage level.

Elevator Stage   A section or sections of the stage floor that can be lowered and raised by hydraulic process.

Entr'acte   (1) Intermission; (2) short scenes performed before the curtain.

Entrance   Actor's appearance on stage.

Epilogue   A scene that follows the end of the play.

Equity   *See* AEA.

Expressionism   From a school of thought that developed in Germany in the late nineteenth century. Really an extension of Impressionism and opposed to Realism and Naturalism. Expressionists are concerned with producing an inner emotional, sensuous, or intellectual reaction. It is this inner emotion that they try to express, and they maintain that it does not necessarily bear a relation to the outer aspect of life.

Exteriors   Settings painted to represent outdoor scenes.

Facing   Decorative trim, painted or applied around doors, windows, flats, etc.

Fade In   Gradual dim up of light or sound.

Fade Out   Gradual dim out of light or sound.

Fall   Rope used with block and tackle.

False Blackout   A blackout that occurs within a scene but does not call for a scenery or prop change. Usually denotes passage of time. *See* Blackout.

False Proscenium   An inner frame especially built for a production to close down a large proscenium, to mask lighting equipment or to give special design to the production. *See* Proscenium.

Fantasy   Play unrestricted by literal and realistic conventions of the theater and usually distinguished by imaginative uses of the supernatural and the mythological.

Farce   Play designed only for entertainment and laughter; there is no serious or sincere attempt to depict character nor is there genuine concern with probabilities or realities.

Farce-Comedy   A form halfway between farce and comedy that contains elements of both.

Feedback   Undesirable noise in sound system; sometimes caused by mike being too close to speaker.

Filament Image   Projection of filament from spot, to be corrected by adjustment of spot or diffusion.

Fill Light   Addition of light to blend areas or reduce shadows.

Fire Curtain   *See* Asbestos Curtain.

Fireplace Unit   A fireplace frame made to fit a flat opening.

Fireproof Curtain   *See* Asbestos Curtain.

First Border   *See* Border.

Flag   *See* Curtain.

Flaking   Paint coming off of flat that needs to be refinished.

Flameproofing   Solution sprayed or brushed on flats or fabrics to retard flames.

Flash Pot   A box device in which a smoke or flash effect is created, also called flash box.

Flat   A wooden frame covered with canvas used as a scenic unit. It may be from 10 to 20 feet in height and vary in widths. The widest flat is usually 5'9" so that it will go through the 6' openings in freight cars. This one is called a "six" or full flat. Other flats are named by their conventional widths.

Flat Paint   Paint that absorbs light, opposed to glossy, which you would not want to use generally for scene paint.

Flies   The space above the stage occupied by sets of lines and hanging scenery.

Flipper   A small piece of scenery hinged to a larger flat.

Float   To lower a covered flat by placing the foot against the bottom rail and allowing it to float down so it is lying flat on the floor. The flat will fall slowly because of air resistance.

Floodlights   Light units that give a general diffused light. Also called olivette.

Floor Cloth   Canvas or duck covering for the stage floor. Also called ground cloth.

Floor Plan   A scale drawing of a stage setting showing the position on the floor of the walls, windows, openings, etc.

Floor Plate   Metal plate with ring used for tying lines to the floor.

Floor Pocket   An opening in the stage floor that contains a receptacle for large stage electrical plugs and is metal covered.

Flown   Term applied to condition of scenery that has been raised into the flies.

Fly   To lift scenery above the level of the stage floor, out of view of the audience by means of lines from the gridiron.

Fly Curtain   A curtain that is raised and lowered.

Fly Gallery   A narrow bridge or gallery running along the side of the stage, well above the floor, from which are operated ropes secured to the pin rail.

Fly Man   Name applied to any stagehand who is to fly scenery.

Fly Rope   *See* Lines, Fly Rope.

Flyboy(s)   Rigger(s).

Follow Spot   A spotlight on a movable joint, operated so as to follow a player on the stage with a beam of light.

Foot   To apply the foot to the bottom rail of a flat or the base of a ladder so that another stagehand can raise it.

Foot-candle   A unit for measuring the illumination given by an instrument: It is equal to the amount of direct light thrown by one international candle on a square foot of surface, every part of which is one foot away.

Foot Iron   A steel brace bolted to the bottom of a piece of scenery or set piece so that it can be fastened to the stage floor by means of a stage screw.

Footlights   Strip lights, a source of illumination for the acting area, which may be portable, permanent, open-trough type, or disappearing. Being used less and less in modern theaters.

Fortuny System   Indirect lighting, using spotlights focused on colored silk fabrics. The silk redirects the light to the stage. It is shadowless, diffuse, and allows for subtle color changes but is impractical because of expense and space required.

Foul   To cause scenery or lights hung in the flies to become entangled with each other.

Fourfold   Four flats hinged together.

Fourth Wall   Name given to the hypothetical wall of separation between the stage and the audience in a proscenium theater.

Foyer   Entrance hall into a theater.

French Scene   The division of an act in which the number of characters is constant. Entrance or exit of character (s) marks the beginning of the next French scene.

Fresnel   Type of spotlight using a Fresnel lens or step lens. Lens is named for French physicist Fresnel who developed it for lighthouse beacons. The Fresnel produces an even field with soft edges.

Front Curtain   *See* Curtain.

Frost   Translucent gel used to diffuse light.

Full   Maximum intensity of lighting or sound.

Full Stage   The entire area of the stage that can be used as the acting area.

Funnel   A cylinder of cardboard or thin sheet metal fastened perpendicularly to a square of the same material. Also called snoot, and highhat.

Fuse   A strip of metal with a low melting point, usually in an insulated fireproof container, which breaks when the current becomes too strong.

Gaffer   Stage crew head.

Gagging   Slang for unauthorized improvisation or revision of lines by an actor.

Gain   Volume control on an amplifier.

Gallery   Highest balcony in a theater.

Gang   (1) To hook together; (2) to move two dimmers together.

Gel Frame   A metal, wood, or cardboard holder for the color medium that is placed in front of a lighting instrument. Also called color frame.

Gelatin (Gel)   Thin, transparent sheet of material for producing colored light.

Generic CADD   One of several CADD programs (Trademark by Generic Software, Inc.).

Ghost   A streak of light that leaks from some light source and falls where it is not wanted. *See* Spill.

Ghost Load   An offstage lighting instrument used to load a resistance dimmer so that it will dim out an onstage instrument properly.

Gimp Tacks   Small roundheaded tacks used for furniture upholstery.

Gimp Tape   A decorative upholstery tape used as a finish strip on the edges of furniture.

Give Stage   To move on stage so that the center of interest will be thrown to another actor.

Glare   Light reflection too uncomfortable for the audience.

Glass Crash   *See* Crash Box.

Glow Tape   Luminous tape that glows in the dark. Used backstage to help actors and crew who must function without a worklight.

Glue Burn   Stain on flats caused by glue.

Glue Gun   Small, hand-held electrical device for heating and applying glue.

Go   Order to take a cue, execute an effect.

Go On   To enter on the stage.

Go Up   To forget one's lines and to be unable to resume without assistance.

Gobo   (1) Metal plate with pattern used in lighting instrument to project pattern on cyc or lighting effect on flat; (2) a louver, usually of metal, used to prevent spill from lighting instrument.

God mic   Public address microphone.

Good Theater   Any piece of business that clicks with the audience, or that communicates surely and easily with the audience.

Gopher (Gofer)   A production assistant who gets his or her title from the fact that he or she is frequently sent to "go fer" something.

Grand Drape   Curtain extending width of the stage opening, which is hung just back of the proscenium and in front of the front curtain. It can be lowered to cut the height of the stage opening.

Grand Valance   The first drapery border in front of the main act curtain, usually of the same material.

Green Room   Waiting or reception room, behind, near, or under the stage, used by authors, directors, and actors, to meet their public. So called because the first "retiring" room in Covent Garden Theater in London was all in green. Most professional theaters do not have green rooms today, but many little community and university theaters provide such meeting places.

Gridiron (Grid)   The framework of steel or wooden beams above the stage, which supports the rigging used in flying scenery.

Grip   A stagehand who assists the master carpenter in moving settings.

Grommet   Metal eyehole, usually found at the top of drapes and through which ties are run.

Ground Cloth   *See* Floor Cloth.

Ground Plans   Layout of the stage showing location of set, properties, and lights for a production. *See* Floor Plan.

Ground Row   (1) A row of lights on the floor to light lower area of a cyc or drop; (2) a low profile of scenery designed to represent rocks, earth, skyline, etc., that stands self-supported on the ground, usually in front of the cyc, and is used to conceal the base of the cyc, the lighting equipment and cables, as well as to help give the illusion of depth and/or horizon.

Grouping   Placing the cast about the stage.

Guy Line   Rope or wire from high scenery to floor used to steady or strengthen.

Gypsy   A dancer, usually one who moves from show to show, or from one summer stock company to another.

Half Hour   Warning by the stage manager a half hour before the curtain goes up.

Ham   An actor who is bad or pretentious, or both.

Hand Prop   Any property that is handled by the actor during the course of the play, but particularly those props that the actor carries onto the stage as opposed to those that are discovered. *See* Properties.

Handle   A word that an actor adds to the beginning of a line, that was not originally written in the script (e.g., *Oh, gee, gosh, well, but,* etc.).

Hang   To install or refocus lighting instruments, as in "to hang the show."

Hanger Iron   Hardware for hanging scenery. It has a ring attached to one end of a steel plate that is bolted to the scenery.

Hanging the Show   Putting up the sets of a play: flats, doorways, lights, etc. So called because originally the show was set with wings and backdrops that had to be hung from the grid. Also called mounting.

Hard Patch   Lighting technician physically connects cable to dimmer or control.

HBV   Hepatitis B virus.

Head Block   Three or more pulley blocks framed together and placed on the grid-iron above the outer edge of the fly floor. The ropes from three or more loft blocks come together at the head block and pass down to the pin rail. Also called lead block.

Heads Up   Order to watch for moving scenery.

Highhat   *See* Funnel.

HIV   Human immunodeficiency virus.

Hold   (1) To sustain an effect for audience response; (2) to pause in delivering a line so that audience can react.

(To) Hold Book   To prompt, take blocking notation, and make notes on line changes and cues during rehearsals.

Hood   *See* Funnel.

Horseshoe Stage   A stage that is surrounded on three sides by the audience.

House   The auditorium and front of the theater, as contrasted with the stage and backstage areas. Also used to refer to the size of the audience, as in "How's the house?"

House Lights   Electrical fixtures that provide light for the audience. Sometimes called auditorium lights.

Humheads   Audio workers.

Hummers   Audio workers.

Hung Up   Condition of being unable to continue one's lines or business because another actor is ad-libbing or because another actor has already taken the position you were to take.

IATSE   International Alliance of Theatrical and Stage Employees. Union for stagehands.

Impressionism   Theory that productions should be concerned with artistic interpretation rather than with reality. Strives for psychological reaction by use of color and line.

In One, Two, Three   "In one" is the area on stage just upstage of the curtain line five or six feet. "In two" is the first area plus the next five or six feet upstage. "In three" adds the next five or six feet upstage or full stage.

Ingenue   Young girl in a play, usually providing the love interest.

Inner Proscenium   *See* False Proscenium.

Inset   A small scene set inside a large one.

Interiors   Sets representing indoor scenes.

Iris Shutter   A manually operated shutter for varying the size of a light beam emitted from a lighting instrument.

Jack   A triangular device made of wood that is hinged to the back of a ground row or other set piece for the purpose of bracing it from behind.

Jackknife Stage   Two portable stages with narrow ends parallel to foots, and on pivots. When one stage has been used, it is swung offstage into the wings. From the wings on the other side of the stage the second stage is swung into position on the acting area. The jackknife stage permits quick changes of scenery, as do elevators and revolving stages.

Jog   A narrow flat.

Juicer   Electrician.

Juvenile   Player of youthful male roles.

Keep Alive   To store scenery or properties so that they will be readily available.

Key Light   The main source of light.

Keyboard   A switchboard, usually with slide controls.

Keystone   A small piece of 3/16" or 1/4" plywood cut in the wedge shape of a keystone and used to reinforce joints in scenery.

Kill   (1) To take an article off a set; (2) to extinguish lights or stop sound effects or other effects.

Klieglight   Trade name for spotlights.

Lamp   Source of light. *See* Bottle.

Lamp Dip   Lamp coloring lacquer that gives a durable translucent color tint.

Lash   To bind two flats together with a lash line.

Lash Cleat   A small metal hook on the frame of a flat, behind which a lash line is thrown to bind the flat to the edge of another flat.

Lash Line   Length of #8 sash cord fastened to the back of a flat and used to lash flats together.

Lash Line Eye   The metal eye to which the lash line is secured.

LDI   Lighting Dimensions International—an annual trade show at which manufacturers of theatrical equipment, not only lighting, display their wares and hold workshops.

Lead   Principal role in a play, or actor or actress playing the role.

Lead Block   *See* Head Block.

Left Stage   The area on stage at the actor's left as he or she stands center stage facing the audience. Stage left.

Leg Drop   A drop from which the entire center portion has been omitted.

Legit   Popular abbreviation for the legitimate stage, live theater as opposed to movies.

Leko   Once a brand name, now a generic term for any ellipsoidal reflector spotlight. (Compare to Fresnel and P.C.)

Lekolite   Trade name for spotlight.

Lens   Glass cut for the purpose of condensing and concentrating the rays of light from lamp source and reflector.

Levels   (1) A platform, set of steps, or ramp that raises the playing space above the level of the stage (also called risers, elevators, and platforms); (2) an imaginary line drawn across the stage at any distance from the curtain line but parallel to it.

Lid   Top of platform or ceiling.

Light Batten   A pipe or batten to which lighting instruments are clamped and along which lighting cables are run.

Light Plot   Sequence of light changes from beginning to end of the play, with lines or business that immediately precede each change. Each change is described.

Light Towers   Poles mounted at the sides of the stage or audience area to mount lighting instruments. Also called light trees.

Light Tree   Tower of pipe or wood used to hang lighting instruments in the wings.

Lightwright   Database program by Rosco that manages lighting designer's reports (Trademark by Rosco).

Line, Lines   Speech or speeches in a play.

Line (of Business)   Type of role or roles in which an actor specializes.

Line Drawings   Blueprints from which sets and set pieces can be constructed without reference to any other drawings or specifications.

Lines, Fly Rope   The ropes from the grid that raise and lower scenery. One end is attached to the batten and the other is secured on the fly gallery. Three ropes are usually used on each batten. The nearest one to the gallery is called the short line. The one in the middle is the center line. The farthest is the long line.

Linnebach Projector   A large metal box with concentrated light source for projecting pictures from a gelatin or glass slide.

Lintel   Horizontal crosspiece over door, window, or arch.

Live Weight   Weight of moving body as opposed to weight of inert body.

Load, Electrical   (1) Amount of current used in a circuit; (2) electrical equipment to be connected to a line.

Load In   Process of moving all of a company's equipment (scenery, props, costumes, etc.) into a theater. *See* Take In.

Load Out   Process of moving all of a company's equipment out of a theater.

Lobby   That part of the theater between the entrance and the last row of seats, usually separated by a wall and doors.

Lobster-Scope   A spotlight effect machine producing a flicker of light.

Loft Block   A pulley block in the gridiron through which a line can be run.

LORT   League of Resident Theatres.

Louvers   (1) Concentric rings of thin metal strips fitted to the front of a projector to cut off all but the straight beam of light (also called spill rings and baffles); (2) parallel strips of wood or metal used to mask a light source from the audience.

Luminaire   Lighting instrument.

Macro Key   One key on console that can be programmed to sequence two or more keys.

Make Fast   To tie off securely or fasten any line.

Manager   There are various types other than stage manager. *Producer:* sometimes called manager. *House Manager:* responsible for all details in management of the theater building. *Business Manager:* handles money, payrolls, accounts, contracts, etc. *Company Manager:* responsible for the company, usually on the road. *Personal Manager:* acts as a representative for an author or actor.

Manual Override   Ability to modify cue during computerized execution of that cue.

Manuscript (ms)   Written or typed play, or the book of a musical. Usually used in rehearsal.

Mark It   Order to record level of intensity of light or sound cue.

Martingale   A two-fer or branchoff connector. Two lines with female plugs spliced into one line with a male plug used to connect two instruments to one cable. (I have heard this term pronounced "Martin-dale" in supply houses on the West Coast. If any reader knows the origin or correct spelling of this term, please let me know. Thanks.)

As a lighting technician who used to spend a lot of time horseback riding, it seems to me that a two-fer bears a good deal of resemblance to an accessory used frequently in horseback riding (English style) to keep the saddle from sliding back on the horse (leather straps with rings or buckle which attach to the top of the saddle and the girth). It is called a martingale. Perhaps this will shed some "light" on the matter.

Barbara Middlebrook
Lighting Technician
Astoria, NY

Mask   (1) To hide from sight, or to conceal from the audience; (2) any sort of cardboard or sheet metal slide to be placed in the guides of a spotlight to restrict the light to various shapes. Also called a mat.

Masking (Piece)   A piece of scenery used to conceal backstage from the audience.

Mat   *See* Mask.

M.C.   Master of ceremonies, introducer of acts or participants in a variety program.

ME   Master electrician.

Medium *See* Color Medium.

Melodrama An exaggerated, romantic, exciting, and improbable play. Incident and situation are important; characterization is not.

Memory Board Lighting board with built-in computer that remembers cues.

Mezzanine (1) Sometimes the first balcony of a theater having more than one; (2) the first few rows of the balcony when separated from the balcony proper.

Mic Abbreviation for microphone.

MIDI Musical instrument digital interface—a standard for keyboard-computer interface allows any MIDI keyboard to communicate with computers.

Mike Slang for microphone.

Milk It Dry To squeeze the maximum laughs out of a line, bit of business, or situation.

Mopboard Baseboard.

Motivation Reason behind all stage action and speech. The skill with which the director and actors find the motivation for characters and incidents will determine the quality of the play.

Mounting *See* Hanging the Show.

Movement Passing of actors from place to place on stage. *See* Blocking.

MR-16 Low-voltage 75-watt tungsten-halogen lamp.

Mugging Excessive facial contortions during a performance.

Mule Block A block with pulley used to change the horizontal direction of a line.

Mullion Slender vertical bar between windows.

Multiple Pin Connector A female receptacle that accepts three male pin connectors.

Muslin Material frequently used for covering flats.

Naturalism Same in external form as Realism but emphasizes the natural function in life as opposed to Realism, which is more selective.

Newel Post that supports handrails of steps, also called newel post.

Notices Reviews, dramatic criticism.

Offstage Area backstage, outside of the acting area.

Ohm Unit of electrical resistance.

Olio A mixture, medley, miscellaneous collection. Usually variety acts following an old-fashioned melodrama.

Olio Curtain A curtain that rolls up from the bottom. Also called drop curtain.

Olivette *See* Floodlights.

Onstage Inside the acting area.

O.P. Opposite prompt, usually the left side backstage.

Open Cold To give the first public performance for critics without out-of-town tryouts or invitational previews.

Orchestra Lower floor of the auditorium.

Organic Blocking Process of blocking in which the director allows the actors to move at will and then uses their movement as the basis for his blocking.

OSHA Occupational Safety and Health Administration.

Out Front (1) The part of a theater that is beyond the front curtain—lobby, box office, seats, etc.; (2) any area occupied by members of the audience.

Outlet Box Heavy metal fireproof box containing two to four female receptacles, porcelain insulated.

Overture and Beginners, Please The British equivalent of "Places, please."

P.A. System Public address system. Microphone and loudspeakers, or any sound amplification equipment.

Pace To the theater what tempo is to music. The timing of lines and business. Not to be confused with speed.

Paper Tech A crew-only technical rehearsal to iron out the mechanical bugs.

PAR Type of lamp used in both amateur and professional theater lighting.

Parallel A collapsible frame support for a stage platform.

Part (1) Character assigned to an actor in a play; (2) typewritten portion of a play that pertains to an actor's scenes and contains all of his or her lines and cues. *See* Side.

Patch *Verb:* to connect cables between luminaire(s) and dimmer, or between any electrical instrument and control (see Hard Patch and Soft Patch). *Noun:* connection of cables and dimmers or controlling devices.

Patch Panel A plugging panel used to interconnect dimmers and outlets, also called plugging panel.

Pay Out Order to allow rope to pass through hands.

P.C. Plano-Convex spotlight. Compare to Leko and Fresnel.

Peephole Stage Stage with definite division between acting area and audience, such as a proscenium arch. Also called a picture frame stage. Compare to central staging and horseshoe stage.

Periactus A three-sided revolving apparatus painted with scenery.

Period Plays Costume plays of other eras.

Perspective Drawing Rendering of floor plan and elevations to perspective of audience.

Phantom Load Added resistance to a dimmer so that it will dim out a spot too small to dim ordinarily.

Picture Frame Stage *See* Peephole Stage.

Pigtail *See* Martingale.

Pilot Light Dim light used by stage manager to follow prompt script.

Pin Rail A rail with holes in it, into which wooden pins are placed to secure lines. *See* Fly Gallery.

Pipe Batten *See* Batten.

Pipe Clamp An adjustable metal jaw for mounting lighting instrument on pipe battens.

Pit Sunken space in front of stage, usually where orchestra performs.

Pivot Stage *See* Jackknife Stage.

Places, Please Signal given by stage manager to the cast for taking their respective positions preparatory to the rise of the curtain.

Plano-Convex Type of lens or type of spotlight using that type of lens.

Plant (1) Member of the acting company who is placed in the audience for the purpose of fostering the illusion that the audience is taking part in the performance; (2) a prop on stage at curtain rise, particularly one concealed from the audience.

Platform A collapsible and portable unit used to add levels to the stage, or to provide an additional acting area.

Playing Space Stage space, inside or outside the set, visible to the audience and used for acting during the play.

Plot (1) List of what is required of each technical department in order to make a play work (light plot, sound plot, property plot, costume plot, special-effects plot, etc.); (2) planned action or intrigue of a play.

Plug (1) A scenic unit placed in or in front of another piece of scenery to change it. For example, an arch for one act may be changed for the next act by placing in it a window plug, a fountain plug, etc.; (2) a male connector with insulated handle, with two strips of copper along the side to make contact with similar strips in the outlet box.

Plugging Box Portable outlet box.

Position An actor's place on the stage as set by the director.

Practical Something that is usable. For example, a pair of French doors might be constructed so that only one opens. The one that does open is the practical one.

Preset To place props, costumes, or any materials in position prior to curtain or prior to use.

Preset (or Preselect) Switchboard   A switchboard where one or more complete changes can be set up in advance without interfering with the lighting of the scene in progress.

Preview   Performance given prior to formal opening.

Principals   Actors who carry major roles in a production.

Problem Play   Play built around a difficulty of society. Its characters personify the various forces and their conflict is the subject matter of the play.

Producer   The individual (amateur or professional) who accepts the responsibility for obtaining the personnel and the materials to make theater happen.

Profile Board   Plywood, 3/16" or 1/4", used to edge a flat.

Projector   Directional floodlight, using a metal parabolic reflector to project parallel light rays.

Prompt Script   *See* Promptbook.

Prompt Side (P.S.)   Side of the stage from which the stage manager runs the show, usually the right side.

Promptbook   Book of the play including all business, action, plans, and plots needed for the production. Also called prompt script.

Prompter   One who stands in the wings or out of sight of the audience, and assists actors with their lines and cues. Usually utters only the first few words of a line that an actor forgets, or significant words of the line.

Prop Box   Box kept offstage in which props are stored.

Prop Table   Table offstage where props are set prior to the curtain. Actors are conditioned to obtain their hand props from the same place on the table at each performance, and return their props there if they carry them offstage.

Properties (Props)   Articles used for a play—hand props, trim props, and set props.

Proscenium   The wall dividing the auditorium from the stage.

Proscenium Arch   The edge of the opening of the proscenium.

Proscenium Opening   The opening in the proscenium through which the audience views the play.

Protagonist   Hero of a play or the character who carries its principal idea.

Protocol   Language in which signal is sent from control to dimmers.

Put-Together   A rehearsal at which all elements of the production are brought together in their appropriate sequence.

Q2Q   Cue to cue.

Quartz-Iodine   A long-life lamp used in lighting instruments.

Quick Study   Hurried and technical memorization of a part and its business by an actor, usually in an emergency when a part must be learned at a moment's notice. Also refers to an actor to whom memorization comes easily.

Quiet, Please   Order for silence.

Rag   *See* Curtain.

Rail   The top or bottom board in the frame of a flat.

Raked Stage   A stage slanted down toward the audience.

Raking   (1) Placing the side walls of a set at an angle to improve the sight lines; (2) slanting stage area, platform, or audience seating area to improve sight lines.

Ramp   Inclined platform.

Rant   To deliver lines in a shouting, melodramatic, and extravagant manner.

Read-Through   Rehearsal at which the script is read from beginning to end.

Realism   Fidelity to nature or real life. Representation without idealization. Adherence to actual fact.

Reflectors   Shiny metal surfaces used in spotlights and projectors in back of the light source to intensify the light and give it direction: spherical, ellipsoidal, or parabolic.

Rehearsal   Repetition of scene or practice of a production in private, preliminary to public performance, and for the perfection of that performance.

Rep Company   Company playing repertory.

Repertory   Collection of plays, operas, or parts that may be readily performed because of familiarity with them on the part of a cast or actor. A repertory company is one in which, instead of performing one play continuously, there are several productions ready and they are varied each night or week. Usually the same actors have parts in several productions.

Reprise   Repeat of a musical number.

Resistance Dimmer   A type of stage dimmer used to decrease intensity of lighting instruments.

Return Piece   A flat set at right angles to the downstage corner of a set. It is parallel with the footlights or curtain and runs offstage to mask the wings.

Reveal   *See* Thickness.

Revolving Stage   One or more circular stages (mounted on top of the permanent stage) electrically or manually revolved to effect scene changes or special effects.

Right Stage   The area on stage at the actor's right as he or she stands center stage facing the audience. Stage right.

Ring Down   To drop the front curtain on the last scene or act. Based on an old theatrical custom of ringing a bell to denote the closing of the show.

Risers   *See* Levels.

Road Irons   Angle irons placed at corners of flats to protect them when they must be moved frequently as on tour.

Road Show   A theatrical production that tours several cities and towns.

Rococo   Overelaborate style of decoration.

Roll Curtain   A curtain that rolls up from the bottom. Also called olio curtain and drop curtain.

Rondel   *See* Roundels.

Rosin Box   A box, large enough to stand in, containing rosin used by actors or dancers to rosin shoes or slippers.

Round, in-the-   Staging a play with audience on all sides of the stage, even if the shape of the stage is rectangular or square.

Roundels   Circular heat-resisting glass color media.

Royalty   Compensation to authors and composers paid for permission to perform their works.

Run   Length of a stage engagement or the total number of performances.

Runway   Extension of stage into audience area.

Saddle Iron   A narrow strip of iron used to brace the bottom of a door flat. Also called door iron and sill iron.

Safety Factor   Safe percentage by which load on ropes, cables, and dimmers may be exceeded.

SAG   Screen Actors Guild. A union for actors working in filmed entertainment.

Sandbags   Canvas bags filled with sand used to weight lines or the jacks behind scenery.

Satire   A form of comedy in which sharp derision is aimed at an idea or individual.

Scene   (1) Setting of an action; (2) division of an act or play.

Scene Dock   A storage area for flats and other scenic units, usually located in either wing area of the stage.

Scioptican   Device used to create moving effects such as clouds, flames, waves, etc.

Scrim   A finely woven material through which light may or may not be seen, depending on how it is lit. Also called theatrical gauze and bobbinet.

Selvage   The edge on either side of a woven or flat-knitted fabric, so finished as to prevent raveling.

Set   To prepare the stage for the scene that is to be performed.

Set Dressing   Props arranged to decorate the set. Also called trim props.

Set of Lines A unit group of ropes hanging from the gridiron used to fly scenery. There are usually three or four lines in a set.

Set Piece A unit of scenery standing alone.

Set Props Props that stand on the stage floor, or other props not carried on by the actors. Compare to Hand Prop.

Set Up To erect a set and install related equipment.

Shift To change scenery and properties from one setting to another.

Shoe A block of wood enforcing the joint between toggle and stile.

Show Curtain A drop or curtain behind the front curtain that is painted to give atmosphere to the particular play being presented.

Showcase Theater A theater whose main purpose is to obtain paid work for members of the cast.

Shtick Slang: business, usually comedy business.

Shutter An apparatus mounted on the front of a spotlight, or designed into it, which cuts entirely, or in part, the rays of light. There are iris, combination, funnel, and slide shutters. Also called cut-off.

Side Page of an actor's part. Usually half the size of a standard typewritten sheet. When bound together, called sides.

Sight Lines Lines, painted or imagined, that divide area the audience can see from area the audience cannot see.

Sitting on Their Hands Phrase used to describe an unresponsive audience.

Situation Relationship of characters to one another or to a condition. A play may have a series of situations. The basic situation refers to that one problem that is central to the play.

Size Water A thin solution of glue and water used in mixing scene paint.

Sky Drop A drop painted blue to represent the sky.

Slider The individual channel control on a manual board or submaster on a memory board controlling groups of channels.

Smoke Pocket Steel channels on each side of the proscenium arch that guide the ends of the asbestos curtain.

Snatch To hook or unhook flown scenery during a scene change.

Snatch Lines Adjustable ropes or chains used to fasten scenery to a counterweighted batten.

Sneak To bring in a light or sound cue imperceptibly.

Snoot *See* Funnel.

Snow Cradle Device for making snow effect.

Soft Light Diffused light with little or no shadow.

Soft Patch Cables of alternative luminaires are all plugged into patch panel, but selection of active cables is done remotely from control board (see Hard Patch).

Soubrette A minor female part in comedies whose characterization calls for pertness, coyness, coquetry, intrigue, etc., and is frequently a show part.

Sound Effects Sounds performed offstage in relation to stage action.

Space Stage Method of staging plays with lights focused on actors so that no setting is necessary.

Spelvin, George Fictitious name used on a program by an actor whose real name already appears in the program. George Spelvin was first used by a minor actor who doubled in the cast of *Brewster's Millions* in 1907. The play was so successful that its author, Winchell Smith, continued to have George Spelvin listed in the rest of his productions for luck. Harry Selby is another name that is similarly used.

Spike To mark the position of a set piece on the stage floor, usually with tape.

Spike Marks Those marks, colored crayon, luminous paint, or tape used to help stage crew position set pieces. Infrequently used to help actors determine where they should be.

Spill   Unwanted light due to a poorly focused or shuttered spotlight. Sometimes spill is unavoidable because it is emitted from a lighting instrument that cannot be shuttered.

Split Stage   Two or more scenes placed on stage simultaneously.

Spot Line   A single rope specifically rigged from the gridiron to fly a piece of scenery that cannot be handled by the regular lines.

Spotlight   Lighting instrument designed to produce a concentrated beam of light.

S.R.O.   Standing Room Only.

Stage   Entire floor space behind the proscenium arch.

Stage Brace   *See* Brace, Stage.

Stage Call   Meeting of the cast and director on stage to discuss problems before a performance or rehearsal.

Stage Directions   Instructions in the script concerning movements and arrangements on the stage.

Stage Manager   The individual who accepts responsibility for the smooth running of the production on stage and backstage in prerehearsal, rehearsal, performance, and postperformance phases.

Stage Pocket   Outlet box distributed about the stage, usually sunken into the floor and equipped with a self-closing slotted cover.

Stage Screw (Peg)   A large, tapered screw with a handle used to secure stage braces to the floor.

Stage Wait   Period of time when there is no dialogue or action on stage, usually an undesirable situation caused by a late entrance or a dropped line.

Stage Whisper   A stage convention in which one actor whispers loud enough for the entire audience to hear, but is assumed to be heard only by those to whom he or she is whispering and not by other actors on stage.

Stagehand   An individual who is always present backstage when an actress or actor has to make a quick change in the wings.

Stand By   An order to be alert for a cue.

Standby   Understudy.

Stands   Metal devices for holding and mounting spotlights, floodlights, and projectors.

Star   Leading actor or actress.

Stile   The vertical piece of wood that forms the side in the frame of a flat.

Stock   Resident company of players performing one play nightly for a week and rehearsing another play for the following week.

Stock Scenery   Flats and other scene units kept on hand for repeated use.

Straight   Refers to a role or performance that is natural, normal, and uncolored by eccentricities.

Strap Hinge   A hinge with long tapered flaps used for hanging windows and doors.

Strike   To clear the stage of scenery, props, etc.

Strip Light   A long, troughlike reflector with sockets for lamps of small wattage, or a row of individual reflectors housed in a rigid sheet-metal structure. Used to produce general illumination.

Stroboscope   An instrument for producing the illusion of motion by a series of pictures viewed in rapid succession.

Subtext   Meaning underlying the lines.

Supernumerary (Super)   An extra or walk-on in a production. A person who merely appears in a mob scene or in the background, and who has no individual lines of her or his own to speak.

Swatch   Sample of material or paint.

Sweep   A method used for setting up and cutting circles or arches.

Switchboard   A combination of switches, dimmer plates, and fuses for controlling light. Also called dimmerboard.

Tab   A sheet of canvas or other material, framed or unframed, narrower than a drop but suspended like a drop, used chiefly for masking offstage spaces. Also called a leg.

Tableau Curtain   A curtain that is gathered up in an ornamental arch. See Curtain.

Tag   Term for the final speech of a scene, act, or play, serving as a cue for the curtain.

Take-In   Process of moving all of the sets and set pieces for the forthcoming production to the acting area for the first time and setting it all up as it is supposed to play. *See* Load In.

Take It Out   Order to raise scenery.

Take Stage   To move into an area of greater prominence on the stage with other actors yielding focus.

Takedown   *See* Dim.

TCI   Theatre Crafts International (magazine).

Teaser   (1) Scenery border suspended from the grid just back of the front curtain used to mask from the audience anything in the flies, edge of a ceiling piece, etc. It can be raised or lowered to change the height of the stage curtain. It is often used in place of a grand drape; (2) any short drop suspended above to mask.

Tech   *See* Technical Rehearsal (Tech) or Technician (Tech).

Technical Director   Individual responsible for construction of scenery and set pieces.

Technical Rehearsal (Tech)   A rehearsal at which the technical aspects of the production are integrated.

Technician (Tech)   An individual who runs lights, sounds, or special-effects equipment.

Template   A pattern made of cardboard or plastic—most useful to the stage manager are those for furniture and lighting instruments.

Template Table   (1) A special type of workbench used in the construction of flats; (2) a pattern.

Theatrical Gauze   *See* Scrim.

Thickness   A width of lumber or other material attached to the edge of an opening—doorway, arch, window—to give the edge the effect of depth or thickness. Also called reveal or return.

Three-Dimensional Scenery   Scenery that will be seen from all sides and is therefore finished on all sides.

Three Fold   Three flats hinged together.

Throw   Distance between lighting instrument and surface to be lit.

Throw It Away   To give no particular emphasis or expression to a speech or line in a play.

Thrust Stage   Acting area of stage that extends into the audience, or the audience is seated on three sides of the apron.

Tie Off   To secure lines to hardware or the pin rail.

Time Sheet   Record kept by stage manager of exact times of each act, scene, and scene change.

Timed Fader   Computer control of cue capable of running at a distinct rate.

Title Role   Character whose name appears in the title of the play, usually the most important role.

Toggle (Bar)   The crosspiece in the frame of a flat.

Top It   To build or increase the volume or emotional intensity of a line to a greater level than the previous line.

Tormentor   Long, narrow curtains or flats, upstage on either side of the proscenium arch, used to mask the wings.

Tormentor Lights   A number of spotlights mounted on a vertical pipe batten on either side of the stage, just behind the tormentors.

Trades   Newspapers and magazines devoted to the theater, or any other special interest.

Tragedy   Drama in which the protagonist fights a losing battle.

Translucency   A sheet of treated, thin material. When backlighted, may be used to produce silhouette effects.

Traps   Trapdoors that open into the basement trap room and permit the use of sunken stairways, scenery, or actors rising from or sinking into the ground.

Traveler   A curtain that opens to the sides.

Treadmill Stage   Machine device consisting of belts running on the stage floor, on which scenery or actors may give the illusion of traveling over a distance.

Trim   To hang and adjust drops or borders so that the lower edge is parallel to the floor.

Trim Props   Those properties that are placed within the set or hung on the walls of the set for ornamentation.

Trip   To elevate the bottom of a drop or other flown scenery with an auxiliary set of lines, to make it occupy a space approximately half its height. Tripping is used on a stage where there is not enough fly space to get a unit out of sight by taking it straight up with one set of lines.

Trip Line   A line or lines to a batten used to adjust its position.

Truck   A dolly.

Tungsten-Halogen   Long-life lamps used in lighting equipment.

Turkey   A show that is a failure. The term originated when bad shows were opened on Thanksgiving Day to clear expenses and make a little money in the two or three holiday performances. Any badly cast or badly produced show.

Turntable   Moving stage, revolving stage.

Twist Lock   Electrical connectors that have to be twisted into place and therefore cannot easily be withdrawn. They are especially useful where cords must lie on the stage floor and are in danger of being kicked out of an outlet.

Two Fold   Two flats hinged together. Also called a wing.

Two-fer   Martingale or multiple connector. Two female plugs spliced into one male plug in order to plug two lighting instruments into a single cable.

Typecasting   Selecting actors for roles because they resemble in real life the characters they will portray.

Ultraviolet Light   *See* Black Light.

Understudy   An actor who must be present or on call, know all the lines and businesses, but who appears only when the person playing that role is taken ill or for some other reason cannot appear.

Uni-Par Can   Plastic par can that accepts Par 46, 56, and 64 lamps.

Unit Set   Set built of scenic units that can be used together in various combinations to form different settings.

Upstage   (1) Away from the footlights or audience; (2) to move upstage of another cast member and thereby compel that cast member to turn his back to the audience if he wishes to speak to the "upstager."

USITT   United States Institute of Theatre Technology—national organization that studies the technology of theater and disseminates information about it.

Valance   Teaser or border.

Vampire Trap   Double-faced section of a flat that revolves on a pivot for fast escapes or disappearance of props.

Velours   Curtains used to dress a stage, made of velour, usually consisting of a backdrop with wing curtains for side masking.

Velveteen   Imitation velvet material used for draperies.

Voltage   The measurement of the force needed for the flow of electricity.

Wagon (Stage)   A low platform on wheels or casters on which a set can be placed and then moved quickly into place.

Walk the Curtain To walk behind the curtain as it closes to ensure that it closes properly.

Walk-On A very small part, with or without lines.

Walk-Through A rehearsal in which actors get out of their chairs and walk through their movements on stage.

Walk Up To raise a flat from the floor to a vertical position, by hand.

Wardrobe (1) Costumes and all articles of dress of a play or production; (2) room in which costumes are stored or fitted.

Wardrobe Person The person in charge of costumes and their upkeep.

Warn A signal that a cue is due within a short time, usually within a minute.

Watt A unit of electric power equal to a current of one ampere under one volt of pressure.

Wing *See* Two Fold.

Wings (1) Space outside the acting area, at the right and left of stage; (2) draperies that hang at the sides of the stage to mask the offstage areas.

Work Light Light for the stage area used during rehearsals, scene shifts, and construction. Work lights are usually controlled by a wall switch instead of from the dimmerboard.

Working Drawings Blueprints made from the designer's drawings. *See* Line Drawings.

Yoke The metal, U-shaped support that holds a lighting instrument.

Zip Cord Lightweight household electrical wire that should not be used for stage lightning, except for practical lights on the set.

Zoom Ellipsoidal luminaire that can be focused manually or remotely.

Suggested Classroom Exercise

Write on the chalkboard those slang theatrical terms, with definitions, used at your theater that are not found in the glossary. Add definitions to your department handbook.

Reader's Comments Form

Does this book meet your needs?

Did you find it easy to read and understand?

Was it organized for convenient use and application?

Was it complete?

Was it well illustrated?

Was it suitable for your theater?

The name of your theater:

❑ Type (circle one): professional—educational—community—
                     showcase—children's—religious

Your name and job title:

Did you use this book (check appropriate lines):

❑ As an introduction to the subject?
❑ For advanced guidance on the subject?
❑ As an instructor?
❑ As a student?

Your comments:

❑ I wish to make reference to Chapter _____
I feel additional information or examples should be included in the area
of _____
Please attach additional pages for your comments if necessary.

    Perhaps in your work you have discovered a management procedure, a method, or a technique that would be of help to future stage managers. Insights into the peculiarities of dance, ballet, opera, ice shows, theme parks, dinner theater, puppetry, magic, variety shows, and festivals would be especially appreciated. Your comments or additions could help to improve the next edition of this manual.

Send to: THE STAGE MANAGER
            P.O. Box 554
            Capitola, CA 95010
            e-mail: lstern@jps.net

Index